Understanding Homicide

Understanding Homicide

Fiona Brookman

SAGE Publications
London • Thousand Oaks • New Delhi

First published 2005

SAGE Publications Ltd
1 Oliver's Yard
55 City Road
London EC1Y 1SP

SAGE Publications Inc.
2455 Teller Road
Thousand Oaks, California 91320

SAGE Publications India Pvt Ltd
B-42, Panchsheel Enclave
Post Box 4109
New Delhi 110 017

British Library Cataloguing in Publication data

A catalogue record for this book is available from
the British Library

ISBN 0-7619-4754-X
ISBN 0-7619-4755-8

Library of Congress Control Number available

Typeset by C&M Digitals (P) Ltd., Chennai, India
Printed in India at Gopsons Papers Ltd, Noida

Contents

Preface

Despite its continued prominence in the media, homicide has received surprisingly little serious analytical attention from criminologists in recent years, especially in Britain. As Rock (1998: 9) puts it, homicide has suffered from 'intellectual neglectfulness'. Fiona Brookman, whose excellent doctoral thesis on the subject I supervised when she was at Cardiff University during the 1990s, has taken some important steps towards ending this neglect, and I am pleased to accept her invitation to write a brief preface to this very welcome book.

The book is a substantial contribution to the recent academic literature on homicide, at the same time being written in a reader-friendly manner which will help it reach a wider audience, including students of criminology and criminal justice. It is informed throughout by the author's now considerable research and teaching experience in this area. Her doctoral work was concerned with explanations of different kinds of homicide, especially those committed by men, and she explored and developed theories around the concept of 'masculinities' and issues of control. She also considered the extent to which homicide should be regarded as a unique kind of crime, deserving of its own theoretical explanations, or whether it should primarily be regarded as the extreme end of the spectrum of violent behaviour (the death of the victim often being the result of behaviour not initially aimed at killing, and to some extent contingent upon fortune – as it were, the difference between a knife hitting the heart or an arm) and hence explicable in the same ways as serious violence in general. In exploring such questions, she undertook extensive analysis of both qualitative and quantitative data, including details of all cases recorded in England and Wales on the Homicide Index and a considerable number of police files. These theoretical interests have been complemented more recently by policy-focused research on behalf of the Home Office, in which she has both examined police investigations and has explored possible ways in which levels of homicide might be reduced in the UK. This book draws on all the above work, bringing together the theoretical with the practical to present a comprehensive overview of the subject. It gives a clear and well evidenced picture of patterns and forms of homicide, discusses competing explanations of why it occurs, outlines key issues in police investigations, and considers the possibilities of reduction and prevention. Whilst focused mainly on the UK, it deals with literature, research and debates from other parts of the world; especially North America, Australia, New Zealand and Canada.

In short, this is a thoughtful, lively and informative book which helps to fill a surprising gap in the recent criminological literature in Britain. It deserves wide readership among students of the subject and non-specialists alike, and I wish it every success.

Mike Maguire
Professor of Criminology, Cardiff University

Acknowledgements

Several people have made this book possible. First, I would like to thank my colleagues at the Centre for Criminology, University of Glamorgan, for their help and support. Special thanks to Harriet Pierpoint, Dr Jon Moran, Dr Katie Holloway, Ian McKim, Maggie McNorton and Professor Trevor Bennett for reading drafts of various chapters of the book and to Ann Williams for her encouragement and support.

A very big thank you to Detective Superintendent Peter Stelfox of the Greater Manchester Police who was kind enough to share with me large chunks of his PhD thesis into the investigation of homicide. As a seasoned homicide investigator and academic, Peter's work was especially insightful. In addition, many thanks to Assistant Chief Constable Tony Rogers of South Wales Police for granting me permission (on behalf of ACPO) to use the Homicide Investigation Manual and extracts from it. Thanks also to Dr Martin Innes (University of Surrey) for allowing me access to the draft copy of his excellent text on the police investigation of homicide prior to publication. Quite simply, I could not have included a chapter on the police investigation of homicide without their generosity. I am also grateful to the Home Office for allowing me to make use of the Homicide Index during both the preparation of this text and my PhD thesis.

Huge thanks to Jane Nolan, a fabulous research assistant who helped me enormously in the final few months of preparing this text. As well as collating and summarising many key articles, Jane also prepared an early draft of Chapter 7 'When Women Kill'. I only wish we'd worked together sooner – very many thanks, Jane.

A very special thank you to Professor Mike Maguire of Cardiff University. Not only did he guide me through my PhD, but he also has continued to support me ever since. As ever, Mike gave me the benefit of his brilliant mind and, most importantly, provided much needed guidance and direction throughout the preparation of this book. Thanks a million, Mike, to you and Jay.

Thanks also to Professor Kenneth Polk of the University of Melbourne for his insightful and generous comments on an earlier draft of the book, and to the Commissioning Editors, Mirander Nunhofer and Caroline Porter at Sage Publications, for their patience and support.

And last, but not least, love and thanks to Pete (thanks for the Gizmo), Mum and Dad (thanks for your support and encouragement and for 'nagging' me about the book, Dad, and ordering millions of copies – you're a star!), Tom and my lovely friends (the 'Ponty' girls).

To my mum, dad and brother (Jan, Ken and Tom Brookman) and Pete

part one
placing homicide in context

1 Deconstructing Homicide

Chapter Overview

Homicide is the most serious form of violent crime. It is uniquely harmful and strikes at the very heart of what most of us hold most precious – our life. As Falk (1990: xi) put it, 'the only possession any of us truly have is our lives'. As well as the obviously devastating consequences to victims of homicide, the effects reach far wider to family and friends of the victim, offenders themselves and the community as a whole. Whilst homicide is undoubtedly a tragic event, at the same time it holds, for many, great interest and, in some cases, fascination. It is the subject of constant press attention and of numerous popular books and films. By contrast, however, homicide has undergone relatively little rigorous study by criminologists in the UK for some significant time. There are a small number of exceptions. For example, some Home Office-funded homicide-related projects, such as possible ways to reduce or prevent homicide in the UK (see Brookman and Maguire, 2003), and an ESRC funded project dealing with homicide in Britain.[1] Generally speaking though, homicide had suffered from academic neglect in the UK and for this reason alone this text is long overdue. Its overarching aim is to fill a glaring gap in the literature by providing an accessible and comprehensive yet challenging overview of homicide for both teaching and research purposes. Whilst clearly focused upon the UK experience of homicide, the text necessarily draws upon international literature, research and debate. At the same time it draws upon the author's own research into homicide in the UK.[2] In traversing different features, aspects and forms of homicide, important questions at the very heart of theoretical debate about this phenomenon will be addressed.

Plan of the Book

The remainder of this chapter comprises a detailed consideration of the meaning of the term 'homicide' – from both a legal standpoint and in terms of how homicide is socially constructed. Although legal categories of homicide may appear clear cut, in reality a very fine, and often artificial, line divides 'murder' from 'manslaughter' or 'accident' or, as Croall (1998: 179) notes, 'licensed killings' by law enforcers or euthanasia. As will be revealed, the divide between acceptable and unacceptable killings is socially, historically and culturally constructed. In addition, this chapter will explore the 'dark figure' of homicide and critically consider the widely held view that homicide is amongst the most 'visible' crimes in society. This is followed, in Chapter 2, by an overview of patterns, trends and forms of homicide in the UK, in other words, a consideration of how homicide in the UK 'looks'. In particular, we will consider a number of socio-demographic characteristics of killers and their victims (such as gender, age, social class and race) as well as features of the homicide event (such as the methods or weapons most often used by killers, and temporal and spatial features of homicide). A basic classification of homicide in the UK is also presented and discussed in Chapter 2; subsequent chapters unravel in much finer detail the particular characteristics and underlying motives of different forms of homicide.

The text then turns, in Part Two, to explanations of homicide. We will consider, in some detail, the three major disciplines of biology, psychology and sociology and their contribution to understanding homicide. Each of these chapters deals with homicide essentially as a 'whole', paying only occasion attention to particular manifestations of homicide.

Chapters 6 through to 9 (Part Three of the text) unravel the nature, circumstances and possible explanations of a number of distinct forms of homicide. There are various ways of classifying or 'slicing up' homicide for the purposes of description and explanation. For example, one can focus upon the 'social relationships' that unite offenders and victims (that is, domestic homicide, stranger homicide, infanticide, gang-related homicide and so forth) or alternatively focus upon issues of motivation (that is, revenge killings, sexually-motivated homicide, robbery homicide and so forth). Chapters 6 and 7 take as their starting point the gender of the perpetrator and victim of homicide. Using case study material we will unravel the nature, circumstances and explanations of different forms of homicide committed by men and women, which is in large part determined by the sex of the victim. For example, male-perpetrated domestic homicide is usually very distinct from those occasions when men kill other men. Chapter 8 is devoted to the killing of infants and children and once again a clear distinction is made between male and female perpetrators of child homicide. Chapter 9 considers the phenomenon of multiple homicide, focusing specifically upon serial, mass and spree killers, terrorism (with a particular emphasis upon Northern Ireland) and corporate homicide. Each of these chapters follows a common format, beginning with discussions of the prevalence of each form of homicide, then providing descriptive examples of each type, followed by evaluations of theoretical explanations.

Finally, in Part Four of the text, we consider how homicide is investigated by the police in England and Wales (Chapter 10) and the potential for reducing or preventing homicide (Chapter 11). The book ends by teasing out some of the most important and recurring issues and themes raised in the text as a whole, as well as taking stock of progress to date in understanding homicide and some potentially useful directions for future research.

The starting point for any comprehensive understanding of the phenomenon of homicide is to make sense of the term itself, to which we now turn.

Defining Homicide

We all think we know what homicide is. Each year, in the very first lecture of the homicide course I teach to final-year undergraduates, I ask the students to write down what they understand by the term 'homicide' and how they would define it. What is most significant about the responses is reference to the term 'murder'. Over half of the class generally include the term 'murder' in their brief explanation. Linked to this, the terms 'deliberate', 'intentional', 'unlawful' and 'unjust' are found in the vast majority of definitions provided by the students. At the broadest end of the spectrum, some students define homicide as the taking of a life, whilst at the narrowest, reference is made specifically to pre-meditated, intentional killing by one human being of another. Each of these are correct – at least in part. What we perhaps do not recognise on initial consideration, however, is the extent to which homicide, like all other crime categories, is socially constructed. Unlawful homicide is not an absolute. Rather, various categories have been constructed over the years that are said to comprise unlawful homicide. Crime cannot exist without the creation of laws by a given society to criminalise particular actions or behaviours.[3] The fact that legal codes vary between different countries and across different historical periods is a clear indication of the socially constructed nature of crime and deviance. Hence the creation of crime categories is a product of societal interaction and reaction to particular behaviours. Very rarely does the image of a large corporation flouting Health and Safety legislation (thereby causing deaths amongst its workers) spring to mind when one thinks of unlawful homicide. This is perhaps not surprising, since the law rarely deals with these 'killings' as homicides. Examples include the slow and painful deaths of thousands of individuals exposed to pernicious dusts, such as asbestos, despite ample evidence, known to employers, of the potentially fatal health risks, or the negligent and fraudulent safety testing of drugs by the pharmaceutical industry, or environmental crimes that cause death due to the dumping of hazardous wastes and illegal toxic emissions (see Slapper and Tombs, 1999 for an overview of corporate crime).

Yet to complicate matters further, whilst, on the one hand, there is little doubt that there exists some sense of a shared meaning of homicide amongst members of a given society, it is also the case that there is considerable blurring at the edges when one moves into the domain of trying to ascertain responsibility, culpability, intent and so forth. So whilst it may be relatively straightforward (some of the time) to discover whether one individual or group of individuals has taken the life of another, any simplicity ends here. The circumstances that surround homicide vary enormously, as does public and media response to different forms of homicide. The death of a young man at the hands of another during a pub brawl is likely to be viewed very differently from the rape and killing of a young woman by an unknown male whilst making her way home at night. The killing of child by a paedophile will tend to be viewed as particularly heinous, whilst the killing of a new-born baby by its mother may be viewed less harshly. As Hazel May observes, 'there is no single social meaning attached to the killing of one person by another' (1999: 489). An interesting question that follows then is what sorts of factors affect our conceptions of homicide?[4] Specifically, what makes some killings seem less heinous than others and why does mass public outrage follow certain killings and not others? According to May (1999), social meanings attached to acts of violence (including homicide) seem to revolve around notions of culpability and victimisation. Culpability refers to the degree to which the perpetrator is seen to be responsible for the violent act and its consequences. There are many ways by which the law of homicide mitigates culpability, which we will examine below in further detail. Suffice it to say, issues such as intent, mental state, self-defence and so forth are often taken into consideration. Beyond the law, however, members of society often make up their own minds about how heinous a particular killing is and how guilty the perpetrator is – often in conjunction with media coverage of the crime. In part, this owes something to the 'status' or 'social profile' of the killer, that is, his or her age, gender, social class and background and relationship to the victim. Hence, when women and children kill this generally provokes greater shock and outrage than when men kill each other. However, another important feature of this decision is, according to May, based upon notions of victimisation. For example, if the victim was seen to have provoked the offender in some way (often referred to as 'victim-precipitated' homicide), they may be viewed as somehow responsible for the violent actions that followed and hence are not wholly innocent. Alternatively, at the other end of the spectrum, victim vulnerability can play an important role in fostering high levels of condemnation toward the offender. So where children or the elderly are killed, emotions generally run very high. Hence, as May puts it, 'culpability and victimization can be seen to be inextricably bound' (1999: 490).

May's work raises further important questions. In particular, what factors affect how victimisation and culpability are conceived in the first instance? Why are we particularly shocked and appalled when the very young or elderly are killed? After all, in some societies under certain conditions, these 'vulnerable' groups would be the first to be left to die. For example, among the Inuit, who live(d) in conditions that Europeans usually considered unsurviveable, infanticide or abandonment of the sick or elderly was not considered a crime in times of food shortage. The hunter was the most valuable member of the family or group, and thus was the last to starve (see Mowat, 1951). There is much evidence that the practice of infanticide, as a method of controlling population size, has occurred in many societies (Resnick, 1972)

and it was not until the nineteenth century that there emerged the beginnings
of a public outcry against infanticide (Lambie, 2001). Despite this, the practice
continued in the UK and throughout Europe, Canada and the US due to financial
concerns and the social stigma associated with illegitimate births (Moseley, 1986).
So in various cultures, under certain circumstances, not only is 'murder' acceptable
but the decisions as to who must be left to die may appear particularly distasteful
and immoral to those not part of that culture. As Levi and Maguire observe in their
discussion of the role of culture in shaping people's attitudes to violence, 'those
who commit "crimes of obedience" define themselves and are commonly defined
in their culture, or at least their narrower reference group, as "loyal" rather than as
being "violent conspirators in a process of genocide"' (2002: 799). Examples of this
cultural 'state of denial' apply, for example, to the murder of some 800,000 Tutsis
in Rwanda during the 1990s or the millions killed in the Nazi Holocaust (see Levi
and Maguire, 2002). Recent research findings from the ESRC (Economic and Social
Research Council) Violence Research Programme found that unlike recent notor-
ious crimes, such as the murders of James Bulger and Sarah Payne, Victorian equiv-
alents failed to ignite widespread social anxieties (Archer et al., 2002). For example,
in 1855, 7-year-old James Fleeson was abducted by two 10-year-old boys who
knocked him to the ground with a half brick and drowned him in the
Leeds–Liverpool canal. All three boys lived in the same street and the entire street
(apart from Fleeson's parents) soon came to realise what had occurred and shielded
the perpetrators' identities from the police. Once caught, the boys were convicted
of manslaughter and imprisoned for one year (Archer et al., 2002). This case, which
bears striking similarities with the abduction and murder of James Bulger 138 years
later in 1993, received a very different public and criminal justice response.[5]
Clearly, many factors, such as cultural and religious values, historical processes,
socio-demographic factors (such as class, age, gender), social conditions and the
effects of the media in reporting crime can impact upon how a given individual or
group of people comes to perceive and react to homicide. The extent to which
homicide, like all crime categories, is socially constructed will be a recurring theme
of this chapter.[6] First, however, it is necessary to outline the legal framework of
unlawful homicide before moving toward a critique.

Study Task 1.1

Make a list of five very different scenarios of killing (that is, the killer(s), victim(s)
and the circumstances of the killing) and consider the extent to which each of
these might cause public outcry and the reasons for such reactions. Be imaginative. Consider examples such as euthanasia, abortion, corporate homicide or fatal
child abuse cases in order that you can explore issues such as 'shared responsibility'
for death. Place your examples on some kind of continuum from 'excusable' at
one end of the scale to 'most unacceptable' and 'heinous' at the other. Consider
what influences your choices and decisions.

The Law of Homicide

It is not possible to discuss the law surrounding homicide in the UK as a whole due to differences in definition across certain jurisdictions. Of the four countries that make up the UK, England and Wales share a common legal system and are treated as a single entity for the purposes of recording crime. Scotland has a very different legal system based on Roman law whereby offence definitions are often inconsistent with those of England and Wales. Northern Ireland has a separate Criminal Justice System that has been profoundly affected by terrorist troubles (Jenkins, 1988). Due to these anomalies, and for the sake of clarity, it will be necessary to deal mainly with the law related to homicide in England and Wales, referring separately to Scotland and Northern Ireland where necessary.

The term 'homicide' refers to the killing of a human being, whether the killing is lawful or unlawful. Examples of lawful homicide would include the killing of another human being during wartime combat, the implementation of the death penalty or the accidental killing of a boxer by his opponent. Where homicide is defined as unlawful it may be legally classified, in England and Wales, as murder, manslaughter or infanticide. Causing death by dangerous or careless driving are generally marked out as separate categories and will be considered later. Where the law in England and Wales makes a distinction between lawful and unlawful killings, in Scotland a similar distinction exists between criminal homicide and non-criminal homicide. The latter includes 'cases of justifiable or excused killing, and casual homicide, that is, where a person kills unintentionally, when lawfully employed and without culpable carelessness' (Gane and Stoddart, 1988: 479).

Murder, manslaughter and infanticide share a common *actus reus* (guilty act) and are currently the three major offences to fall into the category of homicide. However, the issue becomes complicated somewhat in terms of intent or what is often referred to in law as *mens rea* (guilty mind). Whilst it is relatively straightforward to prescribe or define a particular act with particular consequences as a guilty act, it is far from straightforward to determine to what extent the act or its consequences were intended. In other words, it has to be acknowledged that not all killings are intended and that there exists, therefore, different levels of culpability or guilt amongst perpetrators. Let us now consider how the law has met these complex challenges.

Unlawful Homicide

The major criteria under which offences subsumed under the heading of unlawful homicide are differentiated essentially revolve around the issues of culpability or intention, which includes some estimate of the degree of premeditation and the mental capacity of the defendant (Mitchell, 1991). The principal distinction made in English and Welsh law is that between murder and manslaughter – not least because historically there has existed a vast difference in the penalties for murder and manslaughter – murder was a capital offence and manslaughter was not (Murder (Abolition of the Death Penalty) Act 1965). Whilst there is only one definition of murder (and infanticide), there are a number of different ways of defining manslaughter. Moreover, the vast majority of unlawful killings that do not fall under the heading of murder are included in the category of manslaughter which is, therefore, very broad and diverse, encompassing killings under very different sorts of circumstances. The law has also created special provisions for a mother who kills her baby in the form of the Infanticide Act 1938. Table 1.1 gives a definition of unlawful homicide and the penalties are listed in Table 1.2. The various legal categories that comprise unlawful homicide in England and Wales are considered below.

Table 1.1 Summary of the definition of unlawful homicide in England and Wales

A person is liable for murder through causing a person's death, whether by act or omission, either with intent to kill or with intent to cause grievous bodily harm. That liability to conviction for murder may be reduced to manslaughter if the killing stemmed from provocation, diminished responsibility, or a suicide pact. These are commonly referred to as forms of 'voluntary manslaughter'. Alternatively, where there is no apparent intent to murder, an individual may be liable to conviction for 'involuntary manslaughter' if it is shown that they acted in a reckless or grossly negligent manner or that death resulted from an unlawful and dangerous act.

Adapted from Ashworth and Mitchell, 2000.

Table 1.2 Summary of the penalties for unlawful homicide in England and Wales

- *Murder* carries a mandatory penalty of life imprisonment.
- *Manslaughter* carries a maximum penalty of life imprisonment.
- *Infanticide* carries a maximum penalty of life imprisonment but generally attracts a non-custodial sentence (usually a Probation Order).
- *Death by dangerous driving* and *causing death by careless driving when under the influence of drink or drugs* both carry a maximum penalty of 10 years' imprisonment.
- *Causing death by aggravated vehicle-taking* carries a maximum penalty of five years' imprisonment.

Murder

The classic definition of murder, and that which is generally accepted both academically and in practice, is that of Lord Chief Justice Coke from the early seventeenth century;

> [W]hen a person of sound memory, and of the age of discretion, unlawfully killeth within any county of the realm any reasonable creature in rerum natura under the kings peace, with malice aforethought, either expressed by the party or implied by law, so as the party wounded, or hurt, etc., die of the wound or hurt, etc., within a year and a day after the same. (Cited in Card, 1998: 184)

Let us briefly unpick this definition. First of all it is worth noting that Coke's definition was recently amended to exclude reference to 'a year and a day after the same'.[7] The phrase *'rerum natura'* refers to the notion that one can only be held to have killed someone who is 'in being' (as opposed to an unborn child, for example). Finally, the term 'malice aforethought' refers to intent. A conviction for murder requires proof of intention to kill. However, what is not clear from the above extract is that intent to cause grievous bodily harm (that ultimately results in death) is also sufficient for a conviction for murder. We will return to the complex issue of establishing intent below, suffice it to say that intent can be inferred from evidence that the 'defendant foresaw death or grievous bodily harm as a natural and probable (virtually certain) consequence' (Childs, 1996: 54). In essence, the law attempts to distinguish between different categories of homicide in terms of their apparent seriousness or gravity. The extent to which is succeeds is debatable. For example, Ashworth questions whether the 'grievous bodily harm' rule extends the definition of murder too far: 'If the point of distinguishing murder from manslaughter is to mark out the most heinous group of killings for the extra stigma of a murder conviction, it can be argued that the "grievous bodily harm" rule draws the line too low' (1999: 270).

The important point to bear in mind is that murder is a legal category (as, of course, are the other offence categories that we discuss below). A death is not considered a murder in the true sense of the term until a number of legal processes are undergone (see Chapter 10), such as the suspect being charged by the police, committed to Crown Court and ultimately found guilty of murder by a jury (as opposed to a lesser charge of manslaughter, for example or a 'not guilty' verdict). As Adler and Polk point out, 'in a typical jurisdiction only a small number of homicides prosecuted in a year will result in a criminal conviction on the specific charge of murder' (2001: 17). In England and Wales for the period 2000, only 30 per cent of cases resulted in a conviction for murder.[8]

Manslaughter

Generally any unlawful homicide which is not classified as murder is categorised as some form of manslaughter. This offence is 'extremely broad and ranges in its gravity from the borders of murder right down to those of accidental death' (Law Commission, 1996: No. 237, p. 1). There are two generic types of manslaughter: voluntary and involuntary.

Voluntary Manslaughter

Voluntary manslaughter describes cases where the accused intended to cause death or serious injury (that is, kills with malice aforethought), but under circumstances which the law regards as mitigating the gravity of the offence. There are three categories of mitigating circumstance, namely that the accused was:

- provoked to kill; or
- was suffering from an 'abnormality of mind' such that his/her mental responsibility for his/her behaviour was substantially impaired ('diminished responsibility' – commonly referred to as Section 2 manslaughter); or
- he/she killed in pursuance of a suicide pact (where the killer is a survivor of the pact) (Homicide Act, 1957: ss 2–4).

Involuntary Manslaughter

This expression covers cases where there was no intention to kill or to cause serious injury, but where the law considers that the person who caused death was blameworthy in some (other) way. In recent years it has generally been accepted that someone may be convicted of involuntary manslaughter by one of two routes – constructive (or unlawful act) manslaughter or reckless/gross negligence manslaughter. Constructive manslaughter is said to occur where the defendant commits an unlawful and dangerous act likely to cause physical harm such that death is the accidental result of an unlawful act. Reckless/gross negligent manslaughter occurs where a person causes death through extreme carelessness or incompetence. The Law Commission note that 'frequently the defendants in such cases are people carrying out jobs that require special skills or care such as doctors, ships' captains or electricians, who fail to meet the standards which could be expected of them and cause death' (1996: para. 2.8).

Infanticide

Infanticide is a defence to a particular form of murder. It applies when a woman causes the death of her own (biological) child under 12 months while 'the balance of her mind was disturbed by reason of her not having fully recovered from the effects of having given birth to the child, or by reason of the effects of lactation consequent upon the birth of the child' (Infanticide Act 1938: s 1). The Infanticide Act provides that a woman found guilty of infanticide should be dealt with as though guilty of voluntary manslaughter. The creation of this Act has a long and interesting history (see Ward, 1999). For some commentators, the Infanticide Act affords women special treatment and leniency that is no longer appropriate (see Lambie, 2001). The separate form of legislation for mothers was originally introduced in 1624 (Act to Prevent the Destroying and Murdering of Bastard Children – see Gunn and Taylor, 1995) to lessen the penalties for unmarried women who killed their babies during, immediately after, or within a few days of birth in order to conceal the illegitimate pregnancy.[9] This has subsequently been extended to cover the first year following childbirth and is essentially less about social factors of poverty and illegitimate childbirth and more about the association between the effects of childbirth and temporary psychoses. The idea that women are prone to 'temporary madness' following childbirth (Ward, 1999) has a long and persistent history. Some critics argue that there is no need for a specific offence dealing with one form of mental disturbance (that is, post-partum psychosis) when the law offers the general defences of insanity and diminished responsibility (Mackay, 2000). Wilczynski and Morris (1993) argue that many women are treated much more leniently, not simply in terms of the reduction of infant killing from murder to manslaughter, but regarding the sentencing practice and disposals of the female offenders involved. Furthermore, some commentators note that psychiatrists themselves cannot agree upon the nature and aetiology of post-partum disorders (Maier-Katkin and Ogle, 1993) (we will return to the issue of insanity/diminished responsibility shortly).

Scottish legislation, in contrast to the law of England and Wales, makes no special provision for maternal infanticide. A mother or father who kills his or her infant in Scotland is charged with either murder or common law culpable homicide as for any other homicide offence (Marks, 1996). So whilst the parent's mental state may be taken into consideration at trial, there is no legal recognition of a causal link between maternal mental illness and infanticide (Marks, 1996).

Causing Death by Driving

As indicated earlier, the manner in which statistics are collected on homicide in England and Wales is such that only murder, manslaughter and infanticide are grouped together and subsumed under this general heading.[10] However, a great number of deaths occur each year that arise as the result of the dangerous or careless driving of a motor vehicle. That these are not treated as cases of murder or manslaughter owes less to the culpability of the perpetrators and more to the context in which these killings take place. As Clarkson observes, 'when a person has been unlawfully killed, the law's response is strongly influenced by the context in which the killing took place' (2000: 133). Hence in the case of dangerous or careless driving leading to death or fatal breaches of Health and Safety at Work legislation, the most common response is for a prosecution to be brought in relation to the underlying dangerous activity. It is, therefore, important to be clear as to the law surrounding vehicle-related killings.

The law surrounding deaths on the road has changed frequently over the past 15 years and remains in a state of flux. Moreover, there remain calls for more stringent penalties for those who cause death by some form of dangerous or negligent driving. We will return to these debates shortly. For now we will simply deal with the current legislation surrounding death by driving. Most of the provisions we discuss are contained in the Road Traffic Acts of 1988 and 1991.

The most serious charge in connection with a death on the roads is manslaughter (or in Scotland, culpable homicide) for which the courts have the highest penalties available – life imprisonment, unlimited fine and unlimited period of disqualification (DETR, 2000). However, the provision of manslaughter is very rarely used in cases of causing death on the roads (to which we return shortly). What remains, in England and Wales, are three categories of causing death by driving:

- causing death by dangerous driving;
- causing death by careless driving when under the influence of drink or drugs; or
- causing death by aggravated vehicle-taking.

In terms of a hierarchy of seriousness, causing death by dangerous driving ranks highest (Road Traffic Act, 1988: s 1). The offence requires two separate elements. The first is dangerous driving, which is defined under section 2 of the Road Traffic Act 1988 and refers to driving 'far below the standard of driving expected of the competent and careful driver' and 'driving in circumstances which showed complete disregard for any potential dangers'. The second element is that the Crown must prove that the driving caused death, that is, there must be a direct relationship between the driving and the death. If these factors are proven the Court can impose a sentence of up to 10 years imprisonment, an unlimited fine, a period of disqualification (which could be for life) and an extended retest. Forfeiture of the vehicle is also available (DETR, 2000). Causing death by careless driving when under the influence of drink or drugs is next on the seriousness tariff and again carries a maximum prison sentence of 10 years (Road Traffic Act, 1991). Under this offence, drivers' responsibility for death is greatly increased, when compared to the lesser offence of careless driving, by being under the influence of substances known to affect judgement and driving ability (Home Office Department for Transport, 2002). Finally, causing death by aggravated vehicle-taking (commonly referred to as 'joy-riding') carries a lesser maximum prison term of five years. This offence involves the theft and subsequent dangerous driving of a vehicle resulting in death (Aggravated Vehicle Taking Act 1992).

Summary

So far the discussion had centred upon establishing the legal categories of unlawful homicide in England and Wales, with some reference to Scotland.[11] In addition, the often neglected offence categories related to causing death by driving have been outlined. What follows is some critical reflection of these legal boundaries in an attempt to unravel more carefully the term 'homicide' and to move toward an appreciation of its socially constructed nature.

Assessing the Legal Framework of Unlawful Homicide

Many legal professionals have noted problems with the various categories of law relating to unlawful homicide, some of which we will consider here.

The 'Broad' Category of Manslaughter

For many years there has been sustained criticism of the very broad category of manslaughter, which encompasses vastly different sorts of killings. As the Law Commission observes, 'it ranges in gravity from cases that only just fall short of murder (e.g. arson that results in death) right down to cases that are only slightly more serious than accidental death' (1996: 2) (for example, where a person with a particularly thin and fragile skull is subjected to a very minor assault, bangs his or her head and dies of a fractured skull). Because of the enormous breadth of this offence, it has been observed that difficulties exist in delineating where it can logically be seen to begin and end (see Card, 1998; Dine and Gobert, 1998). Furthermore, critics have observed that the 'law is riddled with confusion' in respect of the two categories of involuntary manslaughter as a result of overlap between the two categories amongst other things (Padfield, 1998).

Clear evidence of the difficulties surrounding the existing law in relation to manslaughter becomes evident when considering recent calls for reform. In May 2000, the government published a consultation paper concerned with reforming the law on involuntary manslaughter (unintentional killings). This paper was based upon, and represented a partial response to, the Law Commission's earlier proposals for reform of the law on involuntary homicide (Law Commission, 1996). Both reports reviewed several of the problems with the existing law in relation to involuntary manslaughter. Notably, the Law Commission observed that having one offence of involuntary manslaughter 'to cover such a wide range of mischief presents judges with significant problems, particularly when determining what the appropriate sentence should be in a given case' (Home Office, 2000: 9). A further criticism outlined was the ineffectual nature of current legislation to deal with corporate killings, to which we shall return below. Between them, both documents outline a number of reforms, some quite significant, such as the introduction of two separate offences of 'reckless killing' and 'killing by gross carelessness' and a new offence of 'corporate killing'. In addition, the government proposed the introduction of a third offence of 'death resulting from intentional/reckless causing of minor injury'. This proposal is not in keeping with the Law Commission proposals and in fact goes against one of their main concerns in relation to the law surrounding 'accidental' homicides. Under the current law, a person who commits what would otherwise be a relatively minor assault (either intentionally or as the result of some reckless act) will be guilty of involuntary manslaughter if the victim dies as a result – even if death was unforeseeable. For example, if, during the course of a fight, A gives B a small cut – but A had no way of knowing that B had haemophilia – and B then dies, A would be liable under 'dangerous and unlawful act manslaughter', which carries a maximum penalty of life imprisonment (Home Office, 2000). Essentially, the Law Commission argues that people should not be punished for an unlucky event or 'the lottery effect'. It believes that such events should carry a maximum penalty of five years' imprisonment. The government feel that 10 may be more appropriate (see Home Office, 2000: 12).

Proving Intent

In relation to murder, numerous commentators have observed how reliance on the concept of intention has caused much difficulty in the 'delineation of murder' (Lacey and Wells, 1998: 574). What constitutes intention is a debated issue, as Rock notes:

> [I]ntent is not easy to prove – and it may well reflect judgements about the moral worth of the defendant and his victim, tactical judgements about the prospect of securing a conviction, and the success of defences mobilised around the vexed question of a sound mind, rather than some ontologically absolute distinction between classes of behaviour. (1998: 3)

In short, proving intent presents formidable problems and criminal law has grappled for some time with the evidentiary substance of this requirement.

Diminished Responsibility

Similarly complex issues surround the plea of 'diminished responsibility'. This 'defence' allows for discretion in relation to the sentencing of mentally abnormal offenders charged with murder. Though not intended as such, it has eclipsed and in many respects replaced both the 'insanity' and 'unfit to plead' defences (see Mackay, 2000). Most relevant to the current discussion, critics have argued that 'diminished responsibility is interpreted in accordance with the morality of the case rather than as an application of psychiatric concepts' (Williams, 1983: 693). So, aside from the well-established difficulties of assessing whether an individual is suffering from some mental abnormality (see Davidson and Neale, 2001; Ritsher and Luckstead, 2000; and Rosenhahn, 1973), there are arguments to suggest that the use of this defence is not, in practice, wholly concerned with unravelling the mental health of the defendant. Criticisms have also been made of the medical basis of the Infanticide Act 1938. For example, Ashworth observes that the medical basis of the Act 'is now discredited ... [and] ... reference to the effect of lactation is without foundation' (1999: 292). Whilst not wishing to deny the fact that some women do suffer from psychiatric disorders connected with the after-effects of childbirth, Ashworth (1999) points out that the specific links between lactation and infanticide are somewhat tenuous, whilst recognition of the wider social and situational factors that can give rise to mental disturbance are slowly being acknowledged.

Provocation

Similar difficulties of interpretation surround the defence of provocation. The Homicide Act does not make fully clear the definition of provocation (Jefferson, 1999). This has allowed for significant debate in relation to what amounts to provocation (for example, the law before 1957 took into account only acts; words as well as deeds can now be taken to constitute provocation). Debate has also ensued regarding the notion that a response to provocation is one of 'sudden and temporary loss of self-control'. Hence, any 'cooling-off' time between provocation and reaction to it, weakens the case for using provocation as a defence to murder, since provocation is seen to normally occur on impulse in hot blood. Women are more likely to kill their spouses as a result of planning (often referred to as 'slow burn') than men, who tend to kill in the heat of the moment (Jefferson, 1999). Hence, the provocation defence can be seen to favour men. Yet it has been argued that women may not be able to act on the spur of the moment against a stronger male aggressor and may have to wait to strike back when he is asleep. Because of the 'sexually biased' nature of the provocation defence, several critics have called for its abolition. For example, Horder (1991) argues that the requirements of sudden retaliation fails to capture the reality of the lives of many (battered) women (see also Wells, 2000 and Edwards, 1996). Whatever the rights and wrongs of this issue, it is clear that as one begins to unpick the circumstances of different kinds of homicide, the law seems unable to cope and the notion of any clear-cut or realistic distinctions between particular legal categories quickly dissipates.

Murder and Attempted Murder

An interesting example of the oddity of the law surrounding homicide is illustrated by contrasting the burden of proof and penalties for murder and attempted murder.

The Committee on the Penalty for Homicide (1993) observe that there is a common misapprehension amongst non-legal individuals that a person can be convicted of murder only where it has been established that he or she intended to kill. In fact, the prosecution need only prove intent to cause serious injury. If death ensues, however unexpected and unintended, the offence of murder is established and the mandatory life sentence follows (Committee on the Penalty for Homicide, 1993: 19). It is these cases which form the majority of convictions for murder – not those where an intent to kill has been established. This begs the question of how different in reality many homicides resulting in murder convictions are from those of manslaughter and illustrates the real difficulties in ascribing motives and apportioning distinct levels of culpability. This is exemplified when the offence of murder is contrasted with that of attempted murder. Unlike murder, it is necessary for the prosecution to prove a specific intent to kill (not simply cause serious injury) in cases of attempted murder. So one might suggest that the burden of proof is higher in cases of attempted murder. Yet at the sentencing stage we find that the mandatory sentence of life imprisonment does not apply, sentencing being at the discretion of the judge. Whilst the different penalties for murder and attempted murder obviously reflect, in part, a recognition of the importance of the loss of life, the moral culpability in the offence of attempted murder, with its necessary intent to kill, is often much greater than the offence of murder where 'intent to kill is not a necessary ingredient' (Committee on the Penalty for Homicide, 1993: 19).

Study Task 1.2

As indicated earlier, it has been argued that 'diminished responsibility is interpreted in accordance with the morality of the case rather than as an application of psychiatric concepts' (Williams, 1983: 693). Consider to what extent you agree with this view. Does 'morality' play a role in other legal defences of homicide?

Killings that Don't Count

Because of a range of complexities involved in establishing culpability and guilt and because of the different social meanings attached to homicide, killers are not treated equally. Rather, certain types of killings are rarely prosecuted, or where they are, they are prone to collapse. Put another way, certain groups of individuals are much less likely than others to be held accountable for killing. Of course, the reverse is also true in that certain sections of society are more likely than others to feel the full wrath of the law. The operation of the death penalty in parts of the US is perhaps a very clear example of the arbitrary and discriminatory nature of criminal law. Amnesty International has detailed widespread examples of racially-motivated prosecutions, convictions and death sentences (visit www.amnesty.org). Overall, it has been well established that black and working-class individuals are much more likely than white middle-class individuals to undergo a capital murder trial. Hence, if found guilty, they are sentenced to death, whereas their white counterparts will be sentenced to life imprisonment (see Radelet and Pierce, 1985; Hood, 1996; International Commission of Jurists, 1996). Here I will focus upon some examples of 'killings' that are often treated more as though accidents than acts with some responsible or liable culprit.

Corporate Killings

Though rarely perceived as homicide or prosecuted as such, various forms of corporate crime kill; for example, unsafe working environments or conditions, unsafe pharmaceutical products, unfit food products and illegal emissions into the environment (see Slapper and Tombs, 1999). Corporate (business) crime has been defined as illegal acts or omissions 'which are the result of deliberate decision making or culpable negligence within a legitimate formal organization' (McLaughlin and Muncie, 2001: 56). Hence, corporate killings can be referred to as deaths which result, at least in part, from negligence or deliberate decisions by a corporate body (see Chapter 9). It has been argued that, in terms of the number of lives lost, such deaths represent the most significant single category of homicide the UK (Levi, 1997).

The Law Commission, in its review of involuntary manslaughter in 1996 (report No. 237), noted that many people die each year in factory and building site accidents, many of which could and should have been prevented. Moreover, they found only four prosecutions of a corporation for manslaughter in the history of English Law (1996: 1.10), only one of which resulted in a conviction. The Law Commission observed that part of the reason for the absence of convictions in such cases revolves around the difficulties of mounting a manslaughter prosecution against a large-sale corporate defendant. Significantly, of the four cases mentioned above, it was a one-man company that resulted in a conviction. In short, difficulties arise in identifying individuals to hold responsible who are part of a large company where responsibilities are diffuse and shared. This is further exacerbated, of course, where companies or their components are spread across the globe. Croall (1998) also refers to the 'diffusion of victimisation', whereby the victim is not always identifiable, or may not yet be aware of their victimisation (it may be so minimal that they have not noticed, or will only become apparent over a period of time, thus there is no immediate reaction or detection). For example, the immediate impact of the Chernobyl nuclear power station fall-out in 1986 was blatantly clear, however, the full affects and its wider consequences will only become evident after several decades (Hughes and Langan, 2001).

Finally, it has been suggested that prosecuting authorities fail to adequately investigate such crimes due to a general culture which does not recognise corporate crime as being 'real' crime (Box, 1983, 1996; Slapper, 1993; Wells, 1995). Bergman (1994) estimated that less than 40 per cent of workplace deaths from fatal injuries are typically followed by a prosecution.

It is worth considering some figures for work-related fatalities here briefly. In order to work with confirmed figures and avoid estimates, it is necessary to retreat back a few years. Hence we will consider the period 2001/02. The figures we consider relate to Great Britain (that is, England, Wales and Scotland combined). The Health and Safety Executive (HSE) recorded 292 fatal injuries to workers (that is, employees and the self-employed) during 2001/02 (HSE, 2003: 1). Whilst the HSE claim that their figures for workplace deaths are virtually complete, these figures are, according to several critics, a gross undercount of the 'true' extent of work-related deaths and merely represent a 'headline figure' (see Slapper and Tombs, 1999). Whilst new 'counting rules' have rectified some of these shortfalls (Reporting of Injuries, Diseases and Dangerous Occurrences Regulations (RIDDOR) 1995) under-reporting is still believed to be significant. In particular, it is still the case that deaths whilst driving in the course of employment are not included in the HSE statistics.

Regardless of these and other shortfalls, there remains a further significant category of fatalities that must be considered in order to determine the number of people killed as a result of work activity, that is, deaths arising from occupationally-caused fatal illness. Once again, these statistics are compiled and published by the HSE and, once again, they are a gross under-estimate. Of particular significance here are flaws in the system of death registration and classification, such that doctors and coroners are unlikely to record occupational causes on death certificates (see Slapper and Tombs, 1999: 72). Nevertheless, if we consider the 'official' figure for occupationally caused deaths[12] (that is, asbestos-related deaths of which there are two forms – mesothelioma and lung cancer – and 'other' occupationally-caused diseases, such as farmer's lung and pneumoconiosis[13]) we find a figure of 2,112 (HSE, 2001). Added to our earlier figure of fatal injuries (292), this gives us an official total of 2,404 fatal injuries and diseases to workers, which is *two and a half times greater* than the annual average of recorded homicides for the equivalent jurisdictions. For England, Wales and Scotland combined during 2001,[14] there were 939 homicides recorded (832 for England and Wales and 107 for Scotland).

Finally, we should not forget those relatively rare but highly publicised 'disasters' in which at least an element of corporate negligence can be claimed (Brookman and Maguire, 2003). A quick reckoning of the total deaths in just some of the major disasters in the UK during the last 20 years (such as the Piper Alpha and King's Cross fires, the Bradford Stadium fire and the Hillsborough stadium crush, the Manchester plane fire and the M1 aircraft crash, the sinking of the Marchioness and the Southall and Paddington rail crashes) produces a figure of around 650 deaths (an equivalent of approximately 33 deaths per year). These tragedies have led to growing public concern at the failure of the criminal law to deal effectively with companies whose actions or inaction have played a hand in such disasters and have also played an important role in leading the Law Commission and government to propose the introduction of a new offence of 'corporate killing' (Law Commission, 1996).

Death by Driving

Another important example of killings that are not treated as 'real' homicides comes in the form of fatal road traffic accidents, which invariably do not appear as homicides in the official statistics (the exception being where a vehicle is used as a weapon to kill). Essentially these killings do not fit the conventional definition of homicide, though there is scope to argue that a number of these fatalities could be considered as such. The question is whether the context in which such killings take place justifies the present separate offences, or whether such killings should be brought back within the general homicide offences (see Clarkson, 2000, for a summary of some of the debates surrounding the distinction of death by driving from the category of unlawful homicide).

Around 10 people are killed in road traffic incidents in the UK every day, which translates to approximately 3,500 in an average year (www.roadpeace.org/index. php). RoadPeace, a charitable organisation, continue to campaign for more effective penalties for drivers who kill on the roads. They note that only around 10 per cent of drivers who kill on the roads are charged with causing death by dangerous driving and the manslaughter provision is so rarely used as to be effectively redundant. The important question this raises in the context of the current discussion is what proportion, if any, of these fatal road accidents should 'count' as instances of unlawful homicide? RoadPeace are clearly of the opinion that the proportion is significant. They argue that the existing system of offences is 'a hotch-potch of ineffectively and inconsistently enforced laws' (RoadPeace, 2001: 13) and cite flaws in the processes of investigation and prosecution as underlying explanations for the 'startling low numbers of prosecutions for dangerous driving and manslaughter' (2001: 15–16).

Michalowski (1975) observes that unlike more conventional homicides and assaults, 'vehicular homicides' are seen to represent an impersonal rather than an interpersonal form of violence. This might explain the greater attention given to 'road rage', as it may 'fit' more readily our conceptions of interpersonal violence. However, research by Michalowski challenges the view that these sorts of behaviour are completely separate or discrete. In exploring the possible relationship between violence on the roads (in the form of vehicular homicide) and criminal aggression more generally Michalowski found that the sociological characteristics of vehicular homicide are nearly identical to those of other urban crimes of violence and claims to have found a strong positive relationship between traffic offences and a history of aggression. He discovered that individuals with a prior history of criminal aggression comprised a significant proportion of vehicle homicide offenders.

In December 2000, the government released a consultation paper in relation to road traffic penalties in which it outlined proposals to increase the maximum penalties for those who kill whilst driving a vehicle (See DETR, 2000 and ROSPA, 2001). Examples of some of the proposals include extending disqualification periods to a minimum of three years (and up to life) for causing death by dangerous driving or careless driving while under the influence of drink or drugs and creating an automatic life-long disqualification period for both offences where the offender has previously been convicted of a serious driving-related offence. In addition, it is proposed to increase the maximum term of imprisonment from five to ten years for causing death by aggravated vehicle taking (DETR, 2000). These proposals have now been reviewed (see Home Office Department for Transport, 2002) and are yet to be implemented.

Whilst calls are being made to introduce more stringent penalties for those whose dangerous or careless driving causes death, it seems likely that these offences will remain 'separate' from the general homicide offences. As Clarkson observes, 'the use of motor-vehicles, despite their inherent dangers, is so widespread and accepted that we assign responsibility to (even bad) drivers differently to those who cause deaths in different contexts. Their wrong is "situationally relevant" to ourselves' (2000: 149). Clearly powerful cultural and social factors play a role in our interpretation of these killings as 'less serious' than other forms of homicide.

> **Study Task 1.3**
>
> The last five years have seen increased attention and debate about the penalties for those who kill whilst driving dangerously or carelessly. Consider why such debates might have emerged and what impact they might have upon the laws surrounding unlawful homicide.

Deaths in Custody and During the Course of Arrests

Of equal concern and relevance, albeit a considerably less frequent occurrence, is the issue of deaths in prison or police custody or at the hands of the police in the course of arrests. When police or prison officers cause the deaths of those they encounter (either as suspects or convicted criminals), these deaths are often not viewed as having been committed unlawfully or, where they are, the Crown Prosecution Service (CPS) rarely feels compelled to prosecute. Research conducted by Inquest, a charitable organisation that monitors deaths in custody, indicates that an average of one person a week dies in custody.[15] In 2003 there were 42 known deaths in police custody across England and Wales (which includes road traffic accidents, pursuits and police shootings). In the same year, 76 deaths occurred in prisons across England and Wales that were not believed to have been self-inflicted (www.inquest.org.uk). Inquest believes that many of these deaths are the result of excessive violence on the part of the police towards suspects, or prison officers towards inmates. Even in those cases where an inquest jury[16] confirms that police officers unlawfully killed a suspect, the CPS rarely take action against the officers involved.

Summary

Thus far we have reviewed and critiqued the legal framework of homicide with particular reference to England and Wales. It should now be clear that the law of unlawful homicide is somewhat arbitrary in its application and administration. What is finally included in the relatively broad category of unlawful homicide does not necessarily represent the most serious offences that result in loss of life – either in scale or quality. The important point to retain for the moment, and to carry forward into the second section of this chapter, is that who becomes accountable for causing the death of another individual (or group of individuals) and in what particular manner rests on a complex set of doctrines, some very antiquated. The fact that a number of these anomalies have recently been amended (such as the year and a day rule) and that a number of commentators are arguing for additional reforms (such as the amendments to the law of involuntary manslaughter discussed earlier) only serves further to highlight the problematic nature of the criminal law in this area. There remains a further complication that must be acknowledged. In addition to problems of defining or delineating homicide, the counting of homicides (like the counting of every type of crime) is afflicted by the problem of the 'dark figure', that is, unreported and unrecorded crime. The following section considers this in some detail.

Study Task 1.4

Using a range of resources (that is, the Internet, books, journals and the media), find three examples of proposals to changes in the law of homicide in England and Wales over the last three years or examples of such changes. What do these changes or proposals for change tell us about the nature of the law of homicide?

Counting Homicide

The issue of the 'true' level of crime is a difficult concept. It represents the total amount of crime which takes place in a given country, whether or not it is recog- nised as a crime and whether or not it is reported to and recorded by the police. It is now readily acknowledged by Home Office statisticians, the police, politicians and criminologists alike that recorded crime in England and Wales only represents the 'tip of the iceberg'; below lies an unknown and uncertain mass of hidden crime, known as the 'dark figure'. The problem of the dark figure is common to all the social sciences. Whilst a number of measures have been introduced (essentially since the 1980s in England and Wales) to try and measure the dark figure, these only unearth part of the hidden crime. Examples include self-report studies and local and national victim surveys. The former involves questioning individuals about their own participation in crime and whether that crime has been detected. The latter entails members of the public being questioned about their experiences of crime and whether they have reported all crime known to or experienced by them (for a comprehensive overview of the dark figure of crime, see Coleman and Moynihan, 1996). In short, the statistics of offences recorded by the police, as well as those accumulated via other means (such as self-report studies and victim surveys), provide only a partial picture of the amount of crime committed.

Estimates of the amount of hidden crime vary across offence categories, and hence, the limitations of police statistics are more profound for some categories of crime than others. It is generally asserted that the police come to know about a very high proportion of homicides (Lewis, 1992; Morrison, 1995; Williams, 1996) and, possibly because of this general assumption, researchers often neglect to consider in any real detail the extent of the dark figure of homicide. Yet there are several important ways in which the conventional and authorised version of events may be underestimating or distorting the number of homicides across England and Wales each year. This issue has partly been addressed in the previous section by highlighting the legal 'biases' in counting homicide. Here we focus upon the complexities of unearthing those hidden homicides that *would* tend to be considered 'real crimes', that is, those for which a murder or manslaughter charge would normally apply.

The 'Dark Figure' of Homicide

The seemingly simple question of how many homicides take place in a particular year cannot be easily answered. Several factors influence the official registration of homicides.

Hidden Bodies

First and foremost comes the finding of a corpse. This is without doubt the most common source of discovery of killings which have taken place in the open, in public places, on commercial premises at night and of homicides where attempts have been made to hide the body from the scene of the crime (Morris and Blom-Cooper, 1964: 273). What we do not know, of course, is how many killers dispose of the bodies of their victims without trace. As Polk has pointed out, for some planned murders, 'part of the forethought may consist of disposing of the body in such a manner that its discovery is unlikely' (1994a: 10). Certainly it is not unheard of for the police to unexpectedly discover a corpse in the course of investigating other crimes. Hence, the discovery of a body can sometimes happen by chance, as in the cases of Dennis Nielson whose offences lay hidden for many years. Ultimately he was convicted of 15 murders. During August of 1997, four amateur subaqua divers discovered skeletal remains wrapped in a series of bags and bin liners in the Coniston Waters of the Lake District area in Cumbria, England. Forensic investigations revealed that the remains were that of a female school teacher, Carol Park, who had vanished 21 years previously from her home some 15 miles away. Police subsequently launched a murder investigation, focusing upon Gordon Park, the victim's husband at the time of her disappearance. He was eventually charged with her murder, but the case against him was dropped. In August 2000 a skeleton was discovered in a pub outbuilding in the Welsh village of Ystradgynlais, near Swansea by builders who were converting the beer store into a pub extension. Forensic scientists soon discovered that the remains were that of Barbara Maddocks, the landlady of the pub (the Aubrey Arms), who had disappeared 27 years earlier in 1973, when she was aged 47. At the time of her disappearance, local police officers launched a search and dug up a roundabout and part of a road but found nothing. Her husband, who died eight years previously, had told detectives at the time of her disappearance that he had been visiting friends and that when he returned to the pub, his wife was gone. Some local people believed she had returned to her native Australia after a row with her husband, others believed she had been murdered. A second woman, a friend of Barbara, is also alleged to have disappeared at around the same time. These are just a few of the known examples of hidden bodies that have come to light.[17] Moreover, there are undoubtedly others that have never been discovered.

Missing Persons

Second, there exists a considerable register of 'missing persons'. The National Missing Persons Helpline (NMPH), established in Britain in 1992, estimate that more than 250,000 people are reported missing in the UK each year. The vast majority return safe and sound within 72 hours – but thousands do not. Whilst many of these persons will have deliberately sought obscurity, it is possible that some have become the victim of homicide. Further, there are undoubtedly persons 'missing' who are not registered as such, who again may have become the victims of homicide, but we have no way of knowing. Personal communication between the author and a charity member from the NMPH (January 2003) revealed that roughly 7 per cent of registered missing persons end up dead. Three people on the charity's books are known to have been victims of serial killer Frederick West. A recent Home Office report by the Policing and Reducing Crime Unit suggests that whilst only a small proportion of missing persons are likely to be the victims of serious crime, police procedures for identifying a 'suspicious' missing person are currently underdeveloped (Newiss, 1999). The report recommends a number of measures to assist the police in identifying suspicious cases from the mass of reports they receive.

Establishing Mode of Death

Finally, of relevance to the issue of the dark figure of homicide, it is important to consider some of the complexities that exist in establishing cause of death. In the case of a discovered body, it is not always possible to determine immediately (if at all) whether the death was the result of foul play. Apart from establishing cause of death, one of the key purposes of a medico-legal autopsy is to establish the mode of death. Generally, four modes of death are possible: natural, accidental, suicide or homicide (Geberth, 1996). Distinguishing between the four categories is not always a straightforward procedure. For example, people who have apparently died from overdoses of medicine or 'natural causes' may sometime in fact be homicide victims. In the case of the nurse Beverley Allitt, found guilty in 1993 of murdering four children, it was a matter of contention for some time as to whether or not the children died of natural causes (White, 1995: 130). The now infamous case of Harold Shipman, the doctor convicted of murdering 15 of his patients by lethal injection (but suspected of killing in excess of 200 patients over a 20-year period), illustrates the potential ease with which the medical profession are able to conceal homicide.

Another area in which the complexities involved in establishing mode of death has been well documented relates to infant deaths. It is recognised that distinguishing an infant homicide from Sudden Infant Death Syndrome (SIDS) or 'cot death' can be very difficult (Meadow, 1999). SIDS is characterised by the death of seemingly healthy babies where the cause of death cannot be identified (Beckwith, 1970). It has been estimated that around 20 per cent of SIDS cases are in fact suspicious infant deaths, in that these deaths are thought to be largely attributable to the effects of child abuse (CESDI, 1998; Green and Limerick, 1999; White, 1999). There are many reasons for misdiagnoses, including inadequate police inquiries into the victim's background where suspicion is present (Bacon, 1997; Meadow, 1999), lack of multi-agency co-operation and communication, misdiagnosis by pathologists due to lack of information, a lack of specialism in paediatric pathology, and time pressures in returning the body to the family. Affecting each of these investigative layers would appear to be the inherent problems of handling such sensitive cases, leading some to suggest that professionals err on the side of caution in adopting the SIDS label too readily when in doubt (see Millington and Smith, 1999, for a review of this area).[18]

Study Task 1.5

What does von Hentig mean when he states that 'Murder is not only a legal abstraction but a medical phenomenon' (1938: 112)?

Open Verdicts

Mortality statistics, compiled and disseminated by the Office of National Statistics, provide details of all deaths registered in England and Wales. Perusal of the statistics concerned with death by injury and poisoning reveal some interesting findings. For example, recent mortality statistics (1999) indicate that 'open verdicts' were recorded on over 1,500 people in 1999 in England and Wales (OPCS, 2001). Essentially, these deaths remain unresolved with respect to whether the fatal injuries sustained were accidentally or purposely inflicted, either by the victim (that is, was it accident or suicide?) or some other unidentified person (in which case it could be deemed a homicide). One can only speculate as to what proportion, if any, of these deaths could have been the result of unlawful killings. In addition there exists a category referred to as 'unknown causes of morbidity and mortality', which refers to cases where the underlying cause of death is unknown. There were a total of 915 cases in 1999, 548 of which were given an open verdict (the remainder were classified as accidents or natural causes of unknown origin). Once again, it is possible that some of these deaths may have been the result of undetected 'foul play'. There is a further interesting category from the point of view of questioning the counting of homicide qualitatively. There were 83 recorded cases of 'misadventures to patients during surgical and medical care' in 1999 as determined by an inquest verdict. Could it be that some proportion of these 'misadventures' were due to medical negligence? That these deaths have ultimately been classified as accidental misfortunes may owe more to the complex death registration system than any clear reflection upon the precise circumstances of these deaths. Emmerichs (1999) has argued that a significant number of murders were missed in nineteenth-century England, either deliberately or due to inadequacies in the institution of Coroners' inquests. The extent to which the modern system is less flawed is open to question.

In summary, difficulties involved in certifying the cause of death mean that a number of homicides may go undetected each year. It follows that even if only a small proportion of all deaths regarded as natural were homicides, then the numbers of offences currently recorded as homicides would be an under-estimate. In combination, the effects of undiscovered bodies and misdiagnoses of death could provide for a substantial underestimate of homicides. If we add to this deaths that could be treated as homicides (such as corporate killings, causing death by driving, deaths in custody and during the course of arrest), then we begin to see how the picture of homicide could look substantially different given different definitions, counting rules and perceptions of what it means to commit an unlawful homicide. This statistical bias or imperfection has further implications in respect of theory formulation. As far as the offenders are concerned, we know nothing of those who go undetected. The important ques-tion is whether these 'hidden homicides' are in some way qualitatively different from those we come to know about. Max Atkinson, some 20 years ago, summed up the complexities involved in studying the phenomenon of suicide, drawing attention to both the inaccuracies of suicide statistics and, more particularly, the socially defined (rather than naturally defined) nature of this phenomenon (Atkinson, 1979). Clearly, similar problems present themselves to the would-be homicide researcher.

Chapter Summary and Conclusions

After brief consideration of the socially constructed nature of homicide and the diffi-culties involved in defining homicide, this chapter presented an overview of the legal categories of unlawful homicide in England and Wales before moving on to consider numerous problems with the legal framework. There is little doubt that the law of homicide is a complicated affair. There is considerable debate regarding the need for reform in relation to the law surrounding unlawful homicide. This partly reflects a recognition by many lawyers and penal reformers that the law of homicide presents difficulties of application and consistency (Rock, 1998). Researchers of homicide, in relying upon such legal categories, have to work with a definition that is both arbitrary and, to some extent, restrictive. This is not simply a technical matter; rather, the legal framework has important implications for how we come to view homicide and the kinds of theories that are developed to explain this phe-nomenon. For example, if deaths from negligence and corporate manslaughter were more readily included in the statistics of homicide, the picture would include larger numbers of skilled working-class and middle-class offenders and victims, signifi-cantly altering what is currently a perception of homicide as dominated by work-ing-class individuals. In addition, despite the popular view of the visibility of unlawful homicide, this chapter has illustrated the potential for a 'dark figure'. Moreover, the phenomenon of homicide is somewhat unique in that some of the techniques devised to uncover the dark figure of crime are simply not feasible to adopt. In particular, victim surveys (for example, the British Crime Survey) which have shed light on the dark figure of offences, such as burglary and domestic violence (see Mirrlees-Black et al., 1998; Kershaw et al., 2000), cannot be applied in the case of homicide.

The most important message to take away from this chapter is that homicide, unlike most other forms of crime, is not a concrete phenomenon that we can easily define, count, judge or punish. The 'official' version of events (in the form of criminal statistics compiled by the Home Office) is just that – 'a version'. It by no means captures, nor intends to, all homicides. It is vital to bear this in mind as we proceed to Chapter 2, for here we will be relying upon the official picture in order to provide an overview of patterns and trends of homicide in the UK. Of course, trying to explain and understand homicide is an equally complex task and will be dealt with in subsequent chapters.

Review Questions

- What distinguishes voluntary and involuntary manslaughter? Using examples drawn from the media coverage over the last four years, list two examples of each type of manslaughter.
- What evidence exists to illustrate that unlawful homicide is a social construct?
- How can researchers try to assess the 'dark figure' of homicide and what particular difficulties would they face?
- On 7 May 2003, the Home Secretary (David Blunkett) announced his plans to introduce tougher sentencing 'principles' for the minimum periods that certain life sentence prisoners should serve. Among the particular kinds of murders singled out for increased minimum sentences are the abduction and murder of a child, terrorist-related murders and killings involving the death of a police or prison officer in the course of their duty (Travis, 2003). Access archived news articles and review the proposals along with criticisms from human rights commentators and legal experts. What are the major objections to these proposals?

Further Reading

The most up to date critical review of the law of homicide in England and Wales is *Rethinking English Homicide Law* (Ashworth and Mitchell, 2000: Oxford University Press). Also useful is Barry Mitchell's *Murder and Penal Policy* (1990: Macmillan) and *Law Relating to Violent Crime* (1997: CLT Professional). On the social construction of homicide, refer to Hazel May's 'Who Killed Whom?: Victimization and Culpability in the Social Construction of Murder' (1999: *British Journal of Sociology*, Vol. 50/3, pp. 489–506). An excellent text that deals with many aspects of corporate crime, including corporate homicide, is *Corporate Crime* (Slapper and Tombs, 1999: Longman). A useful chapter dealing with the law surrounding homicide is found in *Principles of Criminal Law* (Ashworth, 1999: Oxford University Press). For an excellent discussion and analysis of the construction and deconstruction of crime, refer to Chapter 1 of *The Problem of Crime* (Muncie and McLaughlin, 2001: Sage). Also Mike Levi and Mike Maguire's chapter 'Violent Crime' in the *Oxford Handbook of*

Criminology (Maguire et al., eds, 2002: Oxford University Press) contains a very useful section on attitudes to and constructions of violence. Finally, for a comprehensive overview of the relationships between legal constructions of crime (generally) and social constructions of crime and criminals, refer to Lacey's excellent chapter in the *Oxford Handbook of Criminology* 'Legal Constructions of Crime' (Maguire et al., eds, 2002: Oxford University Press).

Useful Internet Sites

A very useful Internet site dealing with the law surrounding death by driving is www.oraclelaw.co.uk. The Home Office website www.homeoffice.gov.uk offers a vast amount of information on many aspects of crime and criminal justice. In relation to this chapter, the publications section contains the latest official homicide statistics which, as well as information on the number of homicides recorded and various characteristics of offenders and victims, contain details relating to counting rules and definitional issues pertinent to this chapter. In addition, a search of the subject index will reveal a number of useful links, such as deaths reported to coroners where links to statistical information on deaths in police custody can be found, and motoring offences statistics. The Law Commission is a useful resource for legislative reform www.lawcom.gov.uk. Health and Safety Statistics, such as the number of fatal injuries to workers and occupational diseases, can be found on the Health and Safety Executive/Commission web page at www.hse.gov.uk.

Notes

1 The Economic and Social Research Council (ESRC) funded the Violence Research Programme between 1997 and 2002. One of the 20 projects is concerned with homicide in Britain (see www1.rhbnc.ac.uk/sociopolitical-science/VRP/realhome.htm).

2 Brookman (2000b) analysed a total of 97 covering reports from police murder files as part of her doctoral research (see Brookman, 1999). From these data, case summaries were compiled that comprise condensed versions of important aspects of the cases and provide an understanding of the nature and circumstances of a diverse set of homicides. In addition, analysis of the Home Office HI for the period 1990–2001 (which includes a total of 9,029 cases) has been undertaken. Findings from both data sources will be presented throughout this text. The HI data is clearly more extensive in that it covers a much larger number of homicide cases. By contrast, the police murder file data can be described as intensive in that it contains richer and more detailed information about homicide cases (see Lewis et al., 2003 and Dobash et al., forthcoming for a further discussion of the strengths and weaknesses of such forms of homicide data).

3 See Clarke (2001) for a discussion of social constructionism.

4 See Levi (1997: 843–5) for a similar discussion in relation to the broader category of violent crime.

5 See also Rowbotham et al., 2003 for a similar discussion regarding media coverage, public attitudes and criminal justice responses to the Bulger and Burgess murders, 1993 and 1861.

6 See Lacey (2002) for a comprehensive overview of the legal construction of crime.

7 Until 1996 an individual could not be prosecuted for murder if the individual they had harmed died after a year and a day of the original attack. One of the original rationales for this rule lay in the difficulty in proving a causal connection between old injuries and subsequent

death. However, this rule came under increasing criticism, especially as modern medicine and life-support machines meant that a murderer could avoid liability simply because of lengthy medical attempts to save someone's life. Hence, in 1995 the House of Commons' Select Committee on Home Affairs and the Law Commission produced papers recommending the abolition of the rule, and Parliament did so in the Law Reform (Year and a Day Rule) Act 1996.

8 36 per cent resulted in a conviction for manslaughter, a little over 1 per cent resulted in convictions for lesser offences (such as ABH) and less than 1 per cent of convictions were for infanticide. 13 per cent of cases resulted in an acquittal or proceedings were discontinued (for example, due to a lack of evidence or a decision that it was not in the public interest to prosecute). In a further 5 per cent of cases there were no court proceedings due to the death of the suspect. Proceedings remain pending for 12 per cent of cases from this period.

9 Fear of social disgrace or poverty was seen as the motivation for such actions and hence some protection from the full rigours of the law (that is, the death penalty for murder convictions) in what were perceived as tragic cases emerged.

10 See Flood-Page, C. and Taylor, J. (2003), *Crime in England and Wales: Supplementary Volume* (Chapter 1 by Judith Cotton, 'Homicide').

11 For useful summaries of related legal issues for Scotland refer to Scottish Executive, 1999; Charlton and Bolger, 1999, Soothill et al., 1999 and Christie, 2002 and for Northern Ireland refer to Quinn, 1998, and Hanly, 1999.

12 These figures relate to the period 1999, the most recent year for which accurate figures are available.

13 The Health and Safety Executive, who produce figures for occupationally-caused deaths, acknowledge that they are not always comprehensive. In particular, asbestos-related cancers are believed to be a gross under-estimate since most cases are clinically indistinguishable from tobacco-related deaths (HSE, 2000: 74). The HSE acknowledge that the likely true numbers of asbestos-related cancers are probably at least equivalent to the numbers caused by mesothelioma, of which there were 1,595 in 1999.

14 The homicide figures for 2001 as opposed to 2002 have been included as they are more accurate. Annual totals of homicide are subject to frequent downward revision for the first two or three years after initial reporting, as individual cases are reclassified (see Brookman and Maguire, 2003).

15 This figure includes deaths in police custody and in prison, some of which may have been self-inflicted. The information that Inquest receive from the police and prisons authorities is often limited in detail, making it difficult to determine accurately the circumstances of death (personal communication, June 1999).

16 An Inquest Jury or Coroners' Jury is made up of between seven and 11 members of the public, summoned at random from the electoral roll like other jurors. There are times when a coroner must summon a jury, which include cases where there is 'reason to suspect' that the death occurred in prison, in police custody or as a result of injury inflicted by a police officer or in an industrial accident. The coroner also has discretion to summon a jury in other cases. Any verdict which appears to determine criminal liability on the part of a named person or civil liability is forbidden. However, 'unlawful killing' is permitted as a verdict so long as the killer is not named. The commonest verdicts are: natural causes, misadventure, suicide and open verdict (where there is insufficient evidence to justify any definite verdict) (www.inquest.org.uk).

17 See also the case of Margaret Hogg, whose body was found in 1984 at the bottom of Wastewater lake in Cumbria. Her husband was ultimately found guilty of manslaughter. And Sheena Owlitt, whose body was found in Crummock Water in 1988. Her husband ultimately confessed to her murder and was sentenced to life imprisonment.

18 See also Wilczynski (1997a, Ch. 2) for a comprehensive overview of the 'dark figure' of child homicide and Jackson (2002) for an historical perspective on the issue of child homicide and concealment.

2 Patterns and Characteristics of Homicide in the UK

Homicide can be divided in all sorts of ways from the point of view of describing its patterns, charting trends or trying to unravel its causes. Consider for a moment what you know (or perhaps don't know) about homicide. What are the characteristics of the killers and victims in terms of age, gender, social class and so forth? How do individuals kill one another? To what extent are particular weapons used? Where does homicide occur (that is, what particular locations predominate)? Is it an indoor our outdoor affair, or, put another way, a private or public affair?) Are certain times of the day, week or year significant? And, finally, the all important question, why? What motivates one human being to kill another? This latter question is one that most often ignites the imagination and is, perhaps, the most difficult question posed. Whilst we can chart certain 'facts' about homicide, in terms of the characteristics of those involved where known (question one above), the weapons and methods used to kill (question two above), and where and when (question three), unravelling motivational forces is a far more complex issue to address. Interestingly, though, it is on the basis of the gathering of the 'facts' that theories or explanations of homicide emerge. For example, knowing that homicide is very much a 'masculine' affair (which we discuss below) has led to numerous theories regarding the links between gender or, more specifically, masculinity and homicide. Moreover, the theories that have been developed to address this issue take a number of different forms. Some draw upon biology to explain the over-involvement of males in homicide (for example, exploring the links between the male hormone testosterone and levels of aggression and violence), others draw upon evolutionary psychology to explain why it has been necessary for males to adopt violence. Another body of theories look more to social learning theory to explain why males are socialised more toward aggression or violence. Still others focus upon the wider social structure of society and features such as patriarchy. We will be exploring all of these ideas and more in Chapters 3 to 5.

However, the link between 'facts' and theory formulation is not as simple as might first appear. For example, 30 or 40 years ago, gender was essentially ignored by criminologists as an explanatory variable – yet it was clear even then that males predominated as violent offenders and, to a lesser extent, victims. Yet this was not seized upon and explored – it was simply taken for granted. In stark contrast, many current theories of violent crime are infused with notions of masculinity or masculinities (an issue to which we will return in several chapters of this book).

In this chapter we will consider patterns of homicide along a number of key dimensions. It is not a concern of this chapter to offer explanations of homicide, although it will be useful to flag up some of the perspectives and theories that have been developed to make sense of particular characteristics of homicide. Subsequent chapters will deal with explanations of homicide in detail. At this stage, the emphasis will be upon describing some of the broad patterns of homicide in different ways and alerting readers to the links between what is known about how homicide 'looks' with how it has been explained. We begin with a basic overview of the extent of homicide in the three major jurisdictions of the UK.

Homicide Rates and Trends in the UK

Of the three jurisdictions of the UK, England and Wales has the highest number of homicides each year, as illustrated in Table 2.1. For the financial years 2000/01 and 2001/02, there were 849 and 858 cases of homicide offences recorded by the police in England and Wales respectively (Cotton, 2003). This compares to 105 victims of homicide in Scotland recorded in 2000, and 107 recorded in 2001 (Scottish Executive, 2002). Finally, there were 48 cases of homicides in Northern Ireland in 2000/01 and 52 in 2001/02 (PSNI, 2002, 2003a).

It is not surprising that England and Wales has the largest share of homicide, given that the population of England and Wales is significantly higher than in the other two countries. In order to control for population size and provide a more meaningful measure of the extent of homicide, it is necessary to consider homicide rates.

Homicide Rates

A different picture emerges when we look at the homicide rates per 100,000 population. For the 20-year period 1977–97, the average homicide rate per 100,000 population in England and Wales was 1.3. Scotland was higher at 1.9, although both fade in comparison to Northern Ireland's figure of 5.6 – a figure which increases to 6.2 when the year of 1976 is taken into account, despite the rates for both England and Wales and Scotland remaining the same. These figures are an artefact of what is commonly referred to as the 'security situation' or 'the Troubles' in Northern Ireland (which we discuss in more detail in Chapter 9). This trend continues

Table 2.1   The total number of homicides in the UK in 2001

England and Wales	858
Scotland	107
Northern Ireland	52

Sources: Cotton, 2003; Scottish Executive, 2002; and Police Service of Northern Ireland, 2002.

when we consider preceding years, during the worst period of the Troubles – for example, at the peak of the troubles in 1972, this rate was 24.6 per 100,000 population (Richards, 1999). Further interesting figures emerge upon examining particular cities across the three jurisdictions (see Table 2.2). For example, in Belfast between 1995–97 there was an average 4.37 homicides per 100,000 population, compared to 2.17 per 100,000 in London during the same period, and 2.43 per 100,000 in Edinburgh during 1994–96 (Richards, 1999: 31). For the period 1997–99, the homicide rate (per 100,000 population) in Belfast was 5.23, as compared to 2.36 in London and 1.85 in Edinburgh (although it is interesting to note that Glasgow rates of homicide appear to be more comparable at 4.99) (Scottish Executive, 2001).

Table 2.2   Homicide rates per 100,000 population (averaging over the period 1997–99)

England and Wales	1.4 (London: 2.3)
Scotland	1.9 (Glasgow: 4.9)
Northern Ireland	3.1 (Belfast: 5.2)

Source: Stanko et al., 2002: 30.

Scotland has a high homicide rate (recognised for some time to be one and a half to two times that of England and Wales) and a low violence rate, whereas England and Wales have a high violence rate and low homicide rate. Although there are different recording practices and policies between the two jurisdictions, this difference appears to be real. As Soothill et al. (1999) point out, the differences between the homicide rates in Scotland and England and Wales is not 'across the board', with the victim's gender being crucial. The male victimisation rate appears to account for the major difference in these two regions – specifically, male victims who are killed by 'acquaintances' (with a rate of 12.91 per million in Scotland, compared to 4.72 in England and Wales).

That said, females in Scotland are at greater risk of being killed by a relative than in England and Wales. Soothill et al. (1999) speculate that this may be because the domestic sphere is wider in Scotland with relatives living in closer proximity, resulting in female 'relatives' being at a similar risk of homicide as female 'partners'.

In an attempt to explain the second anomaly (that is, the converse correlation that homicide rates appear to have with violence rates, in both jurisdictions), Soothill et al., compared violence and homicide victimisation rates for the two jurisdictions and went on to calculate a conversion rate for the number of homicides per 10,000 incidences of all violence, 'that is, the rate at which violent incidents of all kinds convert into homicide' (1999: 81). They found that for male victims, the difference between Scotland and England and Wales was huge; in all three categories of domestic, acquaintance and stranger (particularly domestic) incidents, violence was much more likely to end lethally in Scotland than in England and Wales. For females, the conversion rate for domestic incidents was higher in Scotland than in England and Wales, whilst 'acquaintance' incidents rarely converted into homicides (there were no stranger homicides for females in Scotland during the study period of Soothill et al.'s research).

Soothill et al. (1999) emphasise that violence-to-homicide conversion rates deserve further exploration and manipulation (for example, noting a distinction between violence and life-threatening violence). They suggest a number of further reasons for such variations in rates, such as the use of lethal weapons in attacks (bear in mind Scotland has a higher preference for sharp instruments than England and Wales) and the availability of guns. Soothill et al. (1999) also point to the time taken for ambulances to arrive at an injury scene or the distance needed to travel to reach medical facilities, which may affect whether the incident becomes a lethal one. Finally, they also allude to possible cultural differences between the jurisdictions, though caution that because the differences in homicide rates between the two regions are not across the board, explanations which focus upon overall structural or cultural differences between the countries are hazardous.

The extent and trends of homicides in England and Wales and Scotland are potentially difficult to compare with those in Northern Ireland because of the 'security situation' or Troubles mentioned above (see Richards, 1999). Fluctuations in homicide in Northern Ireland have for many years been heavily influenced by terrorist-related killings. Sharp decreases from 1994 onwards, for example, are, by and large, a reflection of the cease-fire agreed by paramilitary organisations – that is, announced by the Irish Republican Army (IRA) in August 1994 and by the Ulster Volunteer Force (UVF) in November of the same year. Increases can be seen for those periods in which the cease-fire was broken. Hence, homicide in Northern Ireland is heavily dependent upon political factors and the cultural and historical context of The troubles (we will return to the issue of terrorist-related killings in the context of Northern Ireland in Chapter 9). That said, Northern Ireland makes a distinction between those homicides attributable to the Troubles and those that are not. As Stanko et al., point out:

> Broadly, violence in Northern Ireland is categorised under two headings. The first is the category 'recorded crime', which is assumed to reflect the kinds of crime in Scotland, England and Wales. The second category refers to 'The Troubles': offences against the state (recorded under the Northern Ireland (Emergency Provisions Act) deaths 'due to the security situation', and 'paramilitary attacks'. (1998: 34)

To make the comparisons in homicide trends in Figure 2.1 more meaningful, terrorist-related homicides have not been included. However, if we were to incorporate security situation homicides into the equation we would find that prior to the end of the 1960s, Northern Ireland experienced relatively few homicides, although after 1969 rates rose drastically. More recently, they tentatively appear to have returned to levels closer to those in the rest of the UK (particularly Scotland) (Richards, 1999: 15).

Figure 2.1   Annual totals of recorded homicides in the UK, 1981–2001

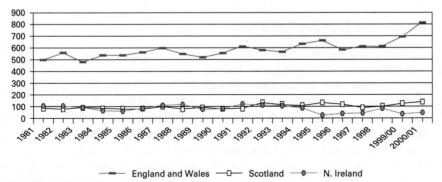

Source: Homicide Index (England and Wales); Scottish HI; PSNI personal communication.

Homicide Trends

Figure 2.1 shows the annual totals of homicides officially recorded in the UK over the 20-year period 1981–2000/01. The figures for England and Wales are derived from the Homicide Index (henceforth HI), a database held and maintained by the Home Office on the basis of incidents reported to it by the 43 police forces. These encompass only those homicides classified as murder, manslaughter or infanticide; 'corporate' homicides and deaths by dangerous driving are not included (refer to Chapter 1). The figures for Scotland and Northern Ireland are taken from similar databases in those two countries.

It can be seen from Figure 2.1 that the annual totals for the UK are consistently well below 900 and that the overall trend is only gradually upwards. For example, the totals in England and Wales for the four five-year periods were: 1981–85: 2,611; 1986–90: 2,785; 1991–95: 3,065; and 1996–2000: 3,369.[1] In Northern Ireland, indeed, the figures in the mid to late 1990s were generally below those of the early 1980s.[2] As illustrated, there has been an increase in the number of homicides in England and Wales, particularly since 1999. At least part of this increase is due to the very large number of victims of the serial killer Harold Shipman, who is estimated to have killed a total of 215 individuals and suspected of a further 45 or more deaths (see Chapter 9). His offences are believed to have spanned a 20-year period from 1978 to 1998 when he was finally identified and arrested. Shipman's offences appear in the HI against the years in which they were recorded and have inflated, in particular, the homicide figures for 1999 and 2000 (as well as 2002, though this is not relevant to our discussion here).

32 Understanding Homicide

In addition, figures for the year 2000 are further unusually inflated due to the deaths of 58 Chinese immigrants (all counted as individual instances of homicide) who were found in a sealed lorry container at Dover. The victims had all suffocated.[3] Finally, it is generally the case that the total number of homicides is revised downwards for the first two or three years after initial reporting.[4] Hence, it will only be possible to assess more accurately the apparent increase in homicide in the last few years in future years.

International Comparisons

In terms of other regions of the world, the UK has a relatively low homicide rate. This is particularly so in relation to England and Wales, which is ranked at 16th highest amongst the 22 countries considered below (Table 2.3) compared to Scotland (ranked seventh) and Northern Ireland (ranked third). South Africa ranks highest with a staggering rate of 564.9 per 100,000 population. The leading cause of death for males aged 15 to 21 in South Africa is homicide. The long history of apartheid and racism is undoubtedly inextricably linked to the high levels of violence experienced in this country.[5] The US ranks second with 62.6 homicides per 100,000 population, followed by Northern Ireland (which we will discuss in more detail in Chapter 9). Finally, the Czech Republic and Spain also exhibit high homicide rates at 28.1 and 26.0 per 100,000 respectively. At the very lowest end of the spectrum are Austria, Switzerland and Denmark.

Table 2.3 Comparison of homicide rates in selected countries and cities, 1997–99

Country	Homicide victims per million population (average per year 1997–99)	Country	Homicide victims per million population (average per year 1997–99)
England and Wales	14.5	Spain	26.0
Scotland	19.8	Netherlands	16.6
Northern Ireland	31.3	Greece	16.9
Ireland (Eire)	13.5	Portugal	13.0
Austria	8.4	Finland	13.9
Belgium	17.5	Switzerland	11.8
Germany	12.8	Czech Republic	28.1
Italy	15.6	Australia	19.1
France	16.3	New Zealand	20.1
Denmark	12.0	USA	62.6
Sweden	19.4	South Africa	564.9

Note: The figures for Spain and New Zealand relate to the average for 1997 and 1998 only and the figures for South Africa and related to the period 1997 only.

Source: Scottish Executive, 2001: 30.[1]

Having considered, in broad terms, the extent of homicide in the UK, we will now move on to consider some particular dimensions of homicide in the regions.

Characteristics of Offender, Victims and the Homicide Event

In this section we will explore some particular dimensions of homicide in terms of victim and offender characteristics and characteristics of the homicide event. We will begin by considering some socio-demographic characteristics of killers and victims in terms of gender, age, race and social class. It is worth noting that detailed information in relation to race and social class are somewhat lacking, particularly for the jurisdictions of Scotland and Northern Ireland. What will be presented here is, in any event, a snapshot or flavour of what is known. We begin by considering the gender of those involved in homicide.

Socio-demographic Characteristics of Offenders and Victims

Gender

In England and Wales males comprised 90 per cent of homicide offenders[6] for the period 2001 and 70 per cent of victims (HI). The over-involvement of males in homicide is even greater when we consider the jurisdictions of Scotland and Northern Ireland with males comprising 89 per cent of homicide suspects and 77 per cent of victims in Scotland (Scottish Executive, 2002) and 93 per cent of offenders and 87 per cent of victims in Northern Ireland (personal communication, Police Service of Northern Ireland)[7].

Interesting patterns appear when we consider the gender 'mix' between victims and killers – that is, the proportion of victims killed by male or female suspects. As illustrated in Tables 2.4 and 2.5, in Scotland a higher proportion of homicides are all-male encounters than in England and Wales (73 per cent compared to 60 per cent respectively). In contrast, a higher proportion of homicides in England and Wales involve males taking the lives of females (28 per cent compared to 16 per cent).[8]

Table 2.4   Gender 'mix' of suspects and victims: England and Wales 1997–2001

Main accused		Main victim	
		Male	Female
Male:	Percentage	60%	28%
	(Number)	(2,445)	(1,144)
Female:	Percentage	9%	3%
	(Number)	(323)	(127)

Source: Homicide Index: total cases = 4,043.

Table 2.5   Gender 'mix' of suspects and victims: Scotland 1997–2001

Main accused		Main victim	
		Male	Female
Male:	Percentage	73%	16%
	(Number)	(513)	(112)
Female:	Percentage	9.1%	1.9%
	(Number)	(66)	(14)

Source: Scottish Executive, personal communication, 2003: total cases = 705.

Age

In this section we will consider the ages of homicide victims and offenders. As illustrated in Figure 2.2, those aged between 21 and 35 exhibit the highest levels of victimisation. Those aged between 0–5 also demonstrate high levels. Moreover, the 5-year age groupings mask the particular vulnerability of babies less than a year old to homicide (see Figure 2.3). In fact, per 100,000 population, babies less than a year old are four times more likely than any other single age group to fall victim to homicide (Brookman and Maguire, 2003). In terms of the 5-year age groupings depicted in Figure 2.2, those aged 31–35 are the most vulnerable, followed by those aged 26–30 and 21–25. Interestingly, those aged 31–35 comprise 7.7 per cent of the population of England and Wales, and those aged 26–30 6.9 per cent (Census, 2001, available at www.statistics.gov.uk/census2001). Hence, it is possible that their greater numbers in the population may have a bearing upon these figures. That said, any relationship is far from simple, in that levels of victimisation for other age groupings do not rise and fall in accordance with population figures. For example,

Figure 2.2   Age of homicide victims, England and Wales: 5-year age groupings 1997–2001

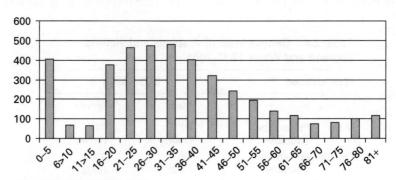

Source: Homicide Index, 1997–2001.

Figure 2.3   Age of homicide victims, England and Wales 1997–2001

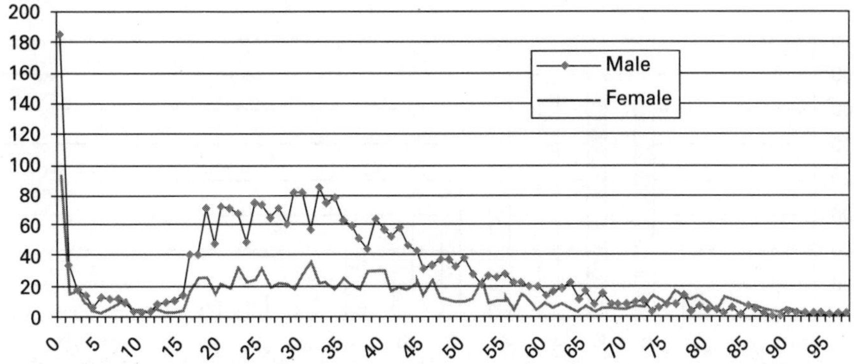

Source: Homicide Index, 1997–2001.

those aged 36–40 comprise a greater proportion of the population than those aged 21–25 (6.3 per cent and 5.9 per cent respectively), yet those in the 21–25 age range have a higher victimisation rate. In addition, those aged 16–20 comprise a smaller percentage of the population (6.1 per cent) than those aged either 6–10 (5.6 per cent) or those aged 11–15 (6.5 per cent), yet the latter two groups fall victim to homicide much less frequently than those in the 16–21 age range.

The picture is much the same in respect of Northern Ireland as in Scotland. For the period 1993–99, the majority of homicide victims in Northern Ireland were aged between 30–49 (45 per cent) and 17–29 (33 per cent). Thus, 78 per cent of all homicide victims were aged between 17 and 49. A further 15 per cent were aged between 50–74, 6 per cent were aged under 17, and finally 1 per cent (1 case) was aged 75 or above (personal communication, PSNI, Central Statistics Unit, 2003). In Scotland 'male victims in the 16 to 29 and 30 to 39 age groups represented the highest rates of homicides per million population; 50 and 48 respectively' (Scottish Executive, 2002).

Consideration of the age of the perpetrators of homicide reveal very similar findings in terms of the peak ages of offending (excluding of course the peak of victimisation for babies). For example, in England and Wales, the peak ages of offending is between the ages of 31 and 35, closely followed by those aged between 21 and 25 (see Figure 2.4). Similarly, in Northern Ireland, figures consistently show that most offenders are aged 25 years or below, with the significant majority of all offenders aged 35 or younger. During the period 1993–99, of those offenders prosecuted, 46 per cent were aged 25 or younger and a further 37 per cent were aged between 26 and 35. Similarly, of those convicted for homicide, 45 per cent were aged 25 or younger and 40 per cent fell in the age group of 26–35 years (personal communication, PSNI, 2003). This trend is also echoed in figures for Scotland, where the majority of all those accused of homicide are males aged 16–29 (Scottish Executive, 2001, 2002).

Figure 2.4   Age of homicide suspects, England and Wales: 5-year age groupings 1997–2001

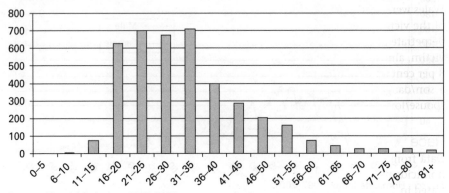

Source: Homicide Index, 1997–2001.

Table 2.6   Child-perpetrated homicides in England and Wales 1992–2001

Age of Suspect	Number of Homicides
< 10 years	5
10	5
11	2
12	6
13	15
14	31
15	73
16	117
TOTAL	254

Source: Homicide Index, 1997–2001.

Homicides committed by children are extremely rare. Nevertheless, they attract significant media and public attention. In England and Wales in the last decade (1992–2001) there have only been 254 cases of child-perpetrated homicide[9] out of a total of 7,641 homicides, which translates to just over 3 per cent of the total number of homicides over this period and an average of 25 cases per year. During the last five years (1997–2001) there has been an average of 30 homicides per year in England and Wales committed by children aged 16 years or younger (a total of 150 cases). The 39 cases of child-perpetrated homicide that occurred in 2001 is the largest number in the last decade. However, it remains the case that child-perpetrated homicides still only accounts for 3.6 per cent of the total number of homicides in an average year. As Table 2.6 illustrates, children's share of homicides increases as they enter their teenage years. It is exceptionally rare for a child under 13 years to kill. Hence, when James Bulger was killed by Jon Veneblesand Robert Thompson (both aged 10) in 1993, media and public interest was intense.

Almost 30 per cent of the victims of child-perpetrated homicide in England and Wales were aged between 0–16 years (8 per cent are aged less than one year[10]). Half of the victims were aged 23 years or below. Eighty per cent of the victims of child-perpetrated homicides were male. In terms of the relationship between killer and victim, almost 29 per cent are classified as strangers, 19 per cent are acquaintances, 8 per cent of victims were a friend or ex-friend, over 5 per cent of the victims were a son/daughter and a further 8 per cent a family member (other than parent or spouse/lover) (HI, 1997–2001).

Race

Data from England and Wales indicate that blacks and Asians are more at risk of homicide than whites when considering their numbers in the population.[11] As illustrated in Table 2.7, ethnic minority groups, as a whole, make up less than 8 per cent of the population of the UK. Asians comprise the greatest share of ethnic minority groups followed by blacks, mixed race groups and finally Chinese and 'other' groups. England and Wales have the greatest ethnic diversity of the regions of the UK at 8.5 per cent and Northern Ireland has the lowest at a mere 0.8 per cent.

Table 2.7   The UK population by ethnic group (percentages)

	England and Wales	Scotland	Northern Ireland	UK Total
White	91.31	97.9	99.0	92.12
Mixed	1.3	0.25	0.2	1.15
Asian	4.4	1.0	0.2	3.97
Black	2.2	0.15	0.1	1.95
Chinese and other	0.6	0.51	0.3	0.81
	All minority ethnic population = 7.88			100%

Note: 'Black' includes black Caribbean, black African and black other. 'Asian' includes Indian, Pakistani, Bangladeshi and other Asian. 'Mixed' includes white and black Caribbean, white and black African, white and Asian and other mixed. Figures have been rounded up to the nearest decimal place.

Source: Census, April 2001, Office for National Statistics available at www.statistics.gov.uk/census2001.

As indicated in Table 2.8, almost 10 per cent of the victims of homicide in England and Wales over the period 1995–2001 were black, despite them only comprising 2.2 per cent of the population of England and Wales (as at 2001, see Table 2.7). Similarly, Asians are over-represented as homicide victims, comprising almost 6 per cent of victims yet only 4.4 per cent of the population of England and Wales. Whites, on the other hand, comprise over 90 per cent of the population of England and Wales but make up only three-quarters of the homicide victim population. A similar picture emerges when considering the ethnic composition of homicide offenders where, once again, blacks and Asians are over-represented (see Table 2.9).

Table 2.8   Ethnic groupings of homicide victims in England and Wales 1995–2001

Victim ethnic group	Number	Percentage
White	4,196	75.5
Asian	323	5.8
Black	525	9.5
Other	211	3.8
Unknown	300	5.4
TOTAL	5,555	100

Source: Homicide Index.

Table 2.9   Ethnic groupings of homicide offenders in England and Wales 1995–2001

Offender ethnic group	Number	Percentage
White	4,173	76.4
Asian	324	5.9
Black	560	10.3
Other	158	2.9
Unknown	340	4.5
TOTAL	5,555	100

Source: Homicide Index.

There are many possible reasons for the over-representation of ethnic minority groups in homicide. Richards (1999) notes, for example, that ethnic minority groups tend to be concentrated in urban areas (where homicide rates are higher). The HI indicates that less than 1 per cent of homicides (between 1995–2001) were racially motivated (36 cases). It seems likely, however, that this figure is an underestimate of the true extent of racially-motivated killings. There is certainly evidence of a rise in racist incidents reported to the police in England and Wales in the last decade, with a dramatic rise between 1998–2000 of 300 per cent, of which half occurred in the Metropolitan London Area (Smith et al., 2002; see also Stanko et al., 2002).

Social Class

There are a number of difficulties in trying to determine the social class of those involved in homicide in the UK. Moreover, there are various ways of calculating one's social class that have changed over time (see Brownfield, 1986). The HI records the economic position of victims and their key occupation at the time of their death, which allows us to gain some sense of social class. This information is not collected in respect of homicide offenders. Moreover, this information is only currently available for England and Wales, hence our discussion will be restricted to these areas. As illustrated in Table 2.10, over a quarter of victims of homicide between 1995 and 2001 have been classified as unemployed at the time of the homicide. The figure for 'no current occupation' in Table 2.11 is larger (at 53 per cent),

Table 2.10 Economic position of homicide victims, England and Wales 1995–2001

Victim's economic position	Number	Percentage
Employed	1,301	23.5
Student	366	6.6
Unemployed	1,462	26.4
Retired	559	10
Economically inactive	170	3.0
Children under school age	422	7.5
Not known	1,275	23
TOTAL	5,555	100

Note: Employed takes priority over student, that is, a 'student' with a job would be categorised as 'employed'. However, student takes priority over unemployed, that is, an unemployed student would be classified as a 'student'. Economically inactive includes housewives/husbands, although other categories take priority.

Source: Homicide Index.

Table 2.11 Key occupation of homicide victims, England and Wales 1995–2001

Victim's occupation	Number	Percentage
Managerial/professional and skilled	367	6.6
Manual (skilled/semi-skilled and unskilled)	775	14.0
Service industry (i.e., police/prison officer; fire-fighter; ambulance staff/paramedics; security staff	116	2.1
Prison inmate	13	0.2
Prostitute	25	0.5
Vagrant	11	0.2
No current occupation	2,947	53.0
Not known	1,301	23.4
TOTAL	5,555	100

Source: Homicide Index.

as it includes students and school children as well as those who have retired or are otherwise economically inactive but not classified as unemployed.

My own (Brookman, 2003) more in-depth analysis of 54 cases of masculine (male-on-male) homicide in England and Wales revealed that 70 per cent of the male victims were unemployed at the time, along with at least 30 per cent of offenders. Moreover, I found not a single case (amongst the 54 analysed) of a professional or skilled worker being killer, or taking the life of another man (2003: 38). Similarly, Dobash et al. (2001) found that 61 per cent of male homicide offenders were unemployed at the time of the homicide. There has been a great deal written about the possible links between social class and homicide, particularly the effects

of unemployment, poverty and inequality on homicide rates, that we will be
exploring in some detail in Chapter 5.

Victim–Offender Relationships

One would be forgiven for assuming that homicide most often occurs amongst strangers,
not least due to the kind of media coverage that such killings attract. In reality, however,
by far the largest proportion of homicides occur amongst spouses (current or former),
other family members or amongst other individuals who are known to each other.

As indicated in Table 2.12, almost one-third of homicides in England and Wales
occur amongst those who are related (or have been) to one another – classed as
domestic homicides in the broad sense of the term.[12] This is followed in volume by
acquaintance homicides at almost one-fifth. Homicides amongst strangers
comprise 15 per cent of homicides in England and Wales.

**Table 2.12   Homicides in England and Wales 1995–2001:
relationship of victim to suspect**

Relationship	Number	Percentage
Domestic:		
Son, daughter (inc. stepson/daughter)	477	8.6
Parent (inc. step parent)	137	2.5
Spouse, lover, boy/girlfriend	949	17
(current and former)		
Other family	179	3.2
Total domestic	1,742	31.5
Acquaintance	1,013	18.2
Stranger	824	15.0
Friend (current and former)	357	6.4
Commercial/business	233	4.2
Homosexual	46	0.8
Criminal associate	30	0.5
Not known	628	11.3
No suspect	682	12.3
TOTAL	5,555	100

Source: Homicide Index.

The figures for Scotland are not directly comparable for all relationship categories (see Table 2.13). For example, the acquaintance category appears much
larger at 47 per cent but includes friends, business and criminal associates and rival
gang members as well as 'other' known persons. The domestic category is lower at 27
per cent (compared to 31.5 per cent in England and Wales) but does not include
ex-partners for the whole time period and it is not clear whether the son/daughter
category includes step-children. Interestingly though, the stranger category, which
would appear to be directly comparable, is somewhat larger than in England and
Wales at 23 per cent (compared to 15 per cent).

These categories begin to provide us with some sense of the nature of homicide
but are, of course, somewhat limited in that it is not clear from the 'relationship'

Table 2.13 Homicides in Scotland 1995–2001: relationship
of victim to suspect

Relationship	Number	Percentage
Domestic:		
Son/daughter (inc. step son/daughter)	23	3.0
Parent (inc. step parent)	39	5.0
Partner (current only pre-2000)	116	16.0
Other family	27	3.0
Total domestic	205	27.0
Acquaintance	347	47.0
Stranger	168	23.0
Not known	12	1.5
No suspect	12	1.5
TOTAL	744	100

Source: Scottish Executive, 2001 and 2002.

classification what factors actually led to the killings. That said, some hint as to the circumstances begins to emerge. For example, knowing that 17 per cent of homicides occur amongst sexual intimates leads one to explore what it is about the relational bond that has broken down. As Polk puts it, such information 'helps us to locate the problem, but it only carries us part of the way to understanding the dynamics of violent behaviour' (1994a: 4). Moreover, categories such as 'stranger' reveal even less. As Polk notes, 'Even more critical is a category such as "stranger", since it becomes an enormous puzzle to determine what would generate the exceptional emotions most often found in a homicide when the people involved are previously unknown to each other' (1994a: 21). Later, in the third section of this chapter, we will be combining information about victim–offender relationships with features of the circumstances of such homicides in an effort to move a stage closer to the 'social reality' of homicide.

Study Task 2.1

Based on the information contained in this chapter, compile a list of the major socio-demographic characteristics of offenders and victims of homicide. What are the similarities and differences between offenders and victims?

Features of the Homicide Event

Aside from certain features that characterise those who become involved in homicide, there are also features of the event itself that ultimately assist in making sense of this phenomenon. It is to a consideration of these that we know turn.

Spatial and Temporal Patterns

It has long been recognised that homicide (and other violent events) are patterned in terms of place or space (spatially patterned) and in time (temporally patterned). For example, certain locations, such as public houses and clubs, or areas of 'spill-over' from these venues, such as nearby 'streets and alleys', feature more heavily as violent locations or 'hot spots'. Similarly, certain times or the day, days of the week and even parts of the year witness greater proportions of homicide than others (see Wolfgang, 1958; Messner and Tardiff, 1985; Sherman et al., 1989; Homel and Tomsen, 1993; Miethe and Meier, 1994; and Leather and Lawrence, 1995).

There is very little information available regarding temporal patterns of homicide in the UK. The HI, for example, contains no information on this matter. However, Brookman (2000b) analysed the temporal distribution of 95 homicides that occurred in England and Wales during 1994 and 1996 (using police murder file data) and found that almost one-third (31 per cent) occurred between midnight and 4:00 a.m., and a further 29 per cent occurred between 8.00 p.m. and midnight. Hence, by far the largest proportion of homicides analysed took place in the evening and early hours of the morning (see also Brookman, 2003).

Once again there is nothing recorded on the HI regarding spatial patterns of homicide in England and Wales, so we will return to earlier data generated by Brookman (2000b) from police murder files. Figure 2.5 indicates the location of homicides observed in three police force areas in England and Wales (where the total number of cases is 95). As illustrated, houses dominate as locations of homicide. This category includes victims' and offenders' houses as well as houses shared by both parties or houses inhabited by offenders or victims friend's. Victims' houses and houses shared by both offender and victim comprise the biggest share with

Figure 2.5   Location of homicides observed in three police force areas in England and Wales 1994–96

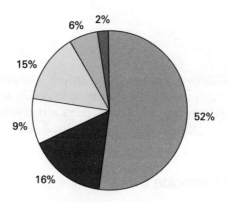

■ House ■ Street/Alley □ Pub/Club □ Open Space ■ Other ■ Not Known
Source: Brookman, 2000b.

21 cases each. A number of previous studies have observed that large proportions of homicides occur in or around pubs, clubs and other places of entertainment (Wallace, 1986; Falk, 1990). However, this does not appear to be the case in England and Wales. Interestingly though, all of the homicides that occurred in or around public houses or clubs involved a male offender and male victim.

Turning now to Scotland, the same basic spatial patterns are revealed (though unfortunately the categories are not exactly the same, making clear comparisons difficult). Houses once again predominate as the location for homicide in this juris-diction at an identical proportion of 52 per cent. Streets/footpaths comprise a fur-ther 24 per cent (higher than the sample from England and Wales). Pubs and clubs comprise only 3 per cent but, in fact, as the Scottish data do not include those homicides that occurred outside or very near to these venues it is likely that the figures would otherwise be very similar (only three of the incidents subsumed under the pub/club category in Figure 2.5 actually occurred within a pub or club – the rest happened just outside such venues).

Figure 2.6   Location of homicide, Scotland 1978–98

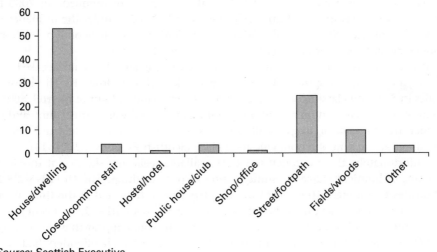

Source: Scottish Executive.

Drugs, Alcohol and Social Settings

There is a large body of literature devoted to the links between alcohol consump-tion and violence (lethal or otherwise). We will be returning to this issue in several of the subsequent chapters of the text. For example, in Chapter 3 we consider the influence of alcohol on individual behaviour from a biological perspective, in Chapter 5 we consider the role of alcohol and the social settings in which a signif-icant proportion of lethal violence occurs and, finally, in Chapter 9 we consider the potential for reducing or preventing alcohol-related violence in and around public houses and clubs. For now, we shall simply consider the extent to which those who become involved in homicide have consumed alcohol or drugs.

Figure 2.7   Percentage of drink or drug status of accused (where known) in Scotland 2000

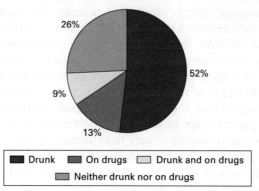

Source: Reproduced from Scottish Executive, 2001: 14.

As indicated in Figure 2.7, over half of those accused of homicide in 2000 in Scotland were classified as drunk and a further 13 per cent under the influence of one or more drug. Nine per cent had consumed both drugs and alcohol prior to the homicide and just over one-quarter were drug and alcohol free.

It is also known that in most cases (86 per cent) where the main accused was drunk and/or on drugs, the victim was also drunk and/or on drugs. For those homicides in Scotland classified as emerging out of some kind of fight or quarrel, 80 per cent of suspects for whom a drink/drug status was known were either drunk and/or under the influence of drugs. In all of these cases the victim was also drunk and/or on drugs at the time the homicide took place (Scottish Executive, 2001: 14).

Unfortunately, there is much less data available regarding the extent to which victims of homicide have consumed either alcohol or drugs. The HI (1995–2001) indicates that a mere 10 per cent of offenders were intoxicated at the time of the homicide, 1.5 per cent under the influence of drugs and a further 1.7 per cent under the influence of both drink and drugs. However, it would appear that this is a significant underestimate – particularly of the extent to which offenders had consumed alcohol. Brookman (2003) found that alcohol had been consumed by either the victim or offender (often to excess) in over half (52 per cent) of all cases of masculine (male-on-male) homicides she analysed. Furthermore, in 30 per cent of cases both the offender and victim had consumed alcohol. Dobash et al. (2001) found that 38 per cent of male homicide offenders in UK prisons were drunk or very drunk at the time of the offence, while 14 per cent were using illegal drugs.

Method of Killing/Weapons

In England and Wales between 1995–2001, the most common method of killing (employed in 30.1 per cent or 1,674 cases of homicide) involved a sharp instrument. This was followed by hitting or kicking (11.2 per cent or 624 cases). A blunt instrument was used to kill a further 530 victims, accounting for 9.5 per cent of

Figure 2.8   Method of killing in England and Wales 1995–2001

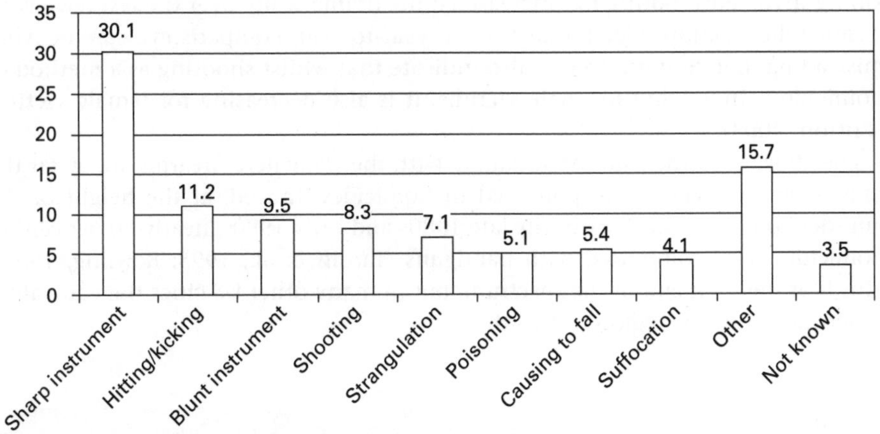

Source: Homicide Index, 1997–2001.

homicide cases, and 8.3 per cent of victims were shot (461). A further 7.1 per cent of victims were strangled, 5.4 per cent pushed to their deaths and 5.1 per cent poisoned. Just over 4 per cent of victims were suffocated and a further 15.7 per cent of victims met their death by 'other' means[13] (see Figure 2.8).

When we break this down by gender of the victim, we find that the primary method of killing male victims involves a sharp weapon (33.4 per cent), hitting and kicking (13.8 per cent), and shooting (10.6 per cent).[14] For those homicides in which a female is killed, the primary method again involves a sharp instrument (25.2 per cent). However, a significant number suffer death by strangulation (17.1 per cent as compared to just 2.6 per cent of male victims). A further 10 per cent were killed with a blunt instrument. An equal number of female victims were hit/kicked to death or suffocated (5.7 per cent respectively). Just over 3 per cent of female victims were shot.

In Scotland, involvement of a sharp instrument dominates the method of killing more so than in England and Wales, accounting for 45 per cent of homicides between 1991–2000, and shootings accounting for an average of 8 per cent (Scottish Executive, 2002). For male victims during this period, 51 per cent were killed with a sharp instrument, 17 per cent by hitting and kicking, 10 per cent by a blunt instrument, and in 8 per cent of male homicides the victim was shot. For females, a sharp instrument was used to kill the victim in 23 per cent of cases, closely followed by strangulation/drowning which accounted for 20 per cent of female homicides. 'Hitting and kicking' and a 'blunt instrument' were the next most common methods of homicide for female victims, comprising 15 per cent each (Scottish Executive, 2002: 11).

Although homicides involving a firearm are relatively rare in the UK, in England and Wales in 2001/02, firearms were used in 12 per cent of homicides – an increase of 32 per cent (23 cases) on the previous year. Cotton (2003) also notes that 2001/02 saw an increase of 41 per cent in the number of male shootings. Although the number of homicides in which the apparent method of killing involved shooting has increased quite dramatically over the last few years, it must be acknowledged that recent year-to-year comparisons can be very misleading. Longer-term trends also indicate that whilst shooting as a method of homicide is increasing for male victims, it is also decreasing for female victims (Cotton, 2003).

The above patterns contrast strikingly with the US, where firearms are by far the most common type of weapon used in homicides. Indeed, at the height of the 'murder boom' in New York in the late 1980s and early 1990s, nearly 80 per cent of homicides were committed with handguns (Tardiff et al., 1995; Bowling, 1999). This is at the high end of the spectrum, but in many other US cities the equivalent proportion is in the region of two-thirds.

Study Task 2.2

Method(s) of killing differ depending upon the gender of the offender and victim. Access homicide statistics for England and Wales (visit the Home Office website and search for Crime in England and Wales 2001/2002: Supplementary Volume, eds Flood-Page and Taylor) or Scotland (visit the Scottish Executive website and search for homicide statistics). Determine what major differences there are in the ways in which males and females meet their deaths. Make a list of the possible reasons for the differences in methods of homicide that you have observed.

Towards a Typology of Homicide: Scenarios and Social Context of Homicide

Thus far we have identified a number of the key socio-demographic features that characterise offenders and victims of homicide in the UK. In addition we have considered some features of the homicide event. In this final section of the chapter an attempt will be made to break down homicide into more meaningful categories.

As stated in the introduction to this chapter, there is no totally satisfactory way of dividing up the 1,000 or so homicides that occur in the UK in an average year. However, in very broad terms it is possible to gain some sense as to the kind of homicide that has occurred by focusing upon the relationship between the offender and victim and aspects of the circumstances of the killing. At the same time, the gender of the offender and victim is a further important consideration when trying to understand the dynamics and context of homicide. Each of these factors has been taken into consideration in the development of the typology below. Before discussing the categories of homicide it is important to make some statements about the difficulties and shortcomings of creating meaningful typologies of homicide, particularly those that provide an indication of motive.

Developing a Typology: Problematic Issues

Existing typologies of homicide are very diverse. Some researchers make very broad distinctions between, for example, 'instrumental' an 'expressive' forms of homicide (based on the classic distinction made in the psychological literature in relation to violence (see Chapter 4). Others have noted a broad distinction between homicides that are 'planned' or 'accidental' (see Chapter 11). According to Tarde (1912), in his review of motive classifications, the distinction between 'simple' homicides and 'premeditated' homicides was recognised by the Romans and perhaps even by the Greeks (Tarde, 1912: 462). Most recently, Block et al. (2001) have suggested that both the instrumental-expressive and planned-spontaneous dimensions be combined, resulting in four 'ideal types' of homicide:

- planned instrumental;
- spontaneous instrumental;
- planned expressive; and
- spontaneous expressive.

Generally speaking, these broad distinctions have been overlooked in recent years as researchers have developed more complex typologies. Regarding the more complex typologies, many researchers seem to confuse issues of motivation with issues of victim–suspect relationships. Take, for example, Harlan's (1950) four-point classification of 'ostensible motive' for homicide in the US county of Alabama:

- killing a family member;
- sex triangle/quarrel over wife or lover;
- quarrel over cards, dice, money and so on; and
- quarrel of relatively trivial origin – an insult, curse or jostle. (Harlan, 1950: 746)

Not only is there some degree of overlap across these categories, but the first category tells us nothing of the factors that led to the homicide; it merely describes the formal relationship between the individuals involved. Similar problems hinder Wolfgang's (1958) motive listing, which includes such categories as domestic quarrel, insult, curse, jostling, accidental and altercation of relatively trivial origin, and has been described by Daly and Wilson (1988: 172) as a 'conceptual hodgepodge'.

Polk suggests that criminologists 're-examine the actual data of homicide to observe if it is possible to obtain more concise and theoretically meaningful groupings of homicide' (1994a: 21). But this is only essentially possible with very detailed data and even under these circumstances is problematic when trying to assess the issue of motive. As Wolfgang (1958: 185) indicated, to determine the 'true' motive of a suspect would require that we know exactly what the suspect was thinking (consciously or subconsciously) at the time of the homicide. One could further argue that the researcher needs to understand the reasoning of the suspect prior to the offence in order to identify any factors that led up to the homicide. The reliability and validity of any judgements in this area are therefore inevitably questionable. As Gibson (1975: 21) acknowledged, the attribution of motive invariably involves some degree of subjectivity: the information available may be inadequate and, in some cases, there may appear to be more than one particular motive for a defendant's actions. In certain types of homicide – for example, where an armed robber shoots a bank clerk – the motive is relatively clear. However, homicides take numerous forms and the motivational factors involved are often diverse and elusive. Invariably the only clues may be the word of the perpetrator(s), and any inferences from such statements are highly questionable since many people attempt to justify or rationalise their actions, to some extent, after the event. That the Home Office were unable to identify the circumstances (their terminology for motive) surrounding 967 (or 23 per cent) of homicides that occurred between 1997 and 2001 illustrates the difficulties involved in attributing motive.

In sum, for all of the above reasons, one can gain no more than a superficial view of the motive or circumstances of homicide from what is the most extensive database of homicide in England and Wales – the Home Office HI. That said, in subsequent chapters, with the benefit of detailed case studies compiled from police murder investigation files and Crown Prosecution files, considerably greater detail and understanding of different forms of homicide will be undertaken (albeit involving smaller samples). For example, in Chapter 6 we will unravel 'masculine' killings and consider two very different forms, that is, 'confrontational' killings and 'revenge' killings, as well as the different circumstances under which men kill their female intimate partners. Later, in Chapter 7, we will consider female-perpetrated homicide, which is very much a domestic affair. In Chapter 8 we deal with the killing of infants and children, and in Chapter 9, the phenomenon of multiple homicide.

A Typology of Homicides in England and Wales

The figures contained in Table 2.14 are derived from analysis of the HI for the 5-year period 1997–2001. A fuller version of this table can be found in the Appendix at the end of this book, including a gender breakdown of several of the categories. As illustrated, of the 10 major categories of homicide displayed, domestic homicides comprise the largest proportion at almost one-third of all homicides. The next largest category (aside from those where the motive is unknown) comprises confrontational homicides. This form of homicide is very much a 'masculine' affair in that 92 per cent of confrontational homicides involved a male offender and male victim (see Appendix). As will be discussed in much more detail in Chapter 6, these homicides differ in several fundamental ways from revenge killings amongst men. For example, revenge killings are generally planned and purposeful, whereas confrontational homicides are often fights or assaults 'gone wrong' – that is, the death of the victim was not necessarily intended. Homicides committed in the course of undertaking some other form of crime, such as burglary, robbery or a sexual attack, comprise the next largest category at 7 per cent of the total proportion of homicides in England and Wales. It is not clear from the data held on the HI to what extent the murder of the victims in these cases was intended. For example, some burglary or robbery homicides may have been intended in order to prevent the victim of the burglary or robbery from identifying the offender. The same may be true of some sexual attacks that result in the death of the victim. On the other hand, an unknown proportion of these homicides may have been intended in that the rape and murder of the victim was intricately connected. Following closely on the heels of crime-related homicides are reckless acts that result in death (at 6 per cent). This includes motor-vehicle related reckless acts, some forms of poisoning and individuals who are pushed to their deaths. A further 4.1 per cent of homicide fall into a category labelled 'unusual cases' and includes serial killing, mass homicide, terrorism and homicide perpetrated by children. Further details of each of these unusual forms of homicide are considered in Chapters 8 and 9. Gang homicides comprise a mere 1 per cent of homicides in England and Wales. Once again, gang homicide is very much a masculine affair; there was only one incident of a gang homicide that did not involve a male offender and male victim (see Appendix). This particular form of homicide tends to attract significant media attention, not least because they often involve firearms and have become associated with drug-related gang turf wars (see Brookman and Maguire, 2003). A recent National Criminal Intelligence Service (NCIS) study noted growing gang violence and the use of weapons and guns in street crime (NCIS, 2002). It is certainly the case that recent years have witnessed an increase in firearms-related homicides from an annual average of 60 incidents in the latter half of the 1990s to a figure of 97 firearms-related homicides in 2001/02. Finally, racial violence accounts for less than 1 per cent of the total number of homicide recorded on the HI, though it is possible, as discussed earlier, that this category is used sparingly. For the remainder of homicides the surrounding circumstances are unclear or unknown.

Chapter Summary and Conclusions

This chapter began by considering some of the broad patterns and trends of homicide in the three jurisdictions of the UK before moving on to consider a number of features of homicide in terms of the characteristics of offenders and victims and particular features of the event itself. Finally, information about victim–offender relationships and features of the circumstances of such homicides was combined in an effort to move a stage closer to the 'social reality' of homicide. Ultimately, all of this information can assist in trying to make sense of homicide. The characteristics of those involved, as well as of the nature and circumstances of the event, are all, in a sense, different pieces of the jigsaw of homicide that, when combined, can help to provide us with a fuller picture of its social context. What Table 2.14 begins to illustrate is that homicide is a very diverse phenomenon. It is not appropriate to think of homicide as one form of crime or type of violent behaviour. Those who kill do so for very different reasons and under different sorts of circumstances. It follows, therefore, that explanations of homicide need to be tailored toward these different forms. As Polk points out, 'there can be no single theory which accounts for the exceptional diversity of homicides' (1994a: 211). With this in mind, subsequent chapters deal much more closely with particular manifestations of homicide in

Table 2.14 Homicide in England and Wales 1997–2001: victim–offender relationships and context (total number of cases = 4,123)

	N	%	Total number	Total percentage
1 **Domestic homicide**			1,287	31.0
Sexual intimacy	717	17.3		
Current or former spouses/lovers	704			
Sexual rivals	13			
Family intimacy	570	13.8		
Parent/child	348			
Child/parent	96			
Other (e.g. siblings/in-laws)	126			
2 **Homicide in the course of other crime**			294	7.0
Robbery	147	(50)		
Burglary	60	(20)		
Other gain	28	(10)		
Sex attack (unrelated individuals)	53	(18)		
Resisting/avoiding arrest	6	(2)		
3 **Gang homicide**			43	1.0
4 **Confrontational homicide** (unrelated individuals)			888	22.0
5 **Jealousy/revenge** (unrelated individuals)			94	2.3
6 **Reckless acts** (unrelated individuals)			248	6.0
7 **Racial violence**			14	<1
8 **'Other' unspecified circumstances** (unrelated individuals)			117	2.8
9 **Context/motive unknown** (some of which unsolved)			967	23.4
10 **Unusual cases**			171	4.1
Serial murder	80			
Mass homicide	58			
Terrorism	4			
Homicide amongst children (under 17) (unrelated)	29			
TOTAL CASES			4,123	100%

Source: Homicide Index.

terms of their characteristics and causes. It is first necessary, however, to consider some of the ways in which different social science disciplines have attempted to explain the phenomenon of homicide more broadly. Hence, in Chapters 3 to 5, we will consider the contributions of biology, psychology and sociology to an understanding of homicide.

Review Questions

- Using at least two criminological theory textbooks, familiarise yourself with 'routine activities theory'. How could you begin to make sense of the temporal and spatial patterns of homicide discussed earlier in this chapter by relying upon routine activities theory?
- Visit the Home Office website and type the word 'homicide' into the search box that appears on the home page. From the list of findings that appear select the document 'Homicide Review' (see Further Reading below for full details of this publication). This document evaluates the quality, completeness and value of the information currently held on the HI. Chapter 6 focuses upon 'gaps in information'. Read this chapter and consider the gaps identified. Can you think of any other features of homicide that could be included on the HI to improve its overall value?
- This chapter has been exclusively concerned with patterns, trends and forms of homicide in the UK. In order to draw some comparisons with homicide in the US, visit the Bureau of Justice Statistics home page (www.ojp.usdoj.gov/bjs/) and select the link to 'Homicide Trends' (under special topics). Select three categories from the contents (for example, demographic trends by age, gender and race, or weapons trends, infanticide and circumstance) and review the statistics for your chosen categories. Compare your findings from the US dataset with those contained in this chapter in relation to England and Wales.

Further Reading

Virtually all of the recommended reading for this chapter is available in electronic format. For example, *Homicide Statistics* (Richards, 1999: House of Commons) can be found at www.parliament.uk. The latest published homicide statistics for England and Wales, *Crime in England and Wales 2001/2002: Supplementary Volume* (Flood-Page and Taylor, eds, 2003: Home Office) are also available to download from the Home Office website, as is *A Review of Information on Homicide: A Discussion Document* (Moxon, 2001: Home Office). The latter is a very useful resource that provides a comprehensive overview of the data currently held on the HI, as well as proposals for its improvement. Scottish homicide statistics are also available online, as are some of those for Northern Ireland (see below). *Taking Stock: What we Know about Interpersonal Violence* (Stanko et al., 2002: ESRC) also contains some information on homicide patterns and is worth consulting. It can be found at www1.rhbnc.ac.uk/socio-political-science/vrp/RESOURCE/TAKING_STOCK_2002.pdf.

Useful Internet Sites

In terms of information and statistics on homicide for the various regions of the UK, the Home Office (www.homeoffice.gov.uk) is obviously the primary source of data for England and Wales. In addition, there are a number of sites which contain official publications and documents, such as www.official-documents.co.uk and www.hmso.gov.uk. National statistics referring to a wide variety of demographic data (and including the results of the recent 2001 UK census) are also available from www.statistics.gov.uk. For Scotland, the Scottish Executive publishes homicide statistics on a yearly basis (follow the link www.scotland.gov.uk/stats), as well as addition relevant sources of information. Finally, the Police Service of Northern Ireland (PSNI) publish data concerning homicide at www.psni.police.uk/index/departments/statistics_branch.htm.

Notes

1 These figures are based on *current*, not *initial*, totals (see also note 4). 2001/02 figures are excluded, as these are still likely to be subject to significant revision as more information about the circumstances of deaths becomes available.

2 It is important to note, however, that the Northern Ireland figures exclude 'terrorist' murders. It is also worth noting that while in England and Wales and Northern Ireland, one homicide is counted for each death, in Scotland multiple deaths in a single incident are counted as one crime. There are (thankfully rare) occasions, such as the Dunblane shootings, when this makes a significant difference.

3 The driver of the vehicle (Perry Wacker) has since been found guilty of 58 charges of manslaughter, as well as four counts of conspiracy to smuggle immigrants into the UK. He was sentenced to 14 years in prison in April 2001.

4 The annual totals of homicides are subject to frequent downward revision for the first two or three years after initial reporting, as individual cases are reclassified by Home Office statisticians on the basis of new information (such as if the police discover an incident is actually a suicide, rather than a homicide). This has the effect of scaling down the totals considerably, typically by around 15 per cent. *Criminal Statistics* each year gives figures both for 'offences *originally* recorded as homicide' and for 'offences *currently* recorded as homicide' (see, for example, Home Office, 1998a: 73).

5 Apartheid is an Afrikaans word meaning 'separation' or literally 'apartness'. In English, it has come to mean any legally-sanctioned system of racial regregation, such as existed in the Republic of South Africa between 1948 and 1990.

6 It is important to note that not all cases have been processed through the courts at this stage, so that although all individuals have been charged with either murder or manslaughter they may not necessarily be convicted.

7 Males comprise less than 49 per cent of the population of the UK as a whole, as well as the three individual regions that make up the UK (48 per cent in Scotland, 48.6 per cent in England and Wales and 48.7 per cent in Northern Ireland) (Census, 2001 available at www.statistics.gov.uk/census 2001).

8 Unfortunately it has not been possible to gain this level of detail for Northern Ireland.

9 'Child' here is taken to mean any person aged between 0–16 years.

10 Homicide amongst children is discussed in more detail in Chapter 8.

11 Unfortunately this level of breakdown is not available for Scotland and Northern Ireland.

12 Criminologists and other social scientists often use the term 'domestic homicide' to refer to homicides that occur amongst current and former spouses or partners (see Chapters 6 and 7). In the context of Table 2.12 it refers to homicides amongst those that are likely to reside (or have done) in the same residence and who have some kind of family bond.

13 The category 'other' includes negligence or neglect, aborting, drowning, explosion, burning/scalding, struck by a vehicle, arson, shaking babies and exhaust fumes.

14 Including shooting by crossbows.

3 Biological Explanations of Homicide

This chapter is concerned to describe and evaluate contributions from the discipline of biology to our understanding of homicide and violence. Biologically-based theories have enjoyed a long and enduring influence among explanations of homicide. Along with psychological theories (to be discussed in the following chapter), biological theories fall within the theoretical approach of individual positivism. This approach views crime as 'being generated primarily by forces located within the individual' (McLaughlin and Muncie, 2001: 149). Theories based on individual positivism have focused almost exclusively upon the individual offender and share a basic premise that, for example, the 'murderer' is a distinct category of person with a biological/constitutional or psychological predisposition to kill. While the crudest forms of positivism – particularly those based solely on biological determinism – went out of fashion in the early part of the twentieth century, many elements of the positivist approach survive today. Indeed, biologically-based theories have seen something of a revival in recent years due to advancements in the fields of genetics and neurochemistry. Moreover, biological theories have proven particularly attractive to those attempting to explain violent, as opposed to property, crime. This is particularly evident when considering some of the most unusual and heinous forms of violent offending (such as serial sexual offending) where, it seems, theorists are often unable to account for such acts without resorting to notions of internal defects.

The first section of this chapter considers the early biologically-based contribution of Lombroso and various applications of his works to homicide. This is followed by a consideration of classic twin and adoption studies, through, in the second section, to the most recent contributions from biology which have taken advantage of significant advances in the field of genetics and neuroscience. Finally, the pharmacological effects of drugs and alcohol and the effects of nutrition and toxins upon violence are considered in the third section. As will be revealed as we work our way through these various theories, one of the principle difficulties of biological theories is that they explain *too few* acts of homicide and tend to neglect the social context within which lethal violence occurs.

Very few commentators believe that homicide, or any other crime – violent or otherwise – has a single cause and, therefore, you should not be reading this chapter (or the other theory chapters that follow) with a view to finding 'the theory' or 'an explanation' to account for homicide. Homicide, though often less frequent than other forms of crime, is no less complex or diverse. Hence, the idea that it can be accounted for by a 'homicidal gene' or 'psychopathic personality' is highly flawed. In fact, what distinguishes many of the most recent contributions from biological and psychological theorists from their predecessors is a keen recognition that crimes, such as homicide, can not be explained by relying upon a single discipline.

Classic Biological Theories

We begin by considering some of the classic contributions from the discipline of biology.

Physical Deficiencies

In their earliest form, over 100 years ago, individualistic explanations focused on biological determinants of homicidal and other criminal (especially violent) behaviour, claiming that the criminal was anatomically or structurally distinct from the non-criminal. Cesare Lombroso (1835–1909) is generally credited as the founding father of the distinct discipline of criminology and was among the first persons to claim a relationship between physical appearance and criminal tendencies. Influenced by the Darwinian theory of evolution (Darwin, 1859, 1872), the central tenet of Lombroso's explanation of criminality was that criminals represented a form of degeneracy manifest in physical characteristics reflective of earlier forms of evolution (Lilly et al., 1995: 20). Physical characteristics such as long lower jaws, big ears, thin lips, curly black hair and aquiline noses were among the characteristics identified by Lombroso as indicative of both primitive man and a tendency toward criminality. Lombroso claimed that a large portion of criminal behaviour was inborn, although he entertained exceptions to this view in his later writings (see Lombroso, 1911). His theories were also modified by his influential successors in the positivist school, such as Raffaele Garofalo (1852–1934) and Enrico Ferri (1856–1929).

This early interest in the links between physique and criminality continued in the work of psychiatrists who began to take an interest in the relationship between the body and the mind (Hall Williams, 1982). Kretschmer (1925), a German psychiatrist, set out to demonstrate a link between body type and certain forms of mental illness. Later still, researchers from both the US and the UK built upon Kretschmer's work, focusing upon physique and its association with criminality. Hooton (1939), Sheldon (1940), and Glueck and Glueck (1956) variously classified humans according to physical endowment (a procedure known as somatotyping), each relating certain body builds in the aetiology of crime. For example, Hooton (1939) claimed that, generally, murderers were older, heavier, larger in the chest, broader in the jaw with heavier shoulders, when compared with other criminals.

Whilst there exists no firm evidence to support an association between physique and criminality, this has not distracted researchers from continuing to pursue this line of research in recent years (see, for example, Wilson and Hernstein, 1985; Eysenck and Gudjonnson, 1989; Rafter, 1992). Cortes and Gatti added a further dimension to the debate about physique and crime claiming that:

> [T]here can be no doubt that mesomorphy [muscular/masculine build] is a variable in delinquency and crime and that mesomorphs possess a greater delinquency potential. (1972: 346)

Whereas Lombroso viewed criminals as physically inferior, this later research was suggesting that criminals were in fact physically 'superior' (Hall Williams, 1982). The notion that criminals may be physically different, at least in appearance, has persisted in some quarters. Bull and McAlpine (1998), for example, suggest that people often have stereotypes of the facial appearance of criminals and that such stereotypes might affect judgements of guilt or innocence in court. The search for a connection between biology and crime continues, albeit in sometimes more sophisticated forms and with an appreciation of additional influencing factors.

Two well-known 'general' theories of crime that appeared more recently represent perhaps the best publicised examples of a return to individualistic explanations of crime (though not exclusively biological in basis) – Wilson and Hernstein's *Crime and Human Nature* (1985) and Gottfredson and Hirschi's (1990) *A General Theory of Crime*. Wilson and Hernstein argue that individuals differ in their underlying criminal tendencies, and that whether a person chooses to commit crime (or not) in a given situation depends upon whether the perceived benefits (for example, material gain, sexual gratification or peer approval) outweigh the perceived potential costs (for example, the risks of being caught and the consequent loss of reputation and employment). The important point for the purposes of the current discussion is the extent to which these authors draw upon constitutional factors in explaining why and how people make the given choice between committing a crime or not. Among the constitutional factors they discuss are physical appearance, genes, intelligence and personality. They also consider developmental factors (for example, broken and abusive families and schooling) and the wider social context such as economic conditions, communities and labour markets). The basic thrust of their argument involves differentiating between criminal and non-criminal groups. For example, they state that:

Offenders are, for example, disproportionately young, male, mesomorphic and nonectomorphic, and from the low, normal or borderline region of the distribution of intelligence test scores. Offenders are also atypical in personality. (Wilson and Hernstein, 1985: 173)

Almost 10 years on, Hernstein and Murray published *The Bell Curve* (1994) in which they claimed that IQ is mainly determined by inherited genes and that people with low IQ are more likely to commit crime because they lack foresight and are unable to distinguish right from wrong (see also Hernstein, 1995).

Gottfredson and Hirschi's (1990) *A General Theory of Crime* is similar to the Wilson and Hernstein theory in that they argue that people differ in their underlying criminal propensities. These differences are argued to appear early in life and to remain stable over much of the life course. The key factor in their theory is 'low self-control' – which refers to the extent to which individuals are vulnerable to temptations of the moment. For Gottfredson and Hirschi, people with low self-control are impulsive, take risks, have low cognitive and academic skills, are self-centred, have low empathy and short time horizons. All of these 'traits' make such individuals likely to respond to the benefits that might be associated with offending and to fail to be sufficiently influenced by the potentially painful costs of future punishment.

As Roshier (1989) has indicated, Lombroso laid the foundations for most of what was to follow in genetic theories of crime. Generally speaking, explanations of violence and homicide – as of crime in general – based purely on the individual's physique have lost favour and credibility in the criminological world. That is not to suggest, however, that biology does not remain influential in criminological thought. In recent years, advances in the field of genetics and an explosion of neuroscience research have fuelled a resurgence of interest in biologically-based tendencies toward violence (see Mednick et al., 1987; Raine, 1993; Reiss, 1994; and Moir and Jessell, 1995). In the UK, at the end of 1994, a new centre for Social, Genetic and Developmental Psychiatry was opened at the Maudsley Hospital in South London to examine what role genetic structures play in determining patterns of behaviour, including crime. A year later a major conference was held behind closed doors to discuss the possibility or isolating a criminal gene – the basis of which remains the study or twins and adoptees (Muncie, 1996), to which we now turn.

Hereditary and Genetics

Twin and Adoption Studies

Twin and adoption studies essentially began in the 1930s to 'scientifically' determine the relationship between inheritance and criminality. Twin studies involve the comparison of levels of criminality among genetically identical (MZ) twins and non-identical (DZ) twins. MZ, or monozygotic twins, are formed when one fertilised egg splits into two (hence their identical genetic makeup). DZ, or dizygotic twins, emerge from the simultaneous fertilisation of two eggs, and are thus no more similar in genetic structure than any siblings. Researchers reason that if levels of criminality are more similar between MZ twins, as opposed to DZ twins, this provides evidence of a link between genetic inheritance and crime. The degree to which a related pair of subjects (in this case twins) both exhibit a particular behaviour (eg, criminal activity) is referred to as 'the concordance rate'. The higher the concordance rate, the greater the similarity between the pairs. The results from the many twin studies conducted over the years are detailed at length in many texts (see, for example, Ainsworth, 2000; Bartol, 1999; Conklin, 1998; and Williams, 2001) and will not be discussed here in any detail. Suffice it to say, the evidence and conclusions from the plethora of twin studies that have occurred is very mixed. Several researchers have claimed to have found strong evidence of a genetic/inherited component to criminality (Lange, 1929; Cortes and Gatti, 1972; and Reid, 1979). Others have reached rather more cautious conclusions (Forde, 1978; Rowe and Rogers, 1989; Rowe 1990), whilst some have categorically denied the involvement of genetics in criminality (Daalgard and Kringlen, 1976). The picture is very much the same in respect of adoption studies (see Hutchings and Mednick, 1977; Mednick et al., 1984; Trasler, 1987; and Bohman, 1995).

Adoption studies have similarly tried to determine the relative effects of heredity and environment/upbringing, by comparing the criminality of adoptees with that of their biological parents and their adoptive parents. Among the most frequently cited adoption studies is a series of longitudinal studies known as the Danish Adoption Studies (Mednick et al., 1987) that have compared the criminal records of adopted children with the criminal records of their biological and adoptive parents. Findings revealed that over 13 per cent of the adopted children had a criminal conviction where neither father (adoptive or biological) had a criminal conviction. This figure rose slightly to 14.7 per cent where the child's adoptive parent had a criminal record. The adopted children were more likely to be convicted of crimes when their natural father had a criminal record (20 per cent). However, if the adoptive father also had a criminal record, the likelihood became even greater (24.5 per cent). These findings can be interpreted in a number of ways. Some researchers have taken these findings as highly suggestive of the role of genetics, whilst others have pointed out that the role of the environment or nurture must be crucial in explaining the finding that the highest proportion (almost a quarter) of adopted boys who gained a criminal record had an extra ingredient of a criminal adoptive father.

The researchers themselves did not claim that the data proved that inherited traits cause criminality. Instead, they cautiously concluded that inherited traits may lead some individuals, who are raised in a certain manner and who live in certain circumstances, to become criminal more often than people in the same situation who lack the inherited traits (Pollock et al., 1983; Mednick et al., 1987). Bohman (1995) has suggested that while genetic transmission may play a part in criminality, the interaction between genes and the environment is vitally important. Bohman found that if biological and adoptive parents both had a criminal record, there was a 40 per cent chance that the child would go on to develop a criminal record. However, in cases where the adoptive parents had no criminal record, the offspring of criminal parents only had a 12 per cent chance of developing a criminal record.

Criticisms of Twin and Adoption Studies

There have been many criticisms of twin and adoption studies, both in terms of the
feasibility of being able to separate and measure the effects of hereditary and environmental influences, and in terms of methodological shortcomings of certain
studies. On the first issue, it has been argued that identical twins are more likely
than non-identical twins to be treated similarly and to experience a similar environment. Thus, any similarities observed may owe as much, or more, to their similar social experiences than any genetic influences. In terms of methodology, many
twin studies have used very small samples of twins, and some of the earlier twin
studies used rather dubious means of determining whether twins were in fact MZ
or DZ. Specifically, early studies relied upon the appearance of twins in order to
categorise them as identical or non-identical (Williams, 2001).

Adoption studies suffer from some of the same methodological difficulties as twin
studies. Crucial to assessing accurately the effects of hereditary over environment in
this instance is the age at which the baby is adopted, a feature that varies across the
studies. The longer the child stays with its natural parent or parents, the greater the
effect of that particular environment upon the infant. Hence, a child's future criminality may in part be explained by certain early pathological experiences with their
natural parents, rather than by genetics (Ainsworth, 2000). Moreover, it is quite feasible that adopted children experience certain negative psychological or emotional
effects associated with having been adopted. They may harbour feelings of rejection
or abandonment that might lead them to engage in destructive, antisocial or violent
behaviour in later life. There is evidence that adoption agencies often try to match
the adopted child with an adoptive family on the basis of the child's socio-economic
and environmental background (Williams, 1991; Bartol, 1999). Hence, once again,
we are confronted by difficulties in terms of separating the relative effects of genetic
and social/environmental influences on any future offending behaviour. Finally,
both twin and adoption studies have been criticised for the manner in which they
measure involvement in crime and delinquency. Linked to this, the absence of a
criminal record does not mean that one has not engaged in criminal behaviour,
rather that the individual may have escaped detection.

It is these difficulties that perhaps explain such a mixed bag of results from these
so-called 'scientific' studies. What is also very interesting is the different manner in
which the results of particular twin and adoption studies are reproduced in the literature. For example, if one considers discussions of the Danish Adoption Studies
(Mednick et al., 1987), the findings and conclusions reached differ depending upon
where one looks. Jones (2000), for example, states that violent (as well as non-violent) crime was found to be greater amongst the adoptees where their biological
father had a criminal record, whereas Conklin (1998) states that the adoptees who
had a biological parent with a criminal conviction had a greater propensity to being
involved in repetitive property crimes, but no greater involvement in violent crime.
There are various other ways in which researchers place their own particular slant
upon the research findings, depending upon their theoretical persuasion, making
definitive conclusions even more difficult to decipher.

In summary, it is virtually impossible to tease out the 'separate' (if this is an
appropriate way to conceive it) effects of heredity over environment, using either

twin or adoption methods. As Farrington points out, 'height has a high heritability, but nutrition in childhood crucially affects the actual height achieved' (1998: 244). Moreover, environmental factors are now thought to exert an influence on behaviour before birth, making the determination of hereditary influence even more difficult (Shah and Roth, 1974). Most reviews of twin and adoption studies now acknowledge that even where genetics play some contributory role in criminality, this occurs in conjunction with environmental and social influences.

Study Task 3.1

Make a list of five possible reasons why identical twins might similarly engage in violent behaviour, other than due to their genetic inheritance.

The XYY Hypothesis

The so-called 'XYY syndrome' exemplifies some of the fundamental problems of biological positivism and is particularly pertinent to male violence. In the mid 1960s much excitement was temporarily generated by what appeared to be a relationship between the possession of an extra Y chromosome and criminality. Researchers, initially in Scotland (Jacobs et al., 1965) and later in the US (Jarvik et al., 1973), claimed that the possession of an extra Y (male) chromosome produced a 'supermale' who was more aggressive and criminal than the 'normal' XY male. Later researchers questioned these assertions and claimed instead that individuals with XYY syndrome were in fact less aggressive than 'normal' XY males and that when they were involved in crime it was rarely of a violent nature, more often property offences (Sarbin and Miller, 1970; Watkin, 1977). In the final analysis, the XYY hypothesis proved to be deeply flawed as an explanation of criminality generally or violence specifically. More importantly, though, as Roshier points out:

> [E]ven if all the possessors of the chromosome anomaly had turned out to be persistent criminals (in the event they did not) then it would still only have been capable of 'explaining' a fraction of 1 per cent of recorded crime, simply because the condition was so rare. (1989: 24)

Neurobehavioural Research: Biochemical Factors and the Central and Autonomic Nervous System

Despite some of the obvious limitations with much of the early biologically-based research considered above, the notion that biology can influence violent behaviour persists. In this section we will consider a range of biologically-based theories that have a bearing on contemporary thinking about violence and homicide. Some of the theories we consider have been developed with the apparent benefit of advancements and refinements in the fields of genetics and neuroscience; others, such as the role of hormones, have their roots in earlier research but persist in some form today.

Hormones

Over the years there have been continued attempts to link certain hormones with aggression and violence. We will consider two examples below, relating to male and female violence respectively.

Testosterone

Much of the research regarding testosterone and violence has been inspired by the knowledge that violent behaviour is predominantly masculine in nature. Hence, the possibility that the 'male' hormone testosterone is responsible for excess levels of violence within the male population is intuitively appealing. The evidence from studies attempting to indicate a correlation between testosterone and violence is, however, far less appealing or convincing. Some researchers claim to have found evidence of a link between testosterone levels and violent tendencies (Olweus et al., 1988; Christiansen and Winkler, 1992). However, Bain et al. (1987) compared testosterone levels among a group of murderers, assaulters and non-violent controls and failed to establish any significant differences in mean random hormone levels across the groups.

The vast majority of the existing evidence on the inter-relationship between hormones, such as testosterone or adrenalin, and measures of aggression and violence, is essentially correlational (Archer, 1991). The fundamental problem with this kind of evidence is that we cannot infer a causal relationship in one direction. Several researchers argue that testosterone levels are raised as a consequence of violent behaviour. In other words, high levels of testosterone do not increase an individual's propensity to violence; rather, violence raises testosterone levels. In essence, this debate must be resolved if hormonal research is to proceed. Similarly, some recent evidence suggests that success in competition, the perception of winning and exposure to erotic films can increase circulating levels of testosterone (Brain, 1990; Archer, 1991). In sum, there is no firm evidence that high levels of testosterone lead to antisocial or violent behaviour. As Lilly et al. note:

> The association between biochemical factors and antisocial behaviour is perhaps the clearest example of the 'chicken or egg' problem facing criminological theory. Which causes which? Or are both interrelated in some complex feedback process? (1995: 211)

Pre-Menstrual Syndrome

In keeping with the criminological literature generally, hormonal research has tended to neglect the role of females and crime. However, one particular area of hormonal research became quite influential in the early 1960s with Dalton's (1961) study of the effect of hormonal changes around the time of menstruation, and female criminality. The clinical syndrome Late Luteal Phase Dysphoric Disorder (APA, 1994) (most commonly known as Pre-Menstrual Syndrome, or PMS) has been associated with an increased propensity to violence and antisocial behaviour in females, in that several of the symptoms associated with PMS, such as increased irritability, concentration problems and emotional changes, including depression and aggression, could facilitate antisocial and violent behaviour. Dalton (1961) conducted research to test this proposition and found that, in a sample of 156 newly-convicted females, 46 per cent of the crimes committed occurred four days prior to or four days following menstruation, a figure higher than the expected chance rate of 29 per cent. A number of subsequent studies apparently supported Dalton's findings (see Fishbein, 1992 for a review). However, critics have pointed out that stress can effect the menstrual cycle and that subsequent arrest and questioning could trigger menstruation. Hence, crime could cause menstruation rather than vice versa (Horney, 1978). It is also possible that women are more likely to be detected for crimes committed at or around the time of menstruation due to deficits in concentration levels. Furthermore, critics have pointed out that Dalton's subjects had almost exclusively committed non-violent crime, thus contradicting a specific link between PMS and violence (Horney, 1978). D'Orban and Dalton (1980) studied 50 consecutive female admissions to a London prison. In this instance, all of the women had been convicted of violent crimes. The research found that 44 per cent of the offences had been committed during the paramenstruum period (defined as the last four days before menstruation and the first four days of menstruation (Dalton, 1990). In addition, a significant number of the offences had been committed on the 28th day of the cycle. Despite these apparently significant findings, only a very small proportion of the women complained of PMS. Specifically, only 4 per cent considered themselves to suffer from PMS, although 34 per cent reported associated symptoms, such as depression and irritability (d'Orban and Dalton, 1980). Of course, these symptoms may or may not have been associated with PMS. It is quite possible, for example, that negative life events could have contributed to the reported feelings of depressions and irritability. To summarise, in keeping with research conducted into the effects of testosterone and crime (reviewed above), the PMS hypothesis has been unable to proceed past the correlational stage.

The Brain and the Central Nervous System

There is a growing area of research probing the possible links between violent crime and brain or central nervous system (CNS) dysfunctions. A well-known modern advocate of a link between homicide and abnormality of the brain is Adrian Raine, a professor of psychology at the University of Southern California. In 1994, Raine and his colleagues reported their findings that murderers had much lower levels of glucose uptake in the prefrontal cortex of the brain than matched controls (Raine et al., 1994). The sample comprised 22 murderers (or individuals who had attempted to commit murder) and 22 carefully matched control subjects. The murderers and attempted murderers were pleading not guilty by reason of insanity

(NGI) in courts of law. Both groups were subject to a positron emission tomography scan (PET), which measures the uptake of glucose, the 'fuel' of the brain, by different brain areas. Raine and his colleagues subsequently expanded their study to include 41 murderers (39 men and 2 women), matched with 41 control subjects (Raine et al., 1997a, 1997b). Again, the group of murderers showed reduced glucose metabolism in the prefrontal cortex, as well as certain other areas of the brain, leading Raine et al. (1997a, 1997b) to suggest that they had discovered the initial indications of abnormal brain processes that may predispose certain individuals to violence (in murderers pleading not guilty by reason of insanity at least). One has to be very cautious in interpreting these findings. Raine and his colleagues studied an unusual sub-category of murderers (that is, those pleading insanity). In England and Wales, a mere 0.4 per cent of homicide suspects were found unfit to plead or found to be not guilty by reason of insanity between 1995 and 1999 (HI, 1995–99). One might add to these figures the further 4 per cent of suspects who committed suicide before the start of or completion of trial. Similarly in Scotland, for the 20-year period 1979–98 only 1 per cent of offenders were deemed to be insane and unfit to plead or insane at the time of the offence, with a further 2.5 per cent of offenders committing suicide before their cases were heard in courts (see Brookman and Maguire, 2003). So even if these findings were reliable, they would only be capable of explaining a very small proportion of all homicides – around 4 per cent in the UK perhaps. We will consider in more detail the methodological limitations of these, and other neurobehavioural studies, in due course, after considering some of the other research findings in this area.

Another modern advocate of the important role of the brain in violent behaviour is Debra Niehoff, author of *The Biology of Violence* (1999). Niehoff (1999) explores the brain and its chemistry in terms of a developing system that is moulded by the environment. Drawing upon neuroscience research, she argues that an 'adaptive behaviour, aggression (the use of physical or verbal force to counter a perceived threat), escalates into maladaptive behaviour, violence (aggression directed toward the wrong target, in the wrong place, at the wrong time, with the wrong intensity)' (Niehoff, 1999: ix). Niehoff's discussion of stress and its effects upon the brain is a good example of her thinking. She argues that the brain is responsive and flexible to challenges from the environment. However, it is only able to operate successfully under certain environmental pressures up to a point. Long-terms stress can lead to an over-reactive or under-reactive nervous system and an inability to cope due to a stress-deadened nervous system. This can ultimately lead to violence. As Niehoff explains:

> This is why bad neighbourhoods, bad homes, and a bad relationship breed violence – not because of a wilful deterioration in moral character but because of a steady deterioration in the ability to cope. As stress wears away at the nervous system, risk assessment grows less and less accurate. Minor insults are seen as major threats ... Surrounded on all sides by real and imagined threats, the individual resorts to the time-honoured survival strategies: fight, flight, or freeze. (1999: 185)

Few would probably disagree that chronic stress can very often lead to adverse physical and emotional functioning. An interesting question that arises is how and why some stressed individuals will take the 'fight' path (that is, resort to violence), whilst others may opt for 'flight' or 'freeze'?

Whilst not without limitations, Niehoff's analysis is valuable in terms of its detailed attention to the interaction between the individual and environmental stimuli and cues, a factor often ignored in early research on the links between biology and violence. Denno also explores the interaction between biological variables and the environment in relation to violence and argues that 'these influences are so interdependent that separate labels designating them as "biological" or "environmental" are not always warranted' (1990: 123). Denno argues that violence occurs due to the combination of predisposing and facilitating factors, but can be offset by various inhibiting factors. Predisposing variables that she considers include genetic, psychophysiological, neurological and social. Facilitating factors include the use of drugs and alcohol, victim provocation, the availability of weapons and the environmental and social context of the situation. Finally, inhibiting factors include social-ethical norms, fear, guilt and the desire to avoid punishment. Once again we see the acknowledgement of the intricate interaction of internal biological factors and external environmental influences. It is this that distinguishes most of the recent biologically-based research into violence, from the early contributions from the discipline of biology. That said, there are also a multitude of studies that continue to link very specific biological or physiological factors with a propensity to engage in violent crime, which we consider below.

Heart Rate

According to Raine (1993), one of the most replicable findings in the literature is the association between low-resting heart rates and antisocial and criminal behaviour. The Cambridge Study (Farrington, 1997) also observed this association. The researchers found that twice as many boys (411 boys in total were studied) with low heart rates (65 beats per minute or less, measured at age 18) were convicted for violence as of the remainder. A low-resting heart rate was also significantly associated with self-reported violence and teacher-reported aggression. Furthermore, a low heart rate was significantly related to all three measures of violence independently of all other variables measured in the project, which included various measures of personality and attainment, as well as family and socioeconomic factors (such as poor child rearing, parents with criminal convictions, low income and poor housing) and finally physical measures (such as low weight). Other studies have looked more broadly at electroencephalogram (EEG) abnormalities. Reviews of this literature by Volavka (1987) and Venables (1987) found what appeared to be strong evidence for EEG abnormalities in criminal offenders, especially violent offenders. However, they, and other critics, note several limitations to the majority of studies in this area. These include clinical judgements to determine 'abnormality' as opposed to computer scoring with established criteria, lack of adequate controls and a lack of attention to environmental factors that may mediate the relationship between cortical arousal and violent criminal outcome (see Volavka, 1987; Venables, 1987; and Brennan et al., 1995).

Neurotransmitters

There are some other prominent biochemical factors that have been associated with violence within the literature, specifically, defects in the neurotransmitters serotonin, dopamine and norepinephrine. Neurotransmitters are the chemicals through which electrical impulses in the brain pass. Serotonin has been implicated in the reduction of aggressiveness by inhibiting behavioural responses to emotional stimuli (Conklin, 1998). Dopamine and norepinephrine are excitatory neurotransmitters that counteract the inhibitory effects of serotonin. Imbalances in the levels of these neurotransmitters has also been associated with mood disorders and aggressive behaviour (Fishbein, 1996). There is some evidence that individuals with lower than average levels of serotonin may be susceptible to violent and impulsive behaviour (Fishbein, 1996). The idea of a 'low serotonin syndrome' (Linnoila and Virkkunnen, 1992) has found some support (see Volavka, 1999 for a review). Fava (1998) found that increasing serotonin levels amongst depressed patients who exhibit anger attacks can lead to a cessation in such attacks. However, this favourable effect was only observed in around half of the patients studied, indicating that impaired levels of serotonin played only a partial role in anger attacks amongst this group.

Cautions and Criticisms of Neurobehavioural Research

There are a number of drawbacks with much of the research related to brain and biochemical dysfunction and its links to violent offending. Most studies in the literature are 'retrospective and anecdotal, with small sample sizes and often inconsistent results' (Filley et al., 2001: 3). Studies often involve unusual population groups, such as individuals pleading insanity defences, or held in institutions for the criminally insane. Hence, findings are skewed toward those who have been apprehended and either imprisoned or hospitalised, making generalisations to the wider population of violent individuals highly spurious. Whether the abnormalities apparently uncovered among such groups were manifest before the crimes were committed, or have developed since the act, is another quandary that besets any solid reliance upon many of these research studies. Individuals awaiting trial, or convicted of homicides and perhaps residing on death row or sentenced to life imprisonment, are likely to manifest a range of psychological disturbances, such as depression and mood swings, that might themselves affect brain functioning and levels of neurochemicals, such as serotonin. In addition, experts in the field agree that neurological identification of brain lesions is imperfect due to limitations in diagnostic classification, neurological examinations, neuroimaging technologies and neurochemical analysis (Filley et al., 2001). Regardless of these methodological limitations, it is virtually impossible to demonstrate a cause-and-effect relationship within the neurobehavioural research literature. Whilst it might be possible to demonstrate that certain individuals who have killed exhibit some form of neurological defect, it is not possible to show that the neurological defect actually caused the individual to kill. For example, physical abuse of a child can cause severe head injuries, including brain damage, that leads to violent outbursts. But children who are the victims of such abuse may have learned to be violent by observing their parents' behaviour – not specifically due to brain damage (Conklin, 1998). Alternatively, damage to the brain may hinder an individual's ability to socialise effectively or to relate to other people, leading to isolation and frustration that may manifest itself in violent behaviour. In this instance, it is the social consequences of the brain damage, not the defect itself, that plays a crucial role. Linked to the issue of cause and effect, many of the studies concerned with exploring the role of biology and violent crime fail to collect information on other potentially important influencing factors, such as the individuals' family, community and social life.

One interesting exception to this trend is a study by Feedman and Hemenway (2000), that examined precursors of lethal violence amongst a death row sample. Extensive, unstructured and open-ended interviews were conducted with 16 men and their accounts cross-validated by extensive record reviews and independent expert assessment and evaluation. These researchers assessed levels of impairment, injury and deficit across four distinct 'ecological'[1] levels. The levels considered were:

- family (for example, experiencing or witnessing family-perpetrated physical and sexual abuse and polysubstance abuse within families);
- individual (for example, brain injury/impairment, depression, polysubstance abuse and post-traumatic stress disorder;
- community (for example, community isolation – being locked away to prevent outsiders gaining knowledge of physical or sexual abuse; and
- social institutions (for example, the failure of key institutions, such as schools, juvenile detention facilities and medical and psychiatric facilities, to identify family and individual deficits and assist).

What is particularly interesting about this piece of research is the finding that for almost all 16 men studied, substantial deficits were found across all four levels examined. All 16 men had experienced family violence and suffered from individual impairment. For example, 14 of the men were severely physically abused as children by a family member, three of whom were beaten until unconscious. At the individual level, 14 of the 16 men were diagnosed with post-traumatic stress disorder and 12 with traumatic brain injury. Twelve men had experienced community isolation and 15 had suffered due to institutional failure.

By examining these individuals within a social and community context, as opposed to examining biological deficits in isolation, the researchers were able to demonstrate the importance of an accumulation of factors. As Freedman and Hemenway put it; 'many factors, although occurring within one level, ripple across the other levels' (2000: 1766). For example, one of the interviewees (described as Mr K) experienced severe physical abuse (family-level injury) and was thus kept away from neighbours and friends in an effort to hide evidence of the beatings (community level) and experienced difficulty in school both as a result of missing school and of cognitive impairments due to traumatic head injuries (individual level). The authors concluded that all of the men in their study 'experienced a

remarkable constellation of pre-disposing factors for lethal violence' (2000: 1767).
Whilst this piece of research has certain limitations, not least the small number of
cases studied and the lack of a control group (that is, non-death sentence murderers),
it is a significant advance upon those studies that focus upon only one aspect of
deficit among samples of murderers.

   In summary, it is critically important that any biologically-based factors are considered in conjunction with various potential effects of the wider environment in
which the individual has grown and continues to live. A recent piece of research
that specifically considers the interplay between biology (in this instance a gene)
and the environment will serve as a useful example. In August 2002, a team of
scientists (based in the UK, New Zealand and the US) published research findings
suggesting that boys who had been physically or sexually abused were more likely
to become violent as adults if they inherited a particular version of a gene known
as MAOA (Capsi et al., 2002). The MAOA gene controls the balance of neurotransmitters in the brain. In its normal state it mops up excess neurotransmitters, helping to keep communications between neurons functioning smoothly. A low-acting
version of the gene fails to fulfil this task effectively and it is this that apparently
elevates the likelihood of antisocial and violent behaviour in men – or rather *some*
men, those who have suffered abuse in childhood. In the absence of abuse, low
activity of the MAOA gene had no bearing upon antisocial or violent behaviour. In
other words, environmental influences are critical. What this research may have
revealed is one (of the undoubtedly numerous) factor that has a bearing upon
whether an abused individual grows up to become violent or not. The findings
from this study have yet to be replicated and it is possible that they may be discredited. That said, research that focuses upon the relationship between biology
and social or environmental factors is clearly an advance upon those that fail to
consider such an interplay.

Study Task 3.2

Make a list of at least five methodological objections to neurobehavioural
research. Should we abandon this form of research because of its flawed nature
or is it important to continue to pursue the possible contribution of the brain
and central nervous system functioning in understanding homicide?

Environmentally Induced
Biological Deficiencies

In this final section of the chapter the possible role of certain chemicals and toxins
in relation to violent offending will be considered. Aside from the possibility of an
innate, internal biological component that might predispose an individual to
engage in lethal violence, it has also been suggested that certain substances can

adversely affect one's biological functioning. Those most frequently discussed are alcohol and drugs, nutrition and lead – each of which will be considered below.

Drugs and Alcohol

There are various ways in which drugs and alcohol can play a critical role in the emergence of violence and homicide. In the case of drugs and violence, Goldstein (1985) suggests that there are at least three distinct levels at which one might uncover a relationship:

- psychopharmacological (that is, the effects upon one's mind and body – which will be considered below);
- economic compulsive (the notion that individuals commit violent crimes, such as robbery, to secure the funds to sustain a drug habit); and
- 'systemic' (which refers to the violence associated with the often very lucrative supply and distribution of drugs, that can lead to territorial disputes within the drugs trade).

The link between drug taking and violence at the pharmacological level is diffi-cult to decipher, and certainly depends very much upon which forms of drugs one considers. According to Levi and Maguire, 'there is no evidence that the *pharmaco-logical* effects of cannabis, hallucinogens or opiates makes people violent, at least when taken alone: if anything, the reverse is true' (2002: 828). There is some evi-dence within the literature of a causal connection between cocaine and opiate ingestion and violence in certain situations (Taylor and Hulsizer, 1998). Situational factors are crucial elements that cannot be isolated from any pharmacological effects. For example, Jones (2000) points out that different drugs gain reputations for having particular impacts, which might lead the taker to expect to experience a particular effect (such as increased aggression). As Fagan aptly states:

[I]ntoxification affects cognitive processes that shape and interpret perceptions of both one's own physiology (that is, expectancy) and the associated behavioural response. The cognitive processes themselves are influenced by cultural and situa-tional factors that determine norms, beliefs and sanctions regarding behaviours following intoxification. (1990: 299)

Reiss and Roth argue that 'for illegal psychoactive drugs, the illegal market itself accounts for far more violence than pharmacological effects' (that is, levels 2 and 3 of Goldstein's 1985 model of the drugs/violence relationship) (1993: 13).

There is a considerable body of evidence suggesting that violent offenders have consumed alcohol immediately prior to committing a violent act. Data from the British Crime Survey indicate that around a quarter of all incidents of stranger violence occur on a weekend in pubs or clubs during the evening or night-time (Mattinson, 2001: 3). In the case of homicide, there is striking evidence of alcohol consumption, particularly amongst male offenders and victims. As detailed in Chapter 2, Dobash et al. (2001) found that 38 per cent of male homicide offenders in UK prisons were drunk or very drunk at the time of the offence and Brookman (2003)[2] found that in over half (52 per cent) of all the male-on-male homicides analysed in England and Wales, alcohol was a prominent feature in that either the victim or offender had consumed alcohol, often to excess. Furthermore, in 36 per cent of these cases, both the offender and victim had consumed alcohol. The data here seem to fall somewhere between that found in other studies. For example, Wallace (1986) found that 47 per cent of homicides amongst men in New South Wales, Australia involved alcohol consumption. Wolfgang (1958), on the other hand, found that 64 per cent of the total male-on-male killings he examined involved alcohol consumption by either the victim or the offender and 44 per cent of all cases involved both men consuming alcohol. Clearly, alcohol consumption is often not confined solely to offenders of homicide; many homicide victims have also consumed alcohol prior to their death. Lindquist (1986) studied homicides occurring in northern Sweden between 1970 and 1981 involving 64 offenders and 71 victims and found that two-thirds of offenders and almost half of the victims were intoxicated at the time of the homicide. Garriott et al. (1986) found that alcohol was present in 63 per cent of the 130 homicide victims in Behar County, Kentucky in 1985. Finally, Goodman et al. (1986) tested the alcohol levels of several thousand homicide victims from Los Angeles for the period 1970–79 and found alcohol to be present in 46 per cent of the cases. In short, very many studies have found that around 50 per cent of the victims of homicide have a high blood alcohol content (for a useful overview of further empirical evidence for the relationship between drinking and violence, see Collins, 1989; and Bartol, 1999: Ch. 12).

Whilst alcohol consumption permeates many incidents of homicide, the link between alcohol consumption and homicide (or other forms of violence) is far from straightforward and certainly not limited to a pharmacological effect. As Levi and Maguire point out, with reference to alcohol use and, to a lesser extent, drug use and violence:

> [I]t is rare for such people to be violent every time that they consume those substances, so it can not be said, for example, that the drink is a sufficient or even necessary explanation of their violence. (2002: 827)

Additionally, of course, many people who consume alcohol never become violent. The bulk of research regarding the role of alcohol consumption and violence is that, whilst it would appear to play some kind of contributory role in a significant proportion of homicides and other forms of violence, its effects are very much influenced by other situational and personal factors operating at the time. Hence, as Collins points out, 'alcohol's capacity to account for violence is virtually always mediated by other circumstances, such as individual personality and situational factors' (1989: 49). Similarly, Gilligan argues that studies on the pharmacology of alcohol use and violence suggest that 'the relationship between the two is a complicated interaction among biological, psychological, social and cultural factors' (2000: 291). Several authors have noted the importance of cultural norms, social interactions and drinkers' expectations in the development of alcohol-related violence (see Tomsen, 1997; Reiss and Roth, 1993; and Levi, 1997). The fact that alcohol consumption – even binge drinking – is commonly observed in some non-European cultures without violent aftermaths is highly suggestive of the importance of social and cultural norms (see Reiss and Roth, 1993). There is some evidence that certain offenders may consume alcohol before their offences in order to steady their nerves or to raise their levels of daring (Cordelia, 1985). The extent to which this 'relationship' applies to homicide is not known. Certainly, many homicides are not planned in the way that some other violent acts tend to be (such as robbery). In any event, the notion that some violent offenders may choose to consume alcohol to facilitate crime is an interesting issue. Finally, research into offenders with mental illnesses or disorders (discussed in the following chapter) have found some important associations between certain forms of mental disorder, coupled with heavy alcohol and/or drug use, that may help to explain some manifestations of homicide. In short, the links between homicide, drugs and alcohol are undoubtedly complex and an area of research that requires further attention. We will be discussing the social and cultural links between drug and alcohol consumption in various other chapters throughout the text.

Nutrition

The idea that nutrition can affect behaviour, as well as health, is not new (see Kanarek, 1994 for a useful review). Cholesterol, vitamin deficiencies and food allergies have all been discussed in relation to violent behaviour, and anecdotal stories of nutritional abnormalities in serial murderers are common (see Mitchell, 1997). For the last two decades theories relating sugar intake to violent behaviour have been particularly prevalent. Interest was sparked after a series of studies conducted by Virkkunen and colleagues where it was suggested that hypoglycaemia (a condition in which the blood-sugar level is less than normal) was common in criminals and delinquents who regularly engaged in violent behaviour (Virkkunen and Huttunen, 1982; Virkkunen, 1986; Linnoila et al., 1990). These same researchers have also claimed an association between cholesterol levels and violence (see, Kanarek, 1994 for an overview of this research). Whilst there would appear to be some evidence from several research studies of an association between hypoglycaemia and violence and low cholesterol levels and violence, the research to date suffers from a number of methodological shortcomings. For example, all of the violent offenders in the studies by Virkkunen and colleagues who were tested for blood-sugar levels had a history of alcohol abuse that often leads to a poor diet as alcohol is substituted for food. Hence, as Kanarek points out, 'it may not be that hypoglycaemia results in violent behaviour, but rather that a lifestyle that encompasses alcohol abuse and other behaviours that contribute to inadequate nutrition results in hypoglycaemia' (1994: 524). Other difficulties with the research relating to both hypoglycaemia and cholesterol levels revolve around inadequate assessments of nutritional intake between violent subjects and controls and a failure to consider other potentially important differences across the two groups – such as activity levels. Other studies have considered aggregate statistical data in their search for a link between nutrition and homicide. For example, Mawson and Jacobs (1978) found that countries with significantly high homicide rates also have significantly high corn consumption. Although, as Mitchell (1997) cautions, such correlations may be spurious. In short, the issue of cause and effect plagues all of the aforementioned studies.

Lead

Numerous studies suggest that sufficient exposure to lead (a metallic neurotoxin) in the environment or diet can promote brain dysfunction. Known as the 'neurotoxicity hypothesis', this position states that lead exposure alters neurotransmitter and hormonal systems and may induce aggressive and violent behaviour (Stretesky, 2001). Few studies have specifically examined violence or homicide, although there is some evidence of an association between lead exposure and delinquent behaviour. For example, Norris (1988) cites experiments in which violent delinquents have shown abnormally elevated lead and cadmium levels. Denno (1990) traced the behavioural patterns of 987 African American youth from birth to age 22 years and found that lead poisoning was among the strongest correlates of delinquency (among the dozens of other sociological and biological factors examined). Needleman et al. (1996) studied bone lead levels and self-reported antisocial behaviour among 301 youths in Pittsburgh. These researchers found that parents and teachers were more likely to report delinquent and aggressive behaviour among children with high bone lead levels. These youths were also more likely to report engaging in delinquent acts than children with low bone lead levels. Finally, Stretesky (2001) examined the homicide rates in all counties in the 48 states of the US whilst examining *estimated* air lead concentrations and blood lead levels. The results suggested an association between lead exposure and violent behaviour. Stretesky controlled for a number of alternative influencing factors, such as other air pollutants and a range of sociological factors that might affect homicide rates (for example, poverty levels and the number of persons aged 16 to 29 years in a given country). However, the author also acknowledged a number of weaknesses with the study. For example, the analysis was based on estimated air lead concentrations, rather than actual measures of air lead, and failed to consider sources of lead in the environment other than air – that is, water and soil concentrations. In conclusion, there have been few studies specifically examining the possible contributory role of lead exposure to either violence or homicide and currently no clear evidence of a causal relationship has been demonstrated.

Chapter Summary and Conclusions

We have considered a number of biologically-based theories of homicide and violence in this chapter, starting with the early contributions of Lombroso and his successors, whose focus lay in the apparent physical deficiencies that characterised murderers and other violent individuals, through to more contemporary research that considers those 'hidden' or unseen biological influences such as neurotransmitters, hormones and the affect of certain drugs and chemicals upon biological functioning.

Many criminologists of a sociological persuasion are highly critical of the role of biology in the aetiology of violent crime, such as homicide – often due to the limitations of the research as outlined above. However, to completely ignore or negate the potential influence of biological factors in the search for explanations of homicide is probably rash and unwise. As Filley et al., reasonably argue, 'Whereas it is unlikely that dysfunction of a discrete brain region, isolated neurochemical system, or single gene will emerge as a direct cause of violence, evidence for a contribution from all of these factors is appearing' (2001: 11). Moreover, they argue that, in contrast to research from the social sciences, neurobehavioural research is still in its infancy. Hence, the role of neurobehavioural factors may be more prominent than has yet been demonstrated or appreciated. That said, even those who strongly support the idea of a biological component or basis to violent offending acknowledge that any comprehensive explanation has to recognise that biology is not destiny. As Filley et al. put it, 'association is not causation, and a brain lesion may alter the threshold for violence but not prove to be its sole direct cause' (2001: 3). Individuals are affected by all manner of experiences, both in their past and at the moment at which violence occurs. It is impossible to understand violence if it is detached from the social, cultural and situational context in which it occurs. What is necessary is a very careful reading and analysis of the existing biological research (to assess its methodological veracity), in conjunction with an awareness that biology alone will not cause an individual to commit homicide. It is possible that for a small number of individuals, certain brain or central nervous system dysfunctions may heighten the potential to react in an impulsive and violent manner when placed in certain situations.

Some of the most promising theories considered in this chapter are those that have focused upon multiple influences of causation. For example, Freedman and Hemmenway's attention to the cumulative effect of deficit or injury in terms of the individual and family as well as community and social effects. The biologically-based theories of Denno (1990) and Niehoff (1999) have also benefited from attention to the links between the individual's biological system in conjunction with environmental influences. In the following chapter we will consider the contribution of psychology to an understanding of violence and homicide. Once again, it will become evident that there are no easy associations to be made concerning individuals' psychological makeup and involvement in violent crime, such as homicide.

Review Questions

- Make a list of the reasons why criminologists might reject biological explanations of homicide.
- Why is it important to look beyond the psychopharmacological effects of drugs in order to understand the role of certain drugs (such as alcohol) in relation to violent behaviour?
- Conduct a search of daily newspapers or newspaper archives (in the library or online) for accounts of homicide. What particular suggestions or explanations are presented as to why the victim may have been killed or, where a suspect has been identified, why he or she has apparently killed the victim? Can you identify which of the theories covered in this chapter most closely fit the assumptions or assertions in the newspaper articles regarding the causes of the homicide?

Further Reading

For an excellent overview of violent crime generally see, 'Violent Crime' *in The Oxford Handbook of Criminology* (Levi with Maguire, 2002: Oxford University Press). Stephen Jones provides a useful review of several theories of violence in *Understanding Violent Crime* (2000: Open University Press). Some excellent chapters are contained in *Pathways to Criminal Violence* (Weiner and Wolfgang, 1989: Sage). Regarding biological theories of homicide and violence more specifically, useful sources to consult are *The Biology of Violence* (Niehoff, 1999: Free Press) and *Biology and Violence* (Denno, 1990: Cambridge University Press). Finally, *The Biosocial Basis of Violence* (Raine et al., eds, 1997: Plenum) contains a number of very pertinent chapters.

Useful journals to consult (always check whether they are available online via your library in the first instance) include: *The Journal of Forensic Science; Behavioural and Brain Sciences; Bioscience; The British Journal of Psychiatry; Archives of Clinical Neuropsychology; Neuropsychobiology; Life Sciences; Science.*

Useful Internet Sites

The *British Medical Journal* online (www.bmj.com) contains a number of very accessible articles concerned with biological or psychological abnormalities and violent crime. Other useful online journals include *The Lancet* online (www.thelancet.com) and *The Crime Times* (www.crime-times.org).

Notes

1 Ecology is a branch of biology concerned with the relations of organisms to one another and to their physical surroundings.

2 A total of 96 cases from police murder files from three police force areas in England and Wales were analysed, 54 of which involved homicides amongst males, that is, a male victim and male offender.

4 Psychological Explanations of Homicide

This chapter evaluates the contribution of psychology to an understanding of homicide. In keeping with biological approaches, psychological theories are essentially located within the positivist tradition (or to be more precise, individual positivism) in that they generally operate on the assumption that the violent offender is somehow distinct from other individuals. For the most part, the task is one of trying to isolate those factors within individuals' psyche or personality structure that 'make a difference'. For some psychologists this means trying to identify violent personality types or trying to unravel the workings of the subconscious mind and the impact upon thought processes and behaviour. For others it involves paying more attention to the social context in which violence occurs and exploring how and why people react to the environment in different ways.

It would be impossible to review here all of the psychological theories that have had an influence upon thinking about violent crime and homicide. What follows is a critical review of a selected number of theories that fall within four distinct branches of psychology:

- psychoanalytic and clinical approaches;
- evolutionary psychology;
- personality theories; and
- social and cognitive psychology.

Psychoanalytic and Clinical Approaches

Psychoanalytical (also known as psychodynamic) approaches to violent crime can be traced back to the work of Sigmund Freud at the end of the nineteenth century (1859–1939). At this time, Freud, and others, began to focus upon the internal workings of 'the mind' and personality configurations, and how these components affected behaviour, including criminality. Psychoanalysis is generally recognised as a branch of psychiatry in that one of its central concerns is the treatment of behavioural problems; as such, psychoanalysis falls under the clinical psychology umbrella. Essentially, psychoanalytic theorists view criminal behaviour to be the result of some mental conflict (that is, in the unconscious or subconscious mind). Moreover, these conflicts are said to be the result of some kind of disruption during childhood 'psychosexual development'.

Freud and Psychoanalysis

Freud argued that the human personality is made up of three sets of interacting forces – the 'id', 'ego' and 'superego'. The id comprises an unconscious area of the mind and the most primitive aspect of personality. It is driven by biological urges and seeks pleasure. Left uncontrolled, the id is seen as potentially damaging as it does not take account of the negative consequences that can occur in the pursuit of urges and pleasure. The ego is largely conscious and develops through learning. The id is formed as individuals learn of the negative and unpleasant consequences that can follow from the uncontrolled pursuits of the id. Finally, the superego, which is basically unconscious in its operation, is seen as that aspect of personality that has internalised the moral and ethical rule and regulations of society. It generally develops via a process of socialisation where the child's carers play a critical role. It represents the fully socialised and conforming member of society. As Williams puts it, 'The ego has two masters, each to be obeyed and each pushing in different directions. The id demands pleasure; the super-ego demands control and repression' (2001: 194).

Freud proposed two different models of criminal behaviour. The first views certain forms of criminal behaviour (such as arson and certain sexual offences) as the result of mental disturbance or illness (Hopkins Burke, 2001). The mental disturbance is seen to be the result of some form of disruption during psychosexual development. The second model proposes that offenders possess a 'weak conscience'. Freud saw the development of the conscience as of fundamental importance in the socialisation of the child and believed that some criminals or delinquents possessed a 'weak conscience' (see Freud, 1920, 1927 and 1930).

Applications of the Psychoanalytic Approach to Violence and Homicide

Several researchers have applied Freud's principles to the study of criminal (including violent) behaviour, most notably juvenile delinquency (see Alexander and

Healy, 1935; Aichorn, 1936; Friedlander, 1947; and Redl and Weineman, 1951). To varying degrees, each of these researchers have claimed a connection between internal psychological conflicts and subsequent involvement in crime. For example, Gallagher (1987) suggested that abnormal and violent behaviour stems from a conflict between the id and the superego due to unresolved childhood experiences.

One of the most direct applications of psychoanalysis to the study of homicide emerged in the 1970s. Guttmacher (1973) utilised psychoanalytic theory in an attempt to classify murderers. He concluded that the 'average' murderer was free of any prominent psychopathology or mental illness, but possessed a defective conscience. The effect of a socially disadvantaged family life, emotional deprivation and inadequate nurturing all apparently contributed to the existence of a defective conscience, causing the killer extreme frustration that could lead to murder. Further, the killer's own experiences of deprivation ensured that he or she failed to appreciate the deprivation caused when he or she killed. Similarly, Wille (1974), in his 10-scale classification scheme of murderers, identified the 'psychopathic' personality, a non-feeling and insensitive individual who has a defective conscience. Further, such individuals suffer from a defective ego structure, failing to profit from experience, repeating the same basic mistakes in judgement and control. A few years later, Tanay (1976) proposed the existence of three 'types' of murderer. The 'ego dystonic' murderer kills against his conscious wishes during an altered state of consciousness, brought about when part of the psychic structure is split off from the rest of the personality. This process of dissociation may be induced by psychological, physiological or pharmacological factors. The second type he calls 'ego syntonic'. Here the murderer deliberately chooses homicide as a method of coping with and resolving psychological conflicts. Finally, Tanay identified the 'psychotic' murderer, an individual who kills in accordance with paranoid delusions and hallucinations. For an excellent overview of psychodynamic theories in relation to serial murder, see Mitchell (1997).

Criticisms of the Psychoanalytic Approach

There are a number of problems with psychoanalytic approaches to understanding crime. To begin with they are highly deterministic. All actions are seen to be determined by unconscious conflicts or tensions. Although many psychoanalytic explanations of criminality recognise environmental factors in the aetiology of crime, the focus is always upon the internal psychological conflicts that the factors influence. A more fundamental problem with the Freudian approach, however, is that it is not easily testable, since it is built upon a complex hypothetical model of human personality or human psyche. It is impossible to directly observe the id, ego or superego (the three core aspects of the human psyche, according to Freud), and extremely difficult to prove (or disprove) their existence, or their apparent influence upon human behaviour. Numerous techniques have been developed by psychoanalysts to try and determine the existence of inner conflicts, for example, dream analysis, hypnosis and Rorschach's inkblot tests.[1]

Some researchers claim that homicidal and normal males show significant differences on the Rorschach inkblot test (for example, Bukowski and Gehrke, 1979).

Homicidal males apparently show factors characteristic of sadism and severity of environment, whereas normal males show factors representative of insight and atonement (see Mitchell, 1997). However, since these techniques are largely subjective, they are susceptible to great variations in interpretation. Most of the literature claiming a connection between psychoanalytic concepts and criminality are based on detailed examination of a few case histories. These analyses start from a presumed consequence – criminality – and proceed to develop an elaborate explanation of why the event occurred or what the behaviour really meant, using essentially anecdotal evidence. As Shoemaker points out, using delinquency as an example:

> [T]he connection between unconscious conflicts and repressed experiences and delinquency is tautological or circular; that is, the effect (delinquency) is taken *as evidence* of the presumed cause (unconscious personality conflicts). (1996: 58, emphasis in original)

The psychoanalytic approach has also been criticised for its strong emphasis on early childhood experiences and its consequent neglect of adult experiences and situational variables in the explanation of behaviour, such as the social context and the influence and role of the victim and any bystanders (Cohen, 1966; Clinard and Meier, 1979).

A Modern Example of the Psychoanalytic Approach

A good example of a modern application of the psychoanalytic approach to violence and homicide is found in Gilligan's (2000) text *Violence: Reflections on our Deadliest Epidemic*. Gilligan's explanation of deadly violence (in particular homicide and suicide) is based on extensive interviews exploring the life histories of extremely violent men in his capacity as a prison psychiatrist over a 25-year period. For Gilligan, the internal psychological conflict that leads to lethal violence is shame and loss of self-respect – defined by Gilligan as the opposite of self-pride. 'The emotion of shame is the primary or ultimate cause of all violence, whether toward others or toward the self' (Gilligan, 2000: 110). There are many factors that can lead one to harbour such feelings. Gilligan pays particular attention to his persistent observation that violent men have been the objects of violence – both physical and psychological, and often of an extreme nature. These men have come to experience feelings of worthlessness, failure, embarrassment, weakness and powerlessness. Gilligan describes several preconditions which can lead men to kill. The first is the feelings of shame or wounded self-esteem already mentioned. Moreover, Gilligan claims that violent men will go to great lengths to hide that fact that they feel ashamed by presenting a defensive mask of bravado and arrogance because 'nothing is more shameful than to feel ashamed' (2000: 111). The second precondition for violence is met when such men perceive there to be no other option, that is, no non-violent means, of diminishing their feelings of shame or low self-esteem – such as socially rewarded economic or cultural achievement, or high social status and prestige. The third precondition for engaging in violent behaviour is that the person lacks the emotional capacities or feelings that normally inhibit violent impulses stimulated by shame (such as love or empathy towards others or fear for one's self). In summary, Gilligan acknowledges that whilst many individuals may suffer dents to their self-esteem or experience the emotion of shame, most either have non-violent means available to them to restore their wounded self-esteem, find themselves in circumstances where violence would not succeed in accomplishing the goal of improving one's sense of pride, or else possess capacities for guilt and empathy that do not allow them to engage in lethal violence (2000: 114).

Aside from his observations of their often violently traumatic childhood experiences, Gilligan extends his analysis to a consideration of the social, economic and cultural features of society that lead certain men to experience overwhelming feelings of shame. In addition, his work covers a number of other important issues, not least the ways in which societies and their criminal justice systems need to alter their response toward violence in order to reduce it. Hence, we shall return to this work in Chapter 11. In addition, there are some interesting parallels among the work of Gilligan and Jack Katz (whom we will discuss later under the heading of Social and Cognitive Psychology, on p. 96).

Study Task 4.1

Compare and contrast the early contributions of psychoanalysts, such as Freud, with the work of Gilligan (2000). What are the main points of similarity and departure?

The psychoanalytical approach to explaining violence represents one quite distinct branch of psychology. There exists a multitude of diverse theories within the psychological discipline that attempt to identify the 'criminal personality' using a variety of research methods and techniques, reflecting the particular clinical or theoretical orientation of the researcher.

Evolutionary Psychological Perspectives

In this section of the chapter we will consider the contribution of evolutionary psychology to an understanding of homicide. Before we evaluate specific theories, it is necessary to outline briefly the basic principles of evolutionary psychology.

Basic Principles

The basic premise of evolutionary psychology (also referred to as socio-biology) is that behaviour is in large part inherited and that every organism acts (consciously or not) to enhance its inclusive fitness – that is, to increase the frequency and distribution of its 'selfish' genes in future generations. This statement requires brief explanation. There are two levels at which one can try to make sense of human behaviour according to evolutionary psychology: proximate and ultimate. Proximate accounts operate in the 'here and now' in that they focus upon the immediate causes or immediate factors responsible for a particular response, such as internal physiology, previous experience, or conditions in the environment. In stark contrast, ultimate accounts look to our evolutionary past to try and decipher how and why certain mechanisms or potentials for behaviours have evolved. For example, if I were to eat a Chinese takeaway meal and later that evening vomit violently, I may find that I had no desire to eat this kind of food in future. A proximate explanation might suggest that the adverse experience of vomiting having eaten a Chinese meal had taught me to avoid this form of food in future, that is, that I had formed a negative association between Chinese food and vomiting. An ultimate explanation would trace this reaction further back in time and might propose that in our evolutionary past it was advantageous (for both my own fitness or genetic posterity and that of my immediate family's) to avoid foods that produce vomiting (they may, for example, be poisonous). In short, evolution may have produced within humans a mechanism to avoid foods that induce vomiting. Both the proximate and ultimate explanations may be correct, and that is not really the issue. What is important is to appreciate the very different levels of analysis and to understand that ultimate explanations do not assume that we are aware or conscious of certain adaptive (or even maladaptive) mechanisms that may be operating within us. As Daly and Wilson explain, human appetites and aversions (in the wider sense) 'have evolved to motivate behavioural choices with the best expected fitness consequences in ancestral environments' (1996: 40). Bearing all of this in mind, one might expect that homicides involving genetically-related individuals would be rare, as they are so costly in terms of inclusive fitness – that is, increasing one's genes in future generations. If I kill my offspring, not only do I lose the genetic inheritance I have passed on to them, but also that which may have been passed on to my grandchildren. Similarly, killing parents or siblings has a dramatic impact upon the continuation of my genes. Such behaviour flies in the face of the very basis of evolutionary psychology, whose central premise is that behaviour has evolved 'to contribute to the single end of manufacturing additional, similar people' (Daly and Wilson, 1996: 39).

Daly and Wilson: Evolutionary Psychology and Homicide

The most well known proponents of evolutionary psychology in relation to homicide are Daly and Wilson (1988) who have written extensively on the subject, covering particular sub-categories of homicide such as infanticide (taken to mean the killing of infants in this context), femicide (the killing of women by men), parricide (killing parents) and male-on-male homicides arising out of altercations and honour. We will consider some examples of their work here.

In keeping with the concept of inclusive fitness, Daly and Wilson (1988) predict that homicide should vary inversely with the degree of genetic relatedness between the offender and victim. In other words, the greater the genetic relationship between two individuals, the less likely they will be to kill one another and vice versa. And according to Daly and Wilson – this is precisely what the data suggest. For example, they point out that whilst it is accurate to state broadly that many homicides occur amongst family members, it is often that case that such killings occur among spouses, who are not, of course, genetically related (Daly and Wilson, 1996). Specifically, Daly and Wilson (1996) report that their analysis of a data archive from the Detroit police records indicates that victim and killer were genetic relatives in just 6 per cent of the total number of solved cases. Data for England and Wales are higher (at around 14 per cent between 1995 and 2000), but still indicate the predominant theme that homicide (whilst often occurring amongst family members or cohabitants) rarely involves genetically-related individuals. The exception to this pattern, however, emerges when one considers the killing of infants.

Infants in the UK, and several other regions of the world (that is, those aged less than one year) are the most likely single age group (per 100,000 population) to be killed (see Brookman and Maguire, 2003). Just over 90 per cent are killed by a natural parent, with 8 per cent being attributable to a step-parent (usually a stepfather), and the remainder by foster parents, other family members or friends. This sort of data would certainly seem to cast some doubt upon Daly and Wilson's arguments. Daly and Wilson make several observations in relation to such data. First, in relation to the killing of infants by their biological mothers, Daly and Wilson (1988) make several predictions, such as:

- infanticidal mothers will be single parents who lack family or social support;
- the probability of infanticide will be maximal for infants and then reduce with the child's age (the parent will have invested more time and energy into the child as it matures and is, therefore, less likely to kill it); and
- infanticidal mothers will be relatively young (as they still have time to reproduce).

They claim to have found evidence to support each of these predictions. Second, they argue that step-parents are the single biggest risk factor for child abuse and infanticide (UK data do not support this argument in relation to infanticide, though step-parents may be responsible for a much greater degree of non-lethal violence against their infants and children). They do not argue that infanticide is an adaptation expressed in step-parents. Rather, they argue that parenting requires an enormous degree of care and attention and that parental care adaptations may fail to activate fully in step-parents due to a lack of genetic relatedness to the offspring. The resulting injuries and deaths are by-products of a *relative* degree of decreased effort, and are not the products of adaptive behaviour. We will return to Daly and Wilson's work in subsequent chapters when dealing with specific forms of homicide.

Burgess and Draper: Evolutionary Psychology and Family Violence

Two other researchers have also applied evolutionary psychology to the study of violence and reached similar conclusions. Burgess and Draper (1989), in their examination of family violence, observe that greater rates of violence against poor and 'physically challenged' children may be understandable in relation to competition for scarce resources and optimising future individual reproductive potential. They also argue, in keeping with Daly and Wilson, that step-parents may be more likely to act with hostility and violence towards their stepchildren due to the fact that they are not genetically related. Their overall arguments and analysis are more sophisticated than this brief snapshot would suggest. They argue, for example, that it is vital to consider ecological, cultural and individual factors in understanding how and why certain evolutionary mechanisms influence family violence.

Criticisms of Evolutionary Psychology

Explanations of homicide in terms of evolutionary psychology have not escaped criticism. For example, Levi and Maguire (2002) have pointed out that Daly and Wilson's argument that it is young mothers who are most likely to kill is flawed. They point out that this theory 'requires the killers to believe that they will not be held accountable, since it is difficult to conceive further children while in most prisons' (2002: 815). Evolutionary psychologists would probably respond by pointing out that their explanations are operating at a very different level. So whilst common sense (or a proximate analysis) might suggest that it is risky and costly to kill one's offspring, in ultimate terms, it is particularly costly to kill one's offspring if there is no further chance to reproduce. Jones (2000) has also challenged some of the assumptions of evolutionary psychology. He points to the work of Levinson (1989), who surveyed 90 pre-literate and peasant societies and found 16 where family violence was virtually non-existent. Evolutionary psychologists might reason that the cultural requirements of these societies has rendered the use of violence unnecessary. However, as Jones points out, if the passing on of healthy genes is as critical as evolutionary psychologists would have us believe, 'it is difficult to envisage circumstances where the use of force against weaker members of the group would not be beneficial' (2000: 34). In summary, evolutionary theory is difficult to either prove or disprove. Several of Daly and Wilson's hypotheses seem to be supported by homicide data; however, others struggle to stand up to scrutiny – not least the notion that step-parents are the most likely to kill infants (which is not supported by data on infanticide in the UK). To date, the subject area has been one where theory outweighs empirical evidence, although this is beginning to change (see, for example, the work of Buss, 1999; Workman and Reader, 2003).

Personality Theories

Embedded within the positivist tradition or framework, the vast majority of personality approaches involve studying violent offenders and comparing them with non-violent individuals, with a view to isolating certain 'psychological traits' that differ among the two groups. It is these psychological or personality traits (such as impulsiveness, excitement-seeking or assertiveness) that apparently account for what is termed 'behavioural consistency' within individuals (see Farrington, 2002). For psychologists, then, individuals with a certain personality type are likely to behave in particular ways in particular situations. As such, psychologists have developed numerous dichotomies and typologies; for example, passive/aggressive typologies, over-controlled/under-controlled personalities, extrovert/introvert/neurotic personalities, to name but a few.

Eysenck and Personality 'Types'

Hans Eysenck's distinction between introverts/extroverts (Eysenck, 1959, 1964) and his later development of the psychopathic personality type (Eysenck and Eysenck, 1968, 1976) is one of the most widely tested and documented typologies in relation to crime and personality. Eysenck's approach has been variously defined as a genetic or biological theory, a version of learning theory or control theory or a derivative of psychoanalysis. Due to the fact that Eysenck combines a number of streams of social scientific thought in formulating his theory, it is a matter of some debate (and ultimately individual researchers' own biases) which aspects of his theory are viewed as the most important. Essentially, Eysenck claimed that certain biologically-based personality features, in conjunction with a particular social upbringing, increased the risk of antisocial behaviour (see Raine et al., 1997a for a useful review of Eysenck's work). Eysenck never specifically focused upon violence or homicide, but was more concerned to develop a general theory of crime; as such, his work will not be elaborated upon further, suffice it to say that Eysenck substantially influenced the discipline of criminological psychology, both directly and indirectly.

Expressive versus Instrumental Violence

Before considering the proposed links between personality and homicide, it is important to note a classic distinction made within the psychological literature between 'expressive' and 'instrumental' violence (see Megargee, 1972, 1982; Block and Block, 1991, 1992). Instrumental violence is said to involve some kind of gain (often financial) and generally begins as a predatory attack (a classic example being a robbery-homicide). Expressive violence, on the other hand, begins as an interpersonal confrontation and is not seen to gain anything specific or tangible (for example, a lethal pub brawl between two young men). As Levi and Maguire note, 'such a bifurcation of motive is far too crude, since many robbers also obtain a "high" from the violence or threats they employ and gangsters may consider that "it is just business" when mutilating and/or murdering their victims, but actually they may be ... psychotic revellers in violence too' (2002: 811). Along similar lines, Felson (1998) observes that fights are usually thought to be expressive because they apparently rarely accomplish anything. Felson notes, however, that this assumption is being reviewed. Tedeschi and Felson (1994), for example, deviate from the traditional distinction between expressive versus instrumental violence, arguing instead that all violence is goal-oriented and that expressive violence does not exist (see also Brookman, 2000a). In short, there is much debate regarding the extent to which the broad distinction between 'expressive' and 'instrumental' violence is a useful classification.

Over-controlled and
Under-controlled Individuals

Megargee (1966) was one of the first investigators to propose a direct link between personality and violence in claiming that violence occurs when the push towards violence (usually arising through anger) is stronger than an individual's ability to control it. Megargee (1966) was particularly concerned to explain why so many apparently mild-mannered individuals should be found among murderers, and as such he made the distinction between 'under-controlled' and 'over-controlled' individuals. The former are viewed as possessing very low inhibitors against aggressive impulses, therefore frequently resorting to acts of violence under perceived provocation. In contrast, over-controlled individuals are rigidly inhibited against the expression of aggression, and violence will occur only if the provocation is intense or has been endured for a very long time; if this occurs, any resultant assaultative behaviour is likely to take the form of an extreme assault of homicidal proportions. Hence, Megargee (1966) predicted that extremely assaultative offenders would, paradoxically, score lower on tests of hostility and aggression than moderately assaultative offenders. In other words, the over-controlled personality would be found in those who have committed acts of extreme violence (such as homicide), but would not be found among those with a history of frequent minor assaults. This hypothesis was apparently confirmed by early studies conducted in the US (Megargee, 1966; Molof, 1967) and the UK (Blackburn, 1968, 1971). For example, Blackburn (1968) compared the personality profiles of a group of 'extreme' violent offenders, convicted of murder, manslaughter or attempted murder, with a group of 'moderate' violent offenders who had committed acts of assault. In keeping with the predictions, the extreme group were significantly more introverted, conforming, over-controlled and less hostile than the moderate group. However, several more recent studies indicate a somewhat more complex picture (Crawford, 1977; McGurk and McGurk, 1979). McGurk and McGurk concluded from their research that:

> Some individuals committing extreme assaultative crimes like homicide are under-controlled and others are more appropriately called controlled than over-controlled. (1979: 47)

McGurk and McGurk also question Megargee's initial concern to explain why generally mild-mannered individuals, as he found them to be in probation interviews, resort to extreme violence;

> [T]he impression of someone, in an interview situation, as mild-mannered is a relative judgement ... and it would probably be true that in comparison with other probation applicants these individuals could be seen as 'over-controlled'. Whether or not these mild-mannered individuals would be seen as particularly mild-mannered relative to non-delinquent people is another question. (1979: 47)

Further doubts about the validity of Megargee's claims come from more recent evidence suggesting that under-controlled and over-controlled types are found in the non-violent population approximately as often as found in violent populations (Henderson, 1983). Finally, Blackburn's classification of violent offenders as 'extreme' or 'moderate' on the basis of their convictions is potentially flawed. Many murders and, of course, instances of manslaughter are not planned attacks and are different from assaults only in outcome, not process. Put another way, it is often a matter of chance whether an assault ends in death. Hence, to separate offenders on this basis may be problematic.

At the very heart of this whole debate are two key issues. First, whether or not personality inventories such as the Minnesota Multi-Phasic Personality Inventory (MMPI) (Hathaway and McKinley, 1967) are a valid and reliable measure of personality types; and second, whether one views an individual's personality as an essentially stable and enduring trait, or alternatively, whether personality should be understood in social learning terms, with the emphasis on a person–situation interaction (see Hollin, 1989). Despite these reservations, the search for unique personality characteristics that might explain involvement in offences of violence continues. In addition, the idea that some individuals are unable to control certain urges or impulses is also reflected in literature that explores the links between mental disorder and violence, to which we now turn.

Mental Disorder and Homicide

The tendency to think of the mentally ill or disordered as dangerous and potentially violent is not a new one (see Monahan, 1981; and Howitt, 1998). The link appears to have been established in the nineteenth century, partly under the influence of the medical profession (Howitt, 1998). This assumption persists today, despite increased knowledge about mental disorders and violent crime, which points to the relative rarity of an association between mental disorder and propensity towards violence. Part of the appeal of the mental disorder–violence connection revolves around the notion that mentally disordered individuals are unpredictable and cannot control their actions (Bartol, 1999). Critically, when individuals commit what appear to be senseless violent acts, they are often labelled as 'crazy'. Judges, passing sentence upon those who have committed brutal murders often label them as 'evil', 'depraved' or 'dangerous' – terms which are readily picked out by the media when reporting such events. Hence, an almost 'natural' connection is made between violence and mental disorder. As Bartol notes, the assumption is often made that 'mentally ill people are dangerous, and people who commit bizarre crimes are mentally ill' (1999: 135). In fact, the bulk of the research evidence suggests that very few homicides are committed by those suffering from a mental disorder. Hence, as Mitchell cautions, 'care must be taken to avoid "circular labelling" – people committing violent crimes are psychopaths and psychopaths are people who commit violent crimes' (1997: 40).

There is a vast body of research that has enquired into the potential links between some abnormality of mental state and involvement in violent crime, such as homicide (see Monahan and Steadman, 1994; and Howells and Hollin, 1989 for useful overviews). In this section we critically review some of the apparent associations. The problem of the often unfounded links proposed between mental disorder and dangerousness will be of particular focus. We begin by clarifying some key terms.

Clarifying Key Terms: Mental Disorder and Mental Illness

Various bodies or organisations have compiled classifications of mental disorder. The Department of Health have highlighted the fact that there is currently no single set of definitions or categorisations of mental disorder, with various definitions being used for different purposes (see House of Commons, 2000). One of the most widely cited definitions is that contained within the Diagnostic and Statistical Manual of Mental Disorders (DSM) (see APA, 1994). It is a guidebook for clinicians who seek to define and diagnose specific mental disorders and is compiled by committees appointed by the American Psychiatric Association (Bartol, 1999). The manual is reviewed and revised periodically to 'conform to the contemporary mainstream thinking of psychiatrists and other mental health professionals' (Bartol, 1999: 135).[2] One example of an interesting change is the removal of homosexuality as a mental disorder after 1973. As Bartol aptly notes, 'mental disorders are whatever the psychiatric profession wishes them to be' (1999: 135). In other words, mental disorder, just like homicide or violence, is a social construct and the reader should bear this in mind as the discussion proceeds.

The terms 'mental disorder' and 'mental illness' are often used interchangeably, yet both terms (whether taken to mean much the same or treated as distinct terms) are defined and used in very different ways by different individuals and organisations. For example, section 1 of the Mental Health Act 1983 sets out definitions of 'mental disorder' of which 'mental illness' is an undefined sub-classification. Generally speaking, the term 'mental disorder' is broader in definition than 'mental illness', although definitions vary across different classification systems. The important point is that one must interpret with care and caution research findings regarding purported links between either mental disorder or mental illness and homicide due to wide variations in the kinds of conditions that are considered. Table 4.1 provides two definitions of 'mental disorder'. As defined by DSM-IV, mental disorders include disorders as varied and distinct as mental retardation and learning disorders, eating disorders, sexual and gender identity disorders, anxiety disorders (such as agoraphobia), substance-related disorders, schizophrenia and other psychotic disorders, mood disorders (such as depression) and personality disorders (such as antisocial, paranoid or obsessive-compulsive disorders). Mental illness, on the other hand, can be (but need not necessarily be) restricted to conditions such as schizophrenia and other forms of psychosis.

Defining and Predicting 'Dangerousness'

According to Menzies and Webster (1989: 116), dangerousness is a 'critical mediating construct' that must be considered in discussions of mental disorder and violent crime. As they explain, dangerousness 'provides the gravitational force that unites the two concepts (that is, insanity and violent crime), allowing practitioners

Table 4.1   Definitions of mental disorder

A clinically significant behavioural or psychological syndrome or pattern that occurs in an individual and that is associated with present distress (e.g., a painful symptom) or disability (i.e., impairment in one or more important areas of functioning) or with a significantly increased risk of suffering death, pain, disability, or an important loss of freedom. In addition, this syndrome or pattern must not be merely an expectable and culturally sanctioned response to a particular event, for example, the death of a loved one. Whatever its original cause, it must currently be considered a manifestation of a behavioural, psychological, or biological dysfunction in the individual.
Source: DSM-IV (APA, 1994: xx1).

Mental and behavioural disorders are understood as clinically significant conditions characterized by alterations in thinking, mood (emotions) or behaviour associated with personal distress and/or impaired functioning. Mental and behavioural disorders are not just variations within the range of 'normal', but are clearly abnormal or pathological phenomena.
Source: World Health Organisation (WHO, 2001: 21).

to see insanity in crime and potential violence in mental illness' (1989: 116). Essentially, they are referring to the fact that it is the potential for dangerousness that allows so-called experts, as well as the general public and the media, to make associations between certain mental disorders and violent crime. It is important, therefore, that we consider further the concept of dangerousness. Those interested in the 'dangerousness debate', which essentially emerged in the 1970s, are referred to Bottoms (1977), Bottoms and Brownsword (1982), Floud and Young (1981), Floud (1982), Prins (1986) and Kemshall (2001).

'Dangerousness' is a highly contentious concept for two reasons at least. The first problem is that of *definition*; how does one define 'dangerousness'? In the UK, dangerous individuals and dangerous behaviour are not specifically defined by statute (Prins, 1986). Both the Butler Committee (1975) and the Scottish Council on Crime (1975) emphasized 'serious' and 'lasting' (or 'irremedial') harm without specifying exactly what these terms meant. Sometimes these limits are expanded to include psychological harm, or even just extreme fear and distress, and this takes into account some robbers and sex offenders whose crimes do not cause serious physical damage to their victims (Brody and Tarling, 1980). Many researchers tend to ascribe dangerousness to those criminals convicted of major robbery, violence and sexual assaults; however, such limited descriptions fail to account for the nature and circumstances of individual offenses. In short, there exists no established definitions to allow one easily to identify those who can be said to be dangerous. As Walker has pointed out:

> Dangerousness is not an objective quality, but an ascribed quality like trustworthiness. We feel justified in talking about a person as dangerous if he has indicated by word or deed that he is more likely than most people to do serous harm, or act in a way that is likely to result in serous harm. (1978: 37)

Attempts to *predict* dangerousness have proved even more problematic. Major criticisms regarding the effectiveness of predicting dangerousness have raged for some time now and often centre around the problem of the so called *false positives*. A false positive occurs when a psychiatrist or other person erroneously predicts that a given individual will be violent when he or she in fact does not end up being so (as judged by follow-up studies of such predictions); conversely a *false negative* refers to an individual who has been released as safe, but then commits acts of violence. Figure 4.1 illustrates this point. In this example, the starting figure is 100 potentially dangerous offenders. The practitioner deems that 30 remain dangerous and will go on to commit further violent offences, and that 70 will not. He or she is correct in 75 cases (that is 10 true positives who did indeed re-offend and 65 true negatives who, as predicted, did not). However, he or she is incorrect in 25 cases. Specifically, 20 individuals deemed to be likely to re-offend do not, and five predicted to be safe go on to offend.

Figure 4.1   An illustration of dangerousness prediction ratings

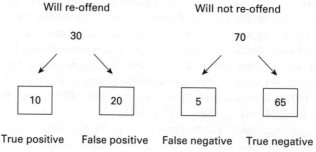

Predictions of 100 individuals:

Will re-offend   Will not re-offend

30   70

True positive   False positive   False negative   True negative

Many of the prediction studies that were undertaken in the 1970s indicated an excessively high percentage of false positives predicted, ranging from 99.7 per cent down to, at best, 54 per cent. In other words, those making the predictions vastly over-rated predictors of violence. More recent research indicates that re-offending rates for released mentally-disordered offenders are approximately equal to those for non-disordered offenders (Murray, 1989) (see Monahan et al., 2001 and Kemshall, 2001 for overviews of more recent developments in dangerousness risk prediction). One of the major objections to such findings is that individuals may be labelled as dangerous and incarcerated for long periods of time, when in fact they would not pose a danger to society.

   In summary, the critical mediating concept of dangerousness, upon which practitioners rely to try and ascertain the likelihood that individuals with mental disorders may commit acts of violent crime, is highly flawed. This, combined with the aforementioned difficulties of defining mental disorder, means that we have to be very cautious in interpreting the research findings regarding homicide and mental disorder. Let us now consider some of the research findings.

Studies and Data on the Link between Homicide and Mental Disorder

Despite widespread misconceptions, and a number of high profile cases, there is no clear evidence to associate mental disorder per se with a significantly increased risk of violent offending (Monahan and Steadman, 1994; Peay, 1997). Equally, it is generally agreed that individuals suffering from mental disorder are responsible for a relatively small proportion of all homicides. However, these broad statements require some important qualification.

As already indicated, it is important, when considering studies of mental disorder, to acknowledge that there are wide variations in definitions of 'mental disorder'. Some analyses are based on diagnoses of mental illness, in the relatively narrow sense of the term normally used by psychiatrists (that is, restricted mainly to conditions such as schizophrenia and other forms of psychosis). For example, a recent estimate by Taylor and Gunn (1999: 10) suggests that around 40 homicides per year in England and Wales are committed by mentally ill individuals; this translates to around 6 per cent of the total homicides in an average year. Furthermore, the authors claim that there has been little fluctuation in the numbers of mentally ill people committing homicide over the 38-year period 1957–95 (1999: 9).

Data from UK homicide databases generally support these estimates. For example, analysis of the Scottish Index for the 20-year period 1979–98 reveals that less than 3 per cent of homicide offenders received hospital orders and a further 1 per cent were determined to be insane and unfit to plead or insane at the time of the offence. If one adds to these figures most of the further 2.5 per cent of offenders who committed suicide before their cases were heard in the courts, a figure of around 6 per cent again emerges. Analysis of the HI (England and Wales, 1995–99) on the same basis produces a similar result (Brookman and Maguire, 2003).

However, if a wider definition of mental illness/disorder is adopted, estimates tend to be rather higher. The *National Confidential Inquiry into Suicide and Homicide by People with Mental Illness* (Appleby et al., 1999) examined the psychiatric reports of 500 people awaiting trial for homicide between April 1996 and October 1997, and concluded that 71 of these (14 per cent) had displayed symptoms of a wide range of conditions including psychoses, personality disorders, chronic substance abuse and affective and organic illnesses. The most common primary diagnosis was personality disorder, identified in 30 of the 71 cases (6 per cent of the total sample), followed by schizophrenia/delusions, identified in 27 cases (also 6 per cent).[3] Cases in which mental disorder was combined with serious alcohol or drug misuse – what are sometimes described as 'dual diagnosis' cases – were also relatively common. This is consistent with findings from the US and elsewhere, which suggest that this combination is a significant risk factor in predicting violence (see Monahan, 1999). For example, Henn et al. (1976) found frequent references to alcoholism, primarily as a secondary diagnosis, in the diagnostic reports of 1,195 defendants referred for psychiatric assessment over a 10-year period in St. Louis, Missouri. Guze (1976) similarly found the diagnosis of alcoholism prevalent among offenders with a diagnosis of antisocial personality disorder. The Appleby Inquiry (Appleby et al., 1999) further concluded that 'mental state abnormalities' had played a 'major role' in the offence in 48 cases – that is, in 10 per cent of the total case sample. Despite this, only 15 subjects had been receiving intensive community care at the time of the homicide.

Comparable results emerged from a review by Dooley (1995) of homicide in southern Ireland between 1972 and 1991. Dooley determined that in 9.5 per cent of cases, the primary motive for homicide was some form of mental disorder. She also found that 12 per cent of offenders had a previous psychiatric history, about three-quarters of these having had in-patient treatment. Once again, the diagnoses covered a very wide range of disorders (Dooley, 1995: 19).

International literature reveals more disparate findings. Mouzos (1999a) reviewed the international research regarding the links between mental disorder and homicide and found that the prevalence of mental disorder amongst homicide offenders ranged from as low as 2 per cent (in Ceylon) to as high as 53 per cent (in northern Sweden). Undoubtedly the vast differences found are a reflection (in part) of different methods of classifying mental disorder and different sampling and testing procedures. For example, the author of the Swedish study (Lindqvist, 1986) acknowledged that the high numbers of mentally disordered homicide offenders observed in his study may be due to the fact that Swedish psychiatrists are more likely to pronounce offenders of homicide as mentally deviant than psychiatrists in other parts of the world. Mouzos's own research of mental disorder and homicide in Australia is much more in keeping with the findings from the UK. Mouzos (1999a) found that only 4.4 per cent of Australian homicide offenders were recorded as suffering from a mental disorder. Mouzos adopted the World Health Organisation (WHO, 1992) definition of mental disorder described in Table 4.1. Mouzos also ascertained the prevalence of mental disorder in the general community and found that at least 18 per cent of the Australian adult population surveyed suffered some form of mental disorder. These findings suggest, as Mouzos concluded, that mental disorder amongst homicide offenders is significantly less than amongst the general population. Moreover, the notion that mentally disordered homicide offenders commit random and senseless attacks against strangers (a popular media conception) is challenged by Mouzos, who found that mentally disordered homicide offenders in Australia (like other homicide offenders) were more likely to victimise a family member in or at some private residence than a stranger on the street.

In summary, the notion that individuals suffering from some form of mental disorder are dangerous and prone to committing acts of violence is clearly not supported by the research literature (which is still evolving). That said, it is important not to ignore the fact that certain subgroups of the mentally disordered may pose a slightly elevated risk (see Toch and Adams, 1994 for a review of the links between mental disorder and violence more generally). The overall message from the literature seems to be that, while there is no justification for regarding the whole 'mentally disordered' population as a special risk group in respect of violent behaviour, there are certain sub-groups which may merit closer attention. The two most important of these appear to be people with severe personality disorder and people with problems of substance misuse.

Study Task 4.2

Visit the *British Medical Journal* online (www.bmj.com) and find at least one article that suggests an association between mental illness or disorder and homicide. You should also be able to find a number of 'response' articles that discuss the contents of your chosen article. Review these too. What conclusions do you draw about the association between mental illness/disorder and homicide?

In the final section of this chapter we will consider some contributions from social and cognitive psychology to an understanding of homicide and violence.

Social and Cognitive Psychology

Social psychology straddles psychology and sociology in that it is concerned with the effects of social situations on human behaviour. However, unlike sociological theories that tend to adopt societal levels of analysis, social psychology focuses upon the individual. In this respect, social psychology is akin to micro-sociological perspectives that focus upon the immediate interpersonal dynamics of violence and the micro-environment of violence (we will be discussing micro and macro sociological perspectives in Chapter 5). In fact, Levi and Maguire describe social psychological explanations as focusing upon 'the immediate cognitive and interpersonal dynamics that "produce" violent behaviour' (2002: 817). Social psychologists look at the power of the situation, rather than the power of individuality. That is, they look at external, situational factors rather than internal, personality factors. In this way they overcome one of the major shortcomings of personality theories that often fail to theorise about the links between elements of personality and individuals' violent behaviour within certain social contexts. Social psychologists recognise that behaviour often occurs in a social situation, which involves two or more individuals. Hence, they study how these social situations affect the behaviour of individuals.

Cognitive psychologists are also interested in how and why individuals act and react to the environment and other individuals, but pay particular attention to the actual mental processes (or cognitions) of individuals, that is, how and why we process information in a particular manner. Beck, for example, views violent responses to external stimuli as the result of distorted cognitions that can lead to hypersensitivity in relation to particular kinds of social confrontations. As Beck puts it, 'the common psychological problem lies in the offender's perception – or misperception – of himself and other people' (1999: 125). One common example that Beck provides is the aggressor's perception of himself as *the victim* who other people disrespect. Such beliefs (or cognitive distortions) can lead quickly to feelings of worthlessness and a reduction in self-esteem that can culminate in violence.

Along similar lines, Huesmann and Eron (1989) argue that aggressive behaviour is largely controlled by programmes or 'scripts' that are learned during early childhood development about what events are likely to occur, how the individual should react to the events and what will result. Of course, ultimately, one cannot appreciate how individuals respond and react to their environment without paying attention to their cognitions or thought processes such that cognitive and social psychology are intricately connected. Huesmann suggests that in order to understand the role that environmental variations play in the process of aggression or violence, 'one must distinguish between *situational instigators* that may precipitate, motivate or cue aggressive cognitions/responses and those more lasting components of the child's *socializing environment* that mould the child's cognitions (schemas, scripts, normative beliefs) and therefore their responses to these stimuli over time, that is, that socialize the child' (1997: 70, emphasis in original). One of the most well-known theories that deals with cognitive processing in social learning and has implications for understanding violent interactions is social learning theory.

Social Learning Theory

Specifically, social learning theory argues that the acquisition of any given behaviour occurs through the process of learning, either through direct experience (that is, being on the receiving end of violence) or by observation (for example, observing violence on the television or amongst parents or siblings). Although formulated by Rotter (1954), social learning theory is generally associated with the American psychologist Albert Bandura and his work on aggression. Bandura (1973a; 1973b) suggested that there are three crucial aspects to understanding aggression:

- the *acquisition* of the aggressive behaviour;
- the process of *instigation* of the aggression; and
- the conditions that *maintain* the aggression.

Evidence exists to suggest that aggressive behaviour can be acquired through direct reinforcement (Hayes et al., 1980) and via observation (Bandura et al., 1963). With regards to instigation, Bandura (1973b) noted that the anticipated outcome of an aggressive encounter, in turn a product of previous learning, was vitally important; such that certain environmental conditions, previously associated with aggression, make aggression more likely to re-occur. Furthermore, social learning theory acknowledges that certain environmental conditions may raise emotional arousal to levels that facilitate the instigation to aggression, such as high temperatures, crowded environments (Rotton and Frey, 1985; Anderson, 1987) and verbal and physical provocation (Dengerink et al., 1978). Finally, the maintenance of aggression is viewed to occur through reinforcement of the behaviour that can occur in several different ways. For example, an individual may gain some sense of pride or achievement from an aggressive display, thus motivating him or her to behave similarly in the future (self-reinforcement). Alternatively, the observation of other people's behaviour being reinforced may motivate the observer to behave in a similar manner (vicarious reinforcement). Finally, external reinforcement occurs whereby behaviour that operates upon the environment to produce positive or favourable results to the aggressor is likely to be repeated again under similar conditions in the future.

This approach goes some way to acknowledging the interplay between an individual's behaviour and the social context, but arguably not far enough. Siann (1985) criticises the social learning approach, not least in terms of the limited scope of laboratory-based studies of aggression and violence that have dominated this research. Siann argues that experimental psychologists have paid insufficient attention to 'real-life instances of aggression and violence ... where violence is fuelled by the social dynamics of the actual situation' (1985: 165–6). Additionally, as Hearn notes:

> [T]he precise nature and relationship of psychological, cognitive, behavioural and social processes in socialisation theories around violence is often left unstated. (1998: 25)

Aside from a number of laboratory-based research studies, however, are those that examine 'real-life' experiences of violence in early life and its affects upon later development.

The Intergenerational Transmission of Violence

There is a long-standing assumption within criminology (and other social science disciplines) that 'violence breeds violence'. That is, that those who experience physical and/or emotional abuse whilst growing up (for example, within the family or at school) are likely themselves to become violent individuals. Hence, Curtis cautioned that abused and neglected children would 'become tomorrow's murderers and perpetrators of other crimes of violence, if they survive' (1963: 386). Such assumptions are based, in part, upon the ideas of social learning (reviewed above), and upon assumptions that negative life experiences, such as abuse, can create psychologically 'damaged' individuals.

There have been very many studies undertaken to assess the validity of the notion that violence begets violence (see Spatz Widom, 1989 for an overview). The majority of studies are retrospective, that is, they involve identifying groups of delinquent or violent individuals and use reverse records checks to determine the incidence of abuse or neglect in these individuals' backgrounds. Other studies examine small numbers of violent or homicidal offenders in clinical settings and ask offenders to recall incidents of abuse, neglect or violence in their earlier family lives. Finally, a few studies have been prospective in nature, whereby children referred to protection agencies for suspected abuse or neglect are traced and followed-up in later life to determine whether they have gained any convictions for delinquency or violence.

In her thoughtful and comprehensive review of the literature regarding the intergenerational transmission of violence, Spatz Widom (1989) observes that many of the research studies that have searched for a correlation between early experiences of violence and subsequent involvement in violence are beset with methodological flaws and problems – which might explain her observation that existing studies present extremely diverse and conflicting findings. She concludes that 'our knowledge of the long-term consequences of abusive home environments remains extremely limited' (1989: 183). One of the major difficulties is how to resolve the fact that findings are so very diverse. In other words, why is it that some mentally and physically abused children become violent offenders, whilst others do not? One possibility is that child abuse or neglect might not cause delinquency or adult criminality directly (1989: 184). Abuse or neglect may lead to a changed environment (for example, being removed from the family home and placed into foster care) that itself may predispose later involvement in violent crime. In other words, they may be 'multiple pathways' that need to be traced in order to understand more accurately the ways in which a violent home environment can lead to later involvement in violent crime. Clearly, negative early life experiences manifest themselves in very different ways, depending upon the individual. For some, the ultimate effect might be future involvement in violent crime, for others, they may become withdrawn, self-destructive, depressed and even suicidal. Alternatively, for those individuals who appear to manifest no negative psychological or behavioural outcomes, certain 'protective factors' may play an important role in offsetting any early negative life experiences. These might include certain personal qualities, such as one's age and gender at the time of the abuse and their cognitive appraisal of such life events, or later positive environmental factors that serve to mitigate against the early affects of abuse. The issue of gender is likely to be particularly significant, bearing in mind what is know about the over-representation of males in crimes of violence, including homicide (refer to Chapter 2). It is possible, for example, that young males' interpretation of their abuse and reaction to it is rather distinct from that of females. In summary, as Spatz Widom suggests, it is 'very likely that our conceptualization of the relationship between child abuse and violence has been overly simplistic' (1989: 184). Hence, future research needs to pay attention to designing more methodologically-sound studies that include adequate experimental and control groups, whilst also focusing upon 'multiple pathways' to delinquency or violence and 'protective factors'.

Let us now consider one fairly comprehensive piece of research that reveals how past negative violent experiences can lead to future violence. The research, conducted by Athens (1989), is an interesting example of the 'violence breeds violence' hypothesis, but is particularly valuable in terms of his attention to the kinds of psychological processes that an abused individual passes through in order to develop into a dangerous violent offender. As is revealed below, however, the research is not without its limitations.

The Creation of Dangerous Violent Criminals

Athens' (1989) research into the creation of dangerous violent criminals has managed to overcome some of the limitations of social learning theories and focuses more specifically upon violence, as opposed to aggression. His theory straddles several theoretical perspectives in what he terms 'an integration of social environment and bio-physiological factors'. His earlier work on *Violent Criminal Acts and Actors* (1980) takes particular account of the situational aspects of violence, and will be considered in Chapter 5. According to Athens, dangerous violent criminals represent the finished product of a lengthy, and at points tortuous, developmental process (1989: 6). Specifically, Athens claims that dangerous violent criminals are created by passing through four experiential stages: brutalisation, belligerency, violent performances and virulency.

Brutalisation amounts to psychological trauma caused by 'violent subjugation' (this essentially involves family authority figures using violence to force the individual to submit to some demand), personal 'horrification' (here the subject witnesses another individual – often a family member – experiencing violent subjugation) and 'violent coaching' (the individual is prompted to act violently by a primary member group who is usually elder). After the experience of brutalisation the individual enters the belligerency stage, a brooding period characterised by repressed rage and feelings of inadequacy and humiliation. During this period the individual resolves to 'hit back' if and when provoked, which leads ultimately to the violent performance stage during which time the subject 'scores his first major victory or violent feat during a physical altercation' (1989: 72). Finally, the individual enters the virulency stage, which essentially sets the seal upon the whole process. During this final phase the individual 'becomes conscious that other people's opinion of him have suddenly and drastically changed in the wake of his violent feat' (1989: 73). In short, the subject embraces his newly-gained violent notoriety and decides to adopt violence even in the absence of provocation. 'He has now gone full circle from a hapless victim of brutalization to a ruthless aggressor – the same kind of brutalizer whom he had earlier despised' (1989: 76). Athens is keen to emphasise that all four stages must be 'successfully' passed through in order for the abused individual to develop into a violent aggressor (1989: 81). So whilst he does not specifically address the issue of 'multiple pathways' or 'protective factors', he does acknowledge that not all children or adolescents who experience what he terms 'brutalisation' will become dangerous violent criminals.

Study Task 4.3

Make a list of four possible 'protective factors' that might mitigate against the psychological trauma discussed above by Athens (1989) and thereby reduce the chances of subsequent involvement in violent offending. You may want to consult Spatz Widom (1989) for some hints, but also draw upon your wider knowledge of criminological theory.

Despite Athens' clear advance on many other social learning theories, his account is not without limitations. Athens fails to theorise about gender in his otherwise detailed account of the creation of violent criminals – despite the fact that he interviewed both violent males and females. His theory cannot explain (nor does it attempt to) why males significantly outnumber females as violent criminals. Are we to assume that boys who undergo brutalisation, belligerency and so forth subsequently become violent but girls do not (or not to the same extent, at any rate)? Or, alternatively, that boys undergo the four-stage process more often than girls? In short, as Hearn notes in his critique of all social learning theories:

> [A]ny learning (of violence or indeed anything else) is done in ways that are thoroughly gendered. Thus, not only may boys learn that violence is possible and is performed by older males, but that this is done in the context of male domination more generally. What is actually called 'social learning' or 'socialisation' is itself imbued with gender and gendering, for example, in what is *valued* and what is *not valued* differentially by gender and for genders. (1998: 27, emphasis in original)

This issue will be expanded upon in Chapters 6 and 7 where we deal with the issue of gender and homicide. Finally, Athens neglects to locate violence within its situational context. Once created, do these dangerous, violent individuals continually act violently? Presumably not. Hence, regardless of the apparently motiveless or unprovoked nature of attacks by such individuals, situational or interactional factors play a role and hence need to be addressed.

Jack Katz, Social Psychology and the 'Meaning' of Homicide

Someone who has paid particular attention to the situational or 'foreground' factors that play a role in lethal violence, as well as the psychological state of killers, is Jack Katz (1988). Once again, his work can be categorised as one that adopts a social-psychological approach in that Katz plays very close attention to the emotional or psychological states of killers and the sorts of social situations and interactions that give rise to homicide, that is, the 'dynamics of interaction' (1988: 5). However, what is particularly novel about Katz' approach is his focus upon such emotions at the moment of violent altercations. So whilst Athens provides a very useful analysis of how individuals can become primed to use violence readily, Katz has taken the analysis of violence (in this instance homicide) a stage further by paying close attention to the emotional states of the killers at the moment in which they become involved in violent altercations. In other words, Katz enquires into the 'subjective experience' of homicide, that is, what it means and feels to kill and what is achieved.

Katz talks at length about three distinct emotional levels or layers that are involved in the 'typical homicide'. For Katz, the typical homicide is heavily laden with emotions, such that the killer commits an 'impassioned attack' or the 'righteously enraged slaughter' of the victim in such a way that the humiliation he has suffered at the hands of the victim is laid to rest. To begin with, the would-be killer must enter into an emotional state whereby he defines himself as righteously defending 'good' against 'evil'. 'He must understand not only that the victim is attacking what he, the killer, regards as an eternal human value, but that the situation requires a last stand in defense of his basic worth' (1988: 18–19). In order to continue on a path of potentially destructive violence, the killer 'must transform what he initially senses as an eternally humiliating situation into a rage' (1988: 19). Where humiliation is transformed into rage, then a violent, and often fatal, confrontation is more likely. Violence is both more likely and more lethal when self-righteous rage is guided into what Katz calls a 'practical project' (1988: 32). This practical project does not necessarily necessitate the death of the victim, rather the objective of righteous rage now becomes one of 'sacrificial violence' whereby the offender transcends humiliation by obliterating the victim (literally or otherwise).

There are some very interesting parallels between the work of Katz (1988), Gilligan (2000) (discussed earlier under the heading of A Modern Example of the Psychoanalytic Approach, p. 78) and Athens (1989) discussed above. For example, all three discuss the importance of the emotions of shame and humiliation prior to acts of violence. As Gilligan states, 'violence toward others, such as homicide, is an attempt to replace shame with pride' (2000: 111). In a similar statement Katz posits 'for the impassioned killer, the challenge is to escape a situation that has come to seem otherwise inexorably humiliating' (1988: 9). Athens also makes reference to humiliation in his discussion of the 'belligerency stage' that follows experiences of 'brutalisation'. So despite the very different starting points and theoretical underpinnings of these three pieces of research, they reach similar conclusions about the role of shame and humiliation in homicide. This issue will be expanded upon in subsequent chapters when we discuss various forms of male-perpetrated homicide, where the issue of masculine pride is increasingly being recognised as an important aspect in understanding why some men resort to lethal violence in response to apparently trivial disputes or challenges.

Another similarity evident in the work of Katz (1988) and Gilligan (2000) is their attention to the *meaning* of violence from the perspective of the perpetrators and hence their ability to challenge the view that homicide is necessarily 'senseless'. For example, both authors pay very close attention to the ritual and symbolism of violence. Gilligan observes that cutting off someone's ear can be symbolic of preventing him from hearing negative things about oneself. As he states, 'cutting off someone's ear does not actually make him deaf, and prevent him from "hearing" bad things about oneself, it only symbolizes doing so' (2000: 85). Katz makes some similar observations, noting that offenders who 'stomp' their victims (for example, kick and stamp on their faces/heads) may succeed in the particular symbolic objective of preventing the victim from staring or glaring at them. Hence, for Katz such actions can serve an important symbolic objective in that 'they remove precisely the condition of the attacker's humiliation, the victim's offending gaze' (1988: 33).

Chapter Summary and Conclusions

This chapter began by considering psychoanalytic and clinical approaches to understanding homicide, followed by the contribution from evolutionary psychologists, personality theorists and, finally, theories derived from social and cognitive psychology. Having cast a critical eye across theories from each of these perspectives, it has essentially been shown that we have yet to discover one single coherent theory that is capable of explaining homicide. In some way or another, psychological theories are found wanting. For example, a major shortcoming of personality theories is a failure to theorise about the links between elements of personality and individuals' violent behaviour within certain social contexts. This has not, however, distracted researchers from searching for violent personality types. A vast array of personality disorders continue to be investigated and implicated as causal factors in violence and homicide (Biro et al., 1992; Blackburn and Coid, 1999; Grann et al., 1999). Other theories that have failed to stand up to scrutiny have tended to operate on a simplistic cause-and-effect model. The 'violence breeds violence' hypothesis is a good example of the problematic nature of such an approach and points clearly to the simple fact that there are no simple explanations (or direct pathways) to account for homicide specifically or other forms of violence more generally.

Whatever the flaws of psychological theories of homicide and violence, they represent an important contribution to understanding some forms of homicide. Whilst some branches of psychology may be limited in their ability to explain many cases of homicide (for example, those that focus upon mental disorder), others may have a wider applicability, such as social and cognitive psychology. Ultimately, one can not ignore the internal workings of the mind as part of the explanation of engagement in violent offending. For whether we believe that individuals are somehow predisposed to violence, succumb to certain internal or external forces or simply choose to commit acts of violence, their thought processes are inevitably involved. The issue is to what extent other factors play a role and how these can be integrated into psychological explanations.

In the following chapter we shall consider the contributions from sociology. Once again, we will find no straightforward answers to the causes of homicide. However, the sociological literature has managed to bridge some of the gaps left by biological and psychological approaches, not least because they take account of the importance of social, cultural, structural and situational factors in facilitating violence. Some sociological theories borrow certain ideas and assumptions from the field of psychology, but are distinct in that they prioritise a notion of 'culture' or 'system' (Hearn, 1998: 29) in order to try and unravel the pushes and pulls towards violence.

Review Questions

- In what ways do psychological explanations of homicide improve upon biologically-based explanations?
- In what respects are biological and psychological accounts of homicide similar?
- Which of the theories discussed in this and the previous chapter could you draw upon to understand and explain corporate homicide? Could it be argued, for example, that those who commit corporate homicide are biologically or psychologically distinct?

Further Reading

Some useful general sources regarding the psychology of violence and homicide are *Psychology and Crime* (Ainsworth, 2000: Pearson Education); *Criminal Behaviour: A Psychosocial Approach* (Bartol, 1999: Prentice-Hall) and *Psychology and Crime* (Hollin, 1989: Routledge). Finally, a very straightforward introduction to the psychology of crime can be found in *Applying Psychology to Crime* (Harrower, 1998: Hodder and Stoughton). More specific and detailed sources include *Prisoners of Hate: The Cognitive Basis of Anger, Hostility, and Violence* (Beck, 1999: Harper Collins); Jack Katz' *The Seductions of Crime: the Moral and Sensual Attractions of Doing Evil* (1988: Basic Books); *Violence: Reflections on our Deadliest Epidemic* (Gilligan, 2000: Jessica Kingsley); *Clinical Approaches to Violence* (Howells and Hollin, 1989: John Wiley); *A Mind to Crime: The Controversial Link between the Mind and Criminal Behaviour* (Moir and Jessel, 1995: Michael Joseph); *The Disturbed Violent Offender* (Toch and Adams, 1994: American Psychological Association); and, finally, several very pertinent chapters can be found in *Pathways to Criminal Violence* (Weiner and Wolfgang, 1989: Sage).

In addition, some of the most pertinent journals to consult include: *The British Journal of Psychology*; *Legal and Criminological Psychology*; *The British Journal of Clinical Psychology*; *The Journal of Police and Criminal Psychology*; *Personality and Social Psychology*; *Aggression and Violent Behaviour*; *Psychology, Crime and Law*; *The European Journal of Personality*.

Useful Internet Sites

- Excellent masters thesis by Mitchell, E.W. (1997), *The Aetiology of Serial Murder: Towards an Integrated Model*: http://users.ox.ac.uk/~zool0380/masters.htm
- *The British Journal of Psychiatry*: http://bjp.rcpsych.org/search.dtl
- *The American Journal of Psychiatry* online: http://ajp.psychiatryonline.org/

Notes

1 The Rorschach inkblot test is a psychological projective test of personality in which a subject's interpretations of 10 standard abstract designs are analysed as a measure of emotional and intellectual functioning and integration. The test is named after Hermann Rorschach (1884–1922), who developed the inkblots, although he did not use them for personality analysis. The test is considered 'projective' because the patient is supposed to project his or her real personality into the inkblot via the interpretation. The inkblots are purportedly ambiguous, structureless entities which are to be given a clear structure by the interpreter.

2 Most recently published in 1994, the manual is currently in its fourth edition (DSM-IV). It has been through many changes (see Bartol, 1999 for a review).

3 This latter finding is very much in line with the estimates by Taylor and Gunn and the figures derived from the HI, which focus upon 'mental illness' in the narrower sense of the term.

5 Sociological Explanations of Homicide

Sociological approaches to the study of crime can be broadly distinguished from biological and psychological approaches due to their emphasis upon the social roots of offending, as opposed to personal predispositions. Put crudely, rather than probing the defects of individuals, sociological criminologists probe the defects of society. It is not possible or necessary to review within this chapter the large and significant contribution of sociology to the discipline of criminology (for very useful reviews, consult Tierney, 1996; Vold et al., 1998; and Rock, 2002). Rather, the aim here is to consider the various ways in which criminologists have drawn upon the discipline of sociology in understanding homicide. With this in mind, it is possible to observe two broadly distinct starting points or approaches to the explanation and analysis of homicide within the sociological literature. These may be called the 'structural'/'cultural' approach and the 'interactional' approach. As the first section of the chapter demonstrates, regardless of their orientation, structural and cultural researchers have been concerned primarily to explain certain striking patterns to be found in the social characteristics of offenders (and sometimes victims) of both violence in general and homicide in particular. They try to unravel, for example, how and why certain factors or conditions, such as poverty, deprivation and inequality, social disorganisation or sub-cultural values, may explain homicide patterns. To these ends, structural and cultural researchers essentially rely upon the statistical analysis of aggregate data. Both approaches originally emerged during the 1930s and persist today, albeit in modified form. In contrast, the interactional approach that will be evaluated in the second section of this chapter questions the degree to which behaviour is determined by structure or culture, emphasising instead the importance of interactional dynamics amongst offenders and victims and the role of the micro-environment (that has both physical and social dimensions). As this chapter unfolds, it will become evident that both approaches have a number of strengths but simultaneously struggle to account comprehensively for homicide when considered in isolation. What is required is a blending of both approaches, and we reflect upon this in the summary and conclusion. We will not explicitly be dealing with the critically important issue of gender in this chapter. Rather, Chapters 6 and 7 will take up this matter, when we consider males and females as homicide offenders respectively.

Structural and Cultural Theories of Homicide

We begin here by considering the board orientation of structural and cultural theory.

Placing Structural and Cultural Theories in Context

Sociological theories of crime are extremely diverse. As Rock (2002: 51) notes:

> ... they extend ... from an examination of the smallest detail of street encounters ... to comparative analyses of very large movements in nations' aggregate rates of crime over centuries, and it is sometimes difficult to determine where their boundaries should be drawn.

Sociological criminology began to flower in the US in the 1930s, with the development of the Chicago School of Criminology and its main intellectual legacy, 'social disorganization theory'. A further boost was provided in 1938 with the first appearance of 'strain theory' in the form of Robert Merton's essay on 'Social Structure and Anomie' (adapted from Durkheim's original use of the term in his study of anomie and suicide, published in 1897). What these and other early sociological theories had in common was the belief that the key to understanding crime was in understanding its social roots (Lilly et al., 1995: 38) merged later in the 1970s, principally because the former retained a positivist orientation that was to become seriously challenged by the late 1960s. In particular, the excessive structuralism that characterised many of the early approaches was challenged and criminologists began to focus more closely upon human agency and, for example, the interactional dynamics between criminals and victims as well as the role of the state in criminalising deviants. Even more recently, postmodernism (which arose in the early 1990s) has challenged structuralism further (see, for example, 'chaos theory', Milovanovik, 1996, 1997). We will not be concerned here with all of these features of sociological thought. Rather, the emphasis is upon some of the theories that have had a particular impact upon thinking about violence and homicide. In this section of the chapter we will consider some of the most relevant contributions from this early sociological phase to an understanding of homicide. In the second section, we will consider some of the later contributions, specifically interactionism and victimology. It is important to emphasise, however, that the broad division highlighted is not perfect and that sociology has waxed and waned over the years between an emphasis upon the influence of structural factors and human agency.[1]

Structural Theories of Homicide: Context and Key Concepts

Essentially, proponents of the structural model assert that certain structural forces, such as poverty or lack of opportunities, create conditions which can ultimately lead to violent crime. The notion that economic conditions can foster violent crime can be traced back as far as antiquity (see Jones, 2000 for historical overviews). Homicide research has focused on the relationship between homicide and two forms of economic deprivation, namely 'absolute' and 'relative' deprivation. Absolute deprivation refers to 'real' deprivation or poverty, that is, access to meagre economic resources that are barely adequate to meet basic needs. Absolute deprivation is generally linked to homicide in terms of the feelings of stress, strain, frustration, alienation, demoralisation and powerlessness that can result from such conditions (see Williams and Flewelling, 1988; and Petterson, 1991). In contrast, relative deprivation refers to inequality in terms of access to economic resources between different groups or sections of society – as opposed to poverty per se. Those interested in relative deprivation focus upon inequality, rather than the absolute amount of deprivation as a source of offending (in particular racial inequality). It is argued that the perception and subjective experience of relative deprivation either motivates or frees individuals to engage in violence (see Messner and Tardiff, 1985; Patterson, 1991; and Messner and Rosenfeld, 1999). Of course, the two measures of deprivation can overlap and are in some senses blurred. For example, those suffering poverty (or absolute deprivation) are, by extension, those suffering inequality and may, therefore, harbour feelings of relative deprivation.

The Chicago School, Communities and 'Social Disorganisation'

Some structural explanations of homicide focus more specifically upon social disorganisation within particular areas or communities and how this can foster violence. This line of thinking can be traced to the work of the Chicago School of Criminology in the late 1920s and 1930s, in particular, the work of Robert Park who studied the ways in which communities evolve and grow using a social ecological model (see Morris, 1966 for a review of Park's work). Essentially, Park and his colleagues argued that certain neighbourhoods had periodically to cope with an influx of outsiders, for example, in the form of new immigrants or business organisations. This could lead to conflict and struggle over space and a general negative effect on the balance or equilibrium of the community. Subsequently, Burgess (1928) identified a particular area or zone within the city of Chicago that was especially criminogenic as a result of such processes and disturbances to the social equilibrium[2] – known as the 'zone of transition'. Later, Shaw and McKay (1969) adopted the work of the Chicago criminologists to study the distribution of juvenile delinquency in the city of Chicago and subsequently advanced their theory of social disorganisation. Social disorganisation 'refers to the inability of a community structure to realize the common values of its residents and maintain effective social control' (Sampson, 1992: 66). Sources of social disorganisation are generally taken to be high residential turnover, population heterogeneity and economic deprivation (see Messner and Rosenfeld, 1999). What unites this research is an emphasis upon the criminogenic nature of particular jurisdictions or specific neighbourhoods as opposed to the individuals who inhabit them. For example, the Chicago criminologists found that neighbourhoods with high crime continued to have high crime rates even when the original inhabitants had moved out, showing that it was not the people but the social characteristics of the neighbourhood that led to crime (Tierney, 1996).

Strain Theory

Another important theory that recognises the importance of the structure of society in leading to crime is 'strain theory', first developed by Merton (1938). Using the concept of relative deprivation, Merton argued that it was not deprivation per se that was important, but rather the ways in which individuals subjectively experienced deprivation (Tierney, 1996: 78). Merton's (1938) 'strain theory' represents a blend of both structural and cultural theory in that he argued that crime arouse due to a conflict between the cultural goals of 'society' and the structural limitations within the social strata. Specifically, Merton (1938) suggested that people in the US had become increasingly encouraged to strive for monetary success, but that lower-class individuals were often prevented from achieving such success through legitimate means (such as education or employment). This, suggested Merton, could lead to frustration and ultimately deviance. However, he recognised that individuals adapted to strain in different ways. For example, some individuals may continue to conform to the cultural goal of material success, regardless of how they were actually performing. Alternatively, the strained individual could adopt one of four deviant reactions: 'innovation', 'ritualism', 'retreatism' and 'rebellion' (see Tierney, 1996; and Vold et al., 1998). Innovation has tended to be most associated with the commission of crime in that it involves individuals remaining committed to the cultural goal of acquiring wealth, but involves them gaining such wealth via illegitimate means (such as robbery or burglary, drug dealing, gambling or various forms of corporate crime – see Chapter 9). Clearly, in terms of homicide, this adaptation could only explain a small proportion of lethal encounters, that is, those that involved the offender gaining some financial benefit from the murder. As detailed in Chapter 2, less than 7 per cent of homicides in England and Wales occur as a direct result of the commission of crime, such as robbery or burglary, indicating that this particular adaptation to strain is only partially helpful in explaining homicide.[3]

Other researchers subsequently developed Merton's ideas to explain the origin of juvenile gangs (for example, Cloward and Ohlin, 1960). More recently researchers have further expanded strain theory, suggesting that the failure to achieve a variety of goals (other than wealth) could produce strain, such as autonomy and status goals – especially the desire of certain males to be viewed and treated as 'real men' (Elliot et al., 1979; Agnew, 1992, 2001). This certainly broadens the potential applicability of strain theory to understanding homicide. As we shall discover in

Chapter 6, the issue of status or reputation has gained further momentum in theories of masculinity(ies) and violence.

A number of criminologists (particularly in the US) have presented evidence and developed theories to suggest that deprivation in one form or another is associated with high rates of homicide (see Sampson and Lauritson, 1990 for a review of research pre-1990; and Messner and Rosenfeld, 1999 for a more up-to-date review). We will consider just a few examples of recent research to provide a flavour of current interest regarding the links between structural factors and homicide. The (English) literature is somewhat dominated by American research which will, necessarily, be reflected in the review below. I will focus upon one particular angle of research as a classic example of the difficulties that have confronted researchers in this area – namely the links between structural factors and the homicide rates of black and white residents. It is, in fact, this line of research that has dominated the research literature in the last 10 years.

Research Evidence Linking Structural Factors to Homicide: Black and White Homicide Rates and the Case of the US

A significant number of American studies have been published in recent years, suggesting an association between the sorts of structural factors described above and rates of homicide. Many of these studies have been particularly concerned to account for the over-representation of black individuals as both offenders and victims of homicide in the US (see Messner and Rosenfeld, 1999). The central assumption that has been made is that blacks suffer significant disadvantage and inequality (that is, both absolute and relative poverty) and are therefore more likely to suffer the subsequent pushes and pulls associated with such disadvantage that can generate lethal violence. Blau and Blau (1982) were among the first researchers to report evidence indicating that racial inequality is positively related to official murder rates in a sample of metropolitan areas in the US. Since that time researchers have reported a somewhat more complex picture and efforts to replicate the Blau's research findings have met with mixed results (see Simpson, 1985; Golden and Messner, 1987; Balkwell, 1990; and Parker and McCall, 1997). Specifically, recent research evidence suggests that indicators of economic deprivation appear to have weaker effects on homicide rates for blacks than whites (Messner and Rosenfeld, 1999: 31). It is beginning to emerge that factors such as segregation and social isolation may be more important predictors of black homicide rates than, for example, poverty (see Logan and Messner, 1987; Peterson and Krivo, 1993; Shihadeh and Maume, 1997).

Parker and McCall (1997) found that absolute and relative deprivation, as well as social disorganisation, adversely affect both white and black intra-racial (within the same race) homicide offending in a number of US cities. However, when focusing more specifically on killings across races (inter-racial homicide), some interesting findings emerged. White-on-black killings were found to be closely linked to economic deprivation. The authors accounted for these (unsurprising) findings by noting that where employment opportunities and other resources are scarce, competition can intensify inter-racial conflict and, ultimately, violence. However, contrary to the researchers' predictions, racial inequality reduced black-on-white homicides (black inter-racial homicide). This runs counter to theories of relative deprivation that would posit that members of disadvantaged groups (that is, blacks) feel antagonism toward their perceived oppressors (whites) and at times respond with violence. It is findings such as these (see also Messner et al., 2001) that are beginning to indicate that simplistic models claiming an association between structural disadvantage and homicide rates do not sufficiently explain patterns of homicide in the US.

Further evidence of the complexity of any links between economic conditions and homicide rates emerges when one considers female as opposed to male offending. Unfortunately, it is very rare for researchers to deviate from the usual populations of male offenders in this context. Among one of the rare recent exceptions is a study by Steffensmeier and Haynie (2000), who compared adult and juvenile homicide rates for both males and females across 178 cities in the US in 1990. The researchers found that structural disadvantage (such as poverty, joblessness and income inequality) robustly affected both male and female adult homicide rates, whereas amongst juveniles the effects of structural disadvantage were large for male juveniles but weak for female juveniles.

The South versus West Debate

Linked to the debate concerning the influences of structural factors upon homicide rates, a raging theoretical and empirical debate has emerged in the US as to whether high rates of homicide in the southern regions of the US (as opposed to western regions) are the result of structural factors or whether, alternatively, they can be attributed to a regionally-based sub-culture of violence (to be considered below). Basically, some scholars maintain that the high homicide rates of the South are due primarily to structural factors, such as poverty (Loftin and Hill, 1974; Parker and Smith, 1979), economic inequality (Blau and Blau, 1982) and limited medical resources (Doerner, 1983), whilst others claim that these differences are due to the existence of a southern subculture of violence (see Harries, 1990 for comprehensive coverage of this debate).

In any event, there is some research evidence which contradicts the very idea that southern regions do have higher homicide rates. For example, O'Carroll and Mercy (1989) found the West to have higher rates of homicide. They argue that previous research has failed to adequately explore the differences in age and race structures between the South and West, relying instead upon crude homicide rates that do not take into account the fact that the southern regions of the US contain much higher proportions of black inhabitants – whose homicide rates are known to be significantly higher. By controlling the age and race compositions at state and regional levels, O'Carroll and Mercy (1989) found that the risk of dying from homicide was highest in the West during 1980. Furthermore, among blacks, the risk of homicide victimisation was found to be lowest in the South. Similarly, Kowalski and Petee (1991) found there to be no significant differences between the South and West in total homicide rates and urge attention to be paid to the 'convergence between the South and West' (1991: 75).

More recently, Parker and Pruitt (2000) conducted research to specifically enquire into the claim that regional patterns of homicide are shifting in the US. Their research findings are interesting and revealing, both in terms of the South/West debate but also ongoing debates about the relative influence of structural and cultural forces and homicide rates. On the first issue, Parker and Pruitt's findings reveal (in keeping with O'Carroll and Mercy, 1989; and Kowalski and Petee, 1991) that mean homicide rates for southern and western regions of the US are comparable. More interestingly, they find that the factors that produce these similarities differ greatly. Specifically, Parker and Pruitt found that whilst structural disadvantage influences black homicide offending in general, the specific form of disadvantage varies by region. Racial inequality was found to have a significant, positive effect on black homicide only in the South. The researchers argue that the unique history of discrimination in southern regions, as well as vast racial differences in education, occupation and income, are at the heart of the racial inequality that characterises southern black homicide offending. In the West, resource deprivation and family disruption were found to be most significantly associated with black homicide offending rates. The picture in relation to whites was found to be quite different. Structural conditions were found to largely affect homicide rates for whites in the West, whilst homicide offending among southern whites could not be accounted for by such structural factors. Rather, a cultural orientation toward violence was viewed to be associated with white homicide offending rates in this region. Clearly, more research is required to further probe the relative effects of structural and cultural factors upon rates of homicide and how they impact upon different regions, races, gender and age groups.

In summary, this most recent research suggests that there may be important differences in the way that certain structural factors, such as poverty, impact upon the homicide rates for white and black citizens in the US, as well as different age and gender groups. Whilst several authors are beginning to offer tentative suggestions to explain these findings, it would seem reasonable to conclude that these issues may only be properly unravelled by paying closer attention to specific communities and the multiple factors that may have a bearing upon rates of violence as well as their cumulative affects. It would seem that the early impact of the Chicago School of Criminology, with its emphasis upon particular communities and crime, has become somewhat lost in the vast majority of US homicide research literature where the dominant trend for the last 20 years has been upon the gathering and analysis of aggregate data. This is an approach far removed from the methodological tradition espoused by the Chicago criminologists of going out into the crime-ridden communities to discover, first hand, what is taking place and conducting ethnographic studies involving techniques of observational research and life histories (see Hammersley and Atkinson, 1995; and Hobbs, 1988).

Some of the most recent sociological analyses of homicide have begun incorporating analyses of specific local conditions and structural factors. A good example of this is Ben Bowling's work on homicide in New York City. Bowling (1999) argues that the surge in murder rates in New York the late 1980s can be explained by the explosive mix of economic decline, severe cuts in welfare benefits, the growth of a lucrative illicit drug economy, the free availability of guns, and low police morale and effectiveness. In essence, the despair fostered by increasing poverty and homelessness fuelled demand for drugs, and the appearance of large supplies of the relatively cheap drug crack cocaine drew numerous young men with no other 'career prospects' into a frenzy of disorganised and violently competitive dealing in search of quick profits. The combined effect, he claims, was to 'transform an area of extreme poverty and marginalization to one of routine serious violence' (Bowling, 1999: 537). There are disputes about the reasons for the equally dramatic fall in homicide rates in the late 1990s – that is, whether it was brought about primarily by 'zero tolerance policing' or whether this was only one factor among a variety of structural and cultural changes. Bowling has convincingly argued the latter (see also Cole, 1999 for a related discussion, albeit a stronger focus on the influence of firearms). In any event, the New York case illustrates the potential value of taking into account wider social problems such as poverty and specific local circumstances – both in terms of understanding and preventing homicide.

Study Task 5.1

What does the South/West debate reveal about the difficulties of researching homicide?

Structural Research: Cautions and Conclusions

Despite a general consensus within the (mostly American) research literature regarding some form of association between poverty, inequality, deprivation, social disorganisation and homicide rates, it is important to note that there are a number of inconsistent and contradictory research findings and conclusions. There are several reasons for this, most notably the use of different definitions and measures of economic conditions such as poverty, unemployment and inequality, and the use of different units of measurement, that is, neighbourhoods, communities, metropolitan areas and nations (see Parker et al., 1999). Moreover, as Vold et al. conclude, 'Both poverty and inequality are clearly associated with crime, especially violent crime, but whether they *cause* crime is another matter' (1998: 121). The most significant association appears to be that between economic inequality and violence, but even this link requires qualification. One of the prevailing difficulties is that those areas or communities with the highest rates of violence tend to suffer a whole host of factors that may cause violence – such as poverty, unemployment, high rates of divorce and single-parent households, high population density, dilapidated housing, poor schools and other social services, frequent population turnover and concentrations of racial and ethnic minorities (Vold et al., 1998). The problem then, as Vold et al. (1998: 118) aptly note, 'is determining which factors actually cause crime' (see also Land et al., 1990).

In summary, the structural perspective is valuable in that it has demonstrated that persons (or communities) with particular socio-demographic characteristics exhibit distinctly higher levels of involvement in homicide (as offenders and victims) than others – most notably young men and, in the US, black residents. However, this line of research has been somewhat less effective at uncovering how and why such individuals are over-represented in lethal violence.

Cultural Theories of Homicide

Cultural and sub-cultural theories of crime have a long history (see Corzine et al., 1999 for an overview). Cultural researchers are interested in the values, ideas and norms of particular cultures or sub-cultures that can encourage involvement in crime. So whilst structural theories focus upon the social conditions that can foster crime, cultural theorists focus upon the ideas and values that particular groups hold and how these can generate involvement in crime. It is essentially argued that complex societies comprise diverse and competing groups whose conceptions of right and wrong differ – some groups will sanction unlawful behaviour to a greater extent than others. Individuals who associate with such group norms are likely themselves to come to favour unlawful acts (including violence) via a process of socialisation. Sutherland's (1939) 'differential association theory' focused upon the transmission of definitions favourable to law-breaking as well as the specific content of what is learned, such as the techniques for committing crime and the rationalisations that accompany criminality (in this respect it transgresses both social learning and cultural theories). Miller (1958) subsequently proposed a cultural theory of gang delinquency, arguing that whilst the middle class has 'values' such as achievement, the lower class has 'focal concerns' which include toughness, smartness (in a 'streetwise' sense), trouble (getting into and staying out of trouble), excitement, fate and autonomy (resentment of authority and rules).

The 'sub-culture of violence' theory (Wolfgang and Ferracuti, 1967) is the most widely-known sub-cultural theory that deals specifically with violent crime and homicide. In this context a 'sub-culture of violence' refers to values favourable to violence. This theory starts from the premise that homicide predominantly occurs amongst individuals from the lowest socio-economic groups in society. Furthermore, Wolfgang and Ferracuti claim that many acts of violence, including homicide, arise from incidents that are relatively trivial in origin – such as minor insults or scuffles. These findings can apparently be explained by the fact that the vast majority of these people share beliefs that are conducive to the use of force and violence when insulted or challenged. These beliefs comprise the 'sub-culture of violence' and include values such an exaggerated sense of honour, courage and manliness. Thus, the use of violence is explained in a cultural context of shared norms and values that favour, if not actively encourage, the use of violence to a much higher degree than 'mainstream' culture or society.

One of the few British studies that has considered the role of culture in generating homicide is Elliot Leyton's (1995) *Men of Blood*. Essentially, Leyton's text is an exploration of the 'historical, social and cultural origins of England's comparatively low homicide rate' (1995: 9). In particular, Leyton focuses upon the cultural differences that keep the English homicide rate one of the world's lowest (1995: 25). Leyton observes that structural factors, such as inequality (discussed earlier), do not sufficiently explain the differences in homicide rates across the world because some low homicide nations, such as England, have profound social and economic disparity. He acknowledges, however, that the vast majority of those who kill in England are from the lowest social spectrum – the 'underclass'. For Leyton, the answer lies in a particular sub-culture that comprises part of this underclass. On the one hand, Leyton argues, England successfully socialised its population through a process of civilisation beginning in the thirteenth century, involving the transmission of non-violent ideals and behaviour (see Leyton, 1995, Ch. 5 for a full discussion of the history and origin of this 'evolution of sensibility'; and Elias, 1982). For Leyton, the 'English achievement' has been to extend the civilisation process, and in particular, self-control, to most of its citizens, including large sections of the working-classes (see Leyton, 1995, Ch. 10). This explains the low homicide rate of England compared to other parts of the world. As for those who do kill, they have not been successfully socialised and form part of a lower-working-class sub-culture who hold values that are conducive to violence. In short, the civilising process has not successfully filtered down to all, such that there remains a 'machismo' remnant. As Leyton explains: '[F]eudal notions of manly vengeance still survive in remnant form in England in the confrontational norms which govern certain sections of the working class' (1995: 243). For Leyton, it is those at the bottom of the social hierarchy whom 'elite propaganda finds it the most difficult to reach – the least educated, with the least prestige to lose (and the most to gain) from violent display' (1995: 234).

Sub-cultural Theories of Homicide Assessed

The sub-culture of violence theory has faced wide-ranging criticisms (for reviews, see McCaghy and Chernkovich, 1987; and Gibbons, 1992). One major bone of contention is that empirical evidence has failed to prove that those who engage in violent behaviour do, in fact, hold different values from other non-violent people (Ball-Rokeach, 1973). Furthermore, there is much debate as to exactly how such sub-cultures develop; what specific factors converge to produce a sub-culture of violence? What are its roots? A variety of plausible explanations have been offered (Wolfgang and Ferracuti, 1967; Hackney, 1969; Bruce, 1979; and Reed, 1982). However, the debate is far from resolved.

Some critics have suggested that the cultural model is nothing more than a circular argument – violent people are people who favour violence! As Wilson states, 'Cultural explanations suggest that groups with high homicide rates actually like violence. It is rarely put in such a bold or vulgar manner, however' (1993: 44). In fact, many cultural models of violence do examine the links between culture and certain structural positions, such as economic inequality (Huff-Corzine et al., 1991; Kposowa et al., 1995). For example, Curtis (1975) adapted Wolfgang and Ferracuti's sub-cultural theory of violence tying it more closely to the structural and social conditions that can generate it. For Curtis, the 'central impulse mechanism' underlying the sub-culture of violence is an exaggerated view of 'manliness', combined with a 'brittle defensiveness' that can lead to heated standoffs in situations that others would find trivial (Curtis, 1975: 37). Moreover, Curtis links these individual responses both to particular social conditions – such as the absence of legitimate opportunities for blacks in parts of the US and repressive violence by the police in black ghettoes, and cultural influences – such as learned ideas and interpretations of these conditions. More promising are studies that examine the connections between gender, social class and culture, in particular the links between marginalisation, masculinity and cultural norms (Messerschmidt, 1986; Gilmore, 1990; and Bourgois, 1996). We shall consider this literature in Chapter 6.

Study Task 5.2

The last few years in the UK have witnessed a number of fatal shooting incidents apparently by gang members (sometimes referred to as 'Yardies'). Access four or more newspaper articles online (a very useful online newspaper in the *Guardian* online at www.guardian.co.uk) regarding gang shootings. What evidence is there within these articles that the individuals involved (as suspects or victims) are gang members or members of a sub-culture of violence? What features can you identify that characterise the gangs and their major activities? In what parts of the UK do gang-related killings predominate? Make a list of the characteristics of the killers and victims (where known) in terms of their age, gender, social class and ethnicity.

Structural and Cultural Theories: The Missing Link

The distinction between structural and cultural models is a blurred one. Both models start from the same basic level of analysis and view violence as the deviant expression of either structural factors (such as poverty, inequality, relative deprivation, racial discrimination or unemployment) or cultural/sub-cultural norms, or, more recently, some combination of both. As such, these theories overlook some potentially vital micro issues, such as complex interactional dynamics. For example, Luckenbill and Doyle (1989) have argued that both cultural and structural approaches fail to specify the situational conditions that channel particular dispositions for violence into concrete lines of action.

Linked to this point, both cultural and structural explanations suffer from the age-old problem of over-prediction. Explanations of relative deprivation or poverty and violence, for example, cannot account for the fact that most people suffering from economic inequality do not engage in violence or criminal homicide. This point is particularly pertinent when gender is entered into the equation. How might we explain the very low rates of female homicide whilst acknowledging that women are among the most disadvantaged of citizens (see Wilson, 1993)? Similarly, not all members of a violent sub-culture engage in violence all of the time, and few become embroiled in lethal violence. The key problem confronting such approaches, as Newburn and Stanko observe, is that 'The subculture activists are generally outnumbered by the conforming majority, despite their common exposure to similar pressures' (1994: 2). Levi, echoing the same point, notes that such accounts 'seldom generate anything close to a causal account which makes sense of non-violence as well as of violence' (1997: 860). Incorporating situational analyses into the equation helps to overcome some of the problems of over-prediction and allows one to begin to unravel the specific circumstances under which violence is likely to manifest. As Luckenbill and Doyle state:

> Violence is performed by individuals in the context of face-to-face interactions and therefore involves a number of psychological and interpersonal processes. (1989: 421)

Despite these criticisms, both the cultural and structural models are valuable in that they have begun to unravel how structural forces and cultural norms can play a role in promoting lethal violence amongst some sections and groups of society. Moreover, in relation to homicide specifically, the description of actual homicide proposed by Wolfgang (1958), and later Wolfgang and Ferracuti (1967), has in fact stood the test of time in that several researchers have identified situations where violence is a 'cultural expectation', or to be more precise, a cultural expectation amongst men (women's violence is generally ignored in these accounts; see, for example, Polk, 1994a and 1994b). McCaghy and Chernkovich (1987), in their 'sub-culture of lethal violence' thesis, argue that rather than reject the notion of a sub-culture of violence, it would be wise to examine closely the specific conditions which contribute to and encourage violence, such as a strong emphasis on masculine honour and physical prowess, victim precipitation, alcohol use and weapon availability. In short, it is becoming increasingly recognised that the most useful way forward may be to combine macro-sociological approaches with micro-analysis of the actual violent event itself. As Zahn notes, 'perhaps the most instructive way of explaining homicide' is to focus upon 'the interactions between structural, cultural and interactional factors' (1990: 385). We will return to this issue in the discussion at the end of the chapter, after considering the contribution of interactional perspectives to an understanding of homicide.

Interactional Perspectives

Generally speaking, 'early' sociological theories, such as those discussed above, have been concerned to explain high rates of crime within lower socio-economic groups. They propose that both the origins and development of crime are structurally determined and also claim to offer a general framework for understanding all crime in asserting that the denial of legitimate opportunities acts as the major precipitating factor. In this regard, they can be clearly located in the tradition of positivist and deterministic modes of analysis (Muncie, 1996). However, by the 1960s, the degree to which behaviour was seen to be determined by structure and class position was being questioned. Matza (1964), for example, claimed that individual gang members were only partially committed to sub-cultural norms and argued that the deviant, rather than forming a sub-culture which stands in opposition to the dominant order, 'drifted' in and out of deviant activity. This was apparently made possible because there is no consensus in society, no set of basic core values, but rather a plurality in which the conventional and the deviant continually overlap and interact.

This line of enquiry was ultimately to provide a critique of all positivist modes of thought in its insistence that pluralism rather than consensus, and interaction rather than determinism, provided a more appropriate means of studying social behaviour. In contrast to positivism, interactionism emphasises the flexibility of individuals' responses to specific situations. This is not the place to review in any detail the remarkable changes that have taken place in criminology from the 1960s to the present day, suffice it to say that by the 1960s, a critique of positivism gathered considerable strength in the form of 'radical' or 'critical' criminology (See Taylor et al., 1973), which in Britain developed in a variety of directions, one of the most important being 'left realism' or 'realist' criminology (see Matthews and Young, 1986; and Young and Matthews, 1992) and, more recently, as discussed earlier, postmodernism.

In short, all of these changes led to a dramatic expansion of criminology's horizons. Of particular importance for the study of violence and homicide came a renewed interest in the victims of crime. The section that follows describes the origins of research interest in victimology and the interactionist perspective more broadly, outlining the importance of this line of research to the study of homicide.

Victimology: Studying the Victims of Crime

Victimology has been defined as a 'branch of criminology which primarily studies the victims of crime and everything that is connected with such victims' (Drapkin and Viano, 1974: 2). As this broad definition implies, criminologists and so-called 'victimologists' have pursued numerous, often diverse, lines of enquiry with regard to victims of crime. Factors such as the extent and nature of victimisation, the impact of crime upon victims and the related issue of fear of crime, the treatment of victims within the criminal justice system and issues of victims' needs and rights therein have all played a part. One major aspect of victimology is of key importance to the study of homicide, namely the criminal–victim relationship and the interactions that take place between them in the lead up to a homicide. It is this strand of thought that in fact sparked major interest in victims of crime in the late 1940s. Later, victimologists looked less at individual interactions and how they result in criminal victimisation and more toward structural understandings of the process of victimisation, for example, by examining the impact of patterns of lifestyle on patterns of victimisation (see Walklate, 2001a: 315). At the same time, there is now a clear recognition that patterns of victimisation are also intricately linked to certain socio-demographic characteristics of individuals. For example, as noted in Chapter 2, homicide victimisation varies significantly in terms of age, gender, social class and race. Mawby and Walklate (1994) view criminal victimisation as 'structural powerlessness', recognising that the impact of criminal victimisation is mediated and rendered more complex by factors such as age, gender and race.[4] We will not be considering structured victimisation in the section that follows; rather, the focus here will be upon the process of victimisation in terms of victim–offender interactions.

Victimology became an identifiable branch of criminology with the publication of Hans von Hentig's *The Criminal and His Victim* (1948). Essentially, von Hentig criticised the traditional offender-oriented nature of criminology, proposing a new and dynamic approach to the study of crime that incorporated clear recognition of the victim's possible role in crime, with particular emphasis on the relationships and interactions between offenders and victims of crime. By classifying victims into typologies based on psychological and social variables, von Hentig suggested that certain individuals were 'victim-prone'. Others, such as Mendelsohn (1956), took up this notion of victim-proneness. Not until Marvin Wolfgang's (1958) study of the patterns of criminal homicide were von Hentig's ideas subjected to systematic, empirical testing. Part of Wolfgang's extensive research of the interpersonal relationships between victims and offenders led him to calculate the proportion of homicides in Philadelphia, between 1948 and 1952 that involved 'victim-precipitation'. Wolfgang defined victim-precipitation as;

> [T]hose criminal homicides in which the victim is a direct, positive precipitator in the crime. The role of the victim is characterised by his having been the first in the homicide drama to use physical force directed against his subsequent slayer ... in short, the first to commence the interplay of resort to physical violence. (1958: 252)

Wolfgang calculated that 26 per cent, or 150 of the 588 homicides known to have occurred in Philadelphia over the study period, were the result of victim-precipitation. Comparative analysis of these cases with those involving no victim-precipitation revealed a number of interesting findings. Significantly higher proportions of certain characteristics were observed among the victim-precipitated homicides, such as, alcohol present in the victim, victims with previous arrest records for assault, 'negro' victims, 'negro' offenders, male victims, female offenders, mate slayings and stabbing incidents (Wolfgang, 1958: 264). Wolfgang concluded that his empirical findings supported von Hentig's theoretical contention that there are cases in which the two distinct categories of offender and victim undergo role reversal, such that the initial aggressor and would-be-offender becomes the victim.

Wolfgang's conclusions inspired many subsequent studies replicating his approach (for example, Amir's 1971 study of victim-precipitated rape and Hindelang et al.'s 1978 study of victims of personal crime). The concept of victim-precipitation introduced valuable insights into the study of homicide. For the first time researchers examined seriously the contention that a homicide may be the result of an interaction between the offender and victim. One implication of this was the recognition that it may be a matter of chance which party becomes the victim in a homicide, hence, reducing the value of studies that examine the characteristics of the offender in isolation (Wallace, 1986). Nevertheless, many criminologists, notably feminists writers, have been critical of the use of terms such as 'victim-precipitation', 'victim-proneness' and 'victim-facilitation'. What started out as a valuable recognition of the importance of victim–offender interactions, soon, according to some critics, developed into value-laden 'victim-blaming' (see Morris, 1987; and Walklate, 1989). Amir's (1971) study of rape victims came in for particularly harsh criticism for this reason, not without some justification (it would today cause an even greater storm), although the author clearly had no conscious intention of making moral judgements to the effect that rape was the victim's 'fault'. However, some other researchers have certainly crossed this line and taken the notion of victim-precipitation to its extreme (see, for example, Allen, 1980, who offers advice to the wife of a man who is prone to violent outburst on receipt of burnt toast to avoid such behaviour lest she become the victim of a homicide!).

Many of the typologies developed by researchers place victims along a continuum according to their degree of provocation or culpability. Such typologies typically range from 'completely innocent' to 'fully responsible'. Critics have noted the problems involved when a researcher has to decide where on the continuum a victim might be placed and note the inevitable involvement of value judgements in reaching such decisions (see Silverman, 1974; and Karmen, 1984). Linked to this, critics have also highlighted problems concerning the methodology by which researchers have come to decide the number of homicides held to be victim-precipitated. Wolfgang, for example, relied upon police files in gathering information regarding victim-precipitation and has therefore been criticised for apparently not forseeing the dangers in relying on what essentially represents the prosecution's version of events (see Wallace, 1986; and Brookman, 1999 for specific discussion of the problems inherent in relying upon police murder investigation files as a 'neutral' form of information).

Combined, these moral and methodological objections have led some criminologists to conclude that the notion of victim-precipitation is too problematic to be of real benefit in understanding crime generally, or violent crime, such as homicide, specifically (Wallace, 1986). In contrast, several researchers have rallied to the defence of the concept of victim-precipitation. For example, Fattah (1991) argues that in a value-free social science there is no reason why it should entail victim-blaming.

As Miethe and Meier state, a murder is impossible 'without the union of an offender and victim in time and space' (1994: 4). Consequently, any explanation of this phenomenon is impossible without attention to both parties. Indeed, it should be noted that there also exists, on many occasions, a crucial third party whose role should be considered, namely the 'audience'. As Decker explains, 'Witnesses can be thought of as representing a third part in many homicide events, expanding the dyad of victim–offender roles to a triad of victim–offender–witness roles' (1995: 440). Witnesses or bystanders can play a variety of roles in homicide events, including instigating, escalating, facilitating or mediating fatal violence (1995). Alternatively, bystanders may intervene to prevent a potential homicide occurring. Ultimately, the role of bystanders is likely to be linked to their association or relationship to the parties involved (if they have any). So aside from 'neutral' witnesses with no links to either the victim or offender, it is typically the case that the nature of the relationship between the witness, victim and offender will have consequences for each of their actions and the potential outcome (see Decker, 1995 for an overview of this literature along with his classification scheme of the role of witnesses in homicide events).

Study Task 5.3

Consider the criticisms of 'victim-precipitation' studies outlined above. Should researchers continue to study the role of the victim in homicide events?

Situational Dynamics of Violent Crime

Following the path carved out by Wolfgang (1958), criminologists have developed increasingly sophisticated analyses of the processual development and interactional dynamics of violent situations (Ball-Rokeach, 1973; Goffman, 1967; Hepburn, 1973; Stark et al., 1974). The major substantive approach that has guided investigations of the processes leading to violence comes from symbolic interactionism. This approach stresses the role of situational identities or self-images in interaction (for example, Becker, 1962; Toch, 1969; Hepburn, 1973; Athens, 1977; Luckenbill, 1977; Felson, 1978). One of the most illuminating analyses of violent interactions has been Luckenbill's (1977) paper 'Criminal Homicide as a Situated Transaction'. Luckenbill was essentially concerned to bridge what he saw as a gap in the literature on victim–offender interactions culminating in homicide. For Luckenbill, at best, some research studies had managed to show that victims can precipitate or contribute to the escalation of violence resulting in their death. What was missing was any clear understanding of how 'transactions of murder are organised and how they develop' (Luckenbill, 1977: 176). Luckenbill's research, based on the analysis of 70 'transactions resulting in murder', describes in detail the dynamic interchange of moves and counter-moves between offenders, victims and oftentimes bystanders of homicide. He sees these interactions as proceeding through six stages, where the key players develop lines of action shaped in part by the actions of each other and predominantly focused towards saving or maintaining 'face' and reputation, and demonstrating character. Similarly, Goffman (1967) claimed that transactions resulting in murder involved the joint contribution of the offender and victim to the escalation of a 'character contest', a confrontation in which at least one, but usually both, attempt to establish or save face at the other's expense by standing steady in the face of adversity (Goffman, 1967: 218–19). Athens (1980, 1997) makes similar observations, noting the importance of adopting an interpretive approach to the study of violent crime that involves unravelling how the perpetrators of violent crime themselves make sense of the situations in which they find themselves and how this impacts upon their actions and reactions. What is especially valuable about Athens' work is his attention to the different ways in which violent offenders interpret the various situations that precede their violent acts. Moreover, Athens also pays attention to those occasion where individuals nearly become involved in acts of violence (near-violent situations), but for various reasons chose to withdraw or abstain due to 'restraining judgements' (1997: 45). Clearly, research has moved on substantially from the early focus upon the victim's possible contributory role in homicide. As Polk notes, focusing simply on 'who started it' provides limited understanding of the nature of the interactions that link victims, offenders and bystanders in unfolding homicide scenarios (1997a: 141). To varying degrees, Luckenbill, Polk and others before them (see Banditt et al., 1970; and Shoham et al., 1973), argue that recognising who initiated the resort to lethal violence is less theoretically meaningful than analysing the content and dynamics of the scenarios surrounding lethal violence (we will be returning to this important issue in subsequent chapters). So whilst victim-precipitation may explain part of the dynamics surrounding homicide, various other important factors need to be considered, which leads to a final important issue in connection to the social context of crime, namely the micro-environment in which crime occurs.

Study Task 5.4

Consider the work of Goffman (1967) and Luckenbill (1977) regarding 'character contests' and the situated transactions that result in homicide. In terms of victim–offender relationships what forms of homicide do their accounts seem most applicable to? Compile a list of the kinds of homicide encounters that their models could not adequately explain. You may wish to refer back to Chapter 2 to reflect upon the various kinds of victim–offender relationships that characterise homicide events in the UK.

The Micro-environment and Homicide

The micro-environment of crime can be defined as 'the social context that unites offenders and victims and comprises both physical and social dimensions' (Miethe and Meier, 1994: 3). From this perspective, crime must be understood not only in terms of the offenders and victims involved, but also 'the setting and the props' (Block, 1977: 74). Previous research clearly indicates that crime, including homicide, is not randomly distributed through time and space. Certain locations, such as public houses and clubs or areas of 'spill-over' from these venues, such as nearby 'streets and alleys', feature more heavily as violent locations (hot-spots) as do certain time periods, so that temporal and spatial patterns become important factors to consider (see Gerson, 1978; Messner and Tardiff, 1985; Sherman et al., 1989; Homel and Tomsen, 1993; and Leather and Lawrence, 1995).

Similarly, alcohol and/or drug consumption permeates many situations in which violence generally and homicide specifically occurs. Whilst it is rare for people to become violent every time they consume such substances (so it cannot be said that alcohol and/or drug consumption is a sufficient or necessary explanation for violence), it is fair to say that in specific situations (for example, where the victim, offender or bystanders are drunk in the course of a confrontation) alcohol and/or drugs can act as a facilitator to violence. Several studies, both in the UK and the US, indicate a strong relationship between crimes of violence and alcohol and/or drug consumption (Evans, 1980; Lucas, 1988; Frieze and Brown, 1989; Field, 1990; Deehan, 1999). Further, a steady literature is growing implicating both alcohol and drug use in the aetiology of homicide specifically (Yarvis, 1994; Brumm and Cloninger, 1995; Parker and Rebhun, 1995). Lucas (1988) conducted a study of drink-related violence in two towns in England (Guildford and Woking). He found that violence in both towns was felt by respondents to be inevitable at weekends, where drinking to excess was the norm for many young men and where competitiveness, bravado and aggression characterised such occasions. Moreover, spill-out areas from pubs and clubs where groups of young men gathered were viewed as particularly conducive to violent altercations. As McHugh and Thompson (1991) suggest, the potential for a downward spiral of misunderstandings is not uncommon in such social settings. A few recent studies have involved interviewing homicide offenders (both male and female) with a view to eliciting their perceptions as to how the murders they committed were related to drug use (Spunt et al., 1995, 1996). A plausible conclusion from this evidence is that alcohol and/or drug consumption amongst offenders, victims and bystanders either promotes the use of violence or reduces the scope for a non-fatal outcome.

Finally, there is the important issue of the availability of lethal weapons, in particular firearms. In areas where firearms are readily available the chances of minor disputes ending fatally is considerably enhanced. As outlined in Chapter 2, the incidence of firearm-related homicides in the UK is very low. For example, less than 6 per cent of all homicides between 1995 and 2000 in England and Wales were shooting incidents (HI), compared to around two-thirds in many parts of the US. However, there is evidence that certain sections of the population are over-represented in fatal shootings in the UK. For example, for the period 1995–99 in England and Wales, 27 per cent of all homicides in which both offender and victim were black involved a firearm (data are not available for the other jurisdictions of the UK). It is probably significant that such homicides occurred principally in cities where most of the media reports of 'Yardie' killings have been focused, especially London, Birmingham and Greater Manchester. It is quite plausible that such homicides are linked to drug-related feuds[5] in a sub-culture that not only legitimates violence under certain circumstances, but also where ready access to firearms is not unusual. Hence the importance of linking sub-cultural features of particular groups to the situational factors that can contribute to homicide.

Sampson and Lauritsen (1994) make a very important point regarding the role of situational factors in violence. They note that it is difficult to establish the independent contribution of situational factors to violent behaviour because most of the data available only contains incidents in which violence occurred. It follows that researchers might gain more from exploring situational factors (such as the availability of lethal weapons or alcohol and/or drug consumption) in relation to both violent incidents and near-violent incidents or homicide and sub-lethal violence. In this way we may learn rather more about the specific combination of factors that can lead to violence and homicide. In summary, it would appear that a number of situational factors feature highly in episodes of violence and hence need to be considered in any comprehensive account of this phenomenon. In short, it is important to recognise the interplay between, at the very least, the offender, victim and facilitating environment.

Chapter Summary and Conclusions

This chapter has examined sociological perspectives of homicide, focusing in some detail on structural, cultural and interactional theories. Whilst there is little doubt that sociology has contributed significantly to the study of homicide, we have observed a number of weaknesses with particular theories. In some senses, 'early' sociological theories, in contrast to biological and psychological perspectives, tend to *overpredict* individuals' involvement in crime. The central problem has been a reliance upon features shared by the whole of the lower classes (for example, inequality or restricted legitimate opportunities) that are very common, whereas homicide is comparatively rare. In short, structural and cultural theories, whilst focusing on why certain people are more disposed to violence than others, generally fail to specify the situational conditions and interactional factors that channel such dispositions into concrete lines of action. The development of the interactionist perspective in the 1960s bridged this important gap, whereupon criminologists became increasingly aware that homicide is better understood undivorced from its various contexts. At the same time, however, interactional perspectives, whilst focusing upon the micro-situational dynamics that characterise homicide encounters, tend to neglect the structural and cultural forces that can set the stage for such events. Clearly, in order to take account of what is potentially a multitude of contributory variables regarding homicide, a blending of these two major sociological approaches is required. Furthermore, there is likely to be some merit in integrating sociological theories or ideas, with those from the disciplines of psychology and even biology.

Finally, it is crucially important to note that homicide is a complex phenomenon that cannot be readily explained without attention to the diverse forms which it takes. To illustrate, the factors that contribute to homicide between sexual intimates are undoubtedly different from the chain of events that culminate in homicide amongst criminal associates. Similarly, the reasons for a parent killing its child will be far removed from the circumstances surrounding a rape-murder, or a robbery-murder. Furthermore, within each of these categories there exists a mass of variation, so that the reasons why men kill their spouse will vary widely, as will the reasons why parents kills their children. Distinguishing between distinct forms of homicide is of particular importance with respect to gender, not least because the picture of homicide becomes increasingly complicated when one enters gender into the (already) complex equation. As Polk notes, many theories of homicide suffer from gender-blind analysis in that they 'fail to examine the critical masculine character of homicide' (1994a: 168). As Wallace notes, 'homicides can and should be qualitatively distinguished. Just as there is no unitary entity called "crime", there is no unitary phenomenon of homicide. Analysis of qualitatively distinct homicides highlights the particular points of conflict between different people, in different situations at different points in time' (1986: 13).

In conclusion, what are ideally needed are theories that focus upon particular manifestations or scenarios of homicide alongside dimensions such as victim-offender and gender relationships. With this in mind, the following two chapters focus upon specific forms of homicide in terms of the gender relationships between the offenders and victims of homicide and distinct manifestations of homicide (such as domestic homicide, 'masculine' – that is, male-on-male – confrontational and revenge killings). The aim is to move a step closer to unravelling the nature and causes of distinct forms of homicide.

Review Questions

- Consider the similarities and differences between structural and cultural theories of homicide. What are the relative strengths and weaknesses of structural and cultural approaches to understanding homicide? On what basis could you convincingly argue that these two approaches should be combined in order to more fully account for homicide?
- What particular forms of homicide are sub-cultural theories most useful in explaining? Is the sub-cultural approach useful for explaining female gang violence?
- Make a list of three key factors that distinguish the interactional approach from structural and cultural approaches to homicide. Why is the interactional approach such a valuable contribution to the homicide literature?

Further Reading

For a general overview of sociological theories of crime, including violence, the reader is referred to John Tierney's *Criminology: Theory and Context* (1996: Prentice-Hall); Vold et al.'s *Theoretical Criminology* (1998: Oxford University Press) and Paul Rock, 'Sociological Theories of Crime', in Maguire et al. (eds) *The Oxford Handbook of Criminology* (2002: Oxford University Press, 3rd edition). For a comprehensive overview of the spatial distribution of offences and offenders, with specific attention to socially disorganised communities and the neighbourhood effects on offending rates as well as opportunity and routine activities theories, see Anthony Bottoms and Paul Wile's chapter 'Environmental Criminology' in *The Oxford Handbook of Criminology* (2002: Clarendon). For an excellent overview of victimology, see Lucia Zender's chapter 'Victims' in *The Oxford Handbook of Criminology*. The best single source regarding the interpretive approach to studying violent crime is Lonnie Athens' *Violent Criminal Acts and Actors: Revisited* (1997: University of Illinois Press). For a useful overview of sociologically-based homicide research, especially structural and cultural theories of homicide, see Smith and Zahn's *Homicide: A Sourcebook of Social Research* (1999: Sage). The journal *Homicide Studies* contains many articles concerned with structural determinants of homicide in the US, although there is a glaring lack of qualitative studies within this journal and a US bias.

Useful Internet Sites

A useful link to the sub-culture of violence theory can be found at www.criminology. fsu.edu/crimtheory/wolfgang.htm. The social science information gateway is a very useful resource with criminology, sociology and psychology links: http://sosig. esrc. bris.ac.uk/www.crimetheory.com. A very useful links site which lists many sociological explanations of crime and references – particularly the further reading page – is at www.crimetheory.com/Reading/ further.htm

Notes

1 'Agency refers to the experiential, everyday world of diverse social relations and interaction. Structure encompasses the world of institutions and structural relations – and their histories – which set the boundaries to social interaction and personal opportunity within society, containing and regulating social relations' (Chadwick and Scraton, 2001: 70).

2 The notion that there is some 'natural balance' that a society achieves is questionable. Postmodernist thought (and in particular 'chaos theory') argues for inherent instabilities and privileges disorder and inherent instability over equilibrium (see Milovanovik, 2001a, 2001b).

3 Strain theory and the adaptation of innovation may well explain a greater proportion of corporate homicide (see Chapter 9). The other adaptations are also limited in terms of their applicability to homicide. For detailed overviews, see Vold et al., 1998; and Tierney, 1996.

4 Victimisation surveys, such as the British Crime Survey in England and Wales, now routinely gather information on the nature and extent of criminal victimisation in terms of victims' age, gender, social class and lifestyle.

5 The link between homicide and drugs in this respect mirrors Goldstein's (1985) 'systemic' category, that is, violence associated with the often very lucrative supply and distribution of drugs, that can lead to territorial disputes within the drugs trade.

part three
making sense of particular
forms of homicide

6 When Men Kill

This chapter is concerned to unravel the nature and circumstances of homicide committed by men and to critically evaluate theoretical explanations of male-perpetrated homicide. The first half of the chapter considers homicide amongst men ('masculine' homicide), the second section examines instances when men kill women ('femicide'). The circumstances surrounding homicides that occur amongst men differ significantly from those occasions when men kill women. For example, a significant proportion of male-on-male homicides take place amongst strangers or acquaintances and are the result of honour confrontations in response to arguments of relatively trivial origin. When men kill women, it is often those with whom they are (or have been) intimately connected (that is, a current or former spouse or lover). Such homicides often occur in response to the breakdown of the intimate relationship at a point when the man believes he is 'losing' his partner. Drawing upon cases studies compiled from police murder files,[1] we will explore in some detail various scenarios of 'masculine' homicide and femicide before moving on to evaluate some of the theories that have been proposed to explain these homicides. The chapter ends with a consideration of some of the challenges that remain in making sense of male-perpetrated homicide. This includes how to strike some sort of adequate balance between gender-based explanations and how these intersect with specific demographic characteristics of particular men (such as the age and social class of those involved in homicide); awareness of the diversity of particular forms of male-perpetrated homicide (such as the similarities and differences between those occasions when they kill other men or women); and, finally, the situational and social context in which such lethal acts unfold.

'Masculine' (Male-on-Male) Homicide

It has been well-established from a host of studies across the world that men predominate as both offenders and victims of homicide in most jurisdictions. In England and Wales males comprised 88 per cent of homicide offenders[2] for the period 1995–2000 and 68 per cent of victims. Moreover, over half of all homicides involved a male offender and male victim (59 per cent) (Home Office Homicide Index, henceforth HI). The picture is much the same for the other two jurisdictions of the UK, with males comprising 89 per cent of homicide suspects and 77 per cent of victims in Scotland (Scottish Executive, 2002) and 93 per cent of offenders and 87 per cent of victims in Northern Ireland (personal communication, Police Service of Northern Ireland).

Some General Characteristics of 'Masculine' Homicide

Before focusing upon some of the specific forms that masculine homicide takes, it is necessary to outline some of the general features of all-male lethal encounters, including some of the characteristics of those involved. The most detailed data available relates to the regions of England and Wales, hence the focus here will necessarily be directed to these locations.

Masculine homicide most often takes place amongst acquaintances or strangers (30 per cent and 20 per cent respectively) or friends and family members (10 per cent and 7 per cent).[3] Stabbing is by far the most common method by which males kill other males and accounts for over one-third of all incidents, followed by hitting/kicking (around 15 per cent), beating with a blunt instrument (12 per cent) and shooting (9 per cent). The choice of weapon very much depends upon other important circumstances that surround a homicide, a point to which we return during later discussions of specific scenarios of male homicide.

Generally speaking, the men who become involved in lethal violence are relatively young. The average age of victims of masculine homicides is 33 years, compared to an average age of 29 for offenders (HI, 1995–2000). The peak age of offending is 22 years and the peak age of victimisation is 21 years. Forty-five per cent of all male suspects (who have killed another male) were aged 25 or below at the time of the killing and 60 per cent of all male victims (killed by another male) were aged 36 or below. Unfortunately, there is a lack of comprehensive data available regarding the socio-economic status of offender and victims. The HI indicates that approximately one-third of male victims of homicides (perpetrated by other males) were unemployed at the time of their death. However, in a further quarter of cases the employment status of homicide victims are recorded as 'unknown' and it is likely that a portion of these unknown cases related to unemployed individuals. Whilst comprehensive datasets do not exist for the jurisdictions of the UK regarding the social class of offenders and victims of homicide, smaller-scale qualitative studies and the quantitative data that do exist would strongly indicate that the working-classes and unemployed are over-represented in homicide.[4] The HI does not currently record this information in respect of suspects. Brookman's (2000b) smaller but more detailed homicide investigation file sample of masculine homicides revealed higher numbers of unemployed men involved in these lethal encounters. Seventy per cent of the victims were unemployed at the time of their death and at least 30 per cent of offenders were known to have been unemployed at the time of the killing. All of the offenders and victims who were employed worked in manual and semi-skilled occupations, and there was not a single example within the police files examined of a professional or skilled worker being killed, or taking the life of another man. Similar observations have been noted in numerous previous studies, in England and Wales and elsewhere (Wolfgang, 1958; Wallace, 1986; Mitchell, 1990; Polk, 1994a). Leyton, with reference to England, has argued that 'nine out of ten homicides, perhaps more, are now committed by members of [the] underclass – persons with little education and no professional qualifications, chronically unemployed and on welfare' (1995: 10). As Cooney argues, 'the criminological literature consistently reports a negative relationship between social status and interpersonal homicide' (1997: 381). Even in the case of intimate femicide linked to prior domestic violence there is evidence of a working-class bias. While it has often been asserted that domestic violence knows no class boundaries, Dobash et al., observe, 'the daily work of advocates in refuges and shelters as well as the police seems to belie this notion in favour of one that suggests a greater frequency of this problem among the working classes and the unemployed'[5] (2003: 2–3).

The HI recording of alcohol consumption by offenders and victims of homicide is currently under-developed. Brookman's (2000b) research revealed (in keeping with data from various other studies from the US and Australia) that in over half of all the masculine homicides analysed, alcohol was a prominent feature in that either the victim or offender had consumed alcohol, often to excess. Furthermore, in over one-third of the cases analysed, *both* the offender and victim had consumed alcohol.

Scenarios of Masculine Homicide

Many different kinds of homicide occur amongst males that are distinct in terms of the circumstances leading up to the killing as well as the underlying motive for the killing (refer to Table 2.14 and the Appendix). It is not possible to discuss all of the manifestations of masculine homicide here. Rather, what follows is a consideration of two predominant yet distinct forms of lethal violence amongst men, as identified by research by Brookman (2000b, 2003) and Smith (1999) with regard to England and Wales, and other authors who have studied Australian homicides (Polk, 1994a; Mouzos, 2000, 2003; Wallace, 1986) and American homicides (Daly and Wilson, 1988). The two scenarios in question are confrontational killings and revenge killings (the latter are also referred to as 'grudge killings' or 'conflict resolution homicides' throughout the literature). Brookman (2000b) found that these scenarios occurred in almost identical proportions and together comprised over two-thirds (68 per cent) of the total number of male-on-male homicides she analysed in England and Wales.[6] Smith (1999) found confrontational homicides amongst men to comprise 40 per cent of all the male-on-male killings he examined for England and Wales, which further translated to one in five of all homicides occurring in this jurisdiction (he did not deal with the revenge category). Similarly, Polk (1994a, 1997a) found that confrontational killings amongst men comprised approximately one in five of all 380 homicides he examined in Victoria, Australia. Together, confrontational and conflict resolution killings comprised almost one-third (32 per cent) of the total number of killings.[7] Figure 6.1 summarises the main characteristics of confrontational and revenge killings. What follows is a detailed exploration of confrontational and revenge killings amongst men.

Figure 6.1 Characteristics of Confrontational and Revenge Homicides in England and Wales

---

Confrontational Homicide
Characterised as face-to-face spontaneous honour contests. Offender and victim become involved in a spontaneous dispute and engage *together* in a violent confrontation that leads to the death of one of them (victim-precipitation evident in some of these killings).

Revenge Homicide
Characterised as planned attacks. The offender plans to kill the victim due to some perceived wrongdoing (against themselves or a third party, such as a family member or female partner). Weapons often secured and the victim sought out and given little or no chance to engage in an altercation. A history of conflict often evident.

Confrontational Homicide

Many studies of homicide have observed that masculine homicide is often the result of a spontaneous confrontation that quickly escalates, resulting in the death of one of the combatants. As Polk puts it, 'confrontational homicide has its source in the willingness of males, first, to lay down challenges to the honour of other males, and second, the masculine readiness to engage in physical violence in response to such challenges' (1994b: 169).

Numerous researchers have paid attention to the apparent triviality of the triggers to lethal violence (Wolfgang, 1958; Wallace, 1986; Daly and Wilson, 1988; Falk, 1990). Falk (1990), for example, referred to such killings as 'sudden anger' and Wolfgang (1958) talked about 'altercations of relatively trivial origin'. Moreover, male 'honour' is a concept that is often used by researchers to characterise men's spontaneous disputes in response to what many deem to be trivial or spurious grievances (Polk, 1994a; Smith, unpublished). Hence phrases such as 'honour' or 'character' contests are consistently found throughout the literature in relation to masculine homicide. Some researchers have gone so far as to locate male honour at the very heart of lethal violence amongst them. Cooney (1998), for example, proposes that honour 'as bravery is part of a larger ethical system'. Similarly, Spierenburg (1998) suggests that passivity is a cardinal feminine virtue, whilst violence may be viewed as honourable. The following is a classic example of the sorts of trivial disagreements that can lead to lethal violence amongst men:

[Case Code: D.06/96]
At around 8.30 p.m. on a Monday evening, Lisa was at home when she heard stones being thrown at her windows and identified the culprits as neighbouring children. This was not the first time this had happened and Lisa decided to complain to the children's parents about these incidents. Accompanied by her 13-year-old son, Lisa made her way to the children's homes. However, their parents were not in and the children had run into a neighbour's house. Lisa's son kicked the door of the house where the children had run to hide. The occupant of the house, Leroy (the offender, aged 29, of mixed race) emerged from his house and was very angry. At this stage, Lisa's boyfriend, Ricky (the victim, aged 33, white), was standing at the corner of the street and was not involved. Lisa began to explain that whilst Leroy's children had not been involved, several of the other children who had run into his house had been throwing stones at her windows. Leroy, apparently uninterested in Lisa's explanation, pushed her against a wall with both hands on her shoulders and shouted at her. He then raised his right hand as if to hit her. At this stage, Lisa's boyfriend, Ricky, shouted out to Leroy, 'Keep your hands to yourself,' to which Leroy replied, 'No fucker speaks to me like that'. Leroy ran into his house and quickly emerged with a wooden baseball bat, whereupon he confronted Ricky and hit him across the back of the head, saying to witnesses, 'That's what he gets for fucking with me'. Ricky died 16 days later.

This case is very typical of the sorts of minor verbal altercations that can result in lethal violence, although more sustained levels of violence are sometimes evident, as illustrated in the following case:

[Case Code: D.05/94]
The victim in this case, Dean (white, aged 35) lived in a neighbouring flat to the offender, Sunil (black, aged 31). At around 2.00 p.m. on a Friday, Dean approached Sunil's flat to complain about the noise of loud music. Dean kicked Sunil's door several times and made racist and derogatory remarks about Sunil's ethnic background and shouted about the level of noise. Sunil responded initially with a verbal threat saying, 'Come near my door again and I'll fucking kill you'. Dean continued to shout abuse at Sunil and the two now came face to face outside Sunil's front door (which by now had been kicked open by Dean). Sunil proceeded to punch and kick Dean and then threw him down a concrete staircase, where the victim collided with a stone wall. Dean was then dragged (now unconscious) down a second flight of stairs and onto a footpath outside the block of flats. What followed was observed by a number of witnesses and amounted to a systematic series of kicks and blows to the victim. At one stage the offender walked away from the victim, only to return and continue his attack. The injuries that Dean sustained were described by the pathologist as consistent with major force of the type normally observed after a high-speed road traffic accident.

Both cases involve an altercation that was not originally instigated by the offender, and commenced on the doorstep of the offenders' homes. The greater levels of violence sustained by Dean may owe something to the fact that he persisted in his verbal assault of Sunil and, of course, made racist remarks that may easily have inflamed the situation. Whilst the response of the ultimate offender may appear excessive, as Wilson and Daly observe, 'The precipitating insult may appear petty, but is usually a deliberate provocation (or is perceived to be), and hence constitutes a public challenge that cannot be shrugged off' (1985: 69). Whilst it could be argued that these cases were to some extent instigated by the ultimate victim, other confrontational killings involve the victim assaulting the offender first, the subject of the next section.

Victim-Precipitated Confrontational Killings

Victim-precipitation refers to those instances where the ultimate victim of homicide (or violence more generally) is the first to have resorted to physical violence (see Wolfgang, 1958; and Chapter 5). In the first case to be considered below, the victim and offender were close friends; the second takes place amongst neighbours. In both cases the violence took place in the presence of an audience, including both males and females and in both cases the victim was the first to resort to physical violence.

[Case Code: B.03/94]
Lenny (white, aged 17), his friend Karl (white, aged 19) and their two girlfriends spent Sunday evening drinking in a local pub before going back to Karl's house with a takeaway meal. Shortly after eating, Lenny fell asleep. As a prank, Karl covered Lenny's head in hair mousse. Lenny woke in a rage and immediately wanted to fight Karl outside. Lenny and Karl went outside, followed by the two girls. Lenny quickly punched Karl in the face, at which stage Lenny's girlfriend grabbed him and broke up the fight. Karl returned to the house and removed a large seven-inch kitchen knife, returning outside moments later. Lenny was being pushed down the road by his girlfriend in an effort to remove him from the area and calm him down. Karl approached Lenny and a fight ensued during which Lenny received a fatal stab wound to the neck. Karl immediately tried to give mouth-to-mouth resuscitation; however, Lenny died shortly afterwards.

[Case Code: D.03/94]
A considerable degree of bad feeling had developed between the victim's and offender's families (who were neighbours) over a period of some years. On the day in question the victim (John, white, aged 33), a heavy drinker, had an argument with his wife. He was in an aggressive mood and went into his back garden to 'cool down'. The offender's sister, Sally, and her young son were also in their back garden. An argument arose between Sally and John and at some stage John threw a lit cigarette over the boundary fence between the two gardens, which struck Sally's son in the face. Sally threw the cigarette back, narrowly missing one of John's children. John became very angry and threw a sweeping brush at Sally, hitting her on the head. He then jumped up on a grass bank near the boundary fence in a threatening manner, at which stage Sally went into her house and telephoned the emergency services in a distressed state saying, 'My neighbour is drunk and is being aggressive,

can you attend please?' Almost half an hour later Sally dialled 999 again and urged the police to attend. She was told that they were on their way. At this time, Mark (white, aged 24), Sally's brother, had returned home and was told of the ongoing problems. Mark went out into his back garden and confronted John about his behaviour. A heated argument developed between the two men. Sally then entered the garden and urged Mark to go back into the house, which he did. John remained at the boundary fence, shouting abuse to the effect that Mark and Sally were having an incestuous relationship. Mark returned to the garden and confronted John once more. A police officer had now arrived at the house and, along with Sally and members of John's family, witnessed the following fatal events. John was clutching a mitre level with a metal rule and as he raised it above his head, as if to attack Mark with it, Mark responded by thrusting a knife into John's chest.

Enquiries which followed revealed that John was a very violent man with a string of previous convictions for violence, including an assault against the police and numerous serious attacks upon his wife and children. John was also receiving medication for depression at the time and it is believed that this, combined with a large intake of alcohol, exacerbated his violent mood. In contrast, Mark had never previously been involved in a violent incident and was described by the police as a man of 'good character'. Evidence suggests that Mark and his sister were petrified of John and had, on many previous occasions, 'backed down' from potentially violent situations. This case is a clear example of a victim-precipitated homicide. The victim was the first to use physical force (in this instance against the offender's sister) and was, according to witnesses (including the victim's wife) the first to threaten force in the confrontation.

Confrontational killings amongst men take place in a variety of contexts. Those considered above occurred on the boundaries of offender's or victim's homes. Others tend to be associated with scenes of leisure activity (that is, in and around pubs and clubs or on the way to or from such venues) and are often associated with heavy alcohol consumption. There is a considerable body of literature that has explored the connections between alcohol consumption and masculine violence – particularly in the context of night-time leisure activity. Among the most illuminating are those that have adopted an ethnographic approach to studying such events. For example, Tomsen's (1997) study of assaults in public drinking venues illustrated how some males 'seek out' violence as part of a 'top night out'. Similarly, Benson and Archer (2002), in their study of sources of conflict between young men on a night out, found that men often used aggression and violence to acquire status and be seen as 'real men'. This predominantly applied among the younger males they observed and interviewed and those of low-status. Implicit in each of these studies is the importance of the social audience. As Polk notes, the presence of an audience 'makes any challenge to honour a visible and public matter' but also 'provides a pool of possible protagonists as the honour contest escalates' (1999: 13). Interestingly, Benson and Archer (2002: 24) found that any notion of 'honour' in status displays amongst men primarily concerned a male audience. Whilst a number of the young females that they interviewed were attracted to a man who was perceived as being able to 'stand up for himself', frequent engagement in violence by men was generally viewed negatively by the women concerned.

The following case exemplifies the classic ingredients of a confrontational homicide in the context of night-time leisure, fuelled by excessive alcohol consumption:

[Case Code: D.06/94]

The victim (Mark, aged 28) spent a Friday evening drinking in local pubs with a male friend. Both men consumed around seven pints of lager and decided to continue from the pubs to a club. They arrived at around 11.45 p.m. The offender (Stephen, aged 36) spent his evening in much the same way with three friends, consuming alcohol in various pubs before finding their way to the same nightclub. Neither party of men were known to one another. Stephen and his friends were positioned between the bar area and dance floor. Between 1.00 a.m. and 2.00 a.m. Mark made several derogatory comments to Stephen and the men in his company whilst moving to and from the bar to purchase alcohol. At one stage he issued threats and was warned to 'fuck off'. On the final occasion, Mark approached Stephen and his friends, at which stage Stephen indicated to his friends that he would hit him if he 'started' again. Mark again made verbal threats, at which stage Stephen punched him with one solid blow to the left-hand side of his face. Mark's head was seen to shoot backward and upwards and he fell to the floor unconscious. Stephen and his friends immediately split up and the victim was attended to by staff at the nightclub. Mark suffered a brain haemorrhage and subsequently died.

Both men had consumed considerable amounts of alcohol and the victim had also ingested a small amount of amphetamine powder at the start of the evening. Mark had a reputation, locally, for becoming involved in fights and for drug taking. Stephen had previously served two separate prison sentences for offences of burglary, theft and actual bodily harm (ABH). It is not clear why Mark was acting in an antagonistic manner toward Stephen and his friends, but what is clear is that neither Mark nor Stephen were strangers to violence. That Stephen declared to his friends his intentions to hit the victim if he persisted, indicates the importance of the social audience within this encounter and his perceived need to control the situation.

The following case involves a lethal altercation on the street as two male friends made their way home after an evening drinking in a city centre:

[Case Code: D.15/94]

James (white, aged 29), an electrical engineer, spent Thursday evening drinking in the city centre with his brother-in-law, Alan. At around 2.00 a.m. both men were making their way home along the street towards Alan's house, where they were going to spend the night. Both men were singing loudly and attracted the attention of four other young men (aged between 17 and 23), one of whom told them to 'shut up and stop singing'. James made a mildly derogatory remark towards the men, at which stage one of the young men in the gang, Darren, produced a knife and challenged James to a fight. Alan removed his belt and began waving it around, whilst James tried to pull him away from a confrontation but was himself pushed aside. Several threatening words were exchanged between James, Alan and Darren (who was still holding the knife). Suddenly, another of the men in the gang snatched the knife from Darren, circled around to the rear of James and plunged the knife into his back, with a single thrust. The young man then removed the knife and all four men ran off. There were several witnesses to the events as many local residents had been woken up, initially by the singing and subsequently by shouting.

The group of four involved in the attack, all of whom were unemployed, were known locally as violent and intimidating men. All four had been drinking and at least two of the gang had been smoking cannabis. In contrast, the victim was apparently a popular, well-liked, mild mannered individual. He too, however, had consumed a large quantity of alcohol on this occasion.

The cases reviewed thus far characterise some of the most common social settings and circumstances of confrontational homicides in England and Wales. Smith (1999) also observed that a significant proportion of confrontational homicides amongst men involve competition amongst men over women. Similarly, Polk (1994b) identified the existence, in Australia, of confrontational killings that revolved around honour and the protection of women – that is, instances where men respond to insults directed at their female companions.

To summarise, confrontational homicides amongst men take place in a variety of contexts and are generally the outcome of a spontaneous dispute between the men involved. These honour contests are as likely to occur amongst strangers as amongst friends or acquaintances. Each of the confrontational killings considered here indicate situations where both the offender and victim entered into a disagreement *together*. In each case there was a period where either the victim or the offender, in some senses, had an opportunity to disengage from the drama. Whilst one of them may play a more forceful or aggressive role than the other, both men essentially 'agree' to allow the confrontation to develop and escalate. Hence, as Katz observes, '[T]o the (eventual) killer, the (eventual) victim, by not trying to brush off or avoid the confrontation, is indicating that neither party may escape the implications of what is to transpire' (1988: 19). In the case of the victim-precipitated confrontational killings, the ultimate victim tended to be the most persistent 'player' in the confrontation, again having many opportunities to leave the scene as the offender issued verbal threats before proceeding to physically assault the victim. Moreover, the consumption of alcohol (oftentimes to excess) pervades many of these lethal encounters. Status or honour contests are not confined to the context of alcohol-fuelled leisure activities, in that many of the confrontations occurred on victim's or offender's doorsteps when neither party had apparently consumed alcohol. That said, the environment in and around pubs and clubs, which often involves the coming together of many young men and heavy alcohol consumption, would appear to exacerbate or heighten the likelihood of confrontations escalating. Lethal confrontations are just one of the ways in which some men kill one another. Closely following on the heels of lethal confrontations in England and Wales are revenge killings, to which we now turn.

Revenge Homicide

It has been suggested that the concepts of revenge and retribution have existed in the philosophies, theologies, literatures and laws of diverse cultures since the dawn of time (Marangui and Newman, 1987). Yet, revenge killings (or 'conflict-resolution' homicides, as Polk, 1994a refers to them) have been the subject of much less attention in the homicide literature as compared to confrontational killings. That is not to suggest that they have not always existed, rather that researchers had not specifically identified them as a coherent sub-category of masculine homicide until Polk identified his 'conflict resolution' category and later Brookman (2000b) identified a comparable scenario labelled 'revenge killings'. Prior to this, these sorts of homicides tended to be found within categories such as 'altercations or arguments over money' (Wolfgang, 1958; Maxfield, 1989) or 'business or drug dealings' (Falk, 1990).

The definitive feature of Polk's conflict resolution category is that at least one of the parties is willing to call upon violence with some degree of planning as a device for resolving a conflict with another person (1994a: 129). This broadly corresponds to Brookman's (2000b: 202) revenge category, defined as killings that are to some extent planned and exhibit a history of ongoing strife between the relevant parties. The principle motive for such homicides is to seek revenge against the victim for some perceived wrongdoing. The essential component that sets these lethal encounters apart from confrontational homicides is the planned nature of the killings. Offenders and victims in these cases are more likely to have known each other than those involved in confrontational killings. Invariably, the individuals who become involved in these revenge killings are friends, relatives (often in-laws), acquaintances or neighbours. Interestingly, a large proportion of the revenge cases identified by Brookman (2000b) were carried out with a firearm (7 cases). Only two other cases from the total sample of police files analysed (97 cases) involved shooting incidents (both of which occurred amongst males).

The kinds of grudges that can lead to revenge killings are quite disparate. In some instances they may be related to apparent 'affairs' between the offender's sexual partner and the victim. In other cases the grudges are 'drugs-related' in that the victim owes the offender money for drugs, for example, and is perceived to have conspired to 'dupe' the offender out of his rightful money. In some instances the victim is killed because of his inappropriate behaviour toward a third party, with whom the offender is closely connected. A classic example of a revenge homicide is illustrated in the following case:

[Case Code: D.10/94]
Since Jeff (white, aged 34) married into the victim's family, a great deal of animosity had occurred between himself and his brother-in-law, Ian (white, aged 39). Specifically, Ian had, on two separate occasions, physically assaulted his sister, Sue (Jeff's wife), in respect of trivial matters. The day before the killing, Jeff went to work at 4.00 p.m. on a night shift. Some time after 10.00 p.m., Ian arrived at his sister's house in a drunken state, shouting to be allowed into the house. On gaining entry he became abusive towards Sue and punched her, breaking her nose. When Jeff arrived home from work he saw his wife's injuries and was informed of the previous night's events, to which he responded, 'I've had a gut's full of him hitting you around'. Jeff went to bed and when he got up he proceeded to put into action his plan to avenge his wife's beatings. He cancelled work for that evening and obtained a shotgun and cartridges from an acquaintance. At around 11.20 p.m. he walked the short distance to Ian's flat, knocked on the door and, without saying a

word, shot him twice in the head at close range. Jeff then telephoned the police to explain what he had done, stating, 'He got what he deserved, he gave my missus a kicking, I hope he dies'.

This case illustrates the key elements of the revenge category of homicide. The offender had built up a considerable degree of resentment against his brother-in-law for his previous actions and clearly planned the killing. No actual confrontation took place between the offender and victim, and the offender apparently felt no remorse at his actions, viewing the killing as justified under the circumstances. The following case also clearly illustrates a revenge-style killing, although unlike the case just considered, there is no evidence of any previous or ongoing grievances between the men involved:

[Case Code: F.11/96]
The offender, Jojo (mixed race, aged 19) had learned that Kofi (the victim, mixed race, aged 30) had sold crack cocaine to his sister. Jojo was incensed by the news and decided to seek revenge. He gathered together three male friends, all of whom armed themselves with baseball bats and knives. They searched for Kofi and eventually found him in a parked car with a friend. Kofi was dragged from the car onto the street, where he was beaten and stabbed to death. Many people witnessed the attack, which took place at around 5.00 p.m. on a Saturday, including a number of small children who were playing close by in a playground.

Whilst this case indicates a fairly clear motive for revenge (albeit an extreme reaction), some of the revenge killings emerged out of what would appear to be rather less significant factors, as the following case illustrates:

[Case Code: F.03/96]
The offender, Mike, and the victim, Phil (both white, aged 22), were acquaintances. Mike and his girlfriend spent the early part of a Sunday evening drinking together in a local pub. Phil, who was also drinking in the pub, started to annoy Mike, making fun of him and his girlfriend. At this stage, Mike had a 'few words' with Phil and the incident went no further. However, on leaving the pub at around 10.00 p.m., Mike, now the worse for wear due to alcohol consumption, decided to 'sort Phil out'. He armed himself with a baseball bat and a large kitchen knife and waited for around an hour for Phil to return home. Mike subsequently stabbed Phil to death.

Incidental Victims of Revenge Killings

'Incidental victims' refers to those cases where the victim was the unintended target of violence and was killed, either because he or she got in the way of a violent incident between the offender and the intended target or, as in the first case to be considered, was mistaken for the intended target. Whilst the victims of these homicides were indeed incidental by-products of violence occurring amongst other men, it remains vital to trace events back to the original motive for the violence in which they became 'caught up', whilst simultaneously acknowledging that these men were not the specific targets of violence.

[Case Code: F.06/94]

Griff, the offender in this case (white, aged 39), had been having a sexual relationship with Sarah. Sarah had recently ended the relationship and Griff had become angry and jealous, suspecting Sarah of having formed a new relationship with another man. Late one Saturday night, Griff broke into Sarah's house and made his way upstairs to see if in fact Sarah had a new boyfriend. On seeing what he believed to be Sarah in bed with another man, Griff stabbed the male, several times. In actual fact, Griff had entered Stephanie's bedroom (Sarah's sister) and stabbed to death Carl (white, aged 22), Stephanie's boyfriend.

This is a rare example of a case of mistaken identify. Had the intended target been killed, as Griff had planned, then of course this case would have represented a clear-cut example of revenge homicide. That Griff killed the wrong man is less important in understanding this killing than his original motive for being in the house, with a weapon, ready to kill. The following case is similar in that the actual victim of the homicide was not the apparent target of a revenge shooting but bore the brunt of the offender's indiscriminate shooting toward the public house in which he worked:

[Case Code: D.14/94]

Danny (white, aged 26) spent Friday evening drinking in a local pub. At some stage he upset one of the barmaids, who informed two of the doormen of the incident. The doormen knew Danny as there had previously been incidents of violence between them. They forcibly removed Danny from the premises, apparently assaulting him in the process. Danny left the area, armed himself with a gun, and returned to shoot the doormen to avenge his earlier beating. Danny fired several shots inside the pub towards the two doormen but missed them. A third doorman (who had not been involved in the earlier incident) approached Danny and was fatally shot.

Finally, some incidental victims of homicide become caught up in what appear to be rival 'gangland' violence, as the following case illustrates:

[Case Code: F.01/96]

Winston (Jamaican, aged 38) was a caretaker and local charity worker. One Monday morning, at around 7.00 a.m., he became caught up in a rival gangland killing in the street. Tyrone (Afro-Carribean, aged 24), part of a gang of six men, had come to the area to kill a member of a rival drugs gang. As their target came out of his car, he was shot. Winston went to the assistance of the victim and was himself shot.

It was not clear from the case file whether Winston was accidentally hit by gunfire or whether he himself became a target as he went to the assistance of the original target of the attack. As outlined in Chapter 2, gang-related homicides involving firearms appear to be on the increase in England and Wales and, by extension, it is possible that certain jurisdictions of the UK will witness an increase in the killing of those directly and indirectly involved, as well as unfortunate bystanders or passers-by that are in no way linked to these masculine feuds.

To recap, the most significant features of revenge killings, which clearly set them apart from confrontational homicides, are the planned nature of the attacks, such that there is always a time lapse between the initial act (which leads the offender to wish to harm the victim) and the actual attack. Unlike confrontational killings, revenge homicides do not involve the active participation of both offender and victim and do not occur spontaneously in the heat of the moment. Rather, the offenders in these cases plan to attack the victim to avenge some perceived wrong-doing (against themselves or a third party) and do so in such a way that the victim has little chance to engage in a confrontation, even if he wished to. This is clearly illustrated by the large proportion of firearms that were used in these killings, as well as in the manner in which some of the offenders lay in wait for their victims or co-opted other men to assist in the attack.

In the following section we explore some of the theories that have been developed that may help to make sense of both scenarios of masculine homicide considered here. The emphasis will be directed toward those theories that explicitly take account of the gendered nature of homicide and readers are referred back to Chapters 3 to 5 for detailed coverage of biological, psychological and sociological perspectives.

> **Study Task 6.1**
>
> Read back through the case studies of confrontational and revenge killings. Make a list of the factors that both kinds of killings share and those factors that are distinct in terms of victim and offender characteristics and characteristics of the event.

Explaining Masculine Homicide

There is a vast array of literature devoted to explaining different forms of lethal (and sub-lethal) violence amongst men. Here we focus upon two main bodies of literature: that which focuses upon the micro-dynamics of violent encounters, exploring how masculine disputes emerge and escalate 'on the ground'; and that which focuses more broadly upon the structural, cultural and social conditions that arguably give rise to such violence, or a willingness to engage in violence. Both approaches have, to varying degrees, acknowledged the need to unravel the maleness of violent crime. Hence, it is important to begin here with a brief overview of the development of what is now a significant body of research concerned with masculinity and crime. The section that follows serves as a backdrop to the more specific explananations of distinct forms of homicide considered later in this section, as well as those explored in the second section of the chapter regarding femicide.

Masculinity and Violence: Taking the 'Maleness' of Violence and Homicide Seriously

It is generally acknowledged that feminists were the catalysts for serious interest in crime and masculinity in that the first theoretical attempts to take the 'maleness' of crime seriously occurred in the works of American radical feminists in the 1970s (Jefferson, 1996; Collier, 1998). The early feminist work paved the way for a vital new focus, but was not without its problems. For example, Jefferson (1996) identifies two broad limitations with the early feminist accounts of the maleness of crime. First, in their attempt to situate specific crimes, such as rapes, within broader social relations, feminism came to equate masculinity with patriarchy or male domination in such a manner that the two were conceptualised as synonymous (see also Segal, 1990). Second, the notion of masculinity deployed was implicitly deterministic such that, regardless of the possible roots of male dominance, the possibility of change was not contemplated.

Jefferson notes a number of challenges to the 'reductionist' and 'essentialistic' tendencies, both within feminism and beyond. Of particular note is the work of Bob Connell (1987), who made an important break with the reductionist angle in arguing for the existence of a range of competing masculinities[8]. Similarly, Brod (1987) observed that gender identities are not naturally given, but are socially constructed and negotiated. In other words, there are various, often competing ways of being a male or 'doing gender'. However, masculinities are not all equally privileged. As Connell (1987) argues, there exists a dominant or 'hegemonic masculinity'[9] along with various 'subordinated masculinities' (Connell, 1987: 183). As Jefferson aptly states, 'some forms of masculinity (as well as all forms of femininity) have to struggle against dominant ideals and practices of "manliness"' (1989: 124). For example, heterosexuality is arguably 'the most important feature of contemporary hegemonic masculinity' and homosexuality 'a key form of subordinated masculinity' (Connell, 1987: 186). For Connell, the value of the concept of hegemonic masculinity is in the recognition of 'the importance of differences among men *in gender terms* as well as in terms of class and race' (2002: 90, emphasis in original). Moreover, it recognises 'a connection between two important social patterns, hierarchy between men and women and hierarchy among men' (2002: 90).

Put another way, whilst certain stereotypes of masculinity – such as aggressiveness, power, independence, strength, dominance, self-confidence, competitiveness, superiority and so forth – may represent the ideals of masculinity across many cultures, it is also the case that there are a number of different ways in which men of different ages and from different backgrounds (in terms of class and ethnicity, for example) may relate to such ideals (Jefferson, 1989). For example, Jefferson suggests that physical prowess is a component of hegemonic masculinity, but that it 'probably holds greater sway among working than middle class males' (1989: 125). He cites the work of Paul Willis, who studied working-class adolescent youths ('the lads') and found that they rejected academic schoolwork and their peers who conformed to the academic ethos, not only because they recognised that the odds against academic success were stacked against them in class terms, but also because 'pen pushing' was regarding as 'cissy' – an expression of femininity. According to the lads, real men chose manual not mental labour (Willis, 1977, cited in Jefferson, 1989: 125).

Jefferson (1994, 1997), adopting a psychoanalytic approach (see Chapter 4 for a discussion of psychoanalysis), observes a number of disjunctions and contradictions that have been felt by both feminists and male researchers in coming to terms with the contradictory and complex nature of masculinities and their various expressions in criminal activity. For Jefferson, some of the clearest examples of the contradictory nature of masculinity come from in-depth, reflexive, case study data on specific criminals – such as the serial, sexual murderer Peter Sutcliffe (Warde Jouve, 1988; Smith, 1989) and the more recent James Bulger case (Jackson, 1995). For example, Jackson notes how the lives of the two young boys who killed James Bulger could be understood as a struggle to straddle different masculine ideals – a framework of powerlessness imposed by regulatory institutions (such as the family and school) collided with the 'idealised fantasy images of hyper-masculine toughness, dominance and invulnerability' (1995: 22) provided by the media and male peer groups. What these kinds of works apparently portray are notions of fragile self-concepts, as opposed to tough, dominant, patriarchal images of masculinity. In sum, for Jefferson, the in-depth case studies are 'transformed by the noticing of, and accounting for, a whole host of apparently inconsequential, overlooked details, thus rendering them theoretically meaningful' (1997: 546). Jefferson believes that incorporating a psychic element can explain why specific men behave in specifically violent ways. Whilst this approach may have gone some way toward transcending the 'social lock' that Jefferson refers to it is also open to criticism. It is, of course, in danger of going down 'the route of celebrating individual differences to its ultimate' (Walklate, 1995: 180), due to its highly individualistic stance (similar criticisms have been made of psychological/psychoanalytic approaches more generally, as noted earlier in Chapter 4). What Jefferson's work achieves, however, is an important move away from the dominant discourse running throughout most other accounts of masculinity which posit a relationship between the power of men, their masculinity and their crimes. Psychoanalytically-grounded accounts instead emphasise the internal struggles and weaknesses of (some) men and their resultant involvement in crime.

Collier neatly summarises what he sees as three stages in theorising masculinity. Stage one comprises those theories that contemplated the relationship between masculinity (in the singular) and crime; stage two consists of those theorists who subsequently focused upon masculinities (plural) and crime; and stage three is characterised by a concern with the way in which some men come to take up certain 'subjective positions' (exemplified in the work of Jefferson, 1994) (see Collier, 2000 for a useful review of masculinities and violence). One might add to this a fourth stage that we could term 'critiquing masculinities'. This final phase in theorising masculinities represents a critique of the very concept itself. It would appear that a debate is emerging (in some small quarters) as to whether the concept of masculinity/ies is merely descriptive, as opposed to explanatory. For example, Walklate notes that 'The maleness of crime ... also becomes the source of its explanation. Thus not only does this reflect a failure to resolve fully the tendency towards universalism, it can also be read as tautological' (1995: 181). Despite these criticisms, it remains the case that criminologists, and other social scientists, continue to search for links between criminality and masculinity.

So how does this growing body of masculinities literature help us to understand specific manifestations of male perpetrated homicide? What follows is a consideration of some of the theories that have been developed to account for confrontational and revenge homicide. Whilst each of these to some extent acknowledge the maleness of homicide, this is much more explicitly unravelled in some theories than others. Some of these theories operate at the micro-level, exploring how violent episodes develop and erupt and in what ways this links to masculine identities and issues of honour. Other theories take as their focus the intersection of socio-demographic factors, such as social class and age, in trying to unravel why particular categories of men become involved in violence and how this links to expressions of masculinity. Examples of both approaches will be considered below.

Explaining Confrontational Homicide

Researchers have generally explained confrontational homicide by stressing the importance of males preserving their sense of dignity or honour in the face of challenges from other men. For example, Luckenbill (1977) provides a particularly useful analysis of homicide that recognises the importance of maintaining face and reputation and demonstrating character. In particular, Luckenbill gives meaning to the apparent triviality of confrontational killings by setting out, step by step, the typical manner in which such confrontations develop and escalate. Luckenbill identifies six stages through which such confrontations develop, beginning with the 'opening move' through to lethal violence (see Figure 6.2).

Figure 6.2   Luckenbill's 6-stage model of the situated transaction of homicide

Stage 1: *Opening Move:* The victim affronts the offender with insults or non-compliance.
Stage 2: *Interpretation:* The offender interprets these as personally offensive.
Stage 3: *Offender Response:* The offender retaliates with a challenge or an actual physical attack and a small number of victims (10 per cent in Luckenbill's sample) meet their demise at this stage.
Stage 4: *Victim Response:* The victim (if not already eliminated) does not comply with the offender's challenge or command or else physically retaliates.
Stage 5: *Working Agreement:* A commitment to do battle is forged.
Stage 6: *The Aftermath:* The victim has fallen (marking the termination of the transaction) and the offender flees the scene, voluntarily remains at the scene or is involuntarily held at the scene by members of the audience or the police.

Source: Adapted from Luckenbill, 1977: 179–85.

The value of Luckenbill's model is that it recognises that, at various stages in the encounter, both the offender and victim have an opportunity to disengage from the drama. That neither disengage is, arguably, what characterises those aggressive or violent interactions that end lethally, from those that end peacefully. For example, at stage 3, having interpreted the victim's behaviour as personally offensive, the offender could excuse the victim's behaviour (judging him drunk or harmless) and leave the scene.

Study Task 6.2

Review stages 1–5 of Luckenbill's 6-stage model and consider in what different ways both offenders and victims could have interpreted and responded to one another, so that a lethal outcome was avoided.

Similar analyses of the process of escalation of violence have been undertaken by Leary (1976), Levi (1980), Felson and Steadman (1983), Felson (1984) and Benson and Archer (2002). For example, Felson and Steadman (1983) identify three major stages, focusing strictly on behavioural elements (as opposed to including cognitive factors) and recognise mediating and evasive actions within their model.

Despite the obvious merits of such approaches, in terms of their attention to detail, such accounts generally fail to acknowledge that not all homicides are the outcome of a 'dynamic interchange' or 'character contest' between the victim and offender. In fact, this conceptualisation only essentially applies to the masculine confrontational scenario discussed here and is not very helpful in understanding revenge killings or many other forms of homicide between males and females. Levi utilised an approach similar to that of Luckenbill, but concluded that it is 'a mistake to try to understand or predict the dynamics of the homicide process solely as a character contest' (1980: 288). Moreover, Polk (1999) finds that even when applied to confrontational masculine homicide, Luckenbill's 'idealised sequence' does not always apply in that some confrontational killings are more complex, involving one or other of the protagonists breaking off from the scene to fetch a weapon, or complications arising where a social audience becomes in some way involved. More critically, Luckenbill's analysis (and many others like it) fail to specifically tackle the gendered nature of this particular form of homicide, nor, for that matter, the importance of social class or age. On the other hand, some researchers have paid rather more attention to some of these issues. For example, Hans Toch (1969) conducted interviews with violent men in prison and, once again, identified the recurring themes of status and reputation. However, Toch more carefully located these themes in relation to masculinity and found that nearly half of his sample fell into one of two categories, namely 'self-image promoters' or 'self-image defenders'. The former refers to men who work hard at manufacturing the impression that they are not to be trifled with; the latter refers to men who are extremely sensitive to implications that others make concerning their integrity, manliness or worth. A clear majority of the men Toch interviewed used violence to respond to challenges (real or imagined) to their ideal (masculine) self-image or 'rep' – which fits well with several of the examples of confrontational homicide discussed earlier.

Daly and Wilson (1988, 1990) have been concerned to account for the masculine character of many homicides, as well as the youth of the offenders (see also Chapter 4). They argue that most masculine homicides arise from competitive struggles for status, resources, mates or a combination of these. However, this competition ultimately arises from evolutionary pressures:

Young men are especially formidable and especially risk prone because they constitute the demographic class on which there was the most intense selection for confrontational competitive capabilities among our ancestors. (1990: 94)

Daly and Wilson's work is, as discussed in Chapter 4, difficult to verify, not least because 'the inner core of their hypothesis cannot be tested directly' (Polk, 1998: 464). Further, whilst they address the youthfulness of most men involved in homicide, Daly and Wilson are not able to unravel why particular young men, as opposed to all young men, engage in lethal violence. Similarly, they say little about the working-class nature of the majority of men involved in homicides, simply arguing that poverty and poor prospects favour risk proneness, since low-status individuals have little to lose by engaging in violence.

Greenberg (1977, 1981) offers an interesting structural interpretation of the relationship between age and crime, combining elements of both strain and control theories. He argues that crime, including violent offending, peaks in the middle- to late-teens. This is a time when adolescents experience difficulties achieving socially-approved goals through conventional means, whilst at the same time being free from the controls or confinements of childhood and the restraining influences of adulthood. Teenagers' precarious position in the labour market does not generate the resources necessary to fulfill the heightened consumption demands of contemporary adolescent sub-cultures. Hence, economic strain leads working- and lower-working-class teenagers in particular to engage in illegal income-generating activities. In terms of 'nonutilitarian' forms of violent offending, Greenberg suggests that the gender role system provokes 'masculine status anxiety' leading to assaultative violence in order to 'provide a sense of potency that is expected and desired but not achieved in other spheres of life' (1981: 131). Violence is then, in part, a desire for a sense of autonomy and self-respect. Hence, 'if age is relevant to criminality, the link should lie primarily in its social significance' (1981: 119). Whilst Greenberg focuses specifically on adolescents, his arguments are useful for understanding the relative youthfulness of violent men. That many violent men have moved beyond their teenage years does not necessarily negate the effects of economic strain (as evidenced by the significant numbers unemployed or in low-paid employment) or the potential for masculine status anxiety. The important issue is that these men are powerless during a time at which their manhood is of crucial importance. What Greenberg neglects to mention is that age has a bearing upon one's lifestyle and activities. Hence, situational influences (discussed earlier in this chapter) may be particularly significant and relevant for younger and, perhaps, unattached men. It is plausible that young males are more preoccupied than their older counterparts in accomplishing their gender identities and 'proving their worth'. Hence, the combined effects of specific social settings that young men frequent and their desire to build a particular form of masculine identity may also play an important role in explaining the youthfulness of violent male offenders.

Polk (1994a) has paid considerable attention to the overwhelming masculine nature of homicide, as well as its class bias. Of equal importance, he has attempted to account for the different forms that masculine homicide can take. On the issue of confrontational homicides, Polk notes that 'extreme violence in defence of honour is definitively masculine and lower or underclass in its makeup' (1994a: 91–92). Drawing upon the work of Gilmore (1990), Polk argues that:

> ... [m]ales who are well integrated into roles of economic success are able to ground their masculinity through methods other than physical confrontations and violence. For economically marginal males, however, physical toughness and violence become a major vehicle for the assertion of their masculinity and a way of defending themselves against what they see as challenges from other males. (1994b: 187)

Thus working- and underclass males elect violence as a way of resolving their disputes due to their disadvantaged position in society which tends to restrict their access to more conventional, legal means of solving their problems. Also focusing upon the working-class nature of homicide, Leyton (1995: 243) argues that confrontational norms govern certain sections of the working-class. Moreover, he argues that this is partly attributed to the fact that the working-classes retain remnants (from feudal times) of manly vengeance. He argues that it is those at the bottom of the social hierarchy whom 'elite propaganda finds it the most difficult to reach – the least educated, with the least prestige to lose (and the most to gain) from violent display' (1995: 234). This is not dissimilar to sub-cultural theories of violence (see Chapter 5) that posit that certain sections of society favour violence as a response to challenges whilst other do not.

As Polk observes, the various scenarios of masculine homicide that have been identified in the literature can be seen as 'different ways of "doing masculinity", of behaving in accordance with understandings of "doing what a man has to do" that apply across a range of situations' (1997b: 3). 'Whilst the violence is exceptional, and the behaviours may be viewed as deviant, the motivations can be seen as residing often in wider norms about masculine behaviour that in fact have wider support' (1997b: 3). A good example of one such situation that may support masculine interpersonal violence is the consumption of alcohol within the environment of pubs and clubs. Consuming alcohol in the presence of other male peers is itself clearly a form of 'doing masculinity', in that alcohol consumption and the forms of socialisation that accompany it are inextricably linked to displays of male bravado and ego. That said, there is evidence that alcohol plays a number of different and complex roles in masculine violence. Brookman (2000a), during interviews with violent men (some of whom had killed), found some evidence that alcohol can act as a disinhibitor, leading to a 'loss of control', whilst on the other hand could act as a 'confidence builder', making some men more daring and removing part of the fear that could be associated with fighting. Other men described alcohol as a relatively concrete part of their lives – a substance they 'turned to' as a crutch in order to deal with stressful life events. In this respect, alcohol may play a more fundamental role in some men's lives than simply fuelling social displays of masculinity. That said, it is likely that the role of alcohol in relation to violence is of greatest significance in relation to the nature of social settings in which such consumption occurs. Canaan (1996) has noted similar complexities regarding the role of alcohol and working-class violence. She observed that young males fought to 'show peers either that they controlled themselves and any opponent(s) – if they won a fight – or, if they lost, that they could take a beating and therefore control bodily pain' (1996: 123). Canaan concluded that drinking and fighting were centrally important to the construction of masculinity within the young men she interviewed, but that drinking engendered both the 'loss and maintenance of control'.

Explaining Revenge Homicide

Revenge homicides have received considerably less attention in the literature on homicide compared to confrontational homicides, which have been the focus of much research ever since Wolfgang (1958) noted the oftentimes trivial triggers to these killings. However, Brookman's research (2000b, 2003) found that revenge and confrontational homicides were comparable in number in her sample of 54 masculine homicides analysed in England and Wales. These revenge killings are arguably more worrying because they are planned and because a majority of offenders show little remorse. Polk's previous work on conflict resolution homicides broadly relates to the revenge scenario discussed in this chapter (though there are some important differences; see Brookman, 2000b, 2003). Polk explains conflict resolution homicides by focusing on their masculine and working-class nature:

> Persons tied more firmly to routine life styles, who possess financial and social resources, can be argued to be more likely to be able to confront such disputes by means other than violence. Obviously, even among the well-positioned, friends can become enemies as disputes emerge around such issues as money, property or even reputation. Economic and social resources permit the well-positioned to cloak their disputes in the rational garb of legal or other arbitration systems, and thus vent disputes through channels that drain away the potential for violence. (1995: 112)

What is unique about Polk's approach is his attention to the different theoretical explanations needed to address distinct scenarios of homicide. Indeed, Polk argues different homicides 'tap into the class distribution at a different point' (1995: 113). Thus, while confrontational homicides often occur within the respectable working-class, homicides committed during robberies and revenge-type homicides are often committed by the most marginalised individuals (1995: 113–14).

There is also a large body of literature concerned with retaliatory violence, a significant volume of which is focused on gang-related homicide. Aspects of this literature are also useful in explaining some of the revenge killings discussed earlier. For example, Topalli et al. (2002) conducted interviews with 20 recently robbed, active male drug dealers in St Louis, Missouri in order to explore how such victims perceived and responded to assaults. In keeping with Polk's (1995) observations, Topalli found that formal avenues of redress (that is, via the Criminal Justice System) were not an available option for these victims due to their illicit status. Rather, informal avenues of redress represented the only means of obtaining justice for these men. The volatile social setting of the drug-dealing world that these men inhabit make them key targets for robbery and violence, and many of the men interviewed in part accepted this as an occupational hazard. At the same time, these men had a particular image to uphold if they were to be respected amongst their street peers and avoid future robberies and assaults. As Topalli et al., state, 'As drug dealers conduct their trade outside the limits of legal protection, a reputation for formidability represents one of the only mechanisms available to them for deterring victimization' (2002: 341). In short, a 'menacing and capable' (2002: 343) street reputation is especially critical for men inhabiting this social setting and they are particularly sensitive to challenges to their courage and character (2002: 340). What these kinds of accounts clearly demonstrate is the intersection between structural disadvantage, cultural adaptations and micro- 'action on the street' (see also Rosenfeld et al., 2003; and Sanders, 1994). We shall be returning to this important issue in the third section of the chapter after considering those instances when men kill women.

Men Killing Women: Femicide[10]

In this section of the chapter we will explore those occasions when men kill women, commonly referred to as femicide. Femicide comprises approximately 30 per cent of the total number of homicides in England and Wales (HI, 1995–2000) and 26 per cent of those in Scotland (Scottish Executive, personal communication).[11]

Some General Characteristics of Femicide

As with all-male lethal encounters, the most predominant means of inflicting death upon women in England and Wales is with the aid of a knife or other sharp instrument (almost 30 per cent of the total number of adult females killed by men met their death in this manner). However, in contrast to those occasions when men kill other men, a large number of women were strangled (20 per cent). A further 12 per cent were beaten with a blunt instrument and around 6 per cent were poisoned. Less than 5 per cent are shot in an average year (HI, 1995–2000). Almost one-third of all victims of femicide were aged between 17 and 30 years, with the peak victimisation of adult females being 25 years. Over two-thirds of victims were aged 35 or below.

Scenarios of Femicide

In stark contrast to the media image of women meeting their deaths at the hands of a stranger, when women are killed by men it is predominantly the case that they are, or have been, intimately connected with them. Of all the women (those aged 17-plus) murdered between 1995 and 2000 in England and Wales, 57 per cent were killed by their current or former husband, boyfriend or lover. In contrast, less than 8 per cent were killed by a stranger. The remaining victims were killed by other family members, friends or acquaintances.

What follows is a detailed exploration of two distinct forms of femicide; intimate and stranger femicide. Once again we will be drawing upon case studies previously prepared from police murder investigation files.[12]

Intimate Femicide

A great deal has been written about violence perpetrated by men against women, particularly in the context of domestic violence (Dobash and Dobash, 1979, 1992; Dobash et al., 1998; Gondolf, 2002). The literature in relation to the killing of women by men is sparse in comparison and a much more recent focal point of the general research on violence against women (Wallace, 1986; Polk and Ranson, 1991; Easteal, 1993; Stout, 1993; Wilson and Daly, 1993). In almost all of these accounts it has been observed that the suspect and victim are often husband and wife or de facto husband and wife (in that they live together as sexual intimates, as if married). Furthermore, it has been regularly noted that a substantial proportion of such killings are in some way connected to pending separation or the threat of separation between the intimates (Showalter et al., 1980; Campbell, 1992; Wilson and Daly, 1992; and Dobash et al., 2003). In relation to this latter observation, research has often suggested that the killer was typically impassioned by sexual jealousy and/or by his concerns about losing his wife/partner. Hence, Polk (1994a: 23) referred to such homicides as motivated by 'jealousy/control' and Wallace (1986: 96) uses similar terms when she talks of 'jealousy/sexual exclusivity'. As Polk and Ranson (1991: 18) indicate, the phrase 'if I can't have you no one will' echoes through the literature on male-perpetrated spousal homicide. Certainly the notion that jealousy may play a role in homicide has been observed in some of the earliest writings on this topic (Jesse, 1952), although the literature has become rather more sophisticated of late, enquiring into the roles of masculine identity and systems of patriarchy, to which we shall return at the end of this section.

   Analysis of police murder file data by Brookman (2000b) broadly confirms previous findings in that the largest proportion of male-on-female homicides occurred between sexual intimates (83 per cent of 19 cases) and of these, approaching half (8 cases) occurred during a time when the female was either in the process of or threatening to leave her male partner, or where she was perceived (rightly or wrongly) as being unfaithful to the male, again posing a threat to the intimate partnership. However, important differences were observed in the sample, which appeared to be dependent upon the length of the relationship between the victim and suspect. In some instances, the victim and suspect had been bound together intimately for a substantial length of time; they had been married or cohabiting between 5 and 10 years, sometimes closer to 20 years. In other cases, the victim and suspect had formed a sexual relationship relatively recently. It appears that the kinds of circumstances that surround homicides between intimates differ according to the extent of intimacy that has developed between the couple. Specifically, the current data suggest that where the victim and suspect had sustained a lengthy relationship, the circumstances surrounding the killing related to issues of what could be termed 'possessiveness/control' on the part of the male, very much in keeping with the previous literature in this area discussed above. All of these homicides were to some extent planned, in that they all involved elements of forethought on the part of the killer who had built up resentment towards his partner and sought revenge for what was ultimately perceived as the female's abandonment of the relationship. Some of these homicides involved a considerable degree of premeditation. In contrast, the more recently-formed partnerships, that were often less regular and more casual, tended to produce violence of a more spontaneous nature, arising out of some kind of argument or quarrel, not originating out of any threat of separation. Here the key issues tended to relate to the male's failing attempt (real or perceived) to control the female's behaviour, leading to anger and rage and ultimately the physical assault of the victim. As such these homicides were termed 'sudden rage' (Brookman, 2000b). In some senses, this division is similar to the confrontational and revenge killings discussed earlier in relation to masculine homicide, in that the distinction between planned and spontaneous killings is evident. The following cases illustrate such differences, starting with three examples of possessiveness/control, followed by two cases of sudden rage.

Possessiveness/Control

[Case Code: F.05/94]

Richard (aged 46) had discovered that Joanne (aged 44), his estranged wife (to whom he had been married for 20 years), was forming a relationship with another man. He became greatly enraged and jealous to the extent that one Monday morning he drove to Joanne's workplace and awaited her arrival. At approximately 8.20 a.m., as she arrived at work, he approached her in the car park and stabbed her, 17 times, to death. He told the police when they arrived at the scene, 'I've just stabbed my wife, I loved her and didn't want her to leave me'.

This is a clear example of jealousy on the part of the suspect, who avenged his estranged wife's involvement with another man by lethal means. Ultimately, his refusal to accept the breakdown of their relationship seems to have provided the trigger to this act. The next case exhibits similar features:

[Case Code: F.13/96]

Ali (aged 38, Pakistan) and his wife Samara (aged 35, Pakistan) had been married for 16 years but had begun experiencing marital problems, apparently instigated by Samara's affair with another man. Several meetings between the couple and family elders had been conducted in order to resolve matters, but to no avail. Samara was due to appear in court with a view to obtaining custody of the children. Ali, realising that his marriage was coming to an end, decided to take drastic action. He lay in wait for Samara in a car park at a railway station and subsequently stabbed her to death.

The issue of child custody was particularly important in this latter case. Ali not only murdered his wife, he also murdered three of their six children beforehand. As such, this case could more accurately be described as a familicide (those occasions when two or more family members are murdered by another family member, see Daly and Wilson, 1988; Wilson et al., 1995 and Chapter 9 of this text).

[Case Code: F.09/94]
Julia (aged 34) was living apart from her husband Karl (aged 38) to whom she had been married for 15 years and both were in the middle of a very acrimonious divorce. The couple apparently hated each other and Karl suspected Julia of having an affair. One Monday evening Karl went to Julia's flat whilst she was out, broke inside and waited behind the living-room door for her to come home. As she did, he hit her over the head with a blunt object, slit her throat and stabbed her in the chest. Investigations later revealed that Karl had tried to hire a hit man some 12 months earlier to kill his wife.

These cases illustrate the planned, revenge-style nature of this kind of femicide and the lengths that some men are prepared to go to in order to avenge their partner's perceived betrayal. As Dobash et al. note, a common thread that runs through such homicides 'is the man's sense of ownership of the woman and his control over the continuation or cessation of the relationship' (2003: 19). The following killings are markedly different in that they are much more spontaneous and not instigated by the male's perception of his partner abandoning the relationship.

Sudden Rage

[Case Code: D.04/94]
Betty (aged 60) had recently struck up a relationship with Billie (aged 73). The couple did not live together but met regularly at a local club. Throughout their partnership, Billie lent various amounts of money to Betty for household goods and recreational activities. Some two weeks prior to the killing, Billie indicated to a number of friends that Betty owed him some money and that he was unhappy that she had not paid up. It appears that Billie had reached a point where he became determined to recover his money. One evening, having drunk a substantial amount of alcohol, Billie made his way to Betty's flat and asked her, in no uncertain terms, to pay back what she owed him. When she refused, Billie strangled her to death. During interview Billie stated, 'I was taken for a ride, I went over there and lost my rag and I think you know the rest ... I lost my temper when she refused to give me the money.'

Billie was described by people who knew him as a very nice man but someone who could display a nasty temper. He had apparently never fully recovered from the death of his wife the previous year and had since drunk heavily when depressed. The following case of rage/control occurs amongst a younger couple whose relationship was rather more developed than the case just considered.

[Case Code: D.07/96]
Tracey (aged 20) and Dean (aged 26) had been living together for approximately one year in what was described by police officers as a 'volatile and tempestuous relationship'. They frequently argued, both invariably the worse for wear due to alcohol and illicit drug (cannabis and Temazepam) consumption. On the day in question, Tracey and Dean spent most of the day and evening drinking alcohol in local public houses with friends, where they argued with each other constantly. Around 8.00 p.m. the couple, still arguing, left

their friends to make their way home. However, before reaching their car, Dean struck a blow to Tracey's head rendering her unconscious. Distraught at his actions and Tracey's condition, Dean returned to the pub and told his male friend that he believed he had killed Tracey. On inspection, it was found that Tracey was in fact alive, whereupon Dean stated he would take Tracey to hospital and they left in his car. For reasons known only to Dean, he decided to drive to a secluded picnic area. Dean claims that Tracey awoke and began to abuse and insult him, at which point he claims to have 'snapped'. He took her from the car and repeatedly kicked and punched her, jumping up and down on her head until he was 'satisfied she was dead'.

Whilst all five cases presented thus far occurred between sexual intimates, it is clear that rather different sets of circumstances led to the killings, dependent upon the nature and intensity of the relationship between the victim and suspect. Specifically, the latter two cases can be distinguished from the earlier examples in that the killings occurred spontaneously, with no evidence of planning or premeditation. The consumption of large amounts of alcohol is a predominant feature of many of these spontaneous killings and a much less apparent feature of the planned killings. Furthermore, the motive for the latter killings do not appear to have been in any way connected to threats of separation. This distinction is an important observation that is unlikely to be unique to homicides in parts of England and Wales, but has rarely been noted in previous literature in this area (see, however, Block et al., 2001). Polk and Ranson (1991) hint at some disparity in intimate femicide in Victoria during 1985 and 1986. They observe:

> When the female victim is a young adult, the homicide seems most often to arise out of sexual possession, commonly mixed with jealousy and some notion of the woman as exclusive property. When the female victim is young, and the partner is also immature and young, there seems to be a similar variant of exclusivity even when the possession may not have been well developed. (Polk and Ranson, 1991: 21)

Brookman's (2000b) research suggests that Polk and Ranson overemphasise the importance of age at the expense of the length of the intrasexual relationship that has developed between the victim and suspect. Specifically, Brookman's data suggest that possessiveness is not restricted to homicide amongst *young* men and women. In fact, the mean ages of the victims and offenders involved in both types of homicide were virtually identical. What does clearly differ across the two scenarios, however, is the length of the intimate relationships. Whilst not all of the files analysed indicated the exact length of intimate partnerships, it is clear that most of the victims and suspects involved in possessiveness/control type homicides had been married for many years, often around 10 years, sometimes around 20 years. In contrast, few of the cases of sudden rage involved such lengthy partnerships. That 'possession may not have been well developed' is a crucial point that Polk and Ranson fail to elaborate upon. The point is, at what stage in a relationship does a male believe that the female partner has become *his property*? Brookman (2000b) suggests that the answer does not rest with the age of the victim (or the suspect for that matter), rather the age of the relationship and hence the male's perceived rights of ownership and control of 'his woman'.

Whilst the possession/rage distinction is accurate for nearly all of the cases considered so far, there are always some exceptions to the rule. In particular, one case exhibited something of a mix of the two major scenarios considered above:

[Case Code: D.16/94]

Debbie (aged 40) and Richard (aged 41) had been married for approximately 12 years and had recently separated as a result of Richard's affair with another woman. The estranged couple were in the middle of a difficult divorce, but had made arrangements to meet at Debbie's house on a Monday afternoon to discuss matters. Richard decided to turn up much earlier than planned, at around 8.00 a.m. During their discussions, matters became very heated and Richard produced a knife, from the sports bag he had brought with him, and stabbed Debbie to death. He then attempted to take his own life, consuming half a bottle of whiskey, an overdose of tablets and by trying to poison himself with carbon monoxide fumes. Police interviews conducted with Richard revealed that he had started living with his girlfriend after leaving Debbie some four months previously. Debbie was clearly very unhappy about matters and had apparently tried, on several occasions, to prevent Richard from seeing his children (aged 13 and 8). Richard said, 'Debbie was trying to destroy my second relationship and kept telling me she would stop me seeing the kids, just totally keeping me in the dark about their welfare, just kept on saying that I walked out on them and that I had no interest in them anymore.'

According to Richard, apart from his concerns regarding access to the children there was also an issue over money. He was paying maintenance charges for the children, but had that morning received a letter from the Child Support Agency demanding additional monthly payments:

'I'm already paying her, I was trying to explain to her that I couldn't exist paying out that sort of money and why was she trying to destroy my second relationship through using the children which she knew were my Achilles heel. She just got hysterical with me, I couldn't make her see sense about trying to cut down on the payments and having more access to the kids so I just, in a frenzy, I grabbed a knife and I stabbed her.'

Whilst this killing was certainly linked to the separation of the intimate partnership and, in particular, access to the children, there is no evidence of jealousy on the part of the suspect, who had in fact instigated the marriage break-up and formed another relationship. So whilst the relationship between the victim and suspect had been a lengthy one, possession on the part of the suspect does not seem to have played a key role. If anything, the female's anger and jealousy at her husband's unfaithfulness may have played a more important role in causing some of their disagreements and, in particular, her disapproval of him seeing the children.

Finally, it is important not to overstate the differences between these homicides at the expense of overlooking their common features. In particular, it is clear that both forms of homicide (possession/control and sudden rage) involve the Killer exerting his will or control over the female partner, albeit for different reasons.

As the latter case illustrates, Richard wished to control his child-care role and maintenance payments, and when his wife would not concede to his wishes he killed her. Whether these women were killed because they were believed to have been unfaithful, because they owed the suspect money or because they were fighting custody battles over children, all of them were ultimately killed because they did not meet the demands of their male partners. We shall now consider those occasions when men kill women with whom they have no intimate bond, or bond of any kind – that is, women who are strangers.

Stranger Femicide

As mentioned earlier, homicides between strangers are rare in comparison with those occurring between intimates (sexual or otherwise). Furthermore, it is often the case that stranger homicides prove particularly difficult to classify as far as motive is concerned. Polk states, in his critical analyses of the usefulness of the relational category 'stranger':

> [I]t becomes an enormous puzzle to determine what would generate the exceptional emotions most often found in a homicide, when the people involved are previously unknown to each other. (1994a: 21)

The answer to this puzzle depends, in part, upon the circumstances surrounding these stranger femicides. Some, for example, occur during the commission of other crimes, such as robbery, and the death of the victim is neither intended nor planned. Mouzos (1999c: 3) found that over half of the femicide victims killed in a stranger relational context died in the course of other crime, including robberies, sexual assaults, abductions and break-ins. Of the 84 stranger femicides that occurred in England and Wales between 1995–2000,[13] 25 per cent occurred in the context of robbery, just over 20 per cent during a burglary and almost 4 per cent during arson attacks (it is not possible to determine whether the victim in these cases was the intended target of a homicide). A further 12 per cent were the result of fatal road traffic accidents where the killer was deemed to have behaved recklessly. So in total, almost two-thirds of stranger femicides would seem to bear no relation to the commonly-held notion of a stranger lurking in an alleyway ready to pounce upon an unsuspecting victim. In such cases the notion of 'exceptional emotions' does not particularly apply, as the following two cases reveal.

[Case Code: B.25/96]
At approximately 11.00 a.m. on a Thursday morning in October, the victim, a 92-year-old lady, left her home and made the short walk to the post office to obtain her state pension. On leaving the post office she was met by two young men who attempted to steal her shopping bag from her grip, causing her to fall violently to the floor and sustain fatal head injuries.

The robbery was apparently committed so that the suspects could purchase drugs with the stolen money. Whilst the 'mugging' of an elderly person leaving the post office was planned, the choice of victim was opportunistic. Clearly, the suspects did not intend the victim to die and did not directly assault her. In the following case the victim was, once again, not the intended target of a homicide:

[Case Code: F.08/96]

The suspect (white, aged 21) set fire to a supermarket where he worked for reasons which had not been established in the file. The fire brigade attended and entered the building. Two oxygen tanks exploded, causing the roof to fall onto the fire-fighters. One of the officers, a female, aged 21, died from her injuries. It later emerged that the suspect had committed two previous arson attacks, although on these occasions no one had been injured.

Whilst by far the largest proportion of stranger femicides occur in the context of other offences where the victim's death was not necessarily intended, unusual and inexplicable homicides do occur. Moreover, some of these, whilst not perhaps planned, certainly ultimately involve the intended death of the victim. Approximately 11 per cent of stranger femicides in England and Wales had a sexual motive and a further 18 per cent have been described as an irrational act, motiveless or the motive unknown. Despite their rarity, cases such as these provoke widespread media attention and public fear – particularly where the suspect is a stranger.[14] In the cases below neither the police nor the defendant could satisfactorily explain the motive for the killing.

[Case Code: R.14/96]

Jane (aged 21) spent a Saturday evening in August drinking in various pubs and clubs with a group of female friends. At around 12.30 a.m. on Sunday she attempted to 'flag down' passing cars which she thought were taxis, in order to make her way home. A car stopped close to the victim and she made her way towards the vehicle and got inside – despite her friend's attempts to stop her. Jane's charred remains were discovered the following day. Numerous pieces of physical evidence link the driver of the vehicle who picked Jane up to the murder, although he denied his involvement and consequently offered no motive for the killing.

The next stranger case is very similar in that it involves a young female attempting to make her way home having spent the evening in the company of a female friend, consuming alcohol.

[Case Code: R.01/96]

The victim, Natasha (aged 23), was walking home alone at around 11.30 p.m., having spent the evening out drinking with a female friend. The suspect, Paul (aged 23), was also walking home when, according to his statement, he 'met the victim and got into a conversation with her' and they walked along together towards the park. Paul claims that he had a 'sudden urge to kill' the victim. He took hold of her with both hands around her neck and squeezed tight until she became semi-conscious. He then removed her T-shirt and continued to strangle her until she was dead. The following morning Natasha's body was discovered. Later the same day, Paul confessed to his sister that he 'had murdered the girl

in the park'. Despite the suspect having made a frank confession to the police, he offered
no clear motive for his actions.

In both cases considered above, the victim and suspect were strangers in the 'true' sense of the term, in that they had not met prior to the evening of the homicide as far as can be determined. In the following case there is some evidence that the victim and offender may not have been complete strangers:

[Case Code: R.26/96]
The suspect in this case (a 36-year-old male) spent the evening amongst friends drinking
alcohol in a local pub. Towards closing time (11.00 p.m.), one member of the group decided
to hold an impromptu party at her house. The suspect was invited to this party. 'Take-
away' alcohol was purchased from the pub and the group made their way to the party.
During the course of the party the suspect viewed a number of hard core pornographic
videos. For much of the time he was alone viewing the videos, as most of the other people
at the party had 'paired off' and gone to bed. At around 3.00 a.m. on Saturday the sus-
pect left the party, sharing a taxi with a friend. On leaving the taxi the two departed in
opposite directions towards their respective homes. According to the police report, the sus-
pect made his way to the victim's house where he made a forced entry, having cut through
the telephone wires. Once inside he made his way to the victim's bedroom where he bound,
gagged and sexually assaulted her. Death was caused by ligature strangulation. It is
suggested in the report that the suspect 'lived out' his sexual and violent fantasies after an
evening of heavy drinking and viewing pornographic videos at the party.

Aside from this case being difficult to categorise in terms of motive, it is also unclear whether the suspect knew the victim. The suspect claims to have been having a sexual relationship with the victim. Extensive police enquires revealed that this was not the case. Apparently, the suspect claimed an involvement with the victim in order to explain the presence of his semen at the crime scene. However, both the suspect and victim lived on the same housing estate and common sense would suggest that the suspect must have known something of the victim, that is, that she was divorced and alone in the house that night, before he decided to make a forced entry. This is an important point because it would appear that the suspect in this case carefully chose his victim, whereas in the majority of stranger femicides, victims appear to have been chosen at random – being in the wrong place at the wrong time.

It has not been possible to determine clearly a motive for any of these homicides, or to trace the events leading up to the killings. Whilst it is tempting to assume that some of these killings may have been linked to a sexual motive (two of the victims having been discovered partially naked), the information contained within the case files is simply too inadequate to even begin to form such an opinion.

Explaining Femicide

Many theories have been developed to explain femicide, though they are considerably fewer than those that explore male-perpetrated domestic violence more broadly.

One theme that permeates much of the literature in this area is the notion of masculine control and possessiveness, often advanced to explain men killing female partners, particularly at a time when the female is threatening to leave the male or has already done so. As Daly and Wilson state, 'We find it highly significant that *men the world around think and talk about women and marriage in proprietary term'* (1988: 189, emphasis in the original).

Daly and Wilson draw on evolutionary biology in arguing that male possessiveness and jealousy has a genetic origin – the evolutionary need of males to control female reproduction (see Chapter 4). They cite numerous examples from diverse ethnic and geographical areas of specific laws and cultural norms explicitly denouncing female infidelity. Although they acknowledge that killing one's spouse is counterproductive in evolutionary terms to the male's ultimate reproduction, they reason that:

> Killing is just the tip of the iceberg: For every murdered wife, hundreds are beaten, coerced and intimidated. Although homicide probably does not often serve the interests of the perpetrator, it is far from clear that the same can be said of sub-lethal violence. (1988: 205)

Basically, Daly and Wilson argue that spousal homicide reflects an extreme manifestation of the same basic conflicts that inspire sub-lethal marital violence on a much larger scale. Violence against wives functions to deter such women from pursuing alternative relationships or opportunities that are not in the interests of the husband (Daly, et al., 1982; Daly and Wilson, 1988; Wilson, 1989; Wilson and Daly, 1992, 1993).

Many other researchers have focused upon culture rather than evolutionary psychology in explaining violence towards women, including femicide. Numerous researchers have claimed that the killing of women by men is linked to masculine control of women (Dobash and Dobash, 1979; Barnard et al., 1982; Martin, 1983; Wallace, 1986; Levinson, 1989; Easteal, 1993; Stout, 1993; Polk, 1994a; Hearn, 1998). In these accounts, violence against women generally, and femicide specifically, are explained by reference to the sexual inequality of females and patriarchal systems of control and domination.[15] Thus, in Scotland, Dobash and Dobash (1979) found that men battered wives when they felt they were not living up to the patriarchal ideal of the 'good wife'. As Dobash and Dobash explain, 'The seeds of wife beating lie in the subordination of females and their subjection to male authority and control' (1979: 33). Additionally, as Websdale and Chesney-Lind (1998) note, the fact that most men do not batter their wives or partners should not be taken to mean that patriarchy does not exist. Rather, men have many means of control available to them, some more consensual (see, for example, Edgell, 1980).

In some cultures, the control of women as a result of patriarchy is particularly extreme. Arin (2001) studied femicide in Turkey, noting the existence of 'honour killings' or 'customary murders' – exercised to control women's sexual life in the broadest sense. The patriarchal system of Turkish culture is one in which women are considered to be the property of the family and are seen to represent its reputation or honour. Women are expected to be virgins when they marry – to be 'clean'. This cleanliness, however, is easily destroyed by acts such as strolling alone in town, requesting a love song on the radio or flirting with a male. Such acts render women 'unclean' and the whole family is 'seen to be dishonoured and their standing in the community diminished' (Arin, 2001: 823). As Arin explains, 'these beliefs are so powerful that families are prepared to sacrifice the life of one of their female members to restore their honour and standing in the eyes of others' (2001: 823). More accurately, men or males are prepared to authorise and undertake such sacrifices or killings. Similarly, Kordvani (2002: 8) notes the continued (albeit sporadic) existence of 'honour killings' in the Middle East and South Asia (the killing of women who have breached, or are suspected to have, a social norm of female sexuality). Kordvani (2002) utilises the term 'adrocracy' to most accurately characterise the gender order in such societies defined (by Remy, 1990: 43) as 'rule of men'. Adrocracy takes two forms – patriarchy (rule of fathers) and fratriarchy (rule of the brotherhood). Whilst men rule the family, the extended family structure is such that particular men (seniors and/or elders) form a fratriarchy (men's club) wherein all decisions relating to women's economic status and sexuality are decided upon and controlled. If a female deviates in any way, it is assumed that the father or husband has failed in his role as controller. To redress this imbalance, the death of the female will likely be called for. This task will fall to a male relative, such as her father, husband or a brother. If an individual fratist does not comply, he will be expelled from the 'men's league'. Hence, to become and remain a member of the all-important men's league, a man must follow the rules and pass the requisites of the league, one of which is to exert controlling power upon female members of the family and to punish deviant women (Kordvani, 2002: 18). Whilst such excessive and ritualised conceptions of control and punishment are clearly less evident in many Western industrialised societies, it remains the case that men are often expected to control their female intimates if they are to be regarded as 'real men'. Hence, phrases such as 'hen-pecked' (in the UK) and 'pussy-whipped' (in the US) signal to individual men that they are not sufficiently dominant within their intimate relationships.

Study Task 6.3

Conduct a literature survey to identify societies from around the world that are based on a matriarchal structure. Make a list of the specific ways and circumstances by which women in these societies control men. Is there any sense in which men still retain certain levels of power and control in the relationship?

An interesting body of research has interrogated men's accounts of violence against women with a view to exploring the role of gender and, in particular, masculinity within such encounters. For example, Fuller (2001), using data from in-depth interviews carried out among men living in three Peruvian cities, found that whilst the men viewed marital reciprocity and solidarity to be the basis of a family relationship, the principle of male authority was seen to underlie the conjugal contract. The men interviewed did not apparently approve of violence, nor perceive themselves as particularly aggressive. They found themselves caught between two competing conceptions of gender system. On the one hand, marital reciprocity and on the other, male supremacy. For example, a large number of the men indicated that marital quarrels would begin when their spouses reproached them for their sexual affairs with other women or for spending too much money and time socialising. Whilst these men admitted that their wives had the right to demand them to be responsible and faithful, at the same time they felt that complying to such demands would mean neglecting their relationships with their peers (no longer belonging to the male circle) and, worse, submitting to female domination. Hence, 'both possibilities would endanger their male status' (2001: 26). These men chose to avoid both possibilities by resorting to violence as a resource to 'reinstate order in situations which had been disrupted' (2001: 28).

Other researchers have suggested that violence is one way of men 'performing' or accomplishing gender (West and Fenstermaker, 1995). For example, Anderson and Umberson conducted in-depth interviews with 33 men who had committed acts of domestic violence and found that 'batterers attempt to construct masculine identities through the practice of violence and the discourse about violence that they provide' (2001: 359). A significant proportion of the batterers claimed their partners to be controlling, demanding, dominating or even emasculating. Anderson and Umberson also noted men's fragile masculinities that necessitate them repositioning themselves as powerful within the relational bond. Both this and Fuller's research appear to acknowledge that maintaining control is of critical importance to these men. As Connell notes, 'research with batterers and rapists indeed detects remorse and shame ... but also detects feelings of entitlement, justifications and the intention to establish control' (2002: 94) (see also Ptacek, 1988; and Lea and Auburn, 2001).

Finally, of importance to the current discussion are some radical feminist contributions to the femicide literature. Radical feminists such as Campbell (1981), Bean (1992), Caputi and Russell (1992) and Radford and Russell (1992) claim that the killing of women by men is inextricably bound up with misogyny, itself a product of patriarchy. In fact, many of these writers actually define femicide (taken here to mean the killing of women by men) as the misogynist killing of women by men (Radford, 1992), thereby altering the theoretical framework within which to explain this phenomenon. For these writers it is assumed that violence directed at women by men, at least in part, is because they are female (see Campbell and Runyan, 1998; and Russell and Harmes, 2001).

To varying degrees, each of the theories or ideas outlined above may help to explain several of the cases of femicide considered earlier, although some of the theories are clearly less relevant or helpful than others. At the outset it is important to recognise that whilst some of the femicides considered here share common features, a diversity of circumstances and motives have also been highlighted. Therefore any one theory will only explain a portion of these femicides. For example, the radical feminist assertion that men kill women due to a general hatred of women (misogyny) is certainly questionable in all but a handful of the cases of femicide (only some of which were reproduced earlier) that Brookman (2000b) analysed. For the majority of cases the notion of misogyny seems extreme and inaccurate. Most of the men who killed their wives or partners appeared to do so out of desperation at the prospect of losing their female partner – not out of some general hatred of women. Instead, the ideas of patriarchy, which would include masculine control, domination and possessiveness and jealousy, seem much more valid explanations of the majority of femicides. Moreover, as Wallace notes, 'violence can be viewed as the ultimate expression of a man's perceived power over his wife; it can equally be viewed as a man's admission that indeed he has no such power' (1986: 108). Wallace is referring particularly to those occasions when a man kills his wife in the context of separation. She notes that for men, marriage may mean something rather different than it does to women. For example, Gove (1972) suggests that contrary to popular wisdom, marriage benefits men more than women in that men are dependent upon women both in an emotional and practical sense. As Gove puts it, 'there appears to be few places where, or people to whom, men are able to openly talk about their feelings and emotions' (1972: 54). Hence, 'when a man loses his wife, he loses not only a companion, but the person most able to help him with that loss' (Wallace, 1986: 107). These accounts point to the fragile nature of masculinity discussed earlier.

In summary, the vast majority of accounts of femicide specifically, or masculine violence toward women more broadly, view men's violence as an expression of their desire to dominate and control women and various aspects of their behaviour. Sometimes such expressions of control and domination are specifically linked to patriarchal structures, on other occasions researchers explore particular manifestations of masculinity. Ultimately, these accounts are not at odds – what differs is the emphasis that they place on structural factors as opposed to more cultural or psychological processes that may be operating (refer to Chapters 4 and 5 for further details of these approaches).

Discussion: 'Some Remaining Challenges'

In this final section of the chapter we will take stock of what is currently known about male-perpetrated homicide and consider some of the difficulties confronting researchers in trying to make sense of male homicide. This section pivots around three main points:

- whether male-on-male homicide and male-on-female are distinct enough to require different explanations;
- the need to strike an adequate balance between acknowledging the importance of macro-structural factors and micro-situational factors; and
- the continuing importance of breaking homicide down into discrete scenarios, in order that explanations are meaningful.

A number of the issues that are raised below are general difficulties that manifest themselves regardless of what particular form of homicide one is concerned to explain. Hence, we shall be returning to some of these issues in the final chapter of this text.

'Masculine' Homicide and Femicide:
Similarities and Differences

Although many commentators stress the role of gender in male-perpetrated homicide, somewhat different language or discourse tends to be used to articulate the role of gender in all-male lethal encounters as compared to femicide. When researchers study the reasons for men killing women, the overwhelming focus is upon issues of domination, power and control, all of which are invariably linked to patriarchy and hegemonic masculinity. Yet when considering homicide amongst men, these issues tend to be less clearly articulated. Researchers talk about men not wishing to 'lose face' or 'back down', but rarely revert to terms such as 'power' and 'control', which feature heavily in the literature on femicide. Yet it would appear that many all-male homicides could just as easily be explained by reference to theories of power and control. Both forms of killing exhibit the basic dichotomy between planned attacks (masculine revenge killings and possessiveness/control homicides) and sponta-neous assaults (confrontational killings and sudden rage femicides). For example, instances where men kill other men to avenge some wrongdoing are not dissimilar to those cases where men kill their wives who are leaving them. Both involve men exerting their will over other individuals (regardless of the victim's gender) in order to avenge some perceived injustice. Put another way, both involve men attempting to regain control over a situation that they cannot, or will not, accept. Similarities are also evident in the more spontaneous forms of male-perpetrated homicide and, interestingly, regardless of the sex of the victim, spontaneous 'confrontational' forms of homicide often involve alcohol consumption by offenders, victims or both.

This point is evident in other areas. For example, Dobash presents examples of the kind of circumstances under which only men kill, stating, 'Men commonly hunt down and kill separated and divorced spouses who have left them; women hardly ever behave similarly' (1990: 13). Whilst interesting and obviously reveal-ing, perhaps we need to ask whether men also hunt down other men who they feel have wronged them in some way (which we have seen from our earlier discussions of revenge killings, they do). In this way we may reveal more about the role of gender in violence than simply observing what men and women do differently. There is no doubt that men and women kill each other for different reasons, but this is not a sufficient observation to explain the intricate role of gender in violence. Whilst it is undoubtedly true that some men want to control women, it is also the case that men often strive to control one another – albeit for reasons other than possession.

In short, some of the reasons that have been identified in the feminist literature for male violence against females are not necessarily exclusive to occasions when men kill women. Power, coercion and control are also vital in explaining male-on-male violence. Unfortunately, a significant portion of the feminist literature often focuses too narrowly upon themes related to issues of gender inequality at the expense of exploring the complexities of masculinity per se. That said, some of the most recent accounts of male-perpetrated violence towards women do indeed recognise some of these issues. For example, the work of Arin (2001), discussed earlier, notes the critical importance of honour in cases of femicide, and the work of Anderson and Umberson (2001) acknowledges the fragility of masculinity and the need for men to reposition themselves as powerful within the relational bond. In different ways these accounts begin to relate to some of the discussions that have, until now, been reserved for all-male encounters of lethal violence.

The difficulty, then, is trying to take account of the issues that pervade male-perpetrated homicide (regardless of the sex of the victim), whilst at the same time acknowledging that the gender of the victim does have an important bearing upon how and why particular homicides unfold. For example, Dobash et al. (forthcoming) have provided some evidence that men who kill their partners tend to 'specialise' in violence against women – an assertion that certainly requires further exploration.[16]

Linking Gender to Socio-demographic Characteristics and Micro-situational Factors

A second, and equally complex, challenge that remains to be further unravelled is in what ways expressions of gender (or masculinity) are linked to the socio-demographic characteristics of the men involved, as well as the particular situations in which they find themselves at the time of the homicide. Put another way, how can we untangle the relative importance or influence of the kinds of men who become involved in lethal violence (vis-à-vis their structural position) and inter-actional factors 'at the scene' of the homicide, so to speak? Explanations and accounts exist for both levels of analysis, but are very rarely effectively combined.

For example, on the issue of structural position, there is sufficient evidence to conclude that the majority of the men involved in lethal interpersonal violence are of a low socio-economic status and relatively powerless. In what ways might this impact upon the likelihood of men committing acts of violence? One prominent line of reasoning has suggested that men with little power feel their masculinity to be undermined or threatened in some way, leading, essentially, to more violent manifestations of masculinity in an attempt to regain a sense of power and manhood. As Segal explains:

> It is the sharp and frustrating conflict between the lives of lower working-class men and the image of masculinity and power, which informs the adoption and, for some, the enactment of a more aggressive masculinity. (1990: 196)

More relevant to the question of domestic violence and homicide, Tolson (1977) and Seidler (1989) argue that because working-class men experience little or no power in their occupational lives, they are more likely than middle-class men to attempt to dominate in the home. For these researchers, the crucial issue is men's social and economic powerlessness and its influences upon the way in which some men 'do gender'. What such analyses begin to do is unravel the links between gender and certain other social and structural factors. As such they alert us to the fact that it is not simply masculinity or maleness that must be accounted for in understanding men's violence. Whilst marginalisation is accorded primacy in the accounts above, other researchers have been keen also to express the important links between, for example, age or race and masculinity (see, for example, Greenberg, 1977, 1981; and Bourgois, 1996). However, few of these accounts also take account of the micro-social settings in which lethal violence occurs. Yet there would seem to be no doubt that certain situations or environments lend themselves to male violence due to the nature of the interactions that are likely to occur within them. To provide one example: young men, from similar backgrounds, coming together and consuming significant quantities of alcohol make for a potentially volatile mix as they mingle together with a shared emphasis on protecting and projecting a tough macho identity. However, these arenas of interaction are not hermetically sealed from the outer world. What occurs in specific settings, whilst in part a product of that particular environment, is also a product of wider structural factors and cultural values that may, or may not, support violence as a form of dealing with conflict. Hence, untangling the relative effects of structure, culture and situational factors is a complex business.

The Significance of Homicide Scenarios

Finally, it must not be forgotten that 'masculine' homicide is not a homogeneous category. Rather, it takes a number of different forms. As indicated earlier, Polk (1994a) is one of the few researchers to have considered the different theoretical explanations required to explain different forms of masculine homicide. He has tentatively explored the possibility that different scenarios of masculine homicide tap into the class structure at different points. He suggests, for example, that con-flict resolution violence appears to be found among those males farthest from the boundaries of conventional community life. In contrast, confrontational violence, while fundamentally lower- and under-class in its makeup, would seem to tap into a slightly less extreme part of the class structure (Polk, 1994a: 207–208). This is clearly an important avenue for further research.

Chapter Summary and Conclusions

This chapter has considered homicides committed by men against other men and women. Within these broad categories, particular manifestations of lethal violence have been explored, including masculine confrontational and revenge homicide and intimate and stranger femicide. The distinctiveness of these particular forms of homicide has been discussed in terms of the circumstances leading up to these killings, the extent to which the killings are spontaneous or planned and the con-text in which such lethal violence occurs. After a brief exploration of masculinity theories, we considered specific theories that have been developed to account for particular forms of male-perpetrated homicide. Finally, in the third section of this chapter, we took stock of the current state of knowledge regarding masculine homi-cide, noting some of the problems still facing criminologists in making sense of male-perpetrated homicide.

Criminologists, and other social scientists, continue to grapple with what is perhaps one of the most complex aspects of criminological theorising, namely, how to keep sight of the maleness of crime, in particular violent crime such as homicide, without losing sight of the fact that not all men (of a particular socio-demographic status) act violently, and those that do are neither continually violent nor do they take part in all forms of violence. Hence, the situational or social context in which lethal violence erupts cannot be ignored. These issues will be elaborated upon in the final chapter of this text when we explore, among other things, some recent criticisms of the value of a gendered approach to understanding homicide.

In the following chapter we explore female-perpetrated homicide. Interestingly, it is once again men's violence that oftentimes leads to lethal violence against men by their female partners.

Review Questions

- In what sorts of different contexts do male confrontational homicides occur?
- To what extent do pride and honour feature in both male-on-male and male-on-female homicides?
- Why is it important to distinguish masculine homicide into discrete scenarios? What is gained from such an approach?
- To what extent do you agree with recent criticisms regarding the tautological nature of links between masculinity and violence? Does the phrase 'men's violence' make more sense than 'masculinity and violence'?

Further Reading

The most useful reference in relation to masculine homicide remains Polk's text *When Men Kill* (1994: Cambridge University Press). Polk considers a diverse range of male-perpetrated homicides and subsequently explores them from a gendered perspective. In addition, Polk has published extensively in a range of journals regarding distinct scenarios of masculine homicide (refer to References at the end of the text). Brookman's (2003) article 'Confrontational and Revenge Homicides Amongst Men in England and Wales' (*The Australian and New Zealand Journal of Criminology*, Vol. 36/1, pp. 34–59) provides a detailed overview of these killings, exploring the distinct nature of these two forms of masculine homicide as well as some important shared characteristics.

Literature more specifically dealing with femicide can be found in Radford and Russell's *Femicide: The Politics of Woman Killing* (1992: Twayne); *Femicide in Global Perspective* by Russell and Harmes (2001: Teachers College Press). Both edited collections contain a number of diverse chapters dealing with femicide from a range of perspectives and locations. A number of pertinent journal articles include: Wilson and Daly's (1993) 'Spousal Homicide Risk and Estrangement' (*Violence and Victims*, Vol. 8, pp. 3–16); Stout's (1993) 'Intimate Femicide: A Study of Men who Have Killed Their Mates' (*Journal of Offender Rehabilitation*, Vol. 19/3, pp. 81–94); Wilson et al.'s (1995) 'Lethal and Non-Lethal Violence against Wives' (*Canadian Journal of Criminology*, Vol. 37, pp. 331–62). In addition, the journal *Homicide Studies* has a special issue dealing with femicide (Vol. 2/4) that contains a number of useful articles. Finally, there is a substantial body of literature that deals with the wider issue of men's violence to women including *Rethinking Violence against Women* by Rebecca and Russell Dobash (1998: Sage), which contains a number of very useful articles. By the same authors, a very useful text dealing with domestic violence is *Violence Against Wives* (1979: Free Press). In addition, Jeff Hearn's *The Violences of Men* (1998: Sage) deals with men's violence to known women and contains many examples of men's accounts of their violent acts, which Hearn interrogates.

For general literature on masculinity(ies) and violent crime, some of the best resources include *Masculinities and Crime* edited by Bowker (1998: Sage) and *Understanding Masculinities*, edited by Mac An Ghaill (1996: Open University Press). Both books contains a number of very interesting chapters on masculinity, several of which relate to crime. James Messerschmidt's *Nine Lives* (2000: Westview Press) makes for a fascinating read. Here, Messershmidt explores in detail the life histories of nine adolescent boys and unravels why some commit acts of violence or sexual offences, whilst others do not. Finally, Richard Collier's *Masculinities, Crime and Criminology* (1998: Sage) is an excellent, albeit quite 'heavy going' text that deals with the maleness of crime and in what ways the relationship between masculinities and crime might best be understood.

Useful Internet Sites

The AIC website is an excellent starting place, with a wealth of information regarding masculine homicide and femicide. The link www.aic.gov.au/publications/ lists all publications, including their Research and Public Policy series (www.aic.gov.au/publications/rpp/), from which you can access Jenny Mouzos's *Femicide: The Killing of Women 1989–1998*. Or alternatively follow the direct link: www.aic.gov.au/publications/rpp/18/full_report.pdf.

The link www.pinn.net/~sunshine/book-sum/femicide.html reviews a number of the most well-known and cited books relevant to femicide, such as Radford and Russell's *Femicide: The Politics of Women Killing*. The 'Men Against Violence' website also contains information regarding male violence (particularly against women), various references and 'readings' and a number of links to other resources: www.menagainstsexualviolence.org/index.html.

An excellent site that concerns masculinities is www.xyonline.net; again, it contains (over 300) links to other websites and resources, online articles and information (www.xyonline.net/links.shtml). Also, the bibliography link that the site has (see www.xyonline.net/mensbiblio/index.html) contains some excellent (and very comprehensive) reading lists for anyone interested in the issue of masculinity, gender, feminism, violence and criminology – that is, particularly the link to male-on-male violence: www.xyonline.net/mensbiblio/violence.html#Malemale.

Finally, the 'Violence Against Women Online Resources' is another good website to visit, and numerous articles and documents can be accessed from it (www.vaw.umn.edu/library/research).

Notes

1 Brookman (2000) analysed a total of 97 covering reports from police murder files as part of her doctoral research (see Note 2, Chapter 1). Of these 97, 56 per cent (54 cases) were all-male (adult) encounters and 26 per cent (25 cases) involved a man taking the life of a woman. From these data case summaries were compiled, comprising condensed versions of important aspects of the cases and providing an understanding of the kinds of circumstances surrounding homicide. In all cases, the names of the victims and suspects and other identifying features have been altered so as to protect the anonymity of the individuals involved. This chapter will draw upon these data, as well as analysis of the Home Office HI.

2 It is important to note that not all cases have been processed through the courts at this stage, so that although all individuals have been charged with either murder or manslaughter they may not necessarily be convicted.

3 For almost 20 per cent of the masculine homicides that occurred in England and Wales between 1995–2000, the relationship between killer and victim has not been established.

4 Though this, of course, ignores the issue of corporate homicide, discussed in Chapter 1.

5 It is possible, of course, that those from the working classes are less able to deal with domestic violence by means other than the law and the assistance of shelters, so that they are over-represented in such agencies figures. Those with ample finances may be able to purchase an alternative residence, whereas those with limited or no disposable income have little choice but to reside in a shelter if and when they make a decision to leave an abusive relationship.

6 These data were obtained from analysis of police murder investigation files from England and Wales as opposed to the analysis of the HI, which does not code data in a manner sufficient to establish such discrete scenarios.

7 Polk does not detail what percentage of the male-on-male homicides these particular scenarios comprised, though it would appear that the figure is in excess of 50 per cent (confrontations comprising around 38 per cent and conflict resolution killings around 18 per cent).

8 In fact, Tolson (1977) had charted similar grounds when he argued that masculinity was not a unidimensional or universal phenomenon which could be understood as the opposite of femininity.

9 'Hegemony' was a term borrowed from Gramsci (1971), referring to the ways in which one class or group in society comes to dominate that society by consent.

10 The term 'femicide' is taken here to refer to the killing of women by men. Some commentators use this term more broadly to refer to the killing of women regardless of the gender of the perpetrator (see Mouzos, 1999b and 1999c), whilst others have defined femicide more narrowly as the 'misogynist killing of women by men' (Radford and Russell, 1992: xi).

11 This figure for Scotland refers to male-on-female homicides generally. It has not been possible to separate out adult killings from the available data. It has not been possible to gain any data on femicide for Northern Ireland.

12 Twenty-five police murder files were examined that involved a man killing a woman. Nineteen of those (76 per cent) occurred between intimates and just 6 cases (24 per cent) occurred amongst strangers.

13 This calculation is based on victims and offenders being aged 16 years or greater.

14 It has been suggested that sexual murders by strangers are of particular concern because of the possible links with psychopathy and/or serial offending (Grubin, 1994: 624). This might explain why the majority of research that has been conducted in the area of sexual murder has focused upon 'sadistic' serial suspects (see Brittain, 1970; Grubin, 1994). According to Jenkins (1988: 7), serial killers account for perhaps only 1 or 2 per cent of murders in England and Wales and the US in an average year.

15 Patriarchy is best defined as 'control by men'. The opposite is 'matriarchy', which means women are in charge and the head of families.

16 As will be revealed in the following chapter, some of these same issues permeate the literature on female-perpetrated homicide, in that researchers are currently grappling with issues of 'sameness' and 'difference' in terms of male and female killers. In short, a number of researchers are beginning to acknowledge that it is vital to take into account not only what female killers share with male offenders, but also what makes them distinct – by virtue of their feminine status and resultant gender inequality, for example.

7 When Women Kill

This chapter explores homicides committed by women or, more specifically, female-perpetrated intimate partner homicide. Despite significant media attention to violent women in recent years and suggestions that violent crime by women has been increasing, women's contribution to homicide in the UK remains low at around 11 per cent in an average year. When women do kill, it tends to be within the domestic setting; specifically, they are most likely to kill their male intimate partner or their own infant. This chapter is only concerned with the former; the killing of children will be considered in Chapter 8. Following a brief discussion of some general characteristics of female homicide, the first section of this chapter will focus upon some of the general characteristics of intimate partner homicides committed by women.[1] This will be followed by a detailed consideration of particular scenarios of female intimate partner homicide. Drawing upon case study data, we shall see that the circumstances in which women kill their intimate partners bear both striking similarities and differences to those intimate partner homicides committed by men. Specifically, the vast majority of female offenders *and* victims of intimate partner killings have experienced a history of domestic abuse at the hands of their intimate male partners. However, when women kill it is not usually characterised by a culmination of violence on their part, nor an attempt to gain control over their male partners. Instead, it is often a final and desperate attempt to gain some degree of control *for* themselves, *from* their partner, at a point in which they feel their life is threatened. Of course, not all domestic homicide perpetrated by women is linked to violence, and we will also consider some financially and sexually motivated killings by women. The third section of the chapter reviews explanations of female partner homicide, with a particular emphasis upon the 'battered woman syndrome'. Finally, we review and critique criminological thought in relation to violent female offenders. During the late 1980s and 1990s a range and variety of female crime was explored more fully than had previously occurred, and the violent female offender became of particular interest. Whilst early studies of female offending located the causes in individual pathology, studies conducted since the late 1980s have observed that female offending can constitute purposeful and meaningful action and that women do not necessarily operate without a sense of agency. However, as we shall discover, despite the more intense focus on women as violent offenders witnessed in recent years, there remains a lack of theoretical or analytical vocabulary to understand female violence that is not grounded in male behaviour (Burman et al., 2000).

Female-perpetrated Homicide: An Overview

As indicated earlier in Chapters 2 and 6, homicide is largely a 'male' activity and females constitute a very small proportion of homicide offenders. Literature from the UK, Australia, Canada and the US all indicate that female-perpetrated homicides account for between 10–12 per cent of the overall homicide rate (Mouzos, 2000; Silverman and Kennedy, 1993; Mann, 1996). In England and Wales during the period 1995–2001, females comprised just over 11 per cent of all known homicide offenders and were implicated in just over 600 homicides (compared to 4,847 cases in which a male suspect had been identified) (HI, 1995–2001). Furthermore, between 1988–97 the ratio of convicted male:female homicide offenders in England and Wales was approximately 8:1 (Chan, 2001). A similar picture is drawn for the rest of the UK. In Scotland, between 1991–2000, females comprised just over 10 per cent of homicide suspects (although the figure for known female homicide offenders has increased to 13 per cent in recent years (Scottish Executive, 2001)). In Northern Ireland, during the four-year period of 1996–99, of 206 homicide offenders prosecuted, only 10 were female (4.9 per cent), and for the same period, of those 95 offenders convicted of homicide, only 5 (4.8 per cent) were female (personal communication, Northern Ireland Office, 2002).[2]

Not only do females perpetrate a very small proportion of homicide, but female rates of homicide offending also appear to be relatively constant. In England and Wales, criminal statistics indicate that between 1980–87, 11.6 per cent of homicide offenders were female (d'Orban, 1990); between 1986–96, women similarly comprised approximately 12 per cent of homicide suspects (Stanko et al., 1998). Finally, analysis of the Homicide Index (HI) for each individual year of the period 1990 and 2001 reveals that the proportion of homicides committed by females has not risen much above 12 per cent and, in recent years, has dropped to below 10 per cent (HI, 1990–2001). In sum, there is no evidence of an increase of female violence in the UK as far as the most serious offence of homicide is concerned.

So, who do women kill? The answer is those closest to them, with whom they live (or have lived) – that is, intimate partners (or ex-partners) and family members (specifically their children). Over the period 1995–2001, intimate partners accounted for 32 per cent of female-perpetrated homicide victims, and sons or daughters comprised a further 30 per cent. Hence, these two intimate relational categories form almost two-thirds of the victims of female killers in England and Wales. A further 5 per cent of victims were friends/ex-friends, 2 per cent of the victims were a parent or step-parent and a further 9 per cent were 'other' individuals known to the offender. Less than 5 per cent of victims were classified as strangers (HI, 1995–2001). Evidence for 1986–96 concurs with this finding, showing that intimate partners formed the largest group of female homicide victims, followed by family members, friends and, finally, strangers (Stanko et al., 1998). Thus, with overwhelming support, Blum and Fisher note female-perpetrated murder to be 'an especially intimate act' (1978: 192).

When comparing patterns of male and female homicide offending, one similarity that can be observed is that of the gender of those whom they victimise. That is, both male and female homicide offenders are most likely to kill men (Foote, 1999; Dobash and Dobash, 1992). However, at the same time, it is clear that male and female killers significantly differ in terms of the overall total of offences perpetrated, and in the distribution and nature of the victim–offender relationship involved. In contrast to females, men kill mostly strangers or acquaintances, or as Jensen states, 'Men, when they kill, are *least* likely to kill intimates, whereas women are *most* likely to kill intimates' (2001: 10; emphasis in original). The victim–offender relationship is, thus, of clear importance and provides us with an interesting starting point at which to examine homicide. As Silverman and Kennedy (1993) point out, the closeness and routine contact between those involved in intimate relationships can not only discourage, but also encourage conflict. They argue that intimate relationships can be intense, volatile, confrontational and explosive (Silverman and Kennedy, 1993: 66).

Female-perpetrated Intimate Partner Homicide: Victim, Offender and Event Characteristics

As already established, intimate partner homicides comprise the largest category of female-perpetrated homicide. In England and Wales, between the period of 1995–2001, intimate partners accounted for around one-third of the victims of female killers (HI, 1995–2001). Figures for Scotland indicate that between 1991–2000, of the 113 homicides committed by women, 92 (81.4 per cent) involved a male victim and 63 per cent of those were intimate partners (Scottish Executive, 2001).[3] Similar patterns have been observed in Australia (Mouzos, 2000), Canada (Silverman and Kennedy, 1993; Dawson, 2001) and in the US (Browne and Williams, 1989; Jurik and Winn, 1990; Mann, 1996; Totman, 1978). Whilst intimate partners form the largest proportion of female killer's victims, it is still the case that within the category of partner homicide, males dominate as offenders. Specifically, males comprise 79 per cent of offenders and females just 21 per cent of offenders in intimate partner homicide (HI, 1995–2001). Similarly, Chan (2001) found female offenders accounted for 24 per cent of 'spousal' homicide offenders for the period 1992–97. However, bearing in mind that females account for only

11 per cent of overall homicide offenders, yet around one-fifth of intimate partner offenders, we can observe that there is some convergence of the gender gap for this particular form of homicide (Browne et al., 1999; Foote, 1999).

Victim and Offender Characteristics

The picture of the typical female intimate partner killer is one aged between 25 and 40 years, with a below-average level of educational attainment, who is likely to be unemployed and from a lower-class background (Mann, 1996; Goetting, 1987). Analysis of the HI for the period 1995–2001 (194 cases) indicates that just over 40 per cent of female perpetrators of intimate partner homicide are aged between 30 and 39, and that the average age of female intimate killers is 35 years. A quarter of these female perpetrators were aged between 21 and 29 years and 55 per cent between 30 and 49 years. Statistics for Scotland reveal similar findings. Between 1991–2000, 22.4 per cent of female offenders who had murdered their partners were aged between 21 and 29, and 48.7 per cent fell in the age group 30–49 (Scottish Executive, 2001). Chan's (2001) qualitative analysis of 50 intimate partner killings (from homicide files in the UK between 1985–91), found that offenders were older than typically reported in other studies, with 40 per cent of female killers aged between 40 and 64, and 28 per cent aged between 20 and 29. She also found that 76 per cent of female offenders had left school without any qualifications, 56 per cent were unemployed and 48 per cent had previous criminal records.

Information regarding the male victims of partner homicide appears to be more limited. Analysis of the HI for the period 1995–2001 indicates that virtually identical proportions of those aged in their thirties and forties fell victim to homicide at the hands of their current of former spouse or lover (29 per cent respectively); the average age of male victims of female-perpetrated intimate homicide being 40 years. Figures for Scotland (1991–2000) similarly indicate that the highest proportion of victims fell in the 30–49 age group (Scottish Executive, 2001). Hence, male victims of female-perpetrated partner homicide are, on average, some five years older than their killers. However, Chan (2001) found that victims were predominantly of the same age group as that of the offender, with 60 per cent falling in the age category of 40–64, followed by 28 per cent between the ages of 30–39.

Characteristics of the Homicide Event

Method of Killing

In the UK, women usually kill their partner with a knife or sharp weapon. For example, analysis of the HI (1995–2001) indicates that 78 per cent of women who killed their partners did so with a sharp instrument (as opposed to 32 per cent of men who stabbed their female partners to death during the same period).[4] The second most significant means of killing is by poisoning (6.2 per cent). The use of a blunt instrument comprised a further 2.6 per cent of cases and arson 2.1 per cent. Shooting incidents comprise just over 2 per cent of such killings.

Whilst the use of a sharp weapon is the predominant method of killing in the UK generally (with figures indicating that one-third of all homicides can be attributed to the use of a sharp instrument[5]), it can be seen that female-perpetrated intimate partner homicides are much more likely to involve such a weapon. In those countries in which firearms are more easily accessible, research has found that a handgun or shotgun appears to be the predominant choice of weapon for female offenders. For example, in the US, Goetting (1987) found that 55.4 per cent of wives shot their partners, and a further 41.4 per cent of victims were stabbed. Similar figures of 51.7 per cent and 44.1 per cent respectively have been cited by Mann (1996). The use of such deadly weapons can be attributed to the likely differential physical stature and strength between victim and offender, in that the level of force ultimately needed for fatal injury would more likely require such a weapon (Jurik and Gregware, 1992).

Temporal and Spatial Patterns

The vast majority of studies show that most spousal homicides occur in the domestic domain of either the offender or victim (or in many cases, their shared residence if they are co-habiting) (Jurik and Winn, 1990; Goetting, 1987, 1989). Available figures for Scotland (1991–2000) show that 86.6 per cent (58 cases from a total of 67) of female-perpetrated partner homicide occurred 'within the dwelling' (Scottish Executive, 2001).[6] Mann (1996) also found that 79 per cent of female-perpetrated partner homicides occurred in the home and, of these, 57.3 per cent took place in a shared residence. It was further noted that if victim and offender were not co-habiting, the murder was usually located in the home of the female offender. In terms of specific locations, studies have found conflicting results, although the most often cited rooms are the bedroom (Totman, 1978; Goetting, 1987, 1989), kitchen (Wolfgang, 1958) and living-room (Mann, 1996). With reference to the particular rooms in which the homicide occurs, it could be argued that there may be a dynamic relationship between the choice of weapon and the location of fatal encounter. That is, the offender may choose a weapon that is readily visible and available in the location in which they find themselves, or alternatively, the offender may purposefully go to a location in which they know an appropriate weapon is kept (for example, collecting a knife from the kitchen).

Although temporal factors of seasonality have been investigated in some studies, the results appear to be somewhat inconclusive[7] and the possibility of such factors influencing the aetiology of female-perpetrated homicide given little credit and much criticism (Mann, 1996). However, in terms of homicide patterns across the week, it has generally been found that the majority of encounters occur at the weekend, between Friday and Sunday (peaking on Saturday) and between 8.00 p.m. to 1.59 a.m. (Wolfgang, 1958; Mann, 1996). For example, Goetting (1987) found that nearly 61 per cent of domestic murders committed by Detroit wives took place between Friday and Sunday. However, figures for Scotland for the period of 1991–2000 indicate that, although 46 per cent of all homicides took place on a weekend, those in which the accused was an intimate partner were more evenly distributed across the week – with Tuesday, Wednesday and Thursday also showing elevated rates of homicide. Overall, 35 per cent of intimate partner homicides (both male and female) occurred over the weekend, and 65 per cent on a weekday (Scottish Executive, 2001).

Substance Use

Numerous studies have investigated the links between substance use (that is, alcohol and drugs) and female-perpetrated partner homicide. Mann (1996) found that 36.2 per cent of female offenders had been drinking prior to the homicide event, and a further 58.3 per cent of victims had consumed alcohol at the time of their deaths (22 per cent of whom were defined as legally drunk) (Mann, 1996). Similarly, Goetting (1987) found figures of 37.5 per cent and 44.6 per cent respectively (Goetting, 1989). Chan's (2001) UK-based research reports higher levels, finding that 60 per cent of female defendants (who had committed intimate partner homicide) had consumed alcohol, and 84 per cent of their victims were under the influence of alcohol.

Mann (1996) found that the link between drug use and female homicide was more difficult to establish; however, she did note that almost 9 per cent of female offenders had taken at least one drug prior to committing the homicide. She further points out that many of those cases which were drug-related were 'particularly heinous' (Mann, 1996: 56). More recent studies have linked the increasing involvement of (and opportunities for) women in the drug market, their increased use of drugs, and their increased use of violence (Brownstein et al., 1994). However, Brownstein et al. (1994: 111) do point out that although homicides may generally involve the use of illegal substances, most killings do not result from drug-induced violent outbursts.

Victim-Precipitation

Following von Hentig (1948), Wolfgang's (1958) concept of 'victim-precipitation' (see Chapter 5) has been an influential one when considering the nature of intimate partner homicide – especially those committed by women (Mann, 1996). Wolfgang's study revealed important findings: 'in the case of intimate partner homicide the killing of men differs substantially from the killing of women' (1958: 260). In the 47 cases in which wives killed husbands, Wolfgang concluded that 28 of the men had precipitated their own deaths by striking the woman or showing and using a deadly weapon. This compared with only 9 of 100 wife killings that Wolfgang deemed 'victim-precipitated'. Overall, in 38 of the 47 cases where wives killed husbands, Wolfgang found that men had 'strongly provoked' the act (Websdale, 1999: 11).

Research surrounding the issue of victim-precipitation generates two important findings of particular relevance to female-perpetrated partner homicide. The first is that homicides which occur in a domestic context are more likely to involve victim-precipitation than non-domestic homicides. Second, female-perpetrated domestic partner homicides are much more likely to involve victim-precipitation than those in which men kill their female partners (Foote, 1999). Following this, Foote importantly points out, 'in exploring why the domestic context produces such a high percentage of victim-precipitated homicides by women, it must first be noted that domestic homicide is the most severe form of domestic violence' (1999: 180). Research investigating this aspect of female-perpetrated partner homicide has generated overwhelming support for the links between physical abuse and domestic homicide (for example, Busch, 1999; Chan, 2001; Goetting, 1988a; Jensen, 2001;

Jurik and Winn, 1990; and Polk, 1991, to name but a few). Websdale found that of 24 cases of female-perpetrated intimate homicide, 20 cases (83 per cent) showed clear evidence of a history of domestic violence, and thus concluded, 'in most cases woman battering was the principal precipitant of the killing' (1999: 124). Furthermore, Jurik and Gregware found that:

> In almost half of the cases in which women killed husbands or male lovers, the victim initiated the use of physical force. In the other half of these cases, the husband made physically threatening moves, verbally threatened physical harm, had beaten the defendant earlier in the day, or had harmed or threatened harm to the defendant's child. Initially, many of the women defendants had passively tried to avoid their victim's violence; only after months or even years of abuse did they finally 'agree' to a violent resolution. (1992: 187)

The concept of victim-precipitation has important implications for intimate homicide. Not only does it give us a much fuller understanding of the preceding context of the homicide, it also provides us with the foundations for developing a richer explanation of the event and the actions of those involved. Perhaps more importantly it shows how domestic violence and domestic homicide are inextricably linked[8] – although it is very interesting to note that whilst male-perpetrated intimate homicide most often results from an incident of 'domestic violence' which went 'too far', female-perpetrated partner killing is most likely to occur in response to or defence from such violence. As Chan argues, 'Homicide between partners and the problem of domestic violence are not unrelated phenomenon. The death of a partner by the other is a logical outcome of a relationship marred by long-term physical and emotional abuse' (2001: 4).

Scenarios of Intimate Partner Homicide

There are, of course, many scenarios of female-perpetrated partner homicide, of which only a few will be considered here. However, there are particular contexts which can be identified as more 'typical' of this type of homicide. As noted above, the influence of victim-precipitation and (the continuum of) domestic violence are significant factors involved in the killing of sexual intimates by women. Two particular scenarios of lethal violence will be discussed in this context, both of which can be regarded as a manifestation of the 'battered woman syndrome' (Walker, 1984, 1989) and considered the primary motivating factor in cases where a woman kills her intimate partner. The first scenario illustrated is that in which the female offender responds immediately to a physical or verbal confrontation by the victim; the second involves delayed retaliation to the confrontation or abuse, whereby a period of time has elapsed and thus the killing is 'unexpected' and the victim often passive.[9] In addition, female-perpetrated spousal killings that are motivated by financial and/or sexual gain shall also be illustrated with examples drawn from previous research. Whilst these latter forms of female-perpetrated intimate homicide account for only a small proportion of cases, it is important to recognise that women do commit homicide in circumstances other than those in which they are victimised, provoked or defending themselves, and thus not all lethal acts committed by females against their intimate partners can be explained by the battered woman syndrome.

The Battered Woman

An important distinction (both contextual and legal) is drawn between those cases of homicide involving battered women as perpetrators, in which sufferers of domestic violence react immediately to the precipitating event (that is, a particular incident of domestic violence), and those cases in which the response is delayed or where there is no apparent catalyst to the event (aside from the current level of violence in which the woman exists, of course). Websdale (1999) gives a useful clarification of these two scenarios with his concepts of 'proximal precipitating violence' (that which immediately precedes, and is central to 'triggering' the killing) and 'distal precipitating violence' (that which is longstanding, and has a grinding and accumulating effect on the homicide) (Websdale, 1999: 125). However, Websdale (1999) also points out that the causal dynamics between these two precipitants are very similar, and that both violence immediately prior to the lethal event and longstanding battering are likely to contribute to the precipitation of homicide. As such, Websdale states that 'it is impossible to distinguish between the roles of each form, or even, perhaps, to argue that they are discrete categories at all' (1999: 125). Nevertheless, the distinction is a useful one and will be adopted below.

Proximal Precipitation

Homicide that occurs in the context of an argument or confrontation is perhaps the most common scenario of female intimate partner homicide. Often such arguments are a common occurrence punctuated with a history of violence against the female partner, and in many cases both victim and offender have been drinking (Chan, 2001). An argument starts (or continues) concerning issues of fidelity, finances or the termination of the relationship, and the women either defends herself from physical attack (actual or feared) or retaliates to such attacks. Thus the offender reacts to proximal precipitation. The following case is a 'typical' example of such a scenario:

Jean
The relationship between the defendant (Jean, a housewife) and the deceased had been an abusive one, whereby the deceased indulged in heavy drinking. He had been verbally, physically and sexually abusive towards the defendant during their relationship. The defendant claimed to live in constant fear of physical violence, and the deceased would not allow her to obtain medical help after an assault. The deceased had threatened to shoot the defendant, her children and members of her family. As well as abusing Jean, the deceased had also frequently abused their children. Although she occasionally tried to leave the deceased, threats by the deceased towards herself and others forced the defendant to return. At the time of the murder, the deceased [had] been abusing the defendant, and the defendant hit the deceased over the head with a cast-iron saucepan. Fearing that the deceased would retaliate, the defendant then strangled the deceased with a ligature. (Adapted from Chan, 2001: 199)

The following two cases clearly illustrate the common themes within the 'fatal argument', which influence the homicide. The first (Case #087), revolves around the attempted termination of the relationship, whilst the second (Case #109) results from the perceived infidelity of the woman. It is worth noting that these same themes, which are centred around the issue of male domination and control, permeate many of those occasions in which men kill their intimate female partners. Hence, as Polk notes, 'masculine possessiveness, and violence, arise even in homicides where men become the ultimate victims' (1991: 153).

Case #087

The woman and her partner had been living together for six years. According to her account she had a drug problem, heroin and coke, and he an alcohol problem. She was trying to get off drugs, but he was not supportive. In fact, he was dealing. She had tried to leave him but that had led to fights. On the night of the killing he was drunk and out of control. When she said she was leaving, he started pushing her. He tried to get a gun, but could not find it. Then he took a knife from his pocket and stabbed her in the thigh. She grabbed a kitchen knife and stabbed him to death. (Adapted from Brownstein et al., 1994: 105)

Case #109

During five years of marriage, both the offender and her husband drank heavily. Things were OK until the last year of marriage, when he would drink and become violent. He would beat her, sometimes to the point where she had to go to the emergency room of a local hospital ... One night, after he had been drinking to excess, he heard her talking on the telephone. He thought it was another man and became enraged. He began to strangle her with the telephone cord. She freed herself and ran into the kitchen. He started to strangle her with his hands. She reached into the sink where she found a knife that she used to stab him to death. (Adapted from Brownstein et al., 1994: 105)

Other fatal fights are not necessarily linked to the perceived infidelity of the woman or her attempts to leave, though the relationship is, nevertheless, marred with violence, as the following case illustrates:

[Case Code: B.06/94]

The defendant and deceased had been married for seven years. The deceased had a long history of violence and antisocial behaviour and regularly beat the defendant. His outbursts of violence were invariably linked to excessive alcohol consumption. On the evening of the homicide, both parties had consumed alcohol. On returning from the pub, the deceased entered the kitchen from where he called the defendant to join him. She found him in a semi-naked state brandishing a knife. He was violent and aggressive toward the defendant and ultimately pinned her back against the kitchen wall, pointing the knife inches from her face. The defendant somehow managed to disarm the deceased and as he backed off he said, 'Well come on bitch, use it'. The defendant claims that she simply threw the knife at him and turned to leave the kitchen. His demeanour quickly changed and he began to plead with the defendant for help. She returned and found him collapsed, at which stage she ran to a neighbour's house to summons help.

Distal Precipitation

Although a woman may be subject to frequent and severe physical abuse, reaction to this (in the form of homicide) may be delayed. In such circumstances, the offender may attack their partner unexpectedly, whilst they are off-guard or incapacitated – as the following case illustrates:

The defendant and her ex-husband (the victim) were living together and attempting rec-onciliation because the victim had promised to see a psychologist for his problems. During their marriage ... he had been verbally and sexually abusive to [the defendant] and her daughter. On the evening of the offence, the defendant and the victim went out drinking at a bar. Afterwards, they began arguing outside the bar in the parking lot. There the victim was seen physically and verbally abusing the defendant. Later that same night, the defen-dant visited a neighbour's carrying a loaded gun and asking for help in what they described as a very hysterical state. The defendant shot the victim later that night while he was sleeping. In her ... interview, she stated that he had sworn to kill her when he awoke.
(Adapted from Jurik and Gregware, 1992: 190)

Despite the distinction between these two scenarios of battered woman syndrome, the typical scene which emerges is one of a woman who has been physically, psychologically or sexually abused (in many cases all three), often over an extended period of time, forcefully enduring a cycle of escalating violence over which she feels she has no control and no perceived escape. The fatal act of violence is thus the final attempt to regain control over their own, and often their children's, lives – whether this be as a result of proximal or distal precipitation (Silverman and Kennedy, 1993; Jensen, 2001; Walker and Browne, 1985).

Financial and/or Sexual Motivations

As a number of commentators have noted, women do not always kill intimate part-ners as a result of violence against them. Studies have found that a small number of female-perpetrated partner homicides are motivated by self-interest – in terms of either financial and/or sexual gain. Chan (2001) argues that such cases highlight a 'darker side' of women's homicide offending. Such cases are thus often planned and premeditated (although they may be opportunistic in terms of the actual 'timing' of the homicide event). The case study that follows is an example of intimate partner homicide motivated by financial gain:

A 26-year-old woman beat and shot to death her estranged husband of the same age after having secured several insurance policies on his life without his knowledge. Three months before the fatal incident, the offender had commented to her mother and sisters that she was going to make them rich, and that she planned to buy a Mercedes Benz. Though at the wake she had to be pulled away from the coffin as she exclaimed, 'All I want to do is tell him that I was sorry to do it,' she never formally admitted her guilt and was acquitted.
(Reproduced from Goetting, 1987: 335)

Often, reasons are both financial and sexual. That is, the female offender simply wants to eliminate her partner for both the financial benefits she may receive as a result of his death, and in order to continue a relationship with another party. In such circumstances, not only is the homicide premeditated, but it often involves more than one perpetrator – usually the female offender and her lover. The following two examples clearly demonstrate the characteristics of such a scenario:

Jenny
The defendant was charged with both murder and attempted murder of her husband. He was the proprietor of several properties and the defendant was motivated by financial reasons to kill her husband. They had been married for five years, but the relationship had soured. The defendant was regarded as the motivator in the conspiracy to kill her husband, having involved her lover, her son and her lover's friend. Although the defendant did not admit guilt to either attempted murder or murder, the testimony of the other parties clearly implicated the defendant. The deceased was shot twice with a sawn-off shotgun, with the second attempt fatally wounding him. (Reproduced from Chan, 2001: 199)

Lucy
The defendant, along with her lover, was charged with the murder of her husband ... Although she claimed that the deceased was violent, there was no evidence to substantiate her claim. The defendant made it known to many people of her desire to 'get rid of' her husband. She had offered a friend money to murder her husband. The deceased was in a motor vehicle with the defendant and her lover when they attacked him with an iron bar. He died as a result of multiple head injuries. (Adapted from Chan, 2001: 200)

Those killings which occur in the context of domestic violence and those resulting from financial and/or sexual motivations are clearly very different. First and foremost, the latter forms of female homicide are very rare – though it is this kind of violence that stirs media and public interest and has, at various stages in recent history, led to suggestions of a new breed of violent female offenders (see Adler, 1975; Simon, 1975; and Heidensohn, 2002 for an overview). More importantly, there are no clear theoretical frameworks to make sense of these forms of female violence. As Bell and Fox note, 'outside the context of the battered woman who kills her abuser, feminists have been unable to posit a rational story which explains the actions of the female killer' (1996: 471).

Bearing these omissions in mind (to which we return in the final section of this chapter) we now turn our attention to those theories that have been developed to explain female homicide, with a particular emphasis upon the predominant scenario of women who strike back at their violent intimate partners.

Explanations of Intimate Partner Homicide

The most dominant explanation of female-perpetrated intimate partner homicide is Walker's (1989) 'battered woman syndrome'. The theory explicitly recognises the importance of domestic abuse against women and the role it plays in the homicides they commit, and recognises that these women are both offenders and victims (Silverman and Kennedy, 1993). Walker (1989) describes the experiences of battered women in terms of a 'cycle of violence' which is committed against them, and the responsive (but passive) strategies of these women are explained through the concept of 'learned helplessness'. Walker argues that male violence against women typically comprises a three-stage cycle. The first is a 'tension-building' phase, in which the man becomes argumentative, giving verbal and/or 'mild' physical abuse. During this stage the female partner will generally try to calm the abuser and pacify the situation, as an attempt to avoid the escalation of violence. As attempts become less effective, the second phase begins, and is characterised by an acute incidence of increasingly frequent and severe beatings – which usually lasts anything from 2 to 24 hours, although in some incidents women have reported a 'reign of terror' for longer than a week (Busch, 1999). At this point the female responsive strategy is that of survival, remaining passive in the fear that attempts of self-protection and retaliation may only provoke further or more severe attacks. Once the battering is over, the third and final stage involves the abuser expressing remorse and showing affection to his partner – he apologises, and promises that the violence and abuse will stop. However, the abuser breaks his promise, and the cycle of violence is repeated.

In an effort to understand why women remain in such abusive relationships, Walker (1979) introduced the concept of 'learned helplessness'. Learned helplessness is a vulnerability pattern (often established in childhood) which develops from the lack of control women have over the violence that they live with. Hence, it is 'a process of learning to believe that nothing one can do will bring about a predictable positive result' (Walker and Browne, 1985: 187) Walker and Browne go on to explain:

> [A] physically, sexually, or psychologically abused woman who has experienced a series of painful, non-contingent attacks begins to perceive fewer and fewer options for dealing with or escaping the violence; her focus is on minimizing injury and coping with pain and fear … Although she sometimes appears not to be taking any action on her own behalf, she may actually be choosing the only option that she believes will facilitate her survival. (1985: 187)

The woman might develop a number of coping strategies (such as learning not to cry out in pain or controlling their breathing during attacks), however, these are at the expense of forming escape tactics. Walker (1979, 1984) explains that many women do not perceive escaping to be a possibility, and even if they were to leave, the danger does not decline. Indeed, as we have seen in Chapter 6, abused women's fear that their partners will find them and retaliate to the separation with lethal consequences is one borne out in reality. Thus, the battered woman can either remain in a situation in which her life is in danger, or attempt to leave the relationship, whereupon a similar (or perhaps greater) threat of death becomes one of many obstacles that she must confront.

It has been suggested that when battered women do respond to the violence inflicted upon them (either in retaliation or self-defence) and kill their abusers, it is when they perceive themselves or their children to be in extreme danger, recognising the incident to be of a much more severe nature than previous attacks. Through the cycle of violence (and having to adapt to their abuser's behaviour), the battered woman become sensitised to her partners' patterns of violence. As Busch puts it, she 'becomes so cognizant of danger signals from her batterer that she is able to perceive a change in the level of abuse foretelling her imminent death' (1999: 36). Like Totman (1978), what Walker argues to be important here is the individuals' perception of the situation (that is, their perception regarding the possibility of escape, or the available options to them) – as opposed the reality of the situation (though this may, in fact, be deadly). Thus, women kill out of terror, and in self-defence.

There is a great deal of support for the main premise of the theory – that many women kill in response to male violence, often after years of abuse. The evidence discussed above regarding victim-precipitation in female spouse killings certainly lends weight to the 'battered woman syndrome'. More recent research has compared battered women who kill their abuser with those who do not (for example, O'Keefe, 1997; Roberts, 1996). These studies have generally found that those who killed had experienced a longer duration of violence, more severe and frequent battering and injuries, experienced more sexual assaults and were more likely to perceive their lives to have been in danger. Furthermore, all note the high involvement of substance use (argued to be an escape route, numbing both the physical and emotional pain of abuse), with a number commenting on the increased likelihood of childhood trauma and abuse (suggesting the cycle of violence may extend much wider than simply that perpetrated by the partner).

However, one could argue that the findings discussed do not necessarily substantiate Walker's theory and the concepts that she employs, but rather it simply shows that many women who kill are battered women. Indeed, a number of well-founded criticisms have been made against the battered woman syndrome. First, a number of commentators strongly argue that the battered woman syndrome, as a 'syndrome', medicalises and pathologises female offending. Walker (1989) argued that women will exhibit signs of living with the cycle of violence which distinguishes them as battered women (such as low self-esteem, hypervigilance and denial of abuse). These form the symptoms of battered woman syndrome, which is itself a diagnosis subsumed under that of 'post-traumatic stress disorder' in the DSM-III (Walker and Browne, 1985; Busch, 1999). In creating a diagnostic classification of battered woman syndrome, Chan argues that a battered woman's experiences of reality are 'transformed into a psychiatric disorder requiring therapeutic or medical intervention' (2001: 152). Thus, the theory implies that battered women are suffering from some form of mental abnormality or psychological defect (Busch, 1999; Chan, 2001; Dobash and Dobash, 1992; Nicolson and Sanghvi, 1993). Ultimately, these women are classified and labelled as patients with a particular collection of symptoms. Consequently, individual elements of a woman's experience are lost. In addition, by focusing on the woman's perceived inability to leave or escape, the concept of 'learned helplessness' further denotes incapacity and passivity – despite the evidence of prior agency contacts (with police and/or support services) and attempts made by the woman to terminate the relationship, which contradict this view. Thus the battered woman syndrome is criticised for relying upon, and perpetuating, traditional and derogatory stereotypes of women. As Nicolson and Sanghvi assert, this medicalised model 'reaffirms the view that when problems arise, women develop headaches, become depressed, take pills and dissolve into nervous wrecks' (1993: 735). Perhaps more importantly, this view of women also denies their agency and responsibility, preventing their actions from being understood as reasonable, rational or purposeful (Dobash and Dobash, 1992).

Further, Chan (2001: 153) has argued that the battered woman syndrome creates a situation of the bona fide battered woman, against which all battered women are judged, and their patterns of behaviour expected to fit. This may prevent some women, who do not meet all of the criteria identified, from being considered a battered woman. This highlights what Schneider (2000) argues to be a general paradox of feminist theory. This argument is not only applied to the diagnostic criteria of the syndrome, but also in terms of the limitations of Walker's (1984) own definitions. First, the theory is restricted to explaining violence that occurs between intimate heterosexual partners, thus excluding same sex relationships (for which research has found similar evidence of domestic abuse and battering). Walker (1979, 1984) also specifies that to be a battered woman one must experience the cycle of violence at least twice. However, some, such as Busch (1999), argue that surely one cycle is enough – with Nicolson and Sanghvi (1993) ironically pointing out that even Walker's own data indicate that not all women experience the entire cycle of violence. Finally, the emphasis given to the physical elements of abuse is argued to result in a neglect of the effects of psychological abuse. Commentators suggest that these weaknesses preclude some women from identifying with the definition of a battered woman, thus preventing their victimisation from being acknowledged.

Perhaps the most important criticism of battered woman syndrome, in the context of homicide research, is that the theory does not necessarily (or at least adequately) explain why some women eventually kill their abusers when others, who may have experienced similar levels of violence and paralleled perceptions of danger, do not. Nor does the theory address the problems faced by these women in terms of the moral and legal aspects of culpability which are inevitably raised by their defences of provocation and/or self-defence. A great deal of (mainly feminist) research has focused on the discriminatory application of the law of defence for females who have killed their partners. They argue that these defences have developed to reflect male experiences and standards of provocation and self-defence, thus neglecting battered women's experiences. As Chan states:

> In order to fulfil the requirement for provocation, a self-defendant must prove that there was a sudden and temporary loss of self-control, imminence in retaliating and that a reasonable person would have reacted to the provocation in the same way. For self-defence, loss of self-control is replaced with proportionality of force in retaliating. (2001: 108)

There have been numerous calls for changes to the law of self-defence in order to include battered women's experiences, which emphasise the need to recognise that violence need not be physically imminent (at that precise moment), for the danger of death to be real for battered women. As Websdale states:

> In short, to understand why women kill their intimate partners, one must transcend the logic of the criminal law and its concern with appropriate defensive force, retreat rules, and perceptions of imminent danger, and instead socially situate the

use of lethal violence amidst that panoply of relationship microdynamics and political forces that precedes and accompanies the homicide. (1999: 121)

Ogle and Jacobs make a similar point and particularly emphasise the importance of examining the entire history and context of the battering relationship. They argue for a need to understand 'cultural, social, structural, and situational forces, as well as the interactional process, that assist the batterer in maintaining the battering relationship and result in the escalation to homicide' (2002: 69).

Important steps in this direction are being taken. Recently in the UK, the courts appear to be recognising the concept of 'cumulative provocation' – which suggests that the defence of provocation should include a whole range and course of behaviour that leads up to and eventually culminates in the homicidal event, as opposed to one violent incident immediately prior to the killing (Chan, 2001: 156; Nicolson and Sanghvi, 1993). However, there is concern surrounding the real possibility that battered women may kill their partners for reasons other than self-protection, and the possibility that revenge killings by women could become subsumed under such defences. There are also unanswered questions concerning the justification of some of these killings, and the legal culpability of battered women generally (Chan, 2001; Silverman and Kennedy, 1993).

Whilst most theorists recognise the importance of domestic violence and abuse as a precipitator to many instances of intimate homicide, several theorists have expanded their explanations beyond notions of the battered woman syndrome to consider wider issues of gender inequality, socio-economic status and powerlessness, as well as the role of the state and its agencies in responding to domestic violence. For example, Peterson (1999) explored the homicidal behaviour of women against intimate partners, using a modification of Black's (1983, 1993) 'self-help perspective'. Essentially, Peterson argues that the vast majority of women who kill their male intimates are those of low social status to whom legal remedies in relation to domestic abuse are often limited and ineffective, or at least are perceived as such. Peterson suggests that various factors can lead such women to perceive formal social controls to be unsatisfactory, including general perceptions of the law as an oppressor rather than a helper, particularly for women who have been 'on the wrong side of the law' (1999: 40); direct or indirect experience of the police and courts as ineffective in dealing with domestic disputes, for example, the half-hearted enforcement of protection orders (1999: 34); and socialisation into a patriarchal environment engendering beliefs that the male-dominated justice system will not be able to resolve her grievance effectively (1999: 40). She cites evidence from research by Grant and Curry (1993), who found that a much higher proportion of the women in their sample who had resorted to lethal violence in response to domestic violence either had never called the police to intervene in a domestic violence episode or had called the police eight or more times. Both reactions suggest that these women did not believe that the police could assist them effectively. Specifically, the absence of any calls is suggestive that this sub-group of women never considered that formal intervention would help, whilst those who had called repeatedly presumably felt they had 'exhausted the viability of that option' (Grant and Curry, 1993: 81, cited in Peterson, 1999: 40). In summary, Peterson's application of Black's self-help model places female homicide in a rather more rational and purposive light (as opposed to suggestions that such women are hapless and helpless). She views their behaviour as 'justice seeking' and as an understandable response to conditions of violence and social isolation, particularly in a context where agencies such as the police and other social services have failed them.

Recent downward trends in domestic homicide in the US and Canada, coupled with the apparent reasons for these declines, offer some support for Peterson's arguments. For example, there is some evidence from the US that spousal homicide generally has decreased in the last two decades (see Dugan et al., 1999; Rosenfeld, 1997). Similar declines have been observed in Canada, although there is some dispute regarding when these declines began and whether they are being maintained (see Dawson, 2001). The general consensus regarding the possible factors leading to the decline of female-perpetrated intimate homicides in these countries include increased gender equality (including a decline in domesticity and the improved economic status of women) and a growth in domestic violence resources – all of which apparently avert domestic homicide by reducing exposure to ongoing violent relationships (see Chapter 11). If correct, this would provide some support for Peterson's (1999) thesis that when women kill a violent male partner, they do so as a form of self-help when they perceive there to be few or no formal or legal alternatives. Hence, as women become less socially and economically isolated and are afforded more options, they may not perceive their situation as one from which they can only escape via lethal means.

Finally, it is worth noting that a significant number of the cases reviewed in this chapter (particularly those amongst intimate partners) occurred at a time when either the victim, offender or both had consumed alcohol. As discussed in several preceding chapters, the role of alcohol in relation to homicide is clearly complex (see Chapters 3 and 6), but there would seem to be little doubt that many instances of domestic violence and homicide are precipitated by heavy alcohol consumption.

Study Task 7.1

It has been suggested that whilst there are many similarities, the experiences of violence against black/minority women differs from that of (white) women in the majority community. Specifically, it is argued that 'Black and minority women confront extra obstacles in escaping abuse' (Siddiqui, 2001: 14). Make a list of the specific sorts of obstacles (from both within and outside minority communities) that black and minority women might face. A useful starting point for information is Southall Black Sisters (SBS), a women's organisation that has campaigned and undertaken policy work aimed at addressing the problem of violence against black women.

In summary, the issues and explanations of women who kill their intimate partners are complex and very difficult to unravel (even when we focus solely on battered women). This is only compounded by the general lack of research surrounding intimate partner killing, especially that which is relevant to the UK experience. However, although the battered woman syndrome has come under much criticism as an explanatory theory, the involvement of victim-precipitation and domestic violence in female-perpetrated partner homicide has central importance in many accounts of why women kill. As such, it is one of the most important issues to consider in understanding why women kill their intimate partners and should not be overlooked.

Locating the Violent Female Offender within Criminological Thought

The field of criminology has been described as 'quintessentially male', with traditional theories and studies of violence and criminality consistently excluding female behaviour (Chesney-Lind, 1997; Daly and Chesney-Lind, 1988; Burman et al., 2000). Research which has been conducted has been undertaken by men, using male samples, to explain male crime. As such, many researchers question whether female crime can be explained by such male-centred theories, and whether such studies can be generalised to the population of women. The applicability of traditional explanations to female homicide offending rest on a number of bold assumptions, mainly that the same factors influence the aetiology, motivations and causal processes for male and female homicide offending, and that men and women respond in the same way to factors which increase or decrease homicide rates (Daly and Chesney-Lind, 1988). The limitations of traditional theories are particularly significant when considering homicide, for which the gender gap is greatest. Even those who advocate the use of traditional theories in explaining gendered patterns of criminal behaviour, such as Steffensmeier and Allan (1996), acknowledge limitations in explaining violent female offending. Furthermore, they argue that such theories cannot adequately address the issue of context, which, as we have seen, is crucial when considering forms of female killings.

The male character of criminology and crime itself has, arguably, resulted in a lack of empirical research and theoretical discourse to make sense of female crime generally and violent offending in particular. The significant under-representation of women in the statistics has only emphasised stereotypical assumptions surrounding the incompatibility of women and crime – to engage in crime is to be male. As Chan illuminates:

> The image of women killing is anathema to prevailing conceptions of womanhood and femininity. Acts of violence have typically been regarded as belonging to the domain of the male species, for whom violent behaviour is more 'natural' and acceptable. Therefore in having to confront women who engage in homicidal acts, the tendency is to fall back on prevailing stereotypes of the 'mad' or insane woman, or the bad 'evil' woman. (2001: 1)

There exist widely-held traditional beliefs (within and beyond criminology) about the nature and morality of women, and normative expectations regarding the nurturing role of women as wife and mother. Femininity and womanhood equate with an absence of criminality, and a woman is judged on the basis of these virtues. Women who do not adhere or conform to patriarchal sex role expectations of what it is to be a good wife, good mother and thus a good woman, are considered to be 'doubly deviant' and punished for both their legal infractions and their refusal to enter into what Eaton (1986) calls the 'gender contract' (Heidensohn, 1996). This is particularly important when considering that the majority of female homicides involve the killing of those closest to them (that is, their spouses, lovers or infants), contradicting all notions of motherhood, wife and woman.

In sum, early theories of deviancy emphasised biological explanations of female criminality locating the causes in individual pathology and personality – the female criminal was (in Lombroso's words) a 'monster' (Chan, 2001: 23; Heidensohn, 1996: 112). Female criminality was dichotomised as either 'mad' or 'bad', troubled or troublesome and thus in need of help or severe sanctions of punishment. By focusing on the mental state of female offenders, it was further possible to deny the intention, agency and culpability of their criminal behaviour – reinforcing the image of women as passive, complying and harmless (Chan, 2001; Heidensohn, 1996). As a result, female homicide offenders are argued to have been treated both more leniently and more severely – depending upon their conformity to the appropriate stereotype (Follingstad et al., 1996; Wilczynski and Morris, 1993).

More recent theories have attempted to take account of gender, focusing on the concept of equality, or conversely inequality. One of the first gendered theories of crime was that of Alder (1975), who suggested that as equality between the sexes increased and women experienced more freedoms that were not available to them previously, their involvement in crime would also increase (see also Simon, 1975). Greater gender equality was argued to lead to higher rates of female crime, as women became more like men. However, the theory has come under a great deal of criticism, with findings not supporting the hypothesis upon which it was based. For example, it has been observed that the largest increases in female offending occurred before the women's movement gained any real momentum (see Bunch et al., 1983; Daly and Chesney-Lind, 1988; Jurik and Winn, 1990; Steffensmeier and Allen, 1996). Furthermore, at the time of heightened equality, female-perpetrated homicide actually decreased. A number of studies linked this decrease of female-perpetrated homicide (particularly the killing of intimate partners) to the provision of women's shelters and support networks which were introduced in the 1970s (Jensen, 2001; Browne and Williams, 1989, 1993). As a result, some theorists have argued the reverse, contending that increased gender equality leads to less female-perpetrated homicide. Put another way, greater gender *inequality* increases female homicide (Baron, 1993; Jensen, 2001).

The latest theoretical developments and debates concerning female violence and homicide have developed these issues of inequality further, stressing the importance not only of women's experience of violence (and subordination), but also their experience of the reality in which they live. For example, Burman et al.'s (2000) UK-based research into girl gangs provides some excellent insights into female responses to, and their experience and definition of, violence. Interestingly, they found that girls' conceptualisations of violence do not necessarily correspond to those of males, adult's or legal definitions. In fact, the girls in their study experienced verbally abusive behaviour (such as threats or name-calling) as more damaging and hurtful than physical violence. As such, like many feminists, Burman et al. (2000) emphasise the differential and gendered experience of violence, which is of implicit importance when considering (and attempting to explain) female-perpetrated homicide. What such works begin to address (unlike the vast majority of research concerned with female violence) is 'the *agency* of women who have few channels of expression yet find their own' (Heidensohn, 2002: 516; emphasis in the original). Along similar lines, Artz' (1998) study of violent schoolgirls emphasises how such violence must be understood in the context of gender issues and the girls' sense of powerlessness. Artz found that through their family relations, and in particular their observations of family conflict and how it was resolved, the girls that she interviewed had learned certain messages regarding men and women, power and relationships. As Artz explains, 'they have seen that men are far more important and more powerful than women, and that men's importance is ... bound up in their being stronger and more forceful than women' (1998: 171). This, according to Artz, makes these girls more susceptible to 'oppressed group behaviour' (a condition whereby those who suffer at the hands of the dominant group – in this instance males – turn upon members of their *own* kind whenever they behave in ways that are deemed unacceptable to the dominant group (see Roberts, 1983; and Friere, 1971). Hence, 'in the hope of gaining a measure of power, they engage in "horizontal violence" – that is, they beat each other up' (1998: 179). Other work which emphasises the importance of status and power and also emphasises the oftentimes purposive nature of female offending, include studies of violent girl gangs (see, for example, Campbell, 1991; Messerschmidt, 1995; and Miller, 2001; and Jurik and Gregware's (1992) large-scale study of female homicide offenders in the US). What such works achieve is a recognition that factors such as status and reputation can be as important for females as for males. For example, Messerschmidt (1995) has attempted to utilise the concept of 'doing gender' (see Chapter 6 for a fuller discussion of this concept) to explain girl gang behaviour. He argues that what is viewed as atypical feminine behaviour outside 'the hood' is normalised within the context of inter-neighbourhood conflict. 'Girl gang violence in this situation is encouraged, permitted and privileged by both boys and girls as appropriate feminine behaviour. Hence, "Bad girl" femininity is situational accomplished and context-bound within the domain of the street' (Messerschmidt, 1995: 182).

Miller observes that there are limitations to understanding female violence in terms of either a 'gender differences' or a 'gender similarities' approach (2001: 199). For Miller the former approach, which tends to essentialise differences between women and men, 'fails to account for similarities in their experiences, and also overlooks important differences *between* women' (2001: 199), for example, in terms of race, class and age. 'On the other hand, the "gender similarities" approach often results in a failure to be attentive to the importance of gender ... [which] continues to play a primary role in creating the opportunities and constrains that frame young women's lives' (2001: 199). For Miller, then, a delicate balance needs to be struck in terms of acknowledging the overlaps and differences in girls' and boys' experiences within gangs (2001: 204) or, for our purposes, 'sameness' or 'difference' between males' experiences and commission of homicide and that of females. Messerschmidt (1995) evades this difficulty to some extent, in that his 'argument attempts to avoid the position of asserting that gang behaviour is in itself masculine, and that girls who engage in such activities are consequently masculinised' (Adler and Polk, 2001: 161–2).

Finally, and perhaps most radically to date, Morrisey explores the ways in which feminist legal discourse and discourses of law and the media represent female killers in such a way as to deny them human agency, thereby confirming that female aggression has no place in our culture (2003: 25). Exploring in detail diverse case studies of female killers (including the battered wife Pamela Sainsbury, who killed her husband as he slept, Aileen Wournos, who murdered seven middle-aged men in Florida, and Karla Homolka, who helped her husband kill two teenage girls in Ontario), Morrisey illustrates how, by denying the possibility of female agency in crimes of torture, rape and murder, feminist theorists deny women the full freedom to be human. According to Morrisey, female agency is denied through three techniques. First, 'vilification/ monsterisation' focuses upon the evil and inhuman nature of the murderess, such that she is considered to have acted not as a human woman. Second, 'mythification' works in a similar fashion, though here she is not just monsterised, but transformed into the living embodiment of mythic evil; 'this strategy is very effective in distancing the female offender from her society' (Morrisey, 2003: 25). Finally, 'victimism' denies agency by insisting upon the powerlessness and oppressed nature of the female killer. This is particularly relevant to the case of female victims of domestic violence who kill their abusers. Representations of the murderess as victim function to deny her responsibility, culpability, rationality and, ultimately, agency. For Morrisey, whilst a strategy of victimism may be helpful in securing the sympathetic legal treatment of such female killers, the more significant benefits of improving general social attitudes to women and challenging negative myths and stereotypes of femininity are denied. In short, women are either demonised in some manner and placed completely outside the boundaries of appropriate female behaviour, or placed into the category of victim – both of which suggest that female violence is unreal. For Morrisey (2003: 168) it is no coincidence that feminists have tended to focus upon the battered murderess, as opposed to instances of female sadists – who do not neatly fit into the contours of the violent female subject.

A classic example of the continued failure to unpack the complexities of gender in terms of female offending is illustrated by Muncer et al. (2001). These researchers note that since the early 1990s the British media have suggested that violent crime by women has been rising as a result of the increased masculine attitudes held by such women (referred to as 'ladettes'). Much like Adler's (1975) gender equality theory, the causal dynamic arguably involved is that of 'masculinisation'; 'these young women are believed to have adopted the attitudes of working-class anti-social males and the rise of female violence is attributed to their emulation of the hard-drinking, swearing, confrontational style of male counterparts' (Muncer et al., 2001: 35). Muncer et al. (2001), however, found no evidence for this in their study. With regards to female homicide, a number of studies have argued that rates of offending are not only increasing, but that victimisation patterns and the types of homicides in which women are becoming involved are also changing (Goetting, 1988b).

For example, evidence has suggested that whilst female-perpetrated spousal homicides have decreased, homicides committed by women against friends, acquaintances and strangers have increased (Brownstein et al., 1994; Mouzos, 2001; Spunt et al., 1996). Such findings have led to what some argue to be the 'resurrection' of the violent female offender. For Heidensohn (1996), the media hype which surrounds female violent crime amounts to that of a 'moral panic'. Certainly, data from the UK do not indicate that female violence, nor female-perpetrated homicide, is on the increase (Stanko et al., 1998). Furthermore, analysis of the HI for the period 1990–2000 does not show any consistent changes in the victimisation patterns of female homicide offenders (with relational categories of partner and child remaining the most dominant victims). Furthermore, evidence from the US also contradicts the image of rising female violence – as Mann states, 'Little support was found in this study for the notion that women are becoming more violent, at least as measured by the commission of homicide' (1996: 176).

Study Task 7.2

Campbell (1993), in her text *Out of Control*, explores the different ways in which men and women understand aggression and violence. She notes a clear distinction in the ways in which men and women view their own violence; women, she claims, perceive outbursts of anger and displays of aggression as a 'loss of control'. Men, on the other hand, view their acts of aggression as a means of 'gaining control'. 'Both sexes see an intimate connection between aggression and control, but for women aggression is the *failure* of self-control, while for men it is the *imposing* of control over others' (1993: 1). Campbell goes on to equate female aggression or violence with expressive theories of violence and males with instrumental theories – in this latter case, violence is seen to serve some larger purpose for the men involved – that is, control of another person's behaviour, or a situation. Consider Campbell's research findings and assertions and to what extent this may explain the forms of female-perpetrated homicide discussed in this chapter.

Chapter Summary and Conclusions

This chapter has focused upon one of the most significant (in volume at least) forms of female-perpetrated homicide; intimate partner homicide. Although the heterogeneous nature of female homicide has been stressed, it is clear that a number of important themes appear to be interwoven in many of the scenarios outlined. Domestic violence, marital discord, childhood experience of trauma, inadequate social and legal support networks and resources, poverty and unemployment, and, often, sheer desperation feature prominently in much of the theoretical and analytical discourse concerning female killings. The limitations of male-centred criminological theorising has also been illustrated, along with the general paucity of research – both empirical and theoretical – that focuses upon female homicide. Whilst female-perpetrated intimate partner homicide has received more attention than most forms of female-perpetrated homicide, criminology has not yet adequately tackled the issue of female violence (lethal or otherwise). Women who commit extreme acts of violence in the absence of any evidence of having suffered domestic violence or abuse are seen as 'abnormal' or 'evil' – neither of which are very helpful terms. Being female and being violent are viewed as an unnatural allegiance as compared to masculinity and violence. As Heidensohn puts it, 'it is striking that we do not have notions of "normal" uses of force and violence by women and girls' (2000: 20). The small amount of research that has been conducted regarding the use of violence by girl gang members (such as Campbell, 1991; Artz, 1998; and Miller, 2001) is an important step in the right direction. Interestingly, these accounts suggest that status and reputation can be as important for females as for males. However, whether it is correct to conceptualise female violence as simply more akin to male violence is questionable (see Miller, 2001). Rather, more critical explorations (such as the work of Morrisey, 2003) of the various ways in which female killers are depicted as operating without agency and simply vilified or victimised point to a continued failure to accept that womanhood and violence can, and do (sometimes) go hand in hand. Finally, the notion that female violence has increased or significantly changed in recent years has been explored, where it was found that there is no clear evidence to support such claims. Just as in the past, women still perpetrate a very small proportion of homicide, and when they do kill, their partners or children are the most likely victims. In conclusion, it seems likely that as research on female-perpetrated homicide continues to grow, and the many aspects and issues of the topic are eventually explored and uncovered, studies will focus on different contexts of female killings and thus 'new' and 'contradictory' findings are highly probable. Whilst some (small but important) steps have been taken in the last 20 years to unravel more carefully female violence, future research needs to develop a more finely-tuned gendered approach to women's violence which can take into account the differential experience of women as compared to men, and the specific influence of the economic, political and social inequalities they face. Only then may we begin to more adequately explain those relatively rare, yet none the less tragic, killings perpetrated by women.

Review Questions

- In what ways are men's violence and possessiveness linked to instances of intimate partner homicide perpetrated by both men and women? Is it simply a matter of chance which of the intimate partners is killed in circumstances where the relationship is marred by domestic violence?
- Early theories of female violence generally located the cause of their violence within a framework of biology. In what ways have theories developed in the last 20 years problematised this view?
- Consider the strengths and weaknesses of the battered woman syndrome as an explanation of female-perpetrated intimate homicide.

Further Reading

For a more in-depth look at women and crime (as both offenders and victims), which discusses the important themes regarding the explanations and understanding of female criminality (from traditional theories to those of feminism), see Frances Hiedensohn's *Women and Crime* (1996: Macmillan Press). For a very useful overview of explanations of female offending and the 'gender gap', see Steffensmeier and Allen's 'Gender and Crime: Toward a Gendered Theory of Female Offending' (*Annual Review of Sociology*, 22, pp. 459–87). For a detailed exploration of feminist thought and criminology, also see Daly and Chesney-Lind (1988) 'Feminism and Criminology', (*Justice Quarterly*, 5/4, pp. 497–538). An excellent text which specifically addresses female-perpetrated killings through a feminist discourse (and the theory of gender equality, or lack of) is Jensen's *Why Women Kill* (2001: Lynne Reiner Publishers), providing both empirical and theoretical analysis regarding a number of different forms of female homicide. Also relevant is Busch's *Finding Their Voices: When Battered Women Kill* (1999: Kroshka Books), which provides a very good critical analysis of the application of battered woman syndrome to the explanation of female-perpetrated partner killings and Ogle and Jacob's *Self-Defense and Battered Women who Kill* (2002: Praeger). Belinda Morrissey's *When Women Kill* (2003: Routledge) is an excellent (although heavy-going in places) text in that it is one of the few that challenges the notion that women kill without a sense of agency. However, that most relevant to the UK experience (and thus highly recommended) is Chan's *Women, Murder and Justice* (2001: Palgrave). Chan looks at cases of female-perpetrated intimate partner homicide in the UK, the circumstances under which they kill and their treatment by the Criminal Justice System. Furthermore, Mann's *When Women Kill* (1996: State University of New York Press) is a good generic text covering many aspects of female homicide.

Useful Internet Sites

The Home Office website contains many publications, statistics, and research findings regarding women and crime, for example, regarding domestic violence against women; see the following link www.homeoffice.gov.uk/rds/violencewomen.html. Also www.domesticviolencedata.org is a domestic violence data source index with some useful links. In addition, Justice for Women www.jfw.org.uk (an organisation that campaigns for and supports women who fight back and kill their male partners) contains useful discussions of the battered wife syndrome, the law of provocation and contains case studies. Also specifically regarding domestic violence against men, www.dvmen.org provides a number of links to when women kill, spousal abuse and family violence perpetrated by women. In addition, www.aic.gov.au/publications/proceedings/16/Polk.pdf is a link to Polk's (1991), 'Homicide: Women as Offenders', in P.W. Easteal and S. McKillop (eds), *Women and the Law*, proceedings of the Women and the Law conference, Sydney, 24–6 September 1991. These conference papers include a number of articles regarding women as offenders, which are useful.

Notes

1 As outlined in Chapter 6, 'intimate partner' refers to a current or former spouse, lover, or co-habitant.

2 It is worth noting, however, that these prosecutions/convictions occurred during 1998–99, and no female defendants were convicted or prosecuted at all during 1996–97 in Northern Ireland.

3 It has not been possible to disaggregate the data for Northern Ireland to obtain this level of detail.

4 See also Stanko et al., 1998 for virtually identical figures for the period 1986–96.

5 Although figures for Scotland between 1991–2000 indicate that 45 per cent of all homicides involved a sharp weapon, and of those killings in which men were victims, 51 per cent involved a sharp instrument (Scottish Executive, 2001).

6 Unfortunately, the location of the homicidal encounter is not recorded in the HI.

7 Goetting (1987), however, did find a clear increase during the months of June, July and December, January and February – which she notes to be the summer and winter holiday periods.

8 Whilst there is undoubtedly a link between domestic violence and domestic homicide, the actual relationship is complex and, as we shall discover in Chapter 11, domestic violence is much more widespread than domestic homicide, making it difficult to determine those women, from the large numbers who suffer domestic violence, who might be seriously 'at risk' of homicide or who might be likely to kill their abusers.

9 As part of her doctoral research, the author accessed and analysed 97 covering reports from police murder investigation files (see Note 2, Chapter 1). Of these, eight cases involved a woman killing a man (seven cases being intimate partner homicide). This small sample, which is neither exhaustive nor fully reflects the diversity of scenarios of female-perpetrated homicide, provides a useful source when combined with case studies compiled by authors from other regions of the world (from similar sources, such as police murder files or prosecutor files).

8 The Killing of Children and Infants

This chapter considers children and infants as homicide victims. The focus will essentially be upon the killing of children in the context of the family unit or domestic setting, though some attention will be paid to stranger killings when discussing males as offenders. In the context of this chapter, a child is taken to be an individual aged between 0–16 years.[1] The first section provides a brief overview of the nature of child homicide in terms of the characteristics of offenders and victims and the events themselves. The second section considers female-perpetrated child homicide, which essentially involves the natural or biological mother (maternal filicide). Here, a distinction tends to be drawn between forms of child killing in terms of the age of the child, whether this be in the first 24 hours of the baby's life (neonaticide), or the first 12 months of life (generally referred to as infanticide). At the same time, a distinction is also emphasised regarding those children killed in the context of fatal abuse, and those who die as a result of an unwanted pregnancy or illegitimate status. The third section of the chapter focuses upon male perpetrators, drawing a distinction between those cases where men kill their own children, or children for whom they care (paternal filicide), and those occasions when men kill children outside the family unit (for example, stranger killings). Finally, we will evaluate some of the most dominant explanations for infant and child homicide, paying particular attention to the different ways in which male and female offenders have been regarded.

The Killing of Children and Infants: An Overview

This section presents a general overview of the extent, nature and circumstances of child and infant homicide.

The Extent of Child and Infant Homicide

The killing of children (through a culmination of abuse, a single violent incident, or through deliberate neglect) is perhaps the most disturbing of all homicides (Unnithan, 1997) and generally provokes considerable attention and outrage (Adler and Polk, 2001; Strang, 1996; Mouzos, 2000). In England and Wales, children (that is, those aged 16 years and below) comprise 14 per cent of homicide victims (HI, 1995–2001).

Children are most at risk from homicide in their earliest years of life. Of the 781 children killed between 1995 and 2001, over 36 per cent (285) were less than a year old (HI, 1995–2001). In fact, as a single (one year) age group, infants of less than 12 months old are the most vulnerable group to homicide in England and Wales. That is (as measured by 100,000 population), children under one year are around four times more likely to fall victim to homicide than any other age group (Brookman, 2000b; Brookman and Maguire, 2003; Richards, 1999), and this has been the case for at least the last couple of decades (Browne and Lynch, 1995; Marks and Kumar, 1993). The greater risk of homicide, not only in the first year of life, but also the first day of life, is a finding supported by international literature from Australia (Mouzos, 2000; Strang, 1996), Canada (Silverman and Kennedy, 1988, 1993) and the US (Crimmins et al., 1997; Mann, 1996; Crittendon and Craig, 1990).

Victim and Offender Characteristics

Boys are more likely than girls to fall victim to child homicide. For example, between 1995–2001, 60 per cent of child homicide victims were male and 40 per cent female. For infants aged less than one year, the corresponding proportions are 59 per cent and 41 per cent.

A startling feature of child homicide is that victims are most likely to be killed by their own parents, a finding more pronounced during the first few years of life. Analysis of the Homicide Index (hereafter HI) (1995–2001) reveals that sons and daughters (aged 0–16 years) account for 50 per cent of the child victims of homicide (rising to 60 per cent for cases involving step-children). However, the relationship category of child–parent increases to almost 84 per cent where female offenders are concerned, and decreases to 30 per cent for male-perpetrated child killings. In other words, when a child aged between 0–16 years is killed by a female, it is highly likely that it is the woman's own child and very rarely the case that the child is a stranger (less than 3 per cent of female-perpetrated child homicides involved a child unknown to the woman during 1995–2001). In contrast, 8 per cent of children killed during this same time period by a male were classified as strangers. In Scotland, figures are higher, indicating that over the last 10 years, 74 per cent of victims under the age of 16 were killed by one of their parents (Scottish Executive, 2001).[2] Overall, very few children are killed by strangers; there were only eight child victims killed by a stranger in 2001/02 (Cotton, 2003: 3). Finally, around 6 per cent of child victims of homicide are killed by other children – 48 cases between 1995 and 2001 in England and Wales (we will discuss homicides amongst children in the third section of the chapter).

The killing of children is the only category of homicide in which female rates of offending begin to approximate those of males – particularly where infants are concerned. Analysis of the HI (1995–2001) reveals that whilst males still significantly outnumber females as offenders, the female share of child homicide is significantly larger than her overall involvement in homicide. Specifically, 71 per cent of child homicides were committed by males and 29 per cent by females. Yet, in terms of all homicides, females comprise just 11 per cent of offenders. The involvement of females increases as the age of the child decreases. Hence, for babies less than a year old, females comprise 40 per cent of killers and males 60 per cent, whereas for children aged between 14 and 16 years, males comprise over 90 per cent of offenders.

Evidence from other studies is somewhat conflicting. For example, Wilczynski and Morris (1993) found that of the 395 parents suspected of child homicides over the period 1982–89, 44 per cent were mothers – although this figure increased to 47 per cent where the victim was under the age of one (Wilczynski and Morris, 1993). Some studies have found that women are the predominant killers (for example, d'Orban, 1979; Wilczynski, 1997a, 1997b), especially with regards to younger victims. Kunz and Bahr (1996) analysed all cases of parental homicide (against victims under the age of 18) between 1976–85, as recorded by the US Federal Bureau of Investigation's (FBI's) Uniform Crime Reports. They found that female parents accounted for 52.5 per cent of offenders, although among those children killed in the first week of life, 90.5 per cent of offenders were women (Kunz and Bahr, 1996). Despite these interesting findings, many argue that the issue of female violence and homicide against their children has been 'virtually ignored' (Adler and Polk, 2001: 4)

Characteristics of the Homicide Event

Because of the particular vulnerability of children and their much smaller physical stature and fragility, the level of force required to kill a child is minimal. It is, therefore, not surprising to find that child homicide is not frequently accomplished using weapons such as knives or firearms, but more often with the offender's own hands or feet. The age of the child has a bearing upon the level of force needed to fatally injure. Generally, research indicates that whilst the youngest victims (that is, newborn babies and infants) are more likely to be suffocated, shaken or drowned, older victims tend to be beaten to death and their killings more likely to involve weapons rather than hands and feet (Crimmins et al., 1997; Silverman and Kennedy, 1993, 1988; Smithey, 1998; Strang, 1996). Mackay's (1993) UK study of a sample of (mainly infant) child homicide cases between 1982–85 (the majority of which were committed by mothers) found that suffocation (27.7 per cent), battering (23.4 per cent) and strangulation (19.1 per cent) were the most frequently used methods of killing. A further 8.5 per cent of victims were shaken to death, and methods of drowning, neglect and stabbing each accounted for 6.4 per cent of deaths (Mackay, 1993). The HI (1995–2001) similarly indicates that the under-ones are particularly vulnerable to shaking (40 per cent) and suffocation (17 per cent).

A further 6 per cent suffered negligence or neglect, and 3 per cent were hit or kicked. However, if we remove babies less than one year from the analysis, other more violent means of death become evident. For example, 17 per cent of children aged 1–16 years were killed with a sharp instrument, 10 per cent were strangled, 9 per cent were hit or kicked, 12 per cent died due to arson and less than 5 per cent were suffocated.

The motive involved in child killing, when it is apparent, can appear very trivial. For example, Brewster et al. (1998) found that 58 per cent of those who had murdered their child stated that the child's crying had preceded the homicide (Mouzos, 2000: 137). Wilkey et al. (1982) identified seven forms of child homicide including neonaticide, infanticide, euthanasia (the parental killing of an abnormal or terminally ill child), physical abuse (non-accidental injury assaults), neglect, those murders in which the parent commits suicide afterwards, and finally those murders which occur in the context of a sexual assault (Mouzos, 2000).

It is generally accepted that there are contextual and qualitative differences between homicides involving very young children and those involving older children. For example, the gender, age and marital status of the offender appear to vary with the age of the child. In addition, victims who are older are more likely to die as a result of fatal abuse and/or as an attempt to discipline the child, whereas younger victims are more likely to be killed as a result of an unknown, unwanted or illegitimate pregnancy. Furthermore, as already indicated, as the child's age increases, so does the level of violence inflicted. It is perhaps because of these factors that cases of filicide (the killing of children) are differentiated according to the age of the victim. 'Neonaticide' is a term used to refer to the killing of a child within the first 24 hours of its life (Marks, 1996). The term 'infanticide' is often used in the international literature to describe the killing of children less than a year old, with some researchers reserving this term for female killers only. However, in England and Wales, infanticide is a legal term which is used more strictly to describe instances in which mothers kill their children, whilst in a disturbed state of mind (Adler and Polk, 2001; Brookman and Maguire, 2003). In order to avoid confusion, 'infant homicide' shall be used to refer to those victims less than a year old, whilst the terms 'infanticide' and 'neonaticide' shall be employed in their more specific contexts.

In the following section we consider cases of child homicide perpetrated by females, followed in the next section by a consideration of male-perpetrated child homicide. Examples of particular forms of child and infant homicide will be provided by drawing upon case studies from the UK and other regions of the world.[3]

Female-perpetrated Child Homicide

As noted earlier, when women kill children it is generally the case that it is their own (biological or adopted) child. It is extremely rare for a woman to kill a child with whom she has no maternal bond. In this section we will focus exclusively upon maternal filicide due to its significance.

d'Orban (1979, 1990) developed Scott's (1973) classification of child homicide to form five groups of maternal filicide. These were neonaticides, battering mothers, retaliating mothers (whose anger against a spouse is displaced and projected onto the child), those who killed unwanted children, and mercy killings (which is altruistic in nature, and similar to Wilkey et al.'s (1982) category of euthanasia) (d'Orban, 1979, 1990). However, these categories are neither exhaustive nor mutually exclusive – for example, it is unclear how different the neonaticide cases are from those who killed their unwanted children (unless this is simply a technical issue of timing). Similarly, it may be difficult to distinguish those cases involving 'battering mothers' and 'retaliating mothers'. Nevertheless, there are undoubtedly distinct types of maternal filicide, and those that seem to recur in the research literature include:

- babies killed at birth (or very soon after) which are usually a result of unknown, unwanted or illegitimate pregnancies (for example, neonaticides);
- those victims murdered as a result of (prolonged) fatal child abuse and/or neglect; or children killed as a result of a fatal injury from one violent incident; and
- those killings in which the mother is convicted of infanticide.

As such, these are the scenarios which will be presented in the next section.

Neonaticide

As previously indicated, neonaticide is a term used to refer to the killing of a child within the first 24 hours of its life. Between 1995–99, babies less than a day old accounted for 17 per cent of infant homicides, with 27 victims over this period (Brookman and Maguire, 2003). Marks (1996), however, suggests a higher figure of around 20–25 per cent.

Neonaticide is almost exclusively perpetrated by the baby's mother, described by Wilczynski as 'young, single, working class girls' (1997b: 243). d'Orban suggest that women who commit neonaticide:

> [D]o not usually suffer from psychiatric disorder. They are significantly younger than other filicides and are single or separated women who conceal illegitimate pregnancy. They are often very passive personalities who dissociate from the pregnancy and do not seek antenatal care or medical help at the time of the birth. They kill the child immediately after birth, usually without any obvious planning or premeditation. (1990: 67)

The immaturity of neonaticidal mothers is an observation that is frequently made. For example, findings from the HI between the period of 1995–99 indicate that the average age of offenders was 22 (as opposed to 27 for those who killed children over the age of 24 hours, but less than one year old) (Brookman and Maguire, 2003). Most often the pregnancy is unknown or unplanned, and the child illegitimate. As a result, 'The motivation for such a killing stems from concealed pregnancy, which if it were to become known, could result in the rejection and ostracism by significant others, such as parents, husbands, or boyfriends' (Mouzos, 2000: 138). It has been suggested that as there is often a total denial of the pregnancy, these women are completely unprepared for the birth. The killing is rarely planned or premeditated, and the offence is not usually elaborately concealed (Adler and Polk, 2001; Brookman and Maguire, 2003; Marks, 1996). Crittenden and Craig (1990) found that the majority (27 per cent) of neonates had been suffocated, 22 per cent had been drowned, and 14 per cent died from exposure. Thus, the violence used could be considered passive as opposed active, in that the neonate was 'discarded' or neglected, as opposed to 'punished' or abused (Marks and Kumar, 1993). The case of Alice is an example of such 'inactive' killing:

Alice

Alice (17 years of age, unmarried) gave birth in the toilet of the family home. Her parents were home at the time. She placed the body in a plastic bag and left it in the laundry. Her mother found the bag the next morning. Her family had thought she had put on a bit of weight, but her sister with whom she shared a bedroom noted that 'At no time did I realise Alice might be pregnant'. Alice did not see a doctor during or after the pregnancy. Sex education had not been discussed in the family. Alice stated to police, 'I was in bed and I started getting pains in the stomach ... the pains got really bad and I went back to the toilet. I got into the room and started to pull down my pants and the baby came ... I didn't know I was pregnant. I was scared ... I thought about being pregnant a couple of times but I didn't think I was ... I effectively closed my mind. I didn't want to know. I was hoping it would go away.' Alice thought that her partner would leave her and that the family would be ashamed. She was also scared of her father's physical abuse in disciplining her. (Adapted from Adler and Polk, 2001: 34)

This example also shows us that it can be difficult in such circumstances to identify whether the child was born alive, died from complications during birth, or was actually prevented from living. However, in some cases this can be determined (as in case study 5221), and in others, the violence is clearly not passive (as in case study 25);

Case Study 5221

The 24-year-old mother claimed that she did not know that she was 'that pregnant' when, as she used the commode, the baby came out head first into the toilet. Neither the offender, her mother, nor her brother would remove the newborn, stating that they were 'afraid to pick up the baby'. The female infant was apparently in the commode for 15 to 20 minutes and was still breathing when the police arrived. She died on the way to the hospital. The police report indicated that the offender attempted to flush the baby down the toilet. The mother, who was a known prostitute with a number of misdemeanour arrests, was sentenced to a six-month jail term and five years probation for the infanticide. (Reproduced from Mann, 1996: 72)

Case Study 25

The offender, who did not want anyone to know that she was pregnant, gave birth and then allegedly cut up the baby with a sharp instrument. The offender then buried the dismembered baby and tried to conceal the body with leaves. A small child subsequently discovered part of the victim's leg, which had been unearthed by neighbourhood dogs. It is alleged that the baby was alive for several minutes and died from multiple injuries. (Reproduced from Mouzos, 2000: 130)

The problem of the 'dark figure' of child homicide[4] is particularly acute in the case of neonaticide. There is greater ease in escaping detection when often the only person to be aware of the pregnancy is the mother – who is herself in denial. Hence, 'should the mother decide either to end the neonate's life or to dispose of a body which she believes to be dead, there would be no observers or official record of the death' (Crittenden and Craig, 1990: 204).

Fatal Child Abuse

Crittenden and Craig point out that 'once children have survived the neonatal period, the factors affecting risk for being killed may change; deaths in early childhood seem more closely related in causation to child abuse and neglect' (1990: 204). Previous research overwhelmingly indicates that in many cases of child homicide there is evidence of violence and abuse inflicted on the child prior to the homicide event (Adler and Polk, 2001; Mouzos, 2000). One to two children are known to die as a result of abuse or neglect in the UK each week, although the true number is likely to be significantly higher as many such deaths still go unreported, uninvestigated and unnoticed (NSPCC, 2001: 5). A number of writers assert that 'child homicide is an extreme phenomenon along a continuum of child abuse' (Unnithan, 1997: 315). For example, Wilczynski (1997a) found that 50 per cent of filicide cases in the UK, between 1989–93, showed a history of prior abuse and injuries. Often in such cases of fatal abuse, the injuries are frequent and extremely severe. As d'Orban found:

> The victims of battering mothers all died as a result of severe physical assault usually from blows or by being thrown against a wall or to the ground. The cause of death was usually intra-abdominal injury, skull fracture or intracranial haemorrhage. (1979: 565)

Furthermore, many victims also suffer neglect, as the following case demonstrates:

Case Study 4216
Harriet, a housewife age 29, was arrested along with her husband and their family doctor for the murder of her three-year-old daughter. Harriet, who birthed eight children, had been tried previously for the murder of her eight-month-old, who choked to death from having been force-fed. There was a recorded history of abuse of all of her children, and Harriet was described as cold and indifferent toward them. According to one social worker, this was a typical case of 'battered child syndrome'. The victim suffered from neglect, pneumonia, emphysema, scars, cuts, bruises, burns and fractures. Harriet claimed her innocence and that the child had just 'stopped breathing'. Although she pleaded 'not guilty', Harriet received 15 years in prison for involuntary manslaughter. Her husband, who stated that he was afraid of Harriet, was sentenced to five years probation for child endangerment. Their

*doctor, who had covered up the abuse and treated the victim both at home and in his office
without reporting the incidents, was also tried for involuntary manslaughter and given two
years probation.* (Adapted from Mann, 1996: 76)

However, not all fatal child abuse victims are found to have experienced a history
of prior violence (see Gelles, 1991).[5] Instead, the death may result from a single
incident of frustration and aggression, in which the offender lashes out in anger or
intolerance. Often these mothers are unprepared for their mothering role, and lacking in adequate parental skills. To a certain extent, such cases appear to bear more
similarity to those of neonaticide than those children who are killed as a result of
extreme child abuse, as the following case (in which the child was unexpected)
clearly illustrates:

Jane
*The pregnancy of Jane (19 years) had not been medically identified until 48 hours before
she gave birth. She went into sudden labour after she discovered she was pregnant. Laurie
was born prematurely and was kept in hospital for six weeks. He had only been home for
10 days when he was killed. Jane gave different explanations for Laurie's injuries, claiming that he had fallen off a bed, and later that he had accidentally bumped into a coffee
table. However, the Coroner found that the injuries sustained by Laurie would have
required the application of considerable force, and it was unlikely they were a result of accidental mismanagement ... [although] the Coroner noted that there were few signs that he
had been abused or roughly handled prior to the events that led to his death. Jane
explained that she was angry and upset that she had been left alone, and expressed concern that her de facto husband might not be returning. A psychiatric report noted that the
lack of ante-natal care and concluded: '[Laurie's] death resulted from an attack by a
mother who was deeply depressed as a result of the child's birth, severely lacking in coping
strategies, totally unprepared for a mothering role and totally unable to tolerate a crying
infant ...'* (Adapted from Adler and Polk, 2001: 53)

Infanticide
The killing of children under the age of 12 months is often referred to as 'infanticide', regardless of whether the infant was killed by its mother or father. However,
as noted earlier, this is not strictly accurate. In England and Wales, infanticide is a
legal term (enshrined in legislation under the Infanticide Act (1938, s1)) encompassing those homicides in which the mental state of the mother is of implicit
importance (refer to Chapter 1 for a full discussion of the Infanticide Act). Motz
describes infanticide as:

> ... a tragic act of violence which can result from a tremendous fear of social stigma,
> feelings of total helplessness in relation to an unplanned baby, or a range of complex
> psychological factors, which result in an almost psychotic panic, in which killing
> seems the only solution. (2001: 131–2)

However, infanticidal acts appear to lack consistency, although different features
may be linked to the type of 'imbalance' the mother experiences (the most

common being post-partum depression and post-partum psychosis) (Maier-Katkin and Ogle, 1993; Motz, 2001). Motz (2001) discusses altruistic and delusional motivations found in infanticide cases. Cases of post-partum depression often appear altruistic in nature, whereby the motivation to kill is to relieve the (real, or imagined) suffering of the child. In some cases the homicide may also be followed by the suicide of the female perpetrator.[6] The dynamic involvement of psycho-social stressors in such depression has also been noted (Motz, 2001). As Adler and Polk note:

> The mother finds her life so unbearable that she cannot go on living and cannot bear to leave her children behind, believing that no one could look after them as well. At the same time there is indication in some cases about the well-being of the child specifically and that these concerns form part of her own unhappiness. (2001: 48)

The altruistic nature of the following case is quite clear, although the disturbance of mind from the effects of childbirth more questionable:

Case F

The defendant asphyxiated her eight-month-old child, who was severely handicapped. On the day of the offence a doctor had explained that the child's prognosis was very poor. Shortly after this the defendant told her husband that she intended to kill the child, but he did not take her seriously. Within an hour she had committed the offence and fully admitted what she had done ... The Director of Public Prosecutions was concerned that if the balance of her mind was disturbed, then this resulted not from childbirth but from her discovery of the child's prognosis. Accordingly, the DPP requested a supplementary report which stated:

'... The balance of her mind was disturbed by reason of her not having fully recovered from the effects of giving birth to this child with its attendant severe handicaps. The new pregnancy (the defendant was pregnant at the time of the offence) would in addition cause hormonal and emotional upsets which would further disturb the balance of her mind ... '

As a result of this report the defendant was charged with infanticide to which she pleaded guilty, receiving an order for two years' probation. (Adapted from Mackay, 1993: 26)

In cases of post-partum psychosis, the female may experience delusions or hear voices which direct her to kill her child (often either to ensure the infant's 'salvation', or because the infant becomes an imagined enemy which must be destroyed). Mouzos' 1999a has referred to cases of 'exorcism' to describe some such killings. As discussed in Chapter 4, drawing associations between mental disorder (of any form) and violent behaviour is a complex business. That said, there would certainly appear to be some occasions when women kill their babies where they have indeed suffered from some psychological imbalance (see Adler and Polk's, 2001 discussion of 'extreme psychiatric disturbance').

Other themes which have been identified (of infanticide and filicide generally) include marital violence or instability and separation, and the experience of childhood abuse and trauma by female offenders (Adler and Polk, 2001; Motz, 2001; Sinclair and Bullock, 2002). Many of the themes discussed are illustrated in the case that follows:

Dawn

Dawn was 28 years old when she was admitted to a regional secure unit following her conviction for infanticide of her 11-month-old son, Gabriel. He had been taken from her care almost from the moment of his birth, following Dawn's frequent admission to psychiatric hospital … Dawn had a long history of psychiatric admissions for severe depression and suicide attempts, but had not previously been charged with a violent offence. She had suffocated and strangled Gabriel after making a special request to spend the night with him at his foster parent's, after a contact visit which was supposed to have lasted only three hours. She had called the police on the evening of the offence and informed them of her intention to kill Gabriel, saying that she felt certain she would go through with it unless they could find her, but she had telephoned from a pay phone, without leaving her name or any other information about her whereabouts. Dawn had been in numerous children's homes throughout her childhood and had vivid memories of waiting anxiously for her mother to visit and reclaim her. In two of these children's homes she had been sexually abused by other residents, and in one of these homes a member of staff had also abused her. Dawn's estranged husband, Gabriel's father, had recently petitioned Dawn for a divorce. Dawn described herself as having been 'devastated' and had been furious with him; she reported that the overwhelming sense of rejection and abandonment made her feel that she would lose her mind. She saw Gabriel as intricately connected to his father, and to herself, and became convinced that he should not be allowed to live. She felt that her own life had been destroyed by her husband leaving her, Gabriel being taken into care, and, finally, being asked to give her husband a divorce. (Adapted from Motz, 2001: 117–18)

The various categories of maternal filicide discussed above, whilst clearly exhibiting distinctions, also overlap in certain ways, such that the categorisations are neither neat nor perfect. For example, not all cases in which women kill their children aged less than one year are ultimately defined as infanticide (the important element here being the state of mind of the offender). In England and Wales between 1995–2001, of all females accused of killing their infant child only 22 per cent were convicted of infanticide. Second, cases of neonaticide may be identified as (and thus subsumed under) infanticide, or alternatively, simply recorded as infant homicide in general. Furthermore, an infanticidal mother may murder the child through inactive neglect, inflict prolonged (and fatal) abuse on her child, or kill the victim as a result of a single violent incident. Thus it is important to bear these complexities in mind.[7]

Study Task 8.1

Having read the case studies of neonaticde, fatal child abuse and infanticide, what common and distinct themes can you identify as leading up to these homicides by women?

Male-perpetrated Child Homicide

In this part of the chapter we will consider two broad categories of male-perpetrated child homicide: those where the perpetrator is the father or stepfather (paternal filicides), and those where the male is not related to the child in any way (that is, stranger killings or non-filicides). Over half (52 per cent) of male-perpetrated child homicide in England and Wales involves either a father (39 per cent) or step-father (13 per cent), making this an important category to focus upon (HI, 1995–2001). The stranger category is much lower at 8 per cent and differs in significant ways from those that occur within family relationships. It is also worth noting that 10 per cent of males who killed a child were themselves aged 16 years or less (we briefly discuss homicide amongst children toward the end of this section).

Paternal Filicide

Adler and Polk (2001) have identified two broad categories of paternal filicide – fatal assaults (comprising 55 per cent of cases) and filicide-suicide (where the father attempts or succeeds to take his own life as well as that of his child). Though not necessarily directly comparable, 59 per cent of paternal filicides in England and Wales (between 1995 and 2001) have been defined as 'child abuse' (158 cases), and in a further 20 per cent of cases of paternal filicide (55 cases) the suspect committed suicide (it has not been possible to determine how many other fathers attempted suicide). Only one case of child abuse involved the offender committing suicide. In summary, there is evidence of two distinct categories that are very similar (if not identical) to those discussed by Adler and Polk. We shall consider each of these 'scenarios' in turn.

Child Abuse/Fatal Assaults

Cases of fatal child abuse or fatal assaults perpetrated by fathers or stepfathers often occur in the context of the parent disciplining the child, though the means used often involve excessive violence and there is sometimes evidence of prior abuse. Ewing (1997: 97) refers to these events as 'corporal punishment run amok', whilst Adler and Polk point out that these cases are characterised by 'the apparent intent to punish or discipline, rather than to kill the child' (2001: 68). The following case is a classic example of this form of child abuse:

Austin was sitting on the floor, eating a packet of chips, and he started crying. I picked him up and whacked him on the bum three or four times with an open hand. I put him down and he was still crying. I picked him up and shook him [to] shut him up ... I didn't lose my cool, I was just annoyed ... I was getting annoyed because I couldn't hear the video. He was getting on my nerves. (Adler and Polk, 2001: 720)

Adler and Polk found several varieties of this form of homicide, some that appeared to be particularly related to asserting or maintaining authority and power over the child and others where the accounts of the perpetrators emphasised an emotional loss of control. The extent to which these killings are actually similar or not is difficult to decipher, bearing in mind that different men will recount their offences in different ways with different sorts of emphases depending upon how they wish to portray themselves and the nature of the lethal act.

Filicide-Suicide

In stark contrast to cases of fatal child abuse are those cases in which the death of the child (or children) is clearly intended and where there seems to be some evidence that the offender is depressed or suffering psychiatric disturbance. Adler and Polk (2001) observed a number of cases of filicide-suicide (or attempted suicide) in their study. A particular feature that dominated many of these homicides was the break-down of the marital relationship. In some cases there were ongoing custody battles for children and the ultimate killings would appear to be linked to the male's perceived failure to resolve these issues and general feelings of 'hopelessness', 'helplessness', 'powerlessness' and 'uselessness' (2001: 80). The following case is such an example;

[Case Nos. 88–0541/2]
Ted was 10 years old and his sister Eleanor was 13 years old when their father, Matthew (41 years), killed them. Matthew and his wife Mona were in the process of divorce, including ongoing custody battles. Having custody of the children for the previous 11 months, Mathew killed them the day after the court gave Mona sole custody. After killing the children and writing a suicide note, he took some medication, cut his wrist and attempted to electrocute himself: he survived. He admitted his action to the police saying, 'I killed my children because we have been living in hell, the situation is horrendous and we've been tormented'. (Adler and Polk, 2001: 78–9)

Adler and Polk have also identified situations in which the mother was the ultimate object of the father's violence. These are scenarios in which there had been a history of jealousy and violence against the mother and where violence against children was used as a means of controlling the behaviour of the mother. Adler and Polk (2001: 81) refer to these homicides as 'mother as object, child as pawn'.

In addition, there are some occasions where men kill their whole family and themselves in what could be described as a mass killing or family annihilation. Some researchers have argued that family annihilation is probably the most common form of multiple murder (Gresswell and Hollin, 1994; see Chapter 9). Turning to the UK, the case of the Mochri family represents a classic example of a father not only killing all of his children, but also his wife and himself. In 2000, Robert Mochri battered to death his wife and four children (aged between 10 and 18) at the family home in Barry, South Wales before hanging himself. There was no evidence of any prior violence by Mochri toward any of his family members. Investigations later revealed that Robert Mochri was in severe debt and suffering from depression and suicidal tendencies. It is believed that, at the time of the killings, Mochri was deluded and believed that there was no alternative to resolving his problems other than killing himself and taking his family with him.

As Adler and Polk point out, we can only speculate about the possible rationales and emotions that lead to such events: 'Is this the ultimate statement of power and control? Are they ultimately not prepared to face the consequences of their actions, or do they think that life would not be worth living without their wife and children?' (2001: 166).

Finally, there are some cases that seem to fall somewhere in between these two broad categories of paternal filicide, as the following case from England illustrates:

[Case Code: B.08/94]
At around midday on a Friday, Davey took a large claw hammer from a drawer in the kitchen and embedded it into his 8-year-old son's head as he lay on the floor crayoning. He repeated this several times. He then turned his attentions to his 10-year-old daughter. He called her downstairs and, as she reached the bottom of the stairs, he attacked her with the claw hammer, again striking several blows to the skull. Both attacks are believed to have resulted in the immediate deaths of the children. Davey went to a friend's house in what appears to be an attempt to summons help. As various neighbours entered the premises and realised the full horror of what had occurred, Davey admitted 'I've killed them'. He subsequently told a member of the ambulance crew, 'The voices told me to do it'. Davey later injured himself deliberately in his cell (a deep laceration to the head), requiring medical treatment. (Brookman, 2000b)

The actual facts of the incident themselves do not necessarily assist in understanding these events. However, when placed in the larger context of the offender's social circumstances and his state of mind, the event becomes somewhat more explicable. In fact, the case was a tragic event 'waiting to happen' and there had been numerous previous incidents of violence that both the school (that the children attended) and Social Services were aware of. Davey was unemployed, a drug user, and had received psychiatric treatment in the past. He had failed to attend follow-up psychiatric appointments, though in the week leading up to the double-homicide he had expressed his desire to see a psychiatrist and had asked his wife to make the arrangements. On the morning of the murders, Davey telephoned his wife at work informing her that their son had been, once again, suspended from school for hitting other pupils and asked her to come home. She felt unable to leave work and told Davey that they would talk about the issues that evening.

This case falls somewhere in between the more usual cases of fatal abuse (where there is not generally any evidence of psychiatric illness, though the perpetrators may have been suffering from some form of depression) and filicide-suicides, where, according to Adler and Polk (2001: 78), there is rarely evidence of previous violence. Furthermore, Davey's self-inflicted injuries, whilst quite severe, were not life-threatening and could not realistically be interpreted as a suicide attempt.

Killing Outside the Family (Non-filicides)

Although much rarer than family-based child killings, the killing of children by men with whom they have no connection is one that causes particular alarm and fear. There were 32 cases of stranger homicides involving a child victim and male adult offender in England and Wales between 1995–2001 (24 male victims and 8 female victims). In addition, there were a further eight cases of child homicide where the perpetrator was himself a child with no apparent prior connection to the victim (bringing the total to 40 cases). We will discuss cases of homicide amongst children later in this section.

Focusing upon the 32 cases, the average age of offenders was 27 years and of victims, 14 years, with the most frequently occurring age being 16 (35 per cent). Around a quarter of these homicides were the result of reckless acts (such as arson or vehicle-related reckless acts) and 16 per cent involved some sort of rage or quarrel. A further 10 per cent involved jealousy or revenge and 3 per cent were the outcome of gang fights or feuds. Twelve per cent were of a sexual nature and involved sexual molestation or a sexual attack (4 cases; 3 male and 1 female victim). In approximately a quarter of cases (22 per cent) no clear motive for the homicide has been established. A quarter of the victims of stranger attacks were stabbed to death; 12 per cent were strangled and a further 12 per cent struck by a motor vehicle. Sixteen per cent were victims of arson attacks and there were two shooting incidents.

Clearly, what the public perhaps fear most in terms of the murder of children, that is, the abduction, sexual assault and murder of a child by a stranger, is very rare. There were only 5 such cases in the 7 year period 1995–2001 in England and Wales, and one of these involved a 15-year-old boy as the offender. In short, there is an average of one per year as compared to around 40 sons or daughters (including stepsons/daughters) per year killed by men. These cases generate huge media and public interest, as, for example, in the case of the abduction and murder of 8-year-old Sarah Payne in July 2000. Moreover, even when the killers are caught, there is often limited understanding of why these killings occurred. In the Sarah Payne case, a 42-year-old labourer (Roy Whiting) was found guilty of her abduction and murder in 2001. He had a previous conviction for the abduction and indecent assault of a 9-year-old girl, for which he received a 4-year prison sentence. The trial judge asserted that Whiting was not insane, but evil. Of course, this does not help to cast any light on the actual causes. More recently, in August 2002, Holly Wells and Jessica Chapman (both aged 10) from Cambridgeshire were abducted and murdered. The school caretaker, Ian Huntley (aged 28) was convicted of their murders and his girlfriend, Maxine Carr, was convicted of conspiring to pervert the course of justice.

Thankfully, such stranger abduction-murders are extremely rare. The majority of cases involve either reckless acts where the death of the victim appears to have been unintended or some combination of confrontations and revenge attacks (some involving gangs) in which male teenagers become embroiled (much like confrontational and revenge homicides amongst male adults considered in Chapter 6). Adler and Polk (2001: 90–100) observe three main categories of non-familial male-perpetrated child homicide, namely honour contests, conflict resolution and killed during the course of other crime, for example, robbery (see also Adler and Polk, 1996). From the available evidence the patterns in England and Wales appear to be similar, with the exception of reckless acts, that predominate.[8]

In addition, there are a small number of cases of male-perpetrated child homicide that fall somewhere in between the two general categories discussed above which involve teenage girls who are intimately linked to the offender. There were six such cases between 1995 and 2001 in England and Wales. All but one of the victims were aged 16 and all six victims were killed by their lover either during an argument or as the result of a reckless act. Adler and Polk (2001) refer to such cases as 'intimate partner homicide'. We will not elaborate on these cases here as they are essentially similar to other cases of male-perpetrated intimate partner homicide discussed at length in Chapter 6.

Study Task 8.2

Make a list of the similarities and differences between male- and female-perpetrated child and infant homicide in England and Wales in terms of:

- the age of the victim;
- the victim–offender relationship; and
- the context of the homicide.

Children who Kill Children

As indicated earlier, there were a total of 48 homicides in England and Wales (1995–2001) involving a child as offender and child as victim, which translates to 6 per cent of the total number of child victims of homicide and less than 1 per cent of the total number of homicides in an average year. All but three of these cases involved a male offender. Regarding the cases involving a female offender, one 12-year-old girl killed a boy aged one and a 10-year-old girl killed a 5-year-old. The 5-year-old was believed to have been pushed to her death by her older friend and the motive and circumstances of the death of the baby are not known. The final case occurred between two 13-year-old girls classified as strangers and involved an argument in which the offender hit and kicked the victim to death.

The cases involving male killers also predominantly involved males as victims (38 boys killed as compared to 7 girls). Three-quarters of the victims were teenagers and of these, 40 per cent were aged 16. Similarly, over 90 per cent of the offenders were in their teenage years and the number of killings increased as the perpetrator's age increased (that is, 13-year-olds accounted for 6 per cent of offenders; 14-year-olds 18 per cent; 15-year-olds 15 per cent and 16-year-olds 36 per cent). In short, homicides amongst children where the perpetrator is male generally involve teenagers as both offenders and victims and are much more likely to involve young boys as victims than young girls. By far the largest proportion involved some sort of confrontation (40 per cent) and a further 9 per cent were gang fights or feuds. There was only one incident that has been classified as of a sexual nature (involving a 15-year-old boy and 14-year-old girl who have been classified as strangers; the girl was strangled to death). Based on the information available, it would appear that many homicides amongst children (particularly teenagers) are essentially not dissimilar to adult masculine scenarios of lethal violence, that is, they revolve around violent interpersonal confrontations or disputes. That said, gang-related homicides are more prevalent amongst teenagers than adults. As illustrated in Chapter 2 (Figure 2.14), gang-related lethal violence comprises just 1 per cent of all homicides in England and Wales. By contrast, 9 per cent of homicides amongst children are related to gang fights or feuds.

More sinister cases, where children seek out and purposely kill other young children, are extremely rare. For example, the case of Jamie Bulger (aged 2), who was abducted and killed by two 10-year-old boys in Liverpool, led to intense international interest. The killers had attempted to abduct another small boy from the same shopping precinct on the same day. It is cases such as this that lead commentators to question the innocence of childhood. As James and Jenks (1996: 32) argue, children (who epitomise morality, purity and innocence) and violent criminality are 'iconologically irreconcilable'. They note that 'the child' has become a symbol not merely of innocence, but of society itself – today's children are tomorrow's adults, they *are* the future. These images of childhood are broken by incidents such as the Bulger case (see also Cavadino, 1996; Ewing, 1990; Heide, 1999; Mones, 1991; and Shumaker and Prinz, 2000 for further information on child-perpetrated homicide).

To recap, when men kill children it is generally the case that the victims are their own sons or daughters (or stepchildren). Within this category there appear to be two broadly distinct forms of paternal filicide; those that involve the excessive disciplining of children leading to their death, and those where the offender kills his child (or whole family) in some sort of desperate act linked to his troubled mental state. A number of previous studies (for example, Adler and Polk, 2001; Mouzos, 2000) have found that the majority of men who kill children within the family setting in the context of child abuse are stepfathers (as opposed to biological fathers). However, the picture in England and Wales shows that biological fathers are more likely to kill their children than de facto fathers. Non-family child homicides generally involve teenage victims and are often the result of reckless acts, lethal confrontations or revenge killings (not dissimilar to adult masculine scenarios of homicide). Very rarely do men seek out and kill children with whom they have no connection in the context of a sexual assault. Finally, killings amongst children very rarely involve female offenders and tend to take place amongst teenage boys who become involved in confrontational assaults, not unlike those that occur amongst male adults, though gang-related disputes are also prevalent.

Explanations of Child Homicide

The killing of children (particularly infants and newborns) has been practised for centuries in various countries and among diverse cultures, with historical studies documenting its occurrence in ancient Rome and Greece. In China, until the nineteenth (some speculate even the twentieth) century, it was common for female infants to be killed at birth, due to the future financial burden parents would face when the child married (Adler and Polk, 2001). Adler and Polk (2001: 32) suggest that the widespread killing of unwanted children in mid-nineteenth century England ultimately led to the implementation of the Infanticide Act 1938.[9] The typical motivations for such killings have been linked to malformation or deformity of the infant, economic distress, illegitimacy and social disgrace (Crimmins et al., 1997). However, as we have seen, there are many different forms of child homicide. It is a diverse offence, with complex interactions between gender, age and social context.

A number of theories have been developed to explain child homicide, which consider both psychological and social aspects of the phenomenon. Psychological approaches focus on the incidence of psychiatric syndromes and the psychosocial factors experienced by those who kill their children. Some criminological theories, such as the 'routine activities' approach, emphasise the shifting patterns of risk as the child grows older and the changing lifestyle and patterns of contact with family members that simultaneously occur. Other criminologists have paid significant attention to gender in their accounts of child homicide. For example, feminist theorists (focusing generally upon female killers) have located child homicide within the wider social context of patriarchal control and domination, arguing that gender inequality and traditional normative expectations and demands of womanhood and motherhood are the primary factors involved in a mother's lethal actions against her child. In the remainder of this chapter we review these various theories.

In her review of the literature, Stroud (1997) identifies two major links between mental disorder and child homicide. First, homicide may be directly associated to the nature and quality of the symptoms of a psychiatric illness. Alternatively, there may be a combination of factors interacting to influence the likelihood of child assault and homicide – such as environmental and psychosocial stressors. Stroud (1997) equates this latter link between mental disorder and child homicide to the circumstances in which children die as a result of fatal abuse. The small number of studies which have investigated mental disorder and female-perpetrated homicide have reported a significant incidence of psychiatric diagnoses (Eronen, 1995; Putkonen et al., 1998, 2001) particularly among those who kill their children (Sinclair and Bullock, 2002; Stroud, 1997; Stroud and Pritchard, 2001). For example, Crimmins et al. (1997) found that 59 per cent of those women convicted of killing a child reported a history of emotional and/or mental health, compared to 37 per cent of women who had killed victims other than children (Crimmins et al., 1997). Research in the UK undertaken by Falkov (1996) also found a clear link between psychiatric disorder and parental filicide. He found that a psychiatric disorder could be identified in one-third of cases examined (Falkov, 1996). d'Orban's (1979) study of female child murderers in the UK found that 43 per cent were diagnosed with a personality disorder, 21 per cent with reactive depression, and 16 per cent were classified as having a psychotic illness.[10] Only 16 per cent (14) of her sample had no psychiatric abnormality (see also d'Orban, 1990). Although various studies find different incidences of particular disorders (compounded by the different diagnostic criteria used in these accounts), the three diagnoses reported by d'Orban appear to generally dominate, and may occur in combination (Stroud, 1997).

There is considerably less literature available regarding the mental state of fathers (natural or de facto) who kill infants or older children. There is, however, evidence that some men who kill their children are suffering mental distress that can manifest itself in depression or rage and the subsequent suicide or attempted suicide of the killer. Strang observes that 'the precipitating factor in these incidents appears frequently to be the desertion of the wife from the marriage, either taking the children with her and thus engendering rage in the offender, or leaving them behind and thus engendering depression' (1996: 6).

Wilczynski (1995) also draws out some important differences between male and female perpetrators of filicide. She notes that general patterns of family violence are much more characteristic of male filicide perpetrators than of female; men who kill their children are more likely to have been violent to the child – and to their partner – before the filicide. Women are more likely to have been diagnosed as suffering from some form of psychiatric disorder. Similarly, Wallace (1986: 115) found that significantly more women than men had undergone professional treatment for mental disorder some time prior to the killing (54 per cent and 20 per cent respectively).[11]

In addition to psychiatric syndromes, studies have also looked at psychosocial factors and sources of stress which are experienced by perpetrators. d'Orban grouped these into three categories:

- 'family stress' (including a family history of mental illness and crime, and parental discord, maltreatment and separation);
- 'social stress' (such as financial and housing problems, marital discord and living alone); and
- 'psychiatric stress' (a history or diagnosis of psychiatric disorder).

'Retaliating' and 'battering' mothers scored highest in these stressors, whilst neonaticide offenders scored the lowest – leading d'Orban (1979: 570) to suggest that these women did not suffer from psychiatric illness, but were 'young women of immature personality'. More recently, Bourget and Bradford (1990) identified similar findings, arguing that exposure to these stressors prior to the homicide was a major factor involved (Stroud and Pritchard, 2001).

There are a number of limitations regarding psychological and biological theories of child homicide. In keeping with criticisms levied against explanations of female-perpetrated intimate partner homicide, theories which locate the aetiology of child homicide in the individual pathology of the female offender present women as irrational, hence negating agency and responsibility from being attached to their lethal acts of violence. Although grounded within a psychological perspective herself, Motz is critical of the Infanticide Act, stating, 'though apparently sympathetic to women, it actually deprives them of moral agency and feeds into the notion of woman as intrinsically hysterical and untrustworthy, literally a product of the unpredictable and terrifying womb which she houses' (2001: 131). Motz argues that 'the woman who commits a crime as serious as killing while distressed following childbirth cannot simply be assumed to be a hapless and passive subject of her hormones; she also displays a complex, and even rational, set of motivations and considerations within a particular social context' (2001: 131). Finally, the most obvious weakness with such an approach is that not all women who kill their children (or, of course, men) are actually diagnosed with a psychiatric disorder, and thus the homicides in these cases remain unexplained.

From a routine activities approach, Silverman and Kennedy (1993) point out that the decline of intra-familial child homicide as the child grows older may reflect the decreased level of contact between family members. With age, the daily activities of children change, taking them away from the family domain, such that they spend large parts of their day at school, for example. Thus the risk they face from family violence and homicide will decrease. In support of this, Adler and Polk note that the increased rates of extra-familial homicide victimisation in the teenage years (especially for boys) may reflect the 'increasing proximity to the contexts and understandings of adulthood' (2001: 125). Furthermore, a number of writers have suggested a link between the over-representation of female perpetrators of child homicide in cases where the victim is in its first few months of life with the disproportionate amount of time mothers spend with their newborns and infants during this period. However, these authors also note a lack of empirical research specifically investigating these arguments (Kunz and Bahr, 1996; Smithey, 1998).

Wallace (1986: 125), in her analysis of the killing of preschool children in Australia, noted that well over one-third of the fatal assaults involving fathers occurred whilst they were alone with the child, or with a number of its siblings, either babysitting or caring whilst the mother was out. Some of these fathers had full-time responsibility for the child. Similar findings have been reported from the US (Gil, 1970) and England (Scott, 1973; see also Adler and Polk, 1996). Moreover, Strang (1996) observes that patterns of filicide in Australia may have seen an increase in the proportion of fathers as killers, perhaps linked to fundamental structural changes in Australian society (presumably changes in child care roles and in the differential pressures suffered by mothers and fathers).

Adler and Polk state that whilst the routine activities approach is useful when attempting to explain rates of child homicide, 'a routine analysis by itself cannot explain why risks of homicide are so low in the middle years of childhood. Neither does this explanation satisfactorily account for the striking gendered patterns of homicide in terms of both victims and offenders with the onset of the teenage years' (2001: 141). Furthermore, the theory may enhance our general understanding of connections between age, risk of victimisation and the victim–offender relationship; but it does little for our understanding of why women or men actually kill their children. Nor does it provide us with any comprehensive understanding of the context, circumstances or micro-dynamics of the homicide.

Adler and Polk (1996) are among the few authors who have paid particular attention to male perpetrators of child homicide and its links to masculinity(ies). Through their analysis of case studies of male-perpetrated child homicide (45 cases) in Victoria, Australia, they found a diversity of violent scenarios that they believe reflects the complex and sometimes contradictory expectations of masculinity. To illustrate, Adler and Polk found that many of the perpetrators of paternal filicide presented themselves as particularly capable and willing carers of their child/children (or stepchildren) to their partners and the wider community (particularly the public environments in which they participated with their children). Moreover, they (and their partners) frequently vehemently denied violence toward the children, indicating that such behaviour was objectionable and not 'manly'. Yet, autopsy reports generally indicated that these men had been violent toward their children on more than one occasion. Hence, Adler and Polk suggest that:

In private the child's actions were interpreted as challenging masculine authority; the violence reaffirms control of the situation. But these same actions cannot be part of a public affirmation of masculinity, in fact they are actions which if made public might be used to question masculinity. (1996: 409)

Interestingly also, Wilczynski discusses two particular forms of filicide that she suggests are generally exclusively the domain of men: 'retaliating killings' and 'jealousy of, or rejection by, the victim' (1995: 168–9). In retaliating killings, anger towards another person (typically the man's sexual partner) is displaced onto the child. 'A common hallmark of these cases was a history of severe marital conflict, often involving physical violence by one or both parties' (1995: 169). Moreover, the male retaliating filicides were often characterised by possessiveness, sexual jealousy and the exertion of power within the marital relationship. Clearly, there are overlaps between this form of homicide and male-perpetrated domestic homicide (discussed in Chapter 6). In jealousy/rejection killings Wilczynski notes that suspicion or knowledge that the man was not the child's biological parent, resentment of the attention that the child received from the mother or 'rejecting' behaviour by the child due to illness or prior abuse were common factors.

Some feminist approaches have also adopted a gendered approach to child homicide. Jensen (2001) addresses women's child killing (as well as other forms of female homicide) in terms of a lack of gender equality, which she defines as social, political-legal and economic inequalities. She argues that these structural and cultural disadvantages restrict the opportunities, power and status that are afforded to women and result in feelings of social and economic entrapment (especially within the domestic environment), contributing to women's lethal violence. Jensen (2001: 51) notes that child-rearing is not in itself oppressive or restrictive, rather it is the patriarchal demand that women do this (usually alone, and with little value attached to it) which leads to stress and feelings of entrapment and isolation. Traditional demands and normative social expectations placed on women dictate their 'nurturing' roles as mother, wife and primary caregiver. Not only is the role expected, but it is financially unpaid and given little external social value or support. The social demand for women to care exclusively for the very young (and very old) means that women are stigmatised for seeking outside help such as child care, and seen as deviating from the role of 'good mother'. Thus, women are often restricted to the domestic sphere with little opportunity for participation in the workforce. Where they are found, women (and especially mothers) are over-represented in low status and low-paid jobs, with fewer opportunities for career advancements and fewer economic resources. The perceived limitations of their social options, compounded by a lack of economic resources, make lethal abuse more likely, with the homicidal event being the final effort to escape an oppressive situation. Emotional stress, anger and frustration is externalised and turned toward the dependent, who is identified as the source of these feelings. Thus, 'like her intimate partner homicide counterpart, the female familial offender will kill the perceived object of her oppression' (Jensen, 2001: 56). Jensen (2001) thus identifies what she believes to be a theme of powerlessness, arguing that the abuse and killing of (powerless) children represents a women's desperate attempt to gain power for herself. Jensen concludes that 'the roots of this powerlessness can be seen as stemming in part from a society that does not offer women equality with men' (2001: 56).

The themes identified in Jensen's (2001) work have a great deal of support with a number of other scholars vigorously stressing the importance of poverty, unemployment, inequality and entrapment as important factors increasing the risk of child homicide (Adler and Polk, 2001; Baron, 1993; Brookman and Maguire, 2003; Browne and Lynch, 1995; Websdale, 1999). Furthermore, support can be found for female 'projection' of violence onto their children, as well as links between domestic violence (that is, battered woman syndrome), childhood abuse and trauma, and female abuse of children (for example, the 'retaliating mother') (Crimmins et al., 1997; d'Orban 1979, 1990; Sinclair and Bullock, 2002; Websdale, 1999). For example, Totman (1978) found that the women in her study viewed their children as irritants, and symbolic of their confinement, frustration and failure. Whilst Motz argues 'for women who have themselves been abused physically, their own violence towards children may reflect the psychological process of identification with the aggressor, in which the mother gives to the child the experience that she herself suffered as helpless victim. She turns her passive role of victim into the active one in which she is in control, as the aggressor' (2001: 97). Finally, Motz (2001: 114) claims that the function of child killing mirrors that of suicide. The mother finds her own inability to provide for, and cope with, the needs of the child intolerable, and thus ends its life (and, in fantasy, their misery).

As indicated earlier, Adler and Polk (1996, 2001) have also focused upon gender in their attempt to explain child homicide. However, they ultimately found that a gendered approach was only partially helpful. For example, they note that whilst the concept of 'doing gender' helps to reveal both the complex and contradictory understandings of masculinity and the ways in which they are achieved differently in different situations, at the same time, 'if we take the notion of the situational accomplishment of gender to an extreme, we would have to argue that there are as many "masculinities" as there are situations in which men find themselves' (Adler and Polk, 2001: 161).[12] Moreover, they note that maternal filicides present even greater difficulties for the 'doing gender' perspective, stating:

> The killing of a child is so antithetical to notions of femininity and motherhood in our society that it is hard to imagine the social context in which a woman's femininity is situationally accomplished by the killing of her child. (Adler and Polk, 2001: 162)

Discontent with the explanatory power of gender alone, Adler and Polk (2001) turn instead to notions of motherhood, fatherhood and childhood. In a not dissimilar vein to Jensen (2001) they note that the fulfilment of expectations of motherhood places considerable stress on some mothers (see also Oberman, 1996). They suggest that '... for many women the options of establishing self-worth are limited, and their position as women, as a valued person is established through their status as mother and wife' (Adler and Polk, 2001: 165). The break-up of the family (which they find characterises many female-perpetrated filicide-suicides in Victoria, Australia) is particularly devastating for these mothers and wives, not simply in terms of their oftentimes economic vulnerability, but also in terms of society's expectations that it is mothers who are held primarily accountable for their children's wellbeing. Hence, mothers who kill themselves and their child or children may be understood as escaping from their perceived failure to live up to society's expectations of them as successful wives and mothers. Adler and Polk (2001) note that family break-up also appears to be a significant contextual feature of filicide-suicides perpetrated by fathers. However, they question whether the family break-up means the same to these men and women or has the same sorts of implications for their self-identity. Whilst they caution at the use of oversimplified distinctions, they note that:

> If one had to characterise these events [that is, filicide-suicides] there is a sense that the mothers' actions can perhaps be described as expressions of feelings of powerlessness, whereas men's actions seem to be expressing or asserting power. (2001: 166–7)

It is interesting, for example, that the Mochri case (discussed earlier) seems to have been precipitated by the father's perceived failure to succeed in the world of employment (that is, his accumulating debts). Hence, for some men their identity as successful fathers may be more closely associated to their success in the world of paid employment (that is, as 'breadwinners' or providers), whilst for mothers their success in the non-paid domestic sphere may be perceived as more crucial. In short, what fathers and mothers perceive as failure is likely to differ and therefore the underlying rationales for the child homicides in which they participate may differ in accordance with wider norms and expectations of motherhood and fatherhood.

In summary, Adler and Polk (2001) suggest that understandings of motherhood and fatherhood and how these relate to understandings of child care responsibilities when combined with broader understandings of gender identity may offer the most fruitful avenue of future research in the area of child homicide. Wallace's (1986) work regarding men's reactions to separation also points to their differential understanding of marriage (as compared to women's) as discussed in Chapter 6.

Study Task 8.3

How have the roles of mothers and fathers (and thereby 'motherhood' and 'fatherhood') changed in the last 50 years? You may reflect upon your own and other people's roles and experiences where appropriate (such as family members) and/or conduct a literature search.
What implications do your findings have for explaining child homicide?

Chapter Summary and Conclusions

This chapter has considered the killing of infants and children, focusing in particular upon the different forms of child homicide perpetrated by male and female
offenders. The focus has been upon the most prominent forms of homicide, with
brief attention to some of the more unusual cases. However, it is important to
recognise that there are other forms of homicide where children are victimised that
we have not considered here, such as nannies or carers who kill (for example,
Louise Woodward the nanny or Beverley Allitt the nurse), 'team' serial killers (for
example, Myra Hindley and Ian Brady or Fred and Rose West) and school shootings.[13] Nevertheless, these are rare cases and it has not been possible to consider
every manifestation of child homicide in one chapter. The important message to
take away from this chapter is that whilst child homicide is indeed diverse, certain
patterns nevertheless emerge particularly linked to the age of the child and the
gender of the offender as well as the context in which the homicide occurs (that is,
within or beyond the family unit). It is the interaction between these factors that
may help to reveal certain patterns and trends of child homicide. At the same time,
however, we must not lose sight of the fact that the social situation in which
offenders find themselves also has an important bearing upon these homicide
events. For example, poverty, social exclusion and other lifestyle stressors can lead
to depression or psychiatric disturbance and can, eventually, lead to homicide.
Ultimately, as Adler and Polk stress, 'child homicides are so varied that ... it is
unlikely that a single, unitary theory of homicide will provide a meaningful understanding' (2001: 168).

Review Questions

- What is the value of focusing upon the distinct nature of male- and female-
  perpetrated child homicide?
- Compare and contrast explanations of neonaticide and infanticide.
- What aspects of child homicide does the routine activities theory help to explain?
- To what extent do you think it is desirable or possible to formulate a general theory
  of child homicide? What might the obstacles be?

Further Reading

Regarding child homicide, the most recent and thorough text that is essential reading is *Child Victims of Homicide* (Adler and Polk; 2001: Cambridge University Press),
which covers many of the themes also contained in *Child Abuse Homicides in Australia*
(Strang, 1996: Australian Institute of Criminology). *Child Homicide* (Wilczynski, 1997:

Greenwich Medical Media) is an important text to consult that deals exclusively with child homicide and 'A Profile of Parental Homicide against Children' (Kunz and Bahr, 1996: *Journal of Family Violence*, Vol. 11/4, pp. 347–62) is also very useful. Other works deal more specifically with female-perpetrated child homicide within general texts of female violence but are worth consulting, such as *The Psychology of Female Violence: Crimes Against the Body* (Motz, 2001: Brunner-Routledge) and *Why Women Kill: Homicide and Gender Equality* (Jensen, 2001: Lynne Reiner).

Useful Internet Sites

A search of the NSPCC's website is recommended, and by following the link www.nspcc.org.uk/inform/CH_Home.asp a search of relevant publications, research and resources will likely prove very fruitful. The same can be said for the World Health Organisation www.who.int/health_topics/violence/en/ website, which contains a world report on violence and health, lists of abstracts and fact sheets on child abuse. Finally, the Australian Institute of Criminology has an excellent website with numerous online articles, research findings and conference papers. For example, the link www.aic.gov.au/research/homicide/aic.html will provide a list of research relating to homicide where articles such as Strang's *Children as Victims of Homicide* can be accessed (www.aic.gov.au/publications/tandi/tandi53. html).

Notes

1 Researchers have adopted various criteria to define child homicide victims, some focusing upon very young children (less than 4 years), whilst others have presented a cut off period somewhere in the teenage years (see Adler and Polk, 2001: 16). Adler and Polk defined a child as under the age of 18.

2 Excluding those victims of the Dunblane incident (Scottish Executive, 2001).

3 As part of her doctoral research, the author accessed and analysed 97 police murder investigation files in relation to homicides from three police force areas (one in Wales and two in England; see Brookman, 1999). Of these, nine cases related to the killing of children. This small sample, which is neither exhaustive (in terms of the number of homicides involving child victims that occurred in the regions) nor fully reflects the diversity of scenarios of child homicide, provides a useful source when combined with case studies compiled by authors from other regions of the world (from similar sources such as police murder files or prosecutor files).

4 As discussed in Chapter 1 of this text, it has been acknowledged that there is a large 'dark figure' of child homicide – that is, those cases which are not recognised as homicides. For example, those in which the case of death is undetected, unproven, undetermined or misclassified, and thus do not appear in the official homicide statistics (Mouzos, 2000; Strang, 1996; Adler and Polk, 2001; Wilczynski and Morris, 1993). Illustrating this, Strang (1996) and Mouzos (2001) point to sudden infant death syndrome (SIDS), commenting that some of these cases may have been deliberately inflicted, but have escaped detection. Although caution must be taken over the small proportion of victims that this would probably apply to, Meadow (1999) found that of 81 children found to have been killed in the UK, 42 were originally certified as having died from SIDS (Adler and Polk, 2001).

5 Although, as Mouzos (2001) warns, it is often difficult to determine whether the fatal act was a culmination of abuse against the child (and what Mouzos refers to as general ill-will towards the child) or the result of a single incident.

6 Although this has been found to be more common in cases where the killer is a male parent (Adler and Polk, 2001).

7 Refer to Chapter 1 for further discussion of the Infanticide Act and some of the recent criticisms and proposed amendments.

8 It must be noted, however, that the HI contains only limited information in terms of motive or circumstance. The author has not analysed detailed case files in respect of stranger child murder (unlike many of the other forms of homicide discussed throughout this text) and therefore, no definitive statements can be made regarding this sub-category of homicide.

9 For a fuller discussion of the Infanticide Act, refer to Chapter 1.

10 When looking more closely at the types of child homicide committed, d'Orban (1979) found that for 'battering' and 'retaliating' mothers, personality disorders were the most common diagnosis, followed by reactive depression. In contrast, 8 of 10 neonaticide offenders were diagnosed as having no abnormality (with only 14 of 89 offenders diagnosed as such in total). The majority of those who were classified as 'mentally ill' in d'Orban's typology were diagnosed with a psychotic illness.

11 Wallace notes, however, that such disparities regarding the mental health of male and female child killers may be 'more apparent than real' due to differences in reporting symptoms and seeking help across the sexes and ultimately to differential patterns of treatment and hospitalisation for men and women.

12 This criticism is ultimately one that applies to any use of the concept of masculinity(ies) in understanding crime, and we shall return to this issue in Chapter 12.

13 There have been a number of cases of school shootings in recent years in the US involving children as perpetrators, whilst in the UK there is the unusual case of the Dunblane massacre.

9 Multiple Homicide: 'Serial Killers', Terrorists and Corporations

This chapter will consider the phenomenon of multiple homicide, though in a somewhat unconventional manner. The concern here is to focus upon relatively rare yet high impact events where one individual or 'body' is responsible for the death of a large numbers of individuals (either during one 'event' or over a longer, more sustained period of time). Mass, spree and serial killings, usually committed by one or maybe two individuals, are perhaps the most obvious examples, and typically the term 'multiple murder' is used to encompass these three types of killings. The term will also be used here for the same generic purposes (as distinct from the chapter's heading of Multiple *Homicide*, which incorporates all three major categories that are covered in this chapter). However, terrorist-related killings and homicide as a result of corporate negligence or neglect are also of importance (though the latter has, until recently, received considerably less attention than 'conventional' homicide). Whilst these homicides are very different in nature, they share common features. All tend to attract significant media attention and fear in the public mind, not least due to the often random nature of victimisation. All represent challenges to the authorities in terms of identifying killers and bringing them to account (particularly so for corporate homicide, where the identification of individual responsibility is complex and prosecutions rare). However, the distinction made here is not necessarily conceptual or analytical, rather one of ease in that the status of multiple victimisation provides a branch under which certain killings can 'hang'. Hence, the different forms of killings (by individuals, corporations and terrorists) are discussed separately, and not comparatively.[1]

Multiple Murder: Mass, Spree and Serial Killing

We begin here by considering some of the difficulties involved in defining and classifying different forms of multiple murder, before moving on to consider the extent of and apparent trends in multiple murder and evaluating some of the dominant explanations offered for this particular form of homicide.

Definitions and Typologies

It is generally accepted that multiple murder, or 'multicide', can be broken down into three further sub-groups; *mass* killings, *spree* killings and *serial* killings (Gresswell and Hollin, 1994; Keeney, 1995; Lester, 1995). These distinctions essentially differentiate between forms of multiple murder in terms of their temporal and spatial characteristics. Mass murder tends to encompass those homicides in which multiple victims are killed in a single episode, and in the same general geographical location. An example of a mass killing in the UK is the 'Dunblane shooting' in Scotland, where, in 1996, Thomas Hamilton walked into a primary school and opened fire on a classroom of children. Hamilton killed 16 children, a schoolteacher and then himself (Coleman and Norris, 2000). Spree killing encapsulates multiple victims who are killed over a slightly longer period (Holmes and Holmes, 2001a, stipulate up to a period of 30 days) and often in different geographical locations. Although these homicides may occur in several sequences, spree killings are considered within the context of one event.[2] The third form of multicide, serial killings, occur repetitively over an extended period; from days, weeks and months, to years (though it is generally specified that this time period must be over that of 30 days; Holmes and Holmes, 1998). An important distinction which is made in serial killings is that of a 'cooling off' period between murders, which is argued to be absent in mass and spree homicide (Gresswell and Hollin, 1994; Holmes and Holmes, 2001a, 2001b). Examples of serial killers from the UK include Peter Sutcliffe (the 'Yorkshire Ripper'), Dennis Nilsen and Harold Shipman. Perhaps of more notoriety are the serial *team* killers involving multiple perpetrators, as well as victims – such as Ian Brady and Myra Hindley (the 'Moors Murderers') and Fred and Rosemary West (see Table 9.1 for an outline of selected multiple killings in the UK).[3]

Further typologies have emerged which refine the sub-categories of mass and serial murder. For example, mass murder has been classified into a number of different types, which include:

- the 'psuedo-commando' (a mass killer fascinated with guns and weaponry);
- the 'disciple' (who kills under guidance from a charismatic leader and is, for example, a member of a cult);
- the 'family annihilator' (who kills members of his family, friends or acquaintances); and
- the 'disgruntled employee/citizen' (who, being resentful towards their place of work, for example, kills those who are responsible for the killer's perceived injustices) (Holmes and Holmes, 2001a, 2001b).

Table 9.1 Multiple murder in the UK: selected cases

Name(s)	Dates active[1]	Victims[2]	Type/Motive
Ian Brady and Myra Hindley 'The Moors Murderers'	1963–65	Convicted 3 Later confirmed 5	Serial (sexual) child killings; sexual assault, torture – Manchester: Saddleworth Moors *sexual*
Patrick Mackay	1973–74	Charged 5 Convicted 3 Suspected 11	Serial robbery-homicides; stabbing, strangulation – London *'pseudo-commando', violence disproportionate to profit*
Donald Nielson 'The Black Panther'	1974–75	5	Serial robbery-homicides; shooting kidnap, strangulation – Lancashire/ Yorkshire *'pseudo-commando', violence disproportionate to profit*
Mark Rowntree	1975–76	4	Spree (8-day period); stabbing – Yorkshire *hedonistic, psychiatric disturbance*
Peter Dinsdale 'Bruce Lee'	1973–80	26	Mass; serial arsonist, fire – Hull *'revenge', psychiatric disturbance*
Peter Sutcliffe 'The Yorkshire Ripper'	1975–80	13 8 escaped assault	Serial; sexual assault, mutilation of prostitutes – Yorkshire *sexual*
Dennis Nilsen	1978–83	15 5 escaped assault	Serial (homosexual) killing; strangulation – London *sexual*
Jeremy Bamber	1986	5	Mass; shooting – Essex *'family annihilator', financial*
Michael Ryan 'Hungerford Massacre'	1987	15 14 injured	Mass/spree, homicide-suicide[3]; shooting – Hungerford *'pseudo-commando'*
Fred West Rose West[4]	1967–87	12 10	Serial; sexual assault, torture – Gloucester *sexual*
Kenneth Erskine 'The Stockworth Strangler'	1987	7 1 attempted	Serial robbery-homicides; sexual assault, manual strangulation – London *sexual*
Beverly Allitt (nurse) 'The Killer Nurse'	1993	4 9 suspected assaults	Serial (child) killer; medical 'intervention' – Lincolnshire *psychiatric disturbance (Munchausen by proxy)*
Colin Ireland 'The Gay Slayer'	1993	5 Suspected of killing inmate	Serial (homosexual) killing; strangulation – London *'missionary'*

(Continued)

Table 9.1   (Continued)

Name(s)	Dates active[1]	Victims[2]	Type/Motive
Peter Moore	1995	4 50 suspected assaults	Serial (homosexual) killing; stabbing – North Wales *sexual, hedonistic*
Thomas Hamilton 'Dunblane Massacre'	1996	17	Mass homicide-suicide; shooting – Dunblane, Scotland *'pseudo-commando', revenge*
Harold Shipman (Dr) 'Dr Death'	1978–98	215 (+) Further 45 (+) suspected	Serial; lethal injection: diamorphine poisoning – Manchester/Yorkshire. The UK's most prolific serial killer *'power and control', financial*
David Copeland 'The Soho Nail Bomber'	1999	3 140 (+) injured	Mass killing; nail bombs – London *'pseudo-commando', 'missionary'*

[1]Active dates are those in which the perpetrator is known to have killed.
[2]Number of victims is approximate unless otherwise indicated.
[3]'Homicide-suicides' do not include the perpetrator in the victim count.
[4]Those victims killed by Rosemary West are included within Fred West's victim count also.

Typologies of serial killers are found in even greater abundance and detail (see, for example, Holmes and De Burger, 1988; Gee, 1988 and Ressler et al., 1988). However, the definition of multiple murder and the typologies proposed to describe these homicides are far from universal. There is much disagreement, for example, regarding how many people must die before a situation is defined as one in which a multiple murder has occurred (Rappaport, 1988). Equally significant is the lack of consensus regarding the distinction between mass and spree homicides. Spree killings appear to be the 'catch-all' or 'in-between' category of multiple murder used when cases do not fit neatly into either group (Fox and Levin, 1998). As Coleman and Norris point out in their discussion of an example from the UK:

> Consider the case of Michael Ryan, who shot and killed one victim, drove to a petrol station and shot at the attendant, and then drove to the town of Hungerford, where he killed fifteen people before shooting himself. Is this a mass or a spree murder? Some feel that the concept of spree murder should be omitted altogether as an unnecessary complication. (2000: 89)

Fox and Levin (1998: 407–8) do just this. They have developed a unified motivational typology for both mass and serial killings, which eliminates the need for the distinction of spree killings, and includes categories of 'power', 'revenge', 'loyalty', 'profit' and 'terror'. Fox and Levin's (1998) unified typology is arguably an important step forward. However, all of the various typologies which have been constructed have their weaknesses. For example, those typologies which are based upon motivation are dependent upon this factor being clearly established. More generally, the range of categories that have been proposed are neither mutually exclusive nor exhaustive (Fox and Levin, 1998). Furthermore, the small number of multiple homicides (in general, and particularly in terms of their further classificatory groupings), in addition to 'an abundance of speculation and a paucity of hard data' (Fox and Levin, 1998: 410), calls into question the validity of such typologies. This is particularly important when we come to consider multiple murder in the UK, where such killings are much rarer than, for example, in the US. In sum, it is questionable as to whether typologies of multiple murder that have been developed to explain such killings in the US are equally applicable, or can be extrapolated, to the UK experience.

Extent and Trends of Multiple Murder

The extent of multiple murder is very difficult to assess, in that statistics which distinguish multiple murder (not to mention the groups subsumed within this term) are not routinely maintained or compiled (Coleman and Norris, 2000). Estimations that have been made have relied primarily upon media accounts and reports. Perhaps the most cited attempt to estimate the prevalence of multiple murder was made by Holmes and De Burger (1988), who suggested that a 'reliable'[4] estimate of serial victimisation in the US ranged from 3,500–5,000 victims each year. This estimate was based upon their assumption that victims of serial killers accounted for between a quarter and two-thirds of the 5,000 or so homicides each year which were unsolved. In addition, they argue that there are a number of undetected victims (especially children) who go missing each year. Such figures have been described as 'preposterous' (Coleman and Norris, 2000; Gresswell and Hollin, 1994) and undoubtedly contribute to what Jenkins (1988, 1994) describes as a moral and social panic. It is generally accepted that this estimate grossly misinterpreted the available data (Egger, 1990: 10), and was built on the flawed premise that unsolved or apparently motiveless killings are attributable to serial killers (Fox and Levin, 1998).

Others, such as Ressler et al. (1988), have placed the figure of multiple (as opposed to serial) murderers active at any one time in the US at between 30 to over 100 individuals. Gresswell and Hollin have attempted to extrapolate these figures to the UK, and note that doing so is fraught with difficulties:

> If the more conservative figures are applied to England and Wales and equated with the smaller population, then one might expect there to be between six and twenty killers active. However, if the general murder rate for England and Wales (six times less than in the United States) is taken into account, but assuming that detection rates are similar in both countries, an estimate of up to four active killers may be more realistic. (1994: 6)

In terms of the UK, cases of multiple killings are relatively scarce but extensively studied. Thus, as Jenkins (1988) argues, those cases which are identified can be confidently considered to be a comprehensive account. However, only a handful of studies have attempted to document the prevalence of multiple and/or serial murder in the UK. Jenkins (1988) studied all serial killings (those involving four or more victims) in England and Wales between 1940–85. He found that there were 12 'individuals' suspected, or convicted, of serial homicide during this period, accounting for *approximately* 107 victims. Jenkins (1988: 5–6) notes that these represent a very small proportion of homicides in England and Wales, accounting for 1.7 per cent of murders in this period. Jenkins (1988) found that the majority of victims were young women (particularly prostitutes), followed by children (a finding in line with the international literature, which emphasises the perceived vulnerability of such victims). Jenkins (1991) went on to analyse all known serial killings (defined as four or more victims killed over a period of more than 72 hours) in England and Wales, for the period 1980–90 and estimated there to have been, perhaps, 25 serial murder cases (compared to a minimum of six or seven hundred in the US) and *approximately* 180 victims.

Gresswell (1994) and Gresswell and Hollin (1994) document incidents of multiple murder in England between 1982–91. These figures indicate that there were 52 'incidents' of multiple murder during this period (defined as three or more victims), involving 58 perpetrators and 196 victims. In addition, another eight incidents were noted (involving 42 victims) in which no perpetrator had been apprehended. Overall, in the 10-year period 1982–91, 3 per cent of homicide victims in England and Wales were killed in episodes of multiple murder.

Analysis of the Homicide Index (HI) for the period 1995–2001 reveals that 4.1 per cent of homicide victims were killed in episodes that could be defined as multiple homicides (that is, three or more victims). Included in this calculation is one incident in 2000 that claimed the lives of 58 victims and accounted for 1.1 per cent of the total victims over the period (that is, the case of 58 Chinese immigrants found dead in a sealed lorry container at Dover). Hence, when this unusual case is removed, the figures are identical to those documented by Gresswell and Hollin above. Returning to Gresswell and Hollin's analysis, they found that a significant number of the victims of multiple murder (51 per cent) were members of the killer's family, and nearly 16 per cent were friends or acquaintances. Interestingly, in 36 per cent of all cases the killer subsequently committed suicide. In all but two of these murder-suicides, the victims were members of the perpetrator's family (Gresswell and Hollin, 1994). Gresswell (1994) analysed the data further, finding that the majority (90 per cent) of offenders were male, 32 per cent were white and the average age of offenders was 31. The primary causes of death were 'shooting' (34 per cent), 'burns' (19 per cent), 'strangulation' (15 per cent) and 'stabbing/cutting' (14 per cent). In addition, in terms of the victim–offender relationship, only 32 per cent of victims were strangers to their killer, whilst 44 per cent of victims were killed in their own home by a member of their family. In fact, of 52 incidents (which involve known suspects), 28 involved family murder (Gresswell, 1994). The predominance of family killers or family 'annihilators' in the UK is an interesting characteristic and one that deserves further exploration considering the rarity of multiple murder in this country (refer to Chapter 8 for a further discussion of family killings).

In terms of patterns or trends in serial murder, although known serial murder has been gradually increasing, in many periods it appears that there were no serial killers active in England and Wales at all, whilst other periods indicate that a number were active at the same time. For example, it was thought that during the mid-1970s, four or five different killers were committing serial homicides (Jenkins, 1988, 1991). In addition, during 1970–79, two particularly active killers (Peter Dinsdale and Peter Sutcliffe) were responsible for the majority (39 of 60) of all serial homicide victims in that period; 26 victims and 13 victims respectively (Gresswell and Hollin, 1994). Gresswell and Hollin (1994) argue that this partly explains why there appeared to be a marked increase in this type of killing in England and Wales for this particular period.

Since the 1980s there has been a great deal of speculation and attention surrounding what was described (quite incorrectly) as a 'new phenomenon' of multiple murder, of epidemic proportions. Interest surrounding multiple murder (and perhaps more specifically, serial sexual murder) has been 'phenomenal' (Danson and Soothill, 1996: 114). A number of scholars have noted the possible benefits to certain agencies of exaggerating the prevalence of multiple murder. In particular, Jenkins (1991, 1994) has drawn attention to the fact that multiple murder provided political and ideological weapons for a number of groups. Soothill (1993: 341) makes a similar point in his reference to the 'serial killer industry'. For example, the FBI's Behavioural Science Unit (BSU) (formed in 1972 at Quantico, Virginia) was keen to expand its resources and activities and establish itself as the 'authority on serial offending' (Coleman and Norris, 2000: 111). Hence, they shared with other groups a 'common vested interest in emphasising certain aspects of the murder problem, above all its very large scale' (Jenkins, 1994: 216; see also Kiger, 1990; and Fox and Levin, 1998). Thus, whilst is it difficult to comment upon more recent trends and statistics regarding multiple killings due to the lack of appropriate (or available) statistical data, it would seem wise to question the extent to which multiple murder has increased, and the manner in which it is portrayed.

Study Task: 9.1

As indicated above, multiple murder (particularly serial sexual murder) is exceptionally newsworthy and has been for many years. More recently there has been intense media and public interest in Internet-based paedophiles. Do you think that paedophiles are replacing serial killers as the as the 'new social menace'? Who might have a vested interest in exaggerating the prevalence of homicide committed by paedophiles that utilise the Internet, and why?

Explaining Multiple Murder

Explanations of multiple murder, particularly serial (and sexual) homicide, tend to focus upon individualistic theories that emphasise abnormality. More so than with 'ordinary' homicide, perpetrators who commit multiple murder are perceived to be 'mad', insane or sick. In his study of multiple murder in England and Wales, Gresswell (1991) found that 45 per cent of murderers had some form of psychiatric history, whilst 24 per cent had a *personal* history of mental illness. Whilst some researchers cite this as evidence supporting the individualistic argument, others point out that 76 per cent of Gresswell's (1991) sample did *not* have a personal history of mental illness. Other forms of mental disorder that have been implicated in the aetiology of multiple murder include 'schizophrenia', 'multiple-personality disorder', 'depression' and, more specifically in relation to serial killers, 'psychopathy' (a term now superseded by 'anti-social personality disorder'). As discussed at length in Chapter 4, many of these disorders are difficult to establish and the particular symptoms that apparently characterise them change over time and are, ultimately, socially constructed. Certainly, 'psychopathy' is a contested concept (Hickey, 1991; Vetter, 1990).

In addition the role of hormones, head injury and, in particular, violent and sadistic fantasy have also been documented (Hickey, 1991; Stone, 2001). For example, in their study of serial sexual homicide, Prentky et al. (1989) argue that fantasy is an internal drive mechanism for repetitive acts of sexual violence. They found that 86 per cent of multiple (sexual) killers engaged in sadistic fantasies, compared to 23 per cent of 'single' killers. Prentky et al. (1989) make a number of interesting points regarding the maintenance of serial offending, and have much theoretical support (for example, Ressler et al., 1988; MacCulloch et al., 1983; and Gresswell, 1991). However, as they point out, it is perhaps more pertinent to question what specific disinhibitory factors enable a sadistic fantasist to 'cross the line' and actually recreate and act out their fantasy in real life. In addition, if, as Prentky et al. (1989) posit, fantasy is an internal drive mechanism for serial sexual assaults, then what is the internal drive mechanism for this fantasy? The underlying cause still appears to be neglected.

A number of researchers have pointed to the increased experience of childhood trauma, abuse and brutality in many studies of multiple killing (Lester, 1995; Gresswell, 1991; Stone, 2001). Hickey (1991), for example, argues that destabilising events or 'traumatisation' (such as an unstable home-life, death of a parent, divorce or physical and sexual abuse) and the inability to cope with such events, can be the triggering mechanism for serial murderers. Hickey describes a 'trauma control' model of serial killing, suggesting that drug abuse, pornography and, in particular, violent sexual fantasy are often 'facilitators' of serial sexual offending (Hickey, 1991).

Other explanations have focused on sociological factors and wider social structures in explaining multiple homicide. Stone (2001), for example, points to the role and (decline in) availability of women for sexual purposes, and the increase in sexual violence and serial sexual offending (Stone, 2001). Also focusing at the societal level, Leyton (1986: 269) suggests that multiple murderers are 'products of their time' and reflect societies' critical tensions. Moreover, Leyton (1986) argues that the social characteristics and origins of killer and victims changes over time. He identifies three broard periods of 'homicidal protest': the 'pre-industrial', 'industrial' and 'modern' era of multiple murder. The 'pre-industrial' murderer belonged to the wealthy aristocracy, attempting to maintain the status of the nobility (who were at that time under threat or challenge from the peasantry). In the context of the Industrial Revolution, when 'new' social classes were created, the middle-class 'industrial' murderer began to prey on members of the lower order – the 'failures' of the system. Finally, by the modern era:

> Both killer and victim had altered their form because the nature of homicidal protest had changed most radically: it was no longer the threatened aristocrat testing the limits of his power; no longer the morbidly insecure new bourgeois checking the threat to his hard-won status; now it was an excluded individual wreaking vengeance on the symbol and source of his excommunication (Leyton, 1986: 287–8).

Grover and Soothill (1997) evaluated Leyton's theory in reference to the UK experience, noting a number of limitations to his thesis. They suggest that the modern British multiple murderer shares more similarities with Leyton's 'pre-industrial' murderer of the US (with victims being drawn from relatively powerless and vulnerable groups, as opposed the relatively powerful middle-classes who symbolise the killer's frustration). However, Grover and Soothill (1997) also add that if the focus of class *position* (the definitive feature of Leyton's argument) is widened to include other social relationships, such as patriarchy and material and social frustrations, then multiple murder as a form of 'homicidal protest' (against those both above and *below* the killer's class position) may still have much conceptual value for the UK.

A small number of academics have considered the issue of gender in trying to account for multiple murder (particularly serial killing). For example, Cameron and Frazer (1987) in their discussion of sexual murder (by men) suggest that such men are extreme products of an exaggerated culture of masculinity, for whom aggression and male sexuality have become inextricably linked. Caputi (1987) views sexual murder by men as the ultimate expression of sexuality as a form of male power. Linked to this, some authors have adopted a psychoanalytic approach incorporating aspects of masculinity to unravel specific cases of serial sexual homicide. For example, Ward Jouve (1988) argues that Peter Sutcliffe's murders can be understood in terms of his perceived failure to live up to social expectations of manliness, leading him first to blame the feminine in himself and hate himself and ultimately to externalise that hatred and destroy women (see also Smith, 1989; and Jefferson, 1997).

Finally, there have been a few attempts to create integrated models to explain multiple murder. For example, Mitchell (1997) presents a model of serial murder that integrates pathological foundations (which can include biological, familial or socio-cultural factors and their interactions) with developmental consequences (for example, the individual experiences psychological and cognitive difficulties and possible sexual fantasies and dysfunction – described under the umbrella phrase 'diathesis-stress syndrome'), which ultimately lead him to kill. He also proposes a cycle of maintenance whereby some form of relief or sexual gratification accompanies the offender's 'first kill', leading to further murders in order to maintain these feelings that might otherwise dissipate (much like any other addiction that needs to be 'fed').

In conclusion, the study of multiple murder has been dominated with concerns to create and refine typologies and definitions and identify its prevalence. In terms of theoretical contributions, it remains the case that biological or psychological approaches dominate, though there are some signs that this may be changing, with researchers incorporating theories of masculinity into their accounts.

Terrorism and the Northern Ireland 'Troubles'

Terrorism and terrorist-related killings generally assume a particular significance in most people's minds, not least since the events of September 11th.[5] Although there have been no terrorist attacks in the UK on this scale, we have experienced some smaller-scale examples of international terrorism, such as the 'Lockerbie Disaster' in

Scotland in 1988. The Lockerbie case (although a complex and confused one) involved a bomb being planted on a Pan Am Boeing 747 (Flight 103) destined for New York, which detonated whilst the plane was flying over the Scottish town of Lockerbie. All 259 passengers were killed when the plane exploded, along with 11 victims on the ground. As such, this remains the worst single terrorist attack in the UK,[6] and the worst incident of mass murder.

Despite Lockerbie being something of an isolated incident of terrorist mass killing, the UK has, for 34 years, experienced sustained, albeit sporadic, terrorist-related killings linked to the Northern Ireland 'Troubles'. As O'Leary and McGarry (1996: 18) note, between 1969 and 1990 more people were killed in Northern Ireland as a result of terrorist incidents and political violence than in all other EC countries put together for the same period. In this section we will briefly explore terrorist and political killings (which often result in mass victimisation – or at least, certainly intend to) within the domestic context of the Northern Ireland Troubles.

Context and Characteristics of the Northern Ireland Troubles

Between 1969 and 2002, 3,344 people were killed in Northern Ireland due to the Troubles (PSNI, 2003c), with much of the killing concentrated in Belfast (Fay et al., 1997; O'Leary and McGarry, 1996; Poole, 1993). In addition, approximately 200 people have been killed outside of the region, for example, in England, the Republic of Ireland, Gibraltar and West Germany (O'Leary and McGarry, 1996: 9). Attacks and killings as a result of the Troubles account for the vast majority of all terrorist attacks directly experienced by the UK as a whole (although no terrorist attacks have taken place in Wales nor, with the exception of Lockerbie, have there been any in Scotland). For example, between 1969–89, of the 107 victims killed by terrorists in England, 83 per cent were killed by 'Irish' terrorists (Clutterbuck, 1990).

As O'Leary and McGarry point out, Northern Ireland:

... has generated the most intense political violence of any part of the contemporary UK, the highest level of *internal* political violence of any member-state of the European Community, and the highest levels of internal political violence in the continuously liberal democratic states of the post-1948 world. (1996: 8)

The Irish Republican Army (IRA), being opposed to British presence in Northern Ireland, have been involved in a persistent fight (or what they would prefer to term 'struggle') for a united Ireland. To these ends they have engaged in terrorist operations which inflict heavy casualties on the security forces and inflict major damage on the viability of Northern Ireland, and thus undermine political stability (Amnesty International, 1994; Clutterbuck, 1990; O'Leary and McGarry, 1996). In contrast, Loyalist paramilitary groups, such as the Ulster Defence Association (UDA) (also known as the Ulster Freedom Fighters (UFF)) and the Ulster Volunteer Force (UVF) fight to retain Northern Ireland as part of the UK (Amnesty International, 1994; Clutterbuck, 1990).

Members of the British security forces are primary targets for the IRA (including those who may be unarmed, off-duty, or even retired), as are members of Loyalist groups, suspected informers, civilian personnel providing services to the security forces, and the general public (Amnesty International, 1994; Dewar, 1996). As Amnesty International explains: 'The stated aim of their operations is to counter the Republican threat to the continued integration of Northern Ireland within the United Kingdom (UK) and this is done in part through intimidation and violence to crush support for Republican activities in Catholic areas' (1994: 7).

Terrorist tactics and methods of killing may involve arson, hostage seizure, hijacking, shooting, and bombing. In Northern Ireland, tactics have most often involved the latter two methods, particularly bombing (Clutterbuck, 1986). Attacks are random and indiscriminate in nature. Sommier argues that this modus operandi rests on two specific rationales: 'one is psychological in nature: random attack is the most likely to create a climate of terror since it strikes anyone anywhere. The other is ideological: indiscriminate killing means that ... each person must side "with us or against us"' (2002: 478).

However, Troubles-related killings are not solely perpetrated by Republican and Loyalist paramilitary organisations. Amnesty International (1994) identify three different 'forms' of political killings in Northern Ireland, including those by members of the security forces and killings by paramilitaries committed with the collusion or complicity of the security forces. Probably the most illustrative example of a security force (mass) killing, is that of 'Bloody Sunday', when 13 people at a civil rights demonstration in Londonderry were shot by members of the Parachute Regiment in 1972. Amnesty International (1994) argue that a series of killings in 1982 (and since this time) have aroused and increased suspicions that 'security force personnel deliberately killed people as an alternative to arresting them', suggesting the possibility of 'an official policy of planned killings of suspected members of armed opposition groups' (Amnesty International, 1994: 6). They point to a significant number of cases in which security forces, such as the British Army, Special Air Service (SAS) and the Royal Ulster Constabulary (RUC)), have killed people in disputed or controversial circumstances.

More recently, Amnesty International (1994) has been investigating and uncovering evidence of collusion between members of the security services and paramilitary organisations (specifically the Loyalists) against the primarily Catholic, Republican community. In addition, the increasing occurrence of paramilitary 'vigilantism' (that is, punishment attacks against members of their own communities) has also been documented (PSNI, 2003d; O'Leary and McGarry, 1996; Silke and Taylor, 2000). For example, Silke and Taylor (2000) argue that since 1970, 115 people have been killed in such attacks and a further 4,000 hospitalised.[7] Table 9.2 summarises some of the major terrorist incidents linked to the Northern Ireland Troubles that have occurred in the UK. There have been a number of bombings in the last few years linked to dissident Republicans, but none have resulted in fatalities.

Extent and Trends of Terrorism Related to Northern Ireland

Fluctuations or trends of homicide in Northern Ireland (especially Troubles-related killings) are obviously influenced by the immediate political context of the time. Sharp decreases in homicide from 1994 onwards, for example, are, by and large, a

Table 9.2   Terrorist incidents in the UK linked to the Northern Ireland Troubles

Date	Group responsible	Place	No. of victims	Method/details
30 Jan. 1972	British Army	Londonderry, Northern Ireland 'Bloody Sunday'	13 13 injured	Members of the Parachute Regiment opened fire on civil rights demonstrators. The shootings caused outrage and an inquiry was set up, which exonerated the army but strongly criticised their actions.
Feb.1972	(O)[1] IRA	Aldershot, Hampshire	7	The first IRA bomb in England (and the only one perpetrated by the (O)IRA), planted in the Officers' Mess in an army barracks.
Feb. 1974	(P) IRA	Bradford, West Yorkshire	12	A bomb placed under an army coach carrying soldiers and their families exploded on the M62.
July 1974	(P) IRA	London	1 41 injured	Bomb placed in the basement of the White Tower, in the Tower of London, exploded.
5 Oct. 1974	(P) IRA	Guildford, Surrey	4 50 injured	Bombs exploded in two pubs frequented by soldiers off-duty from Northern Ireland.
21 Nov. 1974	(P) IRA	Birmingham, West Midlands	21 162 injured	Bombs exploded in two pubs, frequented mainly by young drinkers.
5 Sep. 1975	(P) IRA	The Hilton Hotel, Central London	2 63 injured	Bomb explosion, marking renewed bombing campaign on England.
30 March 1979	(P) IRA/INLA	House of Commons (HOC), London	1	Shadow Northern Ireland Secretary was killed when a car-bomb fitted to his vehicle detonated in the HOC car park.
27 Aug. 1979	(P) IRA	Warrenpoint ('Narrow Water') Ulster, Northern Ireland	18 2 injured	Eighteen soldiers (mostly Paras) were killed and one civilian during an ambush. Two remotely-controlled bombs exploded at opposite sides of the road and at different times along with gunfire.
27 Aug. 1979	(P) IRA	Mullaghmore, County Sligo, North-West Ireland	3	Victims included Lord Mountbatten and his grandson, who were killed on a boat whilst holidaying.

(Continued)

Table 9.2   (Continued)

Date	Group responsible	Place	No. of victims	Method/details
20 July 1982	(P) IRA	Central London	11 50 injured	Two bombs exploded within two hours of each other, the first a nail bomb in a car, the second exploded underneath a bandstand whilst the band was playing.
17 Dec. 1983	(P) IRA	Knightsbridge, London	6 90 injured	Car-bomb exploded outside of Harrods department store, in a busy shopping area.
12 Oct. 1984	(P) IRA	The Grand Hotel, Brighton	5 34 injured	Direct attack on the British government, when a bomb exploded at the Conservative Party Conference.
11 Nov. 1987	(P) IRA	Enniskillen, County Fermanagh, Northern Ireland	12 63 (+) injured	A bomb exploded at a Remembrance Day service. The final victim died in 2000, having never regained consciousness after the bombing.
21 Dec. 1988	Al Megrahi (Libyan terrorists suspected)	Lockerbie, Scotland 'The Lockerbie Disaster	270	Bomb planted on Pan Am Flight 103 exploded over the Scottish town, killing all passengers and 11 people on the ground. Remains the UK's largest mass murder.
22 Sept. 1989	(P) IRA	Deal, Kent	11	A bomb exploded in a recreation centre in an army barracks.
20 March 1993	(P) IRA	Warrington, Cheshire	2 56 injured	Two bombs hidden in dustbins exploded in a busy shopping centre. Those killed were a 3-year-old and a 12-year-old.
9 Feb. 1996	(P) IRA	Docklands, London	2 29 injured	A half-tonne bomb, in a lorry near South Quay, exploded.
15 Aug. 1998	(R) IRA	Omagh, Co. Tyrone, Northern Ireland	29 300 (+) injured	A car-bomb detonated in the centre of the town, in an area in which people were being directed to safety. Described as the worst single atrocity of the Troubles and ended a 17-month cease-fire.

[1]The OIRA (offical IRA) was formed by members of the original IRA which split in 1970. It has carried out very few attacks since a cease-fire in 1972, although in the mid-1970s a feud with the IRSP (Irish Republican Socialist Party) developed.

Source: www.guardian.co.uk/Northern_Ireland/Story/0,2763,209101,00.html

reflection of the cease-fire agreed by paramilitary organisations (announced by the IRA initially in June 1994 and by the Ulster Volunteer Force in November of the same year) and the subsequent peace process inaugurated by the Belfast Agreement of 1998. Increases can be seen for those periods in which the cease-fire was broken. Hence, homicide in Northern Ireland is heavily dependent upon political factors and the cultural and historical context of the Troubles (Fay et al., 1997; Home Office, 1998b, 2001b; O'Leary and McGarry, 1996). In fact, Troubles-related killings account for a *substantial* proportion of all homicide in Northern Ireland. During the period 1987–99, homicides classified as 'security situation-related murders' accounted for an average 73 per cent (704) of all murders (ranging year-to-year from 24 per cent to 92 per cent). In addition, they accounted for 68 per cent of the total homicides in Northern Ireland during the same time frame (personal communication, RUC, 2000).[8]

The Police Service of Northern Ireland (PSNI,[9] 2003b) have also compiled statistics regarding security situation-related deaths, which show that between 1969–2002 a total of 3,344 people have been killed due to the security situation (excluding those killed outside of Northern Ireland). To put this into perspective, O'Leary and McGarry emphasise that:

> Scale matters … If the equivalent ratio of victims to population had been produced in Great Britain in the same period some 100,000 people would have died, and if a similar level of political violence had taken place the number of fatalities in the USA would have been over 500,000, or about ten times the number of Americans killed in the Vietnam war. (1996: 12)

In terms of those killed, PSNI data do not distinguish between civilian victims and those who are members of paramilitary organisations (including the total number of deaths in one 'civilian' category). However, O'Leary and McGarry (1996) suggest that between 1969–90, 32 per cent of victims were Catholic civilians, whilst 21 per cent were Protestant civilians. Thirty-one per cent of victims were members of the security forces, and a further 13 per cent were members of nationalist or Loyalist paramilitary organisations. Fay et al. (1997) analysed the period of 1969–94 and, despite using a more inclusive definition of deaths 'due' to the security situation,[10] found very similar results. In addition, they found that the large majority of those victims who belonged to a paramilitary organisation were members of Republican, as opposed to Loyalist, groups (13 and 3 per cent respectively), and that a significant proportion of victims were relatively young (for example, 70 per cent were under the age of 39). However, both studies noted that Catholic deaths outnumbered Protestant deaths, both in absolute and relative terms[11] (Fay et al., 1997; O'Leary and McGarry, 1996).

Republican paramilitaries have been responsible for the large majority of deaths, followed by Loyalist groups and then security forces. In their study, Fay et al. (1997) found that 59 per cent of deaths were perpetrated by Republicans, 28 per cent by Loyalists and 11 per cent by the British Army and RUC combined. As O'Leary and McGarry put it:

> Between 1969 and 1989 the security forces killed less than half as many people as loyalist paramilitaries; loyalist paramilitaries less than half as many people as nationalist

paramilitaries; and nationalist paramilitaries were responsible for more than half of all deaths. (1996: 35)

From the early 1990s onwards, this picture changed in that Loyalist groups appeared to be responsible for more attacks than Republicans (Amnesty International, 1994). This assertion is supported by recent data from the PSNI (2003d), which shows that of those persons charged with terrorist offences of murder and attempted murder between 2000–02, 78 per cent were from 'Loyalist' groups (with similar findings for other terrorist offences).

In the last five years there have been profound and important developments within Northern Ireland (and between Northern Ireland and Britain) that have undoubtedly changed the landscape of the Troubles. Not least of all, the Belfast Agreement (or the 'Good Friday' Agreement) and the beginnings of the decommissioning of weapons by paramilitary groups. However, since 1998 a significant number of incidents have taken place (both in Northern Ireland and mainland Britain) involving dissident or splinter groups from the IRA (such as the 'Real' IRA – (R)IRA – and the 'Continuity' IRA). Such groups have committed attacks and bombings in protest to the 'Good Friday' Agreement and in response to the increasing politicisation of the (P)IRA and their apparent new passive position over the 'armed struggle' (Alonso, 2001; Dingley, 2001). In England, for example, there have been at least eight attacks between 1998–2002 attributable to such dissident groups, none of which resulted in loss of life, although substantial injury, damage and disruption was caused (BBC News online, 2002). In Northern Ireland, there have been hundreds of bombing incidents within this period (PSNI, 2003e) and dissident groups are held responsible for (at the very least) 30 of such attacks (BBC News online, 2002), including what remains the worst single event in the Troubles: 'The Omagh Bombing' in 1998, which killed 29 people and injured over 300. The situation at present is clearly still a vulnerable one, and the outbreak of political violence still a significant threat. Some commentators, such as Dingley (2001), question whether the (P)IRA are truly sincere in their commitment to the peace process, and whether such 'progress' really does represent what Alonso (2001) refers to as the modernisation of Republican thinking regarding the utility of violence. The long-term implications of these changes on the number of homicides perpetrated by terrorist groups in Northern Ireland and across the UK are yet to be seen.

Explaining Terrorism and the Troubles

Wilkinson has defined terrorism as the systematic use or threat of 'murder and destruction ... to terrorise individuals, groups, communities or governments into conceding to the terrorists' political aims' (1986: 56). Whilst this broad definition clearly encompasses Northern Ireland-related terrorism, terrorism in Northern Ireland could more specifically be described as 'nationalist' terrorism (Clutterbuck, 1990) or 'revolutionary national terrorism' (Wilkinson, 1974). In essence, Republican paramilitary organisations are fighting over territory (and power) that they claim to be 'theirs', in re-claiming the independence of Northern Ireland. As O'Boyle (2002: 28) points out, the IRA use concepts of 'national self-defence', the right to 'national self-determination' and 'independence' to justify their lethal actions. The use of terror is thus a means of overthrowing a government in power, or forcing that government to change its policies. As such, as Crenshaw argues, 'terrorism is a rational choice, deliberately made for reasons that are comprehensible if not justifiable to the outside observer' (1984: 263). Hyams distinguishes between direct terrorism (such as attacks on the 'tenants of power') and indirect terrorism which 'consists in discrediting a government by demonstrating that it cannot protect its own people or their property, cannot maintain law and order: in short, is not fit to be in office at all' (1975: 10). The stated aims of IRA terrorist groups and the tactics which they use, as discussed earlier, fit into such descriptions quite clearly.

In attempting to explain terrorism, a popular view is that terrorists are 'psychopaths' or are mentally ill; however, there is little evidence to support such a proposition[12] (Heskin, 1984; Lyons and Harbinson, 1986; Silke, 2002). For example, in Northern Ireland, Lyons and Harbinson (1986) compared cases of 'political' and 'non-political' murderers referred to them for psychiatric assessment between 1974 and 1984 (47 and 59 cases respectively). They found those offenders who killed for political or terrorist purposes came from a more stable background than those who killed for non-political reasons. In addition, significantly fewer political murderers had a family history of personality disorder, and significantly less were found to suffer from a psychiatric illness (1986: 197). Silke argues that 'the vast majority of research on terrorists has concluded that they are not mentally or psychologically abnormal. On the contrary, many studies have found that terrorists are psychologically much healthier and far more stable than other violent criminals' (2002: 18). Interestingly though, Weatherson and Moran (2003) argue that whilst there is no evidence of a causal connection between mental disorder and engagement in terrorist activity, there may be a connection in the opposite direction, that is, between an individual engaging in terrorist activity and developing a mental disorder(s). Specifically, certain stressors which occur as a result of involvement in terrorist activity may result in psychological disturbance in terrorist individuals.

In exploring the pathway to terrorism, Heskin (1984) puts forward the concept of 'relative deprivation' (both within Ireland and between Ireland and the rest of the UK) as a general source of motivation for paramilitary involvement. Heskin (1984) argues that life experiences and events can provide the motivation or catalyst for involvement. Silke discusses the same themes, although identifies the issue as one of socialisation, arguing that:

> Any given society possesses some minorities and disaffected groups who rightly or wrongly perceive the world is treating them harshly. In some cases, there are genuine and very substantial causes for grievance. Individuals who belong to or identify with such disaffected groups share a sense of injustice and persecution. It is from this that individual terrorists emerge. The move from 'disaffected' to 'violent extremist' is usually facilitated by a catalyst event. Normally this is an act of extreme physical violence committed by the police or security forces or a rival group against the individual, his or her family, friends, or simply anyone they can identify with. (2002: 18–19)

Heskin (1984) also refers to the findings of a number of experimental social psychology studies, such as those of Milgram (1974) and Zimbardo et al. (1973)

which emphasise group conformity, obedience to authority and role-conforming behaviour. Perhaps more importantly, a number of writers comment upon the deep-rooted and historical nature of violence within Northern Ireland, which has legitimised and reinforced the use of political violence and terrorism in the 'armed struggle' and the fight for Irish independence (Clutterbuck, 1990; Crenshaw, 1984; Heskin, 1984). For some, this historical legitimacy, compounded by the antagonistic nature of the Troubles, explains the sheer persistence of terrorism within the context of Northern Ireland (Crenshaw, 1984; O'Leary and McGarry, 1996).

In conclusion, the Northern Ireland Troubles represent one, quite distinct, manifestation of terrorism that has had a particular impact in the context of UK homicide. In the 10-year period 1991–2000 over 450 people died in Northern Ireland alone as a result of terrorist activities. Whilst most terrorists organisations kill in the pursuit of some form of political or ideological change, the ways in which different terrorist groups form, are organised and ultimately pursue their goals are clearly distinct. There is little evidence to suggest that terrorists are psychologically disturbed, rather that they come together to fight some perceived injustice.

Study Task 9.2

Conduct a search (using the Internet and newspaper articles) of terrorist organisations not linked to Northern Ireland (such as Al Qaida and Hamas). By examining the background to the development and emergence of these organisations, assess the similarities and differences, in terms of apparent motivations, terrorist techniques and so forth, between these terrorists and the various manifestations of the IRA that have and continue to exist in Northern Ireland.

Corporate Homicide

In this secion we consider the extent and nature of corporate homicide and also probe some of the explanations that have been offered to try to make sense of this form of homicide.

Nature and Extent

Over the last couple of decades, a number of public disasters and tragedies have brought the issue of corporate homicide to attention (when previously this form of criminality had been very much neglected). As stated in Chapter 1, corporate killings can be referred to as deaths which result, at least in part, from negligence or deliberate decisions by a corporate body.[13] As with other forms of homicide, corporate killings can take a number of forms, and occur in very different contexts. Deaths may result from manufacturing and selling faulty or unsafe products and goods. In addition, consumers can be killed as a result of adulterating or falsely describing contents of food, and manufacturing or selling food produce that is 'unfit for human consumption' (Croall, 1998). An obvious case of such a killing can be seen in deaths which result from food poisoning, incidences of which are increasing (and attributed to the growth of fast food, take-aways and eating out) (Croall, 1998). Killings can also result from breaches of health and safety, whereby organisations fail to comply with regulations regarding the safety of workers, consumers and the general public. For example, employees can be fatally injured in the workplace, killed through exposure (long-term or otherwise) to noxious chemicals and die from occupationally-caused diseases. In addition, corporate killings can result from breaches of environmental law, in terms of illegal emissions and pollution (from industrial waste, for example). Often ignored and undetected, pollution can have wide-ranging effects which are perhaps underestimated (although associated with a wide range of diseases and illness) (Croall, 1998).

Those killings which have attracted greatest attention, unsurprisingly, are those in which there are a large number of victims, particularly when those killed are members of the public, or 'consumers'. Despite the fact that corporate crime is not generally perceived to be 'real' crime, the effects of corporate 'violence' can be devastating. The case of Bhopal, in India, where an explosion released poisonous gas into the atmosphere in 1984, more than illustrates this point. Between 3,000 and 5,000 people were killed and over 200,000 injured. In the areas that were most affected it was estimated that at least 90 per cent of families had experienced either the death or severe incapacitation of one parent or more (Croall, 1998). In the UK, a spate of public 'tragedies' and 'accidents' during the 1980s and 1990s led to hundreds of deaths. Welham (2002) particularly emphasises the period of 1984–89, in which a number of high-profile disasters occurred. Although the number of victims pale in comparison to Bhopal, we can see from Table 9.3 that the number of incidents which have occurred in the UK, and the number of victims such 'incidents' claim, is by no means trivial.

As noted in Chapter 1, the number of deaths in Britain due to corporate negligence or neglect far exceeds the total number of homicides in Britain (by at least two-and-a-half-times). The majority of inquiries which follow these disasters and tragedies reveal negligence surrounding safety procedures, implicating both individuals and corporate bodies themselves (Welham, 2002; Wells, 2001). In addition, it is strongly argued that the majority of such killings (particularly breaches of health and safety legislation) were easily preventable. Yet, prosecutions for these deaths amount to only a handful, and convictions are even rarer.

Explaining Corporate Killings

Attempts to explain corporate killings have focused upon economic changes and market pressures that face companies and organisations in modern industrial and capitalist society. A number of academics argue that the rise in corporate crime (and hence, corporate killings) is an inevitable process of capitalism (Nelken, 2002). Several researchers have drawn upon 'anomie' or 'strain' theory to explain the conditions which foster corporate crime (Waring et al., 1995; Nelken, 1997, 2002). As discussed in Chapter 5, Merton's original (1938) 'strain theory' was a cultural and

Table 9.3   Corporate homicide cases in the UK

Date	Company involved nature of business	No. of Victims	Details/circumstances
1927	Cory Brothers; private mining company	1	The first attempted prosecution for corporate manslaughter was brought against the directors of the company, after a worker fell against an electric fence they had erected around a power house to protect against pilfering during strikes. The prosecution was unsuccessful.
6 March 1987	P&O European Ferries (Dover) Ltd; public transport 'The Zeebrugge Disaster'	192 (154 passengers, 38 crew)	The *Herald of Free Enterprise* capsized when the bow doors were left open upon departure from Zeebrugge harbour, with various bodies at fault. The company and several of the directors and employees were charged with corporate manslaughter; however, the judge in the Crown Court directed acquittals and the case was dismissed (despite the jury returning verdicts of unlawful killing). This was only the third corporate manslaughter case in (English) legal history.
18 Nov. 1987	London Regional Transport (LRT); public transport 'The Kings Cross Fire'	31 60 injured	A fire spread through the London underground station. It was argued that the fire had been caused by a discarded cigarette igniting waste that had been allowed to accumulate under the escalators. In addition, no sprinkler system was in operation, with LRT having ignored recommendations in 1984 to install one. Staff cuts and inadequate training were also blamed.
12 Dec. 1988	British Rail; public transport 'The Clapham Train Crash'	37 500 (+) injured	Two trains collided outside Clapham Junction in London. Signalling failures and lax maintenance blamed.
6 July 1988	Occidental Petroleum; oil company 'The Piper Alpha Oil Rig'	167	An initial explosion set off a fire triggering further explosions. It was argued that the rig was overloaded and dangerous, with inadequate safety procedures.

(Continued)

Table 9.3   (Continued)

Date	Company involved nature of business	No. of Victims	Details/circumstances
19 April 1989	South Yorkshire Police; crowd control 'The Hillsborough Disaster'	95 500+ injured	Spectators surged undirected into Hillsborough football stadium, during an FA Cup semi-final. Victims were crushed to death, when they were pinned to the barricades and fencing at the front of the seating area. This was apparently exacerbated by a fire in a wooden stand. The jury returned a verdict of accidental death, and extra security measures at football stadiums were proposed.
20 Aug. 1989	South Coast Shipping Company Ltd; shipping company 'The Marchioness Disaster'	51 80 injured	*The Marchioness* leisure boat collided with a dredger (*The Bowbelle*) on the River Thames, argued to be caused by the captain of *The Bowbelle* not keeping a lookout.
22 March 1993	OLL Ltd; outdoor activity courses 'The Lyme Bay Canoe Tragedy'	4	The first successful conviction for corporate manslaughter. Four schoolchildren drowned when their canoes capsized on a school expedition, during an outdoor pursuit course run by OLL Ltd. Participants were argued to be ill-equipped and the leaders unqualified to teach the course.
19 Sept. 1997	Great Western Trains; public transport 'The Southall Rail Crash'	7 151 injured	GWT were indicted for manslaughter after a train, en route from Swansea to London, ran through red lights and collided with a goods unit in Southall. The driver had apparently been packing his belongings ready for arrival at the destination of Paddington. Further evidence implicated the company. The company was fined £1.5 million (the highest to date), but the prosecution failed. No charges were brought against the driver.
5 Oct. 1999	Great Western Trains; public transport 'The Hatfield Rail Crash'	31 150 (+) injured	Two trains collided in Ladbrook Grove, West London (the same stretch of line as the Southall crash). Again, signalling failures were blamed.

structural theory of crime presenting a conflict between the cultural goals of 'society' and the structural limitations within the social strata. Merton argued that achieving success goals (of material wealth, prestige and status) had become overemphasised to the point that the legitimate means of achieving these goals (through hard work, honesty and deferred gratification) became weakened and less important. This conflict placed 'strain' on the institutional means, especially for those who could not achieve cultural goals through their use, and meant that forms of deviance were encouraged (Vold et al., 1998).

Similarly, for corporations the shared goal is that of profit maximisation. The institution of business is centred upon profit, therefore this goal is of central priority – without profit, there is no business (Box, 1983; Nelken, 1997; Croall, 1992). However, there is a continuous contradiction between this cultural goal and other elements or 'environmental uncertainties' which mean that within capitalist business, corporations have to juggle the elements of market pressures and organisational priorities within a regulatory environment whilst maintaining and achieving the goal of profit. Box (1983) outlines five major sources that affect the possibility, extent and frequency of these environmental uncertainties, these being:

- competition (in terms of price structures);
- the government (extending regulations which cover corporate activities);
- employees (and demands made by trade unionists);
- consumers (whose demands and needs fluctuate constantly); and
- the public (and the growth of 'environmentalism').

He argues that businesses have to operate within a highly uncertain and unpredictable environment, and that this environment can restrict the legitimate opportunities available to achieve financial success. Thus, as Box states, 'when these environmental uncertainties increase so the strain towards corporate criminal activity will increase' (1983: 37).

In sum, what is argued here is that market forces, organisational contexts and external regulations place 'strain' on corporations to achieve the goal of profit, and that such pressures encourage corporations to 'cut corners'. Thus, health and safety regulations may be breached by corporations (to the detriment of the workforce, consumers and the general public) in a drive to reduce overheads, maximise profits, meet deadlines and so forth. For example, Braithwaite (1984) found that due to a highly competitive market, pharmaceutical companies falsified test results in order to release new products onto the market ahead of their competitors, with fatal results to consumers (Croall, 1992; Nelken, 1997). In the US during the 1970s, Ford Pinto manufactured a vehicle which had a dangerous mechanical fault that the company was fully aware of. However, they did not recall the vehicles and remedy the fault on the basis that the potential payment of damages would prove to be less than the cost of recalling the cars. This decision led to the deaths of between 500–900 people (Nelken, 1997). In addition, many of the cases discussed above (such as Zeebrugge and the GWT crashes) also give support to such explanations. Finally, Passas (1990) makes a similar case regarding the pressure to succeed in terms of profit maximisation, growth and efficiency and desire for these goals to be met by all or any means. Furthermore, he suggests that deviant behaviour within corporations can be maintained and further promoted through processes of interaction that can lead to widespread rationalisations that 'excuse' and 'justify' illegal practices. Ultimately this can lead to deviant activities even in the absence of compelling pressures to perform, deliver or compete.

Theories based on strain or anomie have dominated explanations of corporate crime. Coleman (1987: 161) argues that many theorists remain focused at the social-psychological level concerning themselves with the dynamics of organisations and how group interactions normalise or excuse deviance at the expense of recognising that it is the social structure of industrial capitalism and 'the culture of competition' to which it gives rise that is the root cause of this form of crime. Similarly, Slapper and Tombs (1999: 161–2) argue that the nature of capitalist economy – which constantly pushes people to hit targets, seek promotion, avoid demotion, survive recessions and so forth – is vital in understanding the existence of corporate crime.

Finally, some commentators have recognised links between masculinity and corporate crime. For example, Punch (1996) argues that business is often likened to war and gendered images are common. For example, during company takeovers, the acquiring company is often depicted as 'macho' and the target or taken company as female. Other commentators have noted that successful corporations are often defined through metaphors of masculinity in that they are mean, aggressive, goal-oriented, efficient and competitive but rarely empathetic, supportive or kind (Ackers, 1992) (see also Chappel, 1998).

A very interesting account of corporate homicide that incorporates masculinity into the account is offered by Messerschmidt (1997) in his assessment of the decision-making process leading to the launch of the space shuttle *Challenger*. *Challenger* exploded in mid-air on 28 January 1986, just 73 seconds into flight, killing all seven crew members. The technical cause of the explosion has been well document as a fault with the O-rings (designed to prevent hot gasses escaping). The O-rings failed to seal properly due to the extremely cold temperatures at launch time, allowing hot gasses to escape, ignite and within seconds penetrate the external tank (President's Commission, 1986). The vulnerabilities of the O-rings were well known by both government and corporate officials years before the fateful day. Why, then, in light of the high risk to human life, was the shuttle launched? For Messerschmidt, the backdrop to the launch lies in the various pressures that faced management at both National Aeronautics and Space Administration (NASA) and MTI (the body contracted to design and build the shuttle) to create an economical shuttle, to launch a certain number of flights per year and on time and, for MTI, not to loose their lucrative contract. Hence, despite increased knowledge as to the potentially hazardous nature of the O-rings, management was keen to ignore the problem both in terms of not fixing the defect and not cancelling flights (Messerschmidt, 1997: 94). When engineers and management at MTI made a 'no launch' recommendation to NASA on 27 January due to their concerns at the low temperatures (and the likelihood, therefore, of the O-rings becoming less resilient), they met with serious opposition. Engineers at MTI held firm with their decision, but ultimately MTI management excluded the engineers from their discussions and reversed the 'no launch' decision. As Messerschmidt puts it, 'MTI management engaged in risk-taking behaviour to achieve their corporate objective' (1997: 97). However, Messerschmidt takes the analysis further, unravelling why engineers held firm whilst management yielded to pressure from NASA. He argues that what occurred reflects the differences in managerial masculinity versus engineer masculinity. To begin with, in keeping with Punch (1996) and Akers (1992), Messerschmidt argues that corporations are often defined through metaphors of masculinity – such as careerism, decisiveness and risk-taking. Yet both the managers and engineers were male – so how can we explain their different decisions? For Messerschmidt the answer lies in their differential job roles and masculine status within the corporation. For managers, the key defining aspect of their role as men within the corporation is to take risks and move forward toward the ultimate goal of corporate success. In stark contrast, 'professional-engineer masculinity is to be in command of the particular technology' (Messerschmidt, 1997: 104) and, therefore, to know its limits. Hence, engineers (relative to managers) place very high priority on quality and safety (1997: 104). 'Risk taking is not the appealing masculine prac-tice to engineers that it is to managers. Indeed, for engineers, inasmuch as techni-cal failure threatens their masculinity, it should not be surprising that MTI engineers would exhibit greater caution regarding O-ring capability and argue against launch' (1997: 105).

In short, Messerschmidt links this particular example of corporate crime to both class and gender and the distinct priorities and practices of competing masculini-ties in the context of the organisation of MTI. He goes beyond the issues of pres-sures upon corporations to 'get results' and unravels in much greater detail the complexities of organisational hierarchy and the different ways in which 'mas-culinity' can be played out within corporations. What is particularly interesting about the *Challenger* case is that the mangers must surely have known that if their launch decision was wrong (as indeed it was), the results of their error would be wit-nessed globally in the most dramatic of fashions (as, of course, it was). There would be no opportunity for this corporate homicide to be hidden from public view, yet the risk was still taken.

Study Task 9.3

Conduct a search of newspaper archives via the Internet for the past five years of examples of corporate homicide in the UK. Consider where blame was laid and toward whom, if relevant (that is, an individual within the corporation or the cor-porate body). Do you find any evidence within the accounts of these crimes of links to the wider social or structural features of capitalist society?

In summary, the majority of explanations of corporate crime or homicide recog-nise some element of pressure or strain to perform as crucial to unravelling this phenomenon. Some researchers have paid more attention than others to the wider structural forces of capitalism that give rise to this condition (for example, Coleman, 1987 and Slapper and Tombs, 1999), whilst others, such as Messerschmidt (1997), have been concerned to unravel the links between gender, class and corporate crime. Regardless of their theoretical standpoint, most commentators agree that corporate crime is inadequately policed and prosecuted, and that in this way the criminal justice system contributes to the facilitation of corporate crime as an option for achieving business goals (Slapper and Tombs, 1999: 162).

Chapter Summary and Conclusions

This chapter has considered three distinct forms of multiple homicide in terms of their nature and extent and the dominant explanations put forward to make sense of these killings. Whilst each of these forms of homicide are relatively rare in terms of occurrence,[14] when combined, they account for a significant number of the total homicide count in the UK. Table 9.4 offers an attempt to depict this significance, though it is by no means a perfect measure of the true extent of multiple homicide in the UK. For example, it has not been possible to determine the number of multiple murders in Scotland (as a single case of homicide is counted for each act irrespective of the

Table 9.4   Multiple and non-multiple homicide in the UK

Year	Multiple murder (England and Wales)	Terrorism (N. Ireland)	Corporate homicide (Britain)	Multiple homicide totals	Non-multiple homicide in the UK[1]
1991	9	94	1,865	1,968	820
1992	18	85	1,885	1,988	805
1993	9	84	1,934	2,027	777
1994	24	62	1,925	2,011	802
1995	26	9	2,044	2,079	793
1996	23	15	2,032	2,070	717
1997	15	22	2,079	2,116	735
1998	22	55	2,243	2,320	774
1999	25	7	2,371	2,397	830
2000	86[2]	18	2,321	2,425	920
1991–2000	257	451	20,699	21,407	7,973

[1]These figures were gathered by adding together the total number of homicides in the UK and subtracting the cases of multiple murder in the UK (it has not been possible to do this for Scotland as there is no way of determining this) and also detracting security-related or terrorist killings that occurred in Northern Ireland. In short, these figures are somewhat inflated by the non-removal of multiple murders in Scotland and terrorist-related killings in England (there have been none in Wales). For the purposes of the point being made, however, this is not a crucial issue.
[2]This figure is unusually high due to the incident in which 58 Chinese immigrants were found dead in a sealed lorry container at Dover, having suffocated. Perry Wacker has since been found guilty of 58 charges of manslaughter as well as four counts of conspiracy to smuggle immigrants into the UK. He was sentenced to 14 years in prison in April 2001.

number of victims) and the terrorism figures only related to deaths in Northern Ireland. Regarding corporate homicide, only the three regions that form Great Britain have been included, and a significant number of deaths due to corporate negligence or neglect have not been included.[15] In short, the final figures are an under-estimate of the extent of multiple homicide in the UK – particularly in respect of the corporate homicide category. Nevertheless, even these conservative multiple homicide figures indicate that they significantly outrank 'normal' or non-multiple homicide by threefold.

It is particularly interesting to note that of the three categories of multiple homicide, multiple murder presents the smallest share, yet arguably causes the greatest concern, although recent terrorist events around the globe have heightened people's fear of this particular phenomenon also. But even terrorist killings are dwarfed by those that occur through corporate negligence or neglect (wilful or otherwise). Hence, clearly something other than the number of fatal casualties drives the public (and academic) imagination when articulating concerns or fears of homicide.

Review Questions

- Compare and contrast the explanations discussed in this chapter for the three different forms of multiple homicide. To what extent do the various theories fit in with the three major perspectives discussed in Chapters 3 to 5 of this text?
- Which of the three forms of multiple homicide discussed in this chapter is most prevalent in the UK (in terms of the number of lives lost in an average year)?
- Why do criminologists pay so little attention to corporate homicide?
- What have you learned from this chapter about the difficulties in estimating the extent of multiple *murder* in a country?

Further Reading

The majority of publications in relation to serial and spree killings originate from the US, the most popular being *Serial Murder* (Holmes and Holmes, 1998: Sage) and *Mass Murder in the United States* (Holmes and Holmes, 2001: Sage). Also, *Serial Murder: An Elusive Phenomenon* (Egger, 1990: Praeger) covers a number of important themes and perspectives, whilst Lester's *Serial Killers* (1995: Charles Press) provides a more up-to-date review of the relevant themes and literature. An interesting article that critiques the dominant approaches to determining motives of serial killers can be found in 'Phenomenology and Serial Murder' (Skrapec, 2001: *Homicide Studies*, Vol. 5/1, pp. 46–63). In the UK, any of the handful of studies which have been undertaken are strongly recommended, particularly 'Multiple Murder: A Review' (Gresswell and Hollin, 1994: *British Journal of Criminology*, Vol. 34/1, pp. 1–14); 'British Serial Killing: Towards a Structural Explanation' (Grover and Soothill, 1997: *The British Criminology Conferences: Selected Proceedings, Volume 2*, available online at www.britsoccrim.org/bccsp/vol02/08GROVE.HTM, and *The Aetiology of Serial Murder:*

Towards an Integrated Mode (Mitchell, 1997: MSc thesis available online at http://users.ox.ac.uk/~zool0380/masters.htm.

Regarding Northern Ireland and the Troubles, *The Politics of Antagonism: Understanding Northern Ireland* (O'Leary and McGarry, 1996: Athlone Press) provides one of the most up-to-date and comprehensive accounts of the conflict. In addition, *Political Killings in Northern Ireland* (Amnesty International, 1994: Amnesty International) is also informative and very accessible. Despite being relatively dated, *Terrorism in Ireland* (Alexander and O'Day, 1984: Palgrave Macmillan) is still an excellent compilation of essays regarding various issues particularly relevant to the Northern Ireland experience. In terms of terrorism in general, *Terrorism versus Democracy* (Wilkinson, 2001: Frank Cass) provides an authoritative account.

Amongst the most useful references for corporate homicide are: *Corporate Crime* (Slapper and Tombs, 1999: Longman); *Dirty Business: Exploring Corporate Misconduct* (Punch, 1996: Sage); *White Collar Crime* (Croall, 1992: Open University Press); and Chapter 23 entitled 'White Collar Crime' in *The Oxford Handbook of Criminology* (Maguire et al., 2002: Oxford University Press) is very useful. Chapter 4 (Murderous Managers) in *Crime as Structured Action* (Messerschmidt, 1997: Sage) is worth consulting. Finally, Chapter 10 (Dow Corning and the Silicone Breast Implant Debacle) in *Masculinities and Violence* (Bowker (ed.), 1998: Sage) makes for a very interesting read, where Chapple explores a case of corporate crime against women in her discussion of manufacturers of silicone breast implants (Dow Corning) and how and why they continued to manufacture silicone breasts despite their knowledge of the dangers.

Useful Internet Sites

There are a large number of Internet sites which are dedicated to multiple and serial killing, although few are of any real academic use. However, one site which provides information on a number of killers in the UK is www.murderuk.com/serialkillers/serial.htm. Also BBC News online contains more credible information regarding a number of 'infamous' crimes and criminals www.bbc.co.uk/crime/caseclosed/criminals.shtml, and a simple search of their crime site provides news stories on a variety of relevant issues. Extensive documentation relating to the enquiry into the serial sexual killer Harold Shipman can be found at www.the-shipman-inquiry.org.uk/home.asp. The Police Service Northern Ireland (PSNI) publish data concerning homicide, including information relating to those killed as a result of the security situation; see, for example www.psni.police.uk/index/departments/statistics_branch.htm. Other useful Internet sources regarding terrorism include 'The Lockerbie Trial Briefing' (www.ltb.org.uk), and the 'Bloody Sunday Inquiry' (www.bloody-sunday-inquiry.org.uk/). Also, www.psr.keele.ac.uk/sseal/terror.htm provides a number of useful terrorism links. Finally, the terrorism section on the Home Office website is very useful www.homeoffice.gov.uk/terrorism/index.html, along with links to the UK Resilience website and London Prepared. Also of interest is the coverage of the Shipman Inquiry at www.the-shipman-inquiry.org.uk/reports.asp. A visit to the Law Commission website allows for searches of their latest recommendations in relation to the law surrounding corporate homicide: www.lawcom.gov.uk. The Report of the Presidential Commission on the Space Shuttle Challenger Accident (President's Commission, 1986) can be found at www.science.ksc.nasa.gov/shuttle/missions.

Notes

1 It is perhaps worthwhile to note that many studies exclude certain forms of multiple murder including politically motivated killings, state-sponsored killings, and professional (i.e. contract) killings (e.g., Fox and Levin, 1998; Jenkins, 1991; Gresswell and Hollin, 1994). Often, the assumption here is that such killings are qualitatively different, thus requiring alternative explanations and theoretical analysis. However, as Coleman and Norris (2000) point out, although this may in fact be the case, the interesting similarities between the various forms of multiple murder, *including* those of corporate and terrorist killings, should not necessarily be overlooked.

2 In terms of actually 'counting' such killings for the purposes of homicide statistics, a mass or spree killing in England and Wales would count each victim as an individual example of homicide. In contrast, Scottish counting rules would count the mass or spree event (regardless of the number of victims) as one homicide.

3 The cases selected are those that could be deemed as 'high profile' in terms of the media coverage they received. Those cases with three or less victims have generally been excluded, unless there were a large number of associated victims who were injured but did not die. It is worth noting that a substantial proportion of those cases involving three or less victims take the form of family annihilations (as discussed in Chapter 8).

4 With regards to Holmes and De Burger's (1988) claims of reliability, Kiger quickly makes the important point that 'One can only assume that by a reliable estimate these authors mean an accurate estimate. It should be noted that one could conceivably have a reliable and yet invalid/inaccurate estimate of a particular phenomenon' (1990: 36).

5 On 11 September 2001, four aeroplanes were hijacked by terrorists. Two were flown into the World Trade Centre (the 'Twin Towers') in New York, a third crashed at the Pentagon (outside Washington) and the fourth crashed in a field in Pennsylvania (believed to be an abortive attack possibly aimed at the White House or Camp David).

6 It should be pointed out, however, that the attack was not planned for the UK itself. It is suspected that the bombing was part of a history of retaliation between the US and Libya (e.g., six months prior to Lockerbie, the US accidentally shot down an Iranian Airbus, killing 290). Lockerbie was revenge for this, and other incidents, with Libya and Palestinian terrorist groups strongly thought to be responsible. Although the bomb should have detonated whilst the plane was flying over the Atlantic Ocean, due to delays, Flight 103 took off an hour late and thus the plane exploded over the UK mainland.

7 These 'injury' figures are likely to be under-estimates, with many victims not reporting such incidents or seeking treatment for injuries.

8 Not all security-related deaths are necessarily classified as either murder or 'security-related'.

9 Since the Good Friday Agreement (1998) and subsequent political and governmental changes, a national police service for Northern Ireland (PSNI) has been created, which has replaced the Royal Ulster Constabulary (RUC).

10 Fay et al. (1997) include within their definition every *death* which was Troubles-related as opposed to *homicide*. This includes those deaths resulting indirectly from the conflict, such as those killed by army vehicles and deaths due to trauma, heart attacks and suicide.

11 Although it is important to point out that there are a number of reasons for the over-representation of Catholic victims. For example, more Republican attacks have resulted in the deaths of Catholic civilians, compared to Loyalist attacks which have killed Protestant civilians (for further discussion see O'Leary and McGarry, 1996). Moreover, when we simply

compare civilians killed by the 'other' side (what Fay et al. (1997: 43) argue is at the heart of Troubles), that is, Catholics killed by Loyalists and Protestants killed by Republicans, then the rates of death become much more comparable (Fay et al., 1997).

12 Although Heskin (1984) points out that the proposition that some individuals will be more likely to become involved in terrorist activity than others has more merit.

13 The Law Commission's proposals (1996: Report No. 237) regarding the reform of the law on involuntary manslaughter, and a new offence of 'corporate killing', restricted liability to corporate bodies. However, the government response suggested that the proposed new offence should apply to all undertakings: 'any trade or business or other activity providing employment' (Home Office, 2000). Although this does not affect the nature of our discussion here, the effect it may have upon the scope of the new offence is quite significant, encompassing a much wider range of bodies. The Home Office claims 'We estimate that this would mean that *a total of 3½ million enterprises might become potentially liable to the offence of corporate killing* (2000: 16; emphasis in original).

14 With the exception of fatal work-related diseases and fatal injuries to workers.

15 The figures compiled for corporate homicide only include fatal injuries to workers (which include deaths due to falls from a height, struck by moving vehicles or moving/falling objects and being trapped by something collapsing or overturning) and occupationally-caused fatal diseases where the cause has been specified during death certification. However, the Health and Safety Executive note that there are likely to be very many more lung-related work-deaths that are not recorded as such due to the difficulties in distinguishing asbestos-related fatal cancers from other causes, such as smoking. The HSE (2003: 17) have calculated that the annual number of cancer deaths from work-related causes is 6,000 (with a range of 3,000 to 12,000). Hence, what is relied upon in Table 9.4 is a more conservative figure where the cause has been clearly established. Also excluded from the figures of corporate homicide in Table 9.4 are fatal injuries to members of the public (though many of these will have been the result of negligence or neglect by corporate bodies). Deaths related to OLL Ltd (1994), The Southall Rail Crash (1997) and The Hatfield Rail Crash (1999) (see Table 9.3) have been included, but again, these in no way represent the full picture in terms of deaths due to corporate manslaughter.

part four
dealing with homicide

10 The Investigation of Homicide[1]

Very little has been written about the police investigation of homicide, yet it is an activity familiar to many of us due to the regularity with which it is featured – in both fictional and factual representations – in all forms of media (Innes, 2001: 3). The extent to which these representations are accurate is debatable, of course. Nevertheless, they provide us with some understanding and 'sense of' the manner in which the police go about investigating homicide. This chapter is split into two main parts. The first draws upon 'official sources', in particular the *Murder Investigation Manual* (ACPO, 1999),[2] in order to provide an overview of how homicide investigations work, or are supposed to work, in practice. In reality, homicide investigations are not always conducted in such a 'textbook manner' and can be very chaotic and involve a great deal of inference. The investigation of a suspected homicide is not simply a matter of discovering a victim, labelling his or her death as homicide (as opposed to death due to natural causes, suicide or accidental) and gathering a set of 'facts' as to the cause and motive of the killing and the person or persons responsible. Rather, a complex set of procedures and processes are undergone in order to *construct an account* of what has occurred. Hence, in the second section of this chapter we take a more critical gaze at some aspects of the homicide investigation process. It is not possible to critically review all stages; the focus will be upon the legal context that frames and guides the investigative process, the role of police inference in establishing a suspect's motive and levels of intent, and the role of the forensic science service in making sense of forensic evidence. The theme that unites each of these issues is the constructive nature of the investigative process. As will become evident, just as the 'act' of homicide can be considered a legal and social construct (refer to Chapter 1), so can the investigative process.

Finally, homicide investigations are neither perfect nor foolproof all of the time. Some homicides are never solved, others emerge to have resulted in wrongful convictions. We will be discussing both issues towards the end of this chapter. We begin here by considering the homicide investigation process. It is important to read this section with an eye to identifying important issues, debates and problems that the process of homicide investigation might raise.

The Homicide Investigation Process

There are various ways to break down the homicide investigation procedure for the sake of clarity. However, several authors (such as Stelfox, unpublished;[3] Greenwood et al., 1977; Swanson et al., 1999) note a basic distinction between what can be termed the 'initial response' and 'secondary enquiries'. This division is not perfect and there is, of course, overlap. For example, whilst crime scene preservation and the gathering of evidence are early concerns in a homicide enquiry, these activities continue well beyond the initial phase of an enquiry. Similarly, whilst the identification of any possible witnesses will need to be established immediately, the search for witnesses continues as the investigation progresses. In any event, it is this broad distinction that will guide the subsequent discussion of murder investigations. It is important first to consider, however, the basic organisational structure of a murder enquiry.

The Basic Organisational Structure of a Murder Enquiry

Prior to the early 1980s the investigation of serious crime, such as homicide, was very much autocratically centred on the Senior Investigating Officer (SIO), who was often viewed as having particular 'super-sleuth' expert investigative skills (Innes, 2003: 83). Since that time a number of changes have occurred, which have included the establishment of Major Incident Rooms (MIR), protocols guiding the management and operation of major incidents, for example, the Major Incident Room Standard Administration Procedures (MIRSAP), the introduction of HOLMES[4] and a general rationalised division of labour amongst murder squad officers. Several of these reforms were introduced in response to the criticisms made by Lord Byford in his report of the Yorkshire Ripper Enquiry (see Home Office, 1981).

Innes (2003: 85–6) notes that the current investigative system for major crimes comprises four principal roles:

- the Senior Investigating Officer (SIO);
- the Major Incident Room (MIR);
- the Outside Enquiry Team (OET); and
- Forensic Support.

The SIO (who generally falls within the ranks of Detective Inspector and Detective Superintendent) is in charge of the overall investigation and takes command and control in the development of strategic decision-making and long-term policy planning in relation to the enquiry. He or she does not have 'hands on' involvement in all details of the case. MIR is the administrative core of the investigation and acts as a store for all of the information relating to the enquiry. Personnel within MIR assume particular roles and functions. For example, a typical MIR would comprise an office manager, an administration manager, a receiver (who reviews all documents and identifies what should be indexed), a reader (who reads and summarises all statements, officers reports, and so forth, raising further actions where necessary), an indexer (who indexes the contents of all documents received from the receiver and document reader and raises necessary actions), a telephonist, a typist and a clerk. The OET are the detectives who, under direction from the SIO and MIR, actually perform the physical search and investigation of those people, events and objects which are thought to be of relevance to the enquiry. Finally, Forensic Support undertakes all aspects relating to the collection, identification and analysis of evidence relating to the investigation. We will be returning to each of these functions at various stages throughout the chapter. Let us now consider what occurs during the initial response stage of a homicide investigation. Figure 10.1 depicts the key activities that occur during a homicide investigation and should be referred to as an overall guide when reading this chapter.

Initial Response

The initial response stage of a homicide investigation refers to the activity immediately following the report of a crime and the very early decisions and actions taken by officers who attend the scene of a homicide or possible homicide. The *Murder Investigation Manual* cites five key objectives during the initial response phase, as detailed in Figure 10.2. In slightly more detail, Stelfox (unpublished) suggests that, during the initial response stage of a homicide investigation, there are seven information needs that officers aim to fulfil (see Figure 10.3). What Stelfox includes, and that the *Murder Investigation Manual* critically omits from its list, is the important issue of determining whether a homicide has occurred, an issue to which we now turn.

Discovery of a Dead Body: Has a Homicide Occurred?

Determining that death is a homicide and identification of the victim are two important information needs during the initial stages of a murder investigation (Stelfox, unpublished). Essentially, the investigation of a homicide (or suspected homicide) starts from the moment the police discover or, as is the case in most instances, respond to a report of a 'dead body' (or an individual who is seriously injured and might die). There are occasions when the police launch a murder investigation in the absence of a corpse, for example, where an individual has gone missing in suspicious circumstances.[5]

The initial police response in relation to the report of a suspicious death is generally to dispatch uniformed officers to the scene. The first task facing these officers is to determine whether the victim is actually dead. If not, they must

Figure 10.1   Flow chart indicating key activities in response to possible homicide

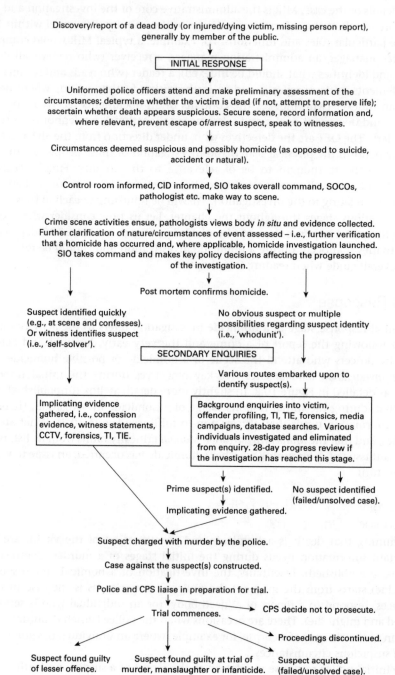

Discovery/report of a dead body (or injured/dying victim, missing person report), generally by member of the public.

INITIAL RESPONSE

Uniformed police officers attend and make preliminary assessment of the circumstances; determine whether the victim is dead (if not, attempt to preserve life); ascertain whether death appears suspicious. Secure scene, record information and, where relevant, prevent escape of/arrest suspect, speak to witnesses.

Circumstances deemed suspicious and possibly homicide (as opposed to suicide, accident or natural).

Control room informed, CID informed, SIO takes overall command, SOCOs, pathologist etc. make way to scene.

Crime scene activities ensue, pathologists views body *in situ* and evidence collected. Further clarification of nature/circumstances of event assessed – i.e., further verification that a homicide has occurred and, where applicable, homicide investigation launched. SIO takes command and makes key policy decisions affecting the progression of the investigation.

Post mortem confirms homicide.

Suspect identified quickly (e.g., at scene and confesses). Or witness identifies suspect (i.e., 'self-solver').

No obvious suspect or multiple possibilities regarding suspect identity (i.e., 'whodunit').

SECONDARY ENQUIRIES

Various routes embarked upon to identify suspect(s).

Implicating evidence gathered, i.e., confession evidence, witness statements, CCTV, forensics, TI, TIE.

Background enquiries into victim, offender profiling, TI, TIE, forensics, media campaigns, database searches. Various individuals investigated and eliminated from enquiry. 28-day progress review if the investigation has reached this stage.

Prime suspect(s) identified.

No suspect identified (failed/unsolved case).

Implicating evidence gathered.

Suspect charged with murder by the police.

Case against the suspect(s) constructed.

Police and CPS liaise in preparation for trial.

Trial commences.

CPS decide not to prosecute.

Proceedings discontinued.

Suspect found guilty of lesser offence.

Suspect found guilty at trial of murder, manslaughter or infanticide.

Suspect acquitted (failed/unsolved case).

Subsequent appeal (which may or may not be upheld).

Figure 10.2   Key objectives during initial response

- Preservation of life
- Preservation of the scene
- Securing evidence
- Identifying victim(s)
- Identifying suspect(s)

Source: ACPO, 1999: 48–50.

Figure 10.3   Information needs during initial response

- Has a homicide offence occurred?
- What is the victim's identity?
- Can the scene be identified?
- What are the circumstances of the offence?
- Is the identity of any suspects known?
- Is the location of the suspect known?
- Can a case be made against this suspect?

Source: Stelfox (unpublished).

administer first aid and arrange for an ambulance. The *Murder Investigation Manual* alerts officers to be sure to ascertain carefully whether the victim is actually dead:

Murder Investigation Manual Caption
REMEMBER:
There have been cases in the past where police officers believed a victim to be dead, only for police surgeons to discover vital signs of life through medical examination. (ACPO, 1999: 48)

On those occasions when the victim is removed from the scene to be taken to hospital, officers have to be mindful of the potential for evidence to be destroyed or lost at this early stage. Hence, they are required to observe exact detail of scenes, particularly the location of the victim, ensure that the removal of the victim occurs with a minimal disturbance to the scene and carefully manage the route into and out of the scene, and identify and record all individuals entering and leaving the scene along with anything which is moved, noting the original and eventual location (known as a crime log) (ACPO, 1999). Stelfox (unpublished) notes that the importance of identifying and preserving the scene of a potential homicide is 'drummed into all officers during basic training'. In short, it is vital that the crime scene, which might transpire to become a murder scene, is carefully protected and monitored from the outset.

Where the victim is dead, it is the task of officers to determine whether death is suspicious. The police are called to the scene of many deaths, most of which are the result of natural causes or suicide, and many of which are the result of accidents of one sort or another (Stelfox, unpublished). Ultimately, it is the task of a pathologist to determine cause of death. However, it is important for police officers attending the scene of a death to arrive at a preliminary view as to the likelihood of death being a homicide, in order that evidence can be secured and steps towards arresting the offender(s) taken at the earliest opportunity. Attending officers are, therefore, tasked with making an interpretation of the circumstances they find at the scene or from information received from witnesses. In some instances the circumstances are highly suggestive of a homicide event. However, other scenes are much less clear cut and can give rise to the question 'Did she fall or was she pushed?' Also, some natural deaths can be very 'messy', making them appear to be murders in the first instance.

Launching a Murder Enquiry

Where the police make an initial assessment that the death is indeed suspicious and likely to be the result of 'foul play', they will notify the police control room. At this stage a range of appropriate personnel are called upon in order that a murder investigation can be launched, including informing the Divisional Commander that a major investigation may be launched and the Criminal Investigation Department (CID) (who will assume responsibility for the investigation). The Head of CID will take steps to appoint an SIO from a pool of appropriately trained officers. Aside from the major Metropolitan forces who retain 'specialist murder squads', police forces draw upon officers from the CID who have received specialised training for this function. Once the Divisional Commander and the SIO have attended the scene and assessed the situation, the investigation proper will commence (Innes, 2003: 88). SIOs are keenly aware of the importance of making a correct assessment of the scene at the earliest opportunity (2003). Where innocuous scenes are misinterpreted as murder scenes and a murder investigation launched, SIOs will be subject to criticism for wasting valuable resources. On the other hand, if a death is attributed to natural causes or suicide and later emerges to have been the result of foul play (for example, via the post mortem), then the effectiveness of the investigation is likely to have been impeded, as vital early clues are lost.[6]

As well as police investigative personnel being alerted and attending the scene, other specialists will be making their way to the area, including specialist Scenes of Crime Officers (SOCOs), police photographers and a Home Office pathologist. Each play an important role in terms of gathering evidence and assisting to determine the circumstances of the death. It is generally the case that the initial assessment of the first officers at the scene that the circumstances are a homicide is subject to a process of verification by a senior officer (that is, the Divisional Commander and Head of CID) before a pathologist is called.[7]

Whilst every homicide may require varying sorts of responses during the initial stage – depending, for example, on factors such as whether the offender is present at the scene and the availability of witnesses and so forth – there are a number of basic decisions and actions that tend to characterise most investigations during the initial phase in order that the investigation can progress.

Managing and Resourcing a Murder Investigation

A host of decisions have to be made in the early stages of a homicide investigation (and, of course, beyond). SIOs are required to record systematically key decisions in a Policy File, which is subject to ACPO guidelines in terms of the kind of decisions that should be recorded and under what headings. It is not possible to consider all such decisions here, suffice it to say they revolve around issues such as setting up the investigation, staffing, finance, administration and enquiry parameters/lines of enquiry. For example, in the early stages of the investigation the SIO will need to identify and select officers to work on the murder enquiry (which generally means removing them from other duties and enquiries) and assign them to particular roles and duties. In addition, organising accommodation to house the enquiry and acquiring equipment, as well as ensuring that officers are given time to eat and rest during what can be a very time-consuming and demanding murder investigation are all important tasks. Vitally, community and family issues have to be taken into account. For example, a Community Impact Statement must be completed within the first four hours of the launching of the homicide investigation. The purpose is to assess the impact of the homicide upon the local community, which can vary significantly depending upon the nature of the homicide and the character-istics of the victim. For example, where a young child has been abducted and murdered, concern may be high within the community. Similarly, killings with a racial or homophobic element can cause fear amongst the 'black' or 'gay' com-munity and resentment against the police if they are not seen to be treating the murder seriously. In addition, the Community Impact Statement may reveal the need to protect certain members of the public (such as witnesses or informants) and may alert the police to the possibility of a revenge attack against the family of the suspect.

An additional vital decision is the appointment of a Family Liaison Officer (FLO) to the investigation. The role of the FLO is to provide support to the immediate family of the deceased and to act as a liaison between the enquiry and the family. At the same time, FLOs should endeavour to gather detailed information from the family (for example, by constructing a family tree) that may help to explain the victim's death. Factors such as the family's ethnicity may be important in terms of assigning the most appropriate officer to undertake this role.[8]

These issues, and all other aspects of the investigation, are underpinned by finan-cial considerations and constraints. The decision as to how many officers should be assigned to the investigation and the extent to which resources should be allocated generally is based on an assessment of the scale, gravity and complexity of the homicide. Current ACPO guidelines recommend the grading of homicides via the A, B, C system – a three-fold classification of murders outlined below:

Category A: A major crime of grave public concern, for example, if the victim is a child or where multiple murder or the murder of a police officer occurs.

Category B: Routine major crime where the offender is not known.

Category C: A major crime where the identities of the offender(s) is apparent. (ACPO, 1999: 84)

We will not delve any further into the issue of financing murder enquiries, suffice it to say that setting up and maintaining a homicide investigation requires a host of resources that have to be accounted for and paid for and can have an important impact upon the nature and extent of resources drawn upon. Moreover, some investigations, particularly those that are complex and protracted, cost vast sums of money whilst simultaneously draining the capacity to investigate and solve other crimes in the area.

Study Task 10.1

Whilst comon sense would predict that resources will necessarily vary in accordance with the complexity of a homicide case and its potential to be solved, the grading scheme does raise several questions in terms of victim status. Why, for example, should the killing of a child or police officer have been singled out in this scheme? Innes (2003: 92) suggests that the boundaries that are established between the categories above in the three-fold classification of murder 'appear to reflect broader public opinion about murder'. Put another way, he suggests that the classification scheme provides some evidence that the police response to homicide is, to a certain degree, structured according to 'the particular symbolic status that is attributed to different types of murder' (2003; 92). To what extent to you agree with this reasoning? Refer back to Chapter 1 where we considered the moral status of homicide victims and societies' response to different forms of homicide.

Identifying Suspect(s) and Witnesses During Initial Response

In contrast to the rather more extensive enquiries that occur during the secondary response phase of a homicide investigation to trace and interview witnesses and possible suspects (which we deal with below), police officers arriving at the scene of a homicide or potential homicide are required to take immediate steps to gather information as to the possible identity of the suspect(s). This generally involves speaking to those who are at the scene as well as canvassing for witnesses at premises overlooking, or in the immediate vicinity of, the crime scene.

In the majority of homicides, the suspect (or suspects) can be identified during the initial response phase of the investigation. Innes (2002: 672), for example, indicates that around 70 per cent of homicides tend to be categorised by the police as 'self-solvers' in that a suspect is identified at an early stage. Similarly, Stelfox (unpublished) found that suspects were identified during the initial response phase in 29 out of 40 cases analysed in the Greater Manchester Police Force area for the period 1998/99, which translates to 72 per cent. There were various ways in which this occurred, including:

- *Identification at the Time of the Report*: Suspect informs the police and admits responsibility or informs solicitor or family member who contacts police on his or her behalf.
- *Identification by Witnesses*: Witnesses present at the scene provide the name of a suspect to the police. Includes cases where the eye-witness knew the offender and was present during the fatal incident as well as non eye-witness information, that is, where witnesses were in close proximity and saw the suspect apparently fleeing the scene.
- *Identification by Police Inference*: The police infer the identify of the suspect from other information readily available at the scene.

In summary, both suspects and witnesses are often present at the scene of the homicide (and contact the police to report the incident/killing) allowing the speedy apprehension of the killer. Interestingly, the *Murder Investigation Manual* specifically alerts officers to the possibility of offenders being at the crime scene under some other guise:

Murder Investigation Manual Caption
REMEMBER:
It is not unusual for offenders to present themselves in the guise of a witness. Offenders often return to the scene amongst crowds of spectators to observe initial activity. (ACPO, 1999: 53)

Crime Scene Analysis and Forensics

Homicide scenes are treated with a reverence that wouldn't be out of place for a holy shrine. They are protected from the elements, guarded and only the select have a right of entry. (Stelfox, unpublished)

The investigation of crime scenes and the analysis of evidence recovered is a critical aspect of the modern investigation of a homicide. The principles of forensic science are based on Edmund Locard's (1920) 'theory of interchange', summed up in the now famous phrase 'every contact leaves a trace'. Locard's theory indicates that when someone commits a crime they will always leave something at the scene which was not there before, and take away with them something which was not on them before they arrived (Gallop and Stockdale, 1998: 47). Forensic science is, therefore, concerned to identify and analyse 'trace and contact' evidence. Walker and Stockdale define forensic science as 'the systematic and painstaking identification, analysis and comparison of the physical residues of crime in order to establish what happened, when, where and how it happened, and who might have been involved' (1999: 121).

The *Murder Investigation Manual* identifies the possibility of five significant scenes that may require some level of analysis, as well as the routes between them. Hence, aside from the most obvious murder site scene (where the victim will often be discovered), it is important to be aware that the murder site can be distinct from the site where the body is discovered, as well as various other sites where the victim and offender may have been prior to or after the homicide (see Figure 10.4).

Figure 10.4   Significant Scenes

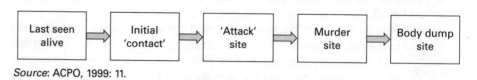

Source: ACPO, 1999: 11.

One of the key decisions to be made in relation to crime scene examination is whether or not the to call upon the Forensic Science Service (FSS). The FSS tend to be called where the scene presents a particularly difficult problem of interpretation or where specialist skills are needed to recover evidence (Stelfox, unpublished). For example, the analysis of patterns of blood splashes, or expert advice where attempts have been made to destroy evidence could involve the assistance of the FSS at the crime scene (Weston, 1998: 43). The expert assistance of a specialist firearms investigator in shooting incidents is also commonplace and can provide invaluable information about the type of weapon used and the distance over which it was fired, as well as the position of the firer and victim (1998: 43). Under certain circumstances, additional expert support may be drawn upon to attend the crime scene. For example, where fatal fires have occurred, Fire Brigade Officers will identify the cause and seat of the fire and be able to offer their insight as to whether the fire was deliberately started. Where the scene is not so complex, Scenes of Crime Officers (SOCOs) perform the function of searching, seizing and analysing physical evidence. Crime scene examination can reveal a host of samples or pieces of evidence such as clothing, fingerprints or palm prints, foot marks, blood, hair, semen, saliva or body tissue, fibres, weapons, tyre marks and gun cartridges. The analysis of most forms of physical evidence is undertaken by the FSS at various laboratories throughout the country.

Offender Behavioural Assessment

There is a further important dimension related to crime scene assessment more broadly, namely behavioural assessment of the offender. This may take the form of an offender profile (also termed 'psychological' or 'criminal profile') or geographical profiling. Essentially, offender profiling operates on the assumption that expert offender profilers can infer or deduce certain *offender* characteristics on the basis of his or her *offence* characteristics (see Holmes and Holmes, 1996; Canter and Alison, 1999; Turvey, 1999; and Ainsworth, 2001 for comprehensive overviews of various forms of offender profiling). Geographical profiling involves the analysis of geographical boundaries of the offence (or linked offences where relevant) in an effort to identify the most likely place of residence, work or locations frequented by the offender (see Rossmo, 1999). Police forces in England and Wales can access accredited profilers via the National Crime Faculty in Bramshill, Hampshire. Finally, the police have at their disposal, where necessary, various national databases, such as the Homicide Index (HI), CATCHEM (Centralised Analytical Team Collating Homicide Expertise and Management), BADMAN (Behavioural Analysis–Data Management–Auto Indexing–Networking), CCA

(Comparative Case Analysis); and SCAS (Serious Crime Analysis Section), which can assist them in their search for suspects in difficult-to-solve investigations.

The Role of the Pathologist

As often depicted in television detective dramas, the pathologist is a key figure in providing information about the manner in which the victim met his or her death. However, unlike some media depictions of the pathologist's role, he or she does not 'play detective' and try to determine a motive for the killing. Rather, it is the task of the pathologists to determine, where possible, *mode of death*, that is, was the death due to natural causes or the result of an accident, suicide or possible homicide (refer to Chapter 1 for further discussions of the difficulties involved in determining mode of death) and *cause of death* (for example, which injury was responsible for death). In addition, pathologists can, using educated guesswork, provide estimates of time of death, though often the best evidence is that based upon the last known sightings of the victim and when he or she was found dead. Toxicology reports (for example, blood alcohol levels) and weapon and injury analysis are also commonly undertaken by pathologists. Regarding the latter, the pathologists may be able to indicate how particular injuries on a victim can be interpreted (for example, some indication of the level of force involved in an attack) in order to reconstruct the interactional dynamics of an assault (Innes, 2003: 90). In most circumstances the pathologist will attend to examine the body *in situ* at the crime scene. This enables the pathologist to gather contextual information which aid later interpretation of the circumstances under which injuries to the victim were caused and generally assist in the subsequent autopsy (also known as post-mortem examination). The autopsy (which would actually fall into the secondary response phase of the investigation, but will be considered here for the sake of clarity) is a detailed medico-legal examination conducted by the pathologist and usually attended by one or two senior members of the murder squad. In addition, the Coroner (or one of his or her officers) may attend the autopsy and will at some stage hold his or her own enquiry into the cause of death. To satisfy the legal requirements in England and Wales, a Coroner must be informed of the death and assumes responsibility for the body until released for burial (Weston, 1998: 40). At some earlier stage (generally prior to the autopsy) the body will have been identified to the pathologist and to the Coroner's Office. In most cases, the identity of the victim will be known and they can be positively identified by a relative or friend. Where the identity of the victim is unknown or the body badly decomposed or otherwise unsuitable for visual identification, there are several other methods available to aid in the identification process, such as fingerprints, dental records, DNA profiling, tattoos, scars or other unusual marks, property and clothing, jewellery or facial reconstruction.

Thus far we have considered the major activities that ensue in the initial response stage of a homicide enquiry with a particular focus upon early considerations as to whether a homicide had occurred, the launching of a homicide investigation and resourcing and staffing issues and, finally, initial crime scene considerations and the role of forensic science, pathology and offender profiling. We will now move on to consider the major activities that occur during secondary enquiries.

Secondary Enquiries

The secondary investigation process is used to formalise the information already gathered during the initial response (Stelfox, unpublished). This is achieved by carrying out a range of routine activities, such as, post-mortem examinations, scene examination, interviewing suspects and formally recording the statements of witnesses who were identified during the initial response. Some of these activities will have already been conducted during the initial response, depending upon the nature and circumstances of the homicide. Hence, as Stelfox (unpublished) notes, it is difficult to define the exact point at which the initial response ends and the secondary enquiries begin. Ultimately, what occurs during the secondary response phase of a homicide investigation is dependent upon what has already been achieved during the initial response. For example, where a suspect has already been identified, suspect-related activities will be focused around gathering implicating evidence. In contrast, where no suspect is apparent, activities will be centred around establishing his or her identity. It is oftentimes these latter cases (which, as we have already discussed, tend to comprise the smaller proportion of homicides) that pose the most difficulties for homicide investigators.[9] Stelfox's (unpublished) research reveals that secondary enquiries can be sub-divided into three distinct phases, as detailed in Figure 10.5: suspect development, case building and case management. We will now consider each of these phases.

Figure 10.5   The phases of an investigation

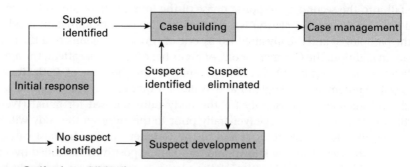

Source: Stelfox (unpublished).

Suspect Development

The suspect development phase of a homicide investigation occurs where there are no immediate or obvious suspects identified in the early initial response stages of an enquiry. The key objective, therefore, becomes identifying a credible suspect or suspects. SIOs have been found to meet this critical need via two distinct strategies or 'sub-processes'. The difference between these two strategies lies in the level of information that is needed to undertake them (Stelfox, unpublished). On the one hand, there are activities that can be undertaken without specific details of the circumstances of the case – such as tracing and interviewing the victim's family and associates, carrying out house-to-house enquiries in the immediate area, making media appeals and examining the crime scene and evidence extracted from it. These activities require little information other than the identity of the victim and the location of the scene. On the other hand, certain kinds of activity are 'case dependent' and require specific kinds of information in order to occur – such as 'identifying the tall, blond man seen near the scene' or 'tracing the black BMW seen speeding away from the scene'. These latter, case-specific enquiries are generally called 'lines of enquiry'. Similarly, reconstructions of the event, in order to 'jog' witnesses memories and raise the profile of an investigation, generally require certain case-specific details. Such reconstructions tend to occur on the same day, place and time of the following week or, in very protracted cases, may occur a year to the day (anniversary reconstruction). Much of the activity that ensues during the suspect development phase involves the police having to 'trace and interview' or 'trace, interview and eliminate' potential witnesses and suspects (known as TI and TIE enquiries respectively).

Tracing and interviewing witnesses may be relatively simple, that is, where the police have clear knowledge as to whom they are seeking and where to find them, for example, the victim's brother or employer. On other occasions, tracing a witness can be difficult due to limited information in terms of a description or the whereabouts of the witness. Similarly, the process of interviewing witnesses whom the police successfully trace can be conducted with ease or difficulty, depending upon factors such as the witnesses' decision to co-operate with police questioning. Some witnesses may be in some way involved in the homicide or other criminal activity and not be willing to assist the police with their investigations. Others may be inclined to provide inaccurate information (we will deal with this issue later). The interview process, known as the 'cognitive interview technique', takes a standard format and is conducted according to a structure known by the acronym PEACE (Planning and Preparation; Engage and Explain; Account, Clarification and Challenge; Close; Evaluate) (see Milne and Bull, 1999).

On other occasions the police may attempt to trace, interview and eliminate (TIE) particular individuals from the enquiry. Stelfox (unpublished) identifies two connected ways in which this option is used. First, where an individual falls within a general suspect set, but there is no specific information linking him or her to the murder, then steps will be taken to eliminate such general suspects. For example, the murder of a man during a domestic burglary could lead to the tracing, interviewing and (where appropriate) elimination of all domestic burglars known to operate in the location. The main point of the exercise is to eliminate suspects, but it is recognised that because of their criminal networks they may hold relevant information. Alternatively, elimination enquiries are used in relation to those who it is believed may have some information relevant to the investigation but who are also potential offenders. This most often includes those who were known to be at the scene, the victim's immediate family and close associates. The main aim in relation to this second group is to obtain information that they are believed to hold, but it is also recognised that because of their relationship with the victim or their connection with the incident itself, they are potentially the offender. It is now generally recognised that it is often difficult to eliminate entirely anyone from an investigation (ACPO, 1999) unless there is very good evidence, such as a detailed description of the offender or DNA evidence. The most common cause of failure to eliminate suspects is the lack of sufficiently narrow elimination criteria. For example, no forensic evidence and only a very vague description of the offender.

Case Building
The case building phase is entered where a credible suspect or suspects exists. For the vast majority of homicide investigations, suspects are identified in the initial response phase of an investigation, meaning that the case moves quickly to the case building phase that essentially involves concentrating on discovering evidence that either implicates or eliminates a suspect from the enquiry. Strategies employed to these ends include interviewing any suspects and searching their homes and places of work. In addition, it involves formalising information gathered throughout the investigation and converting it into a format that is acceptable to the courts. For example, turning witnesses' verbal accounts into written witness statements and interviewing suspects using a tape recorder under the provisions of the Police and Criminal Evidence Act 1984 (PACE). Where the case building phase provides sufficient evidence to charge a suspect, the investigation enters what Stelfox (unpublished) refers to as the 'case management phase'.

Case Management
The case management phase essentially involves producing a file of evidence for the Crown Prosecution Service (CPS) and the overall management of the case through the criminal justice process to trial. It involves such activities as preparing files of evidence, liaising with the CPS and the barrister who is to represent the prosecution, dealing with the logistics of getting witnesses, evidence and exhibits to court for trial, witness liaison and, where appropriate, witness protection. According to Stelfox (unpublished), this is possibly the most routine phase of a homicide enquiry and is usually delegated to a Detective Sergeant who carries out the work under the supervision of a local Detective Chief Inspector or Detective Inspector, with only occasional input from the original SIO where key decisions need to be made.[10]

Innes (2002: 672–8) outlines a slightly more detailed model that distinguishes between what he terms 'self-solvers' and 'whodunit' homicides. *Self-solvers* generally involve three main stages of activity:

- Initial response: initial definition of the situation and determination as to whether a homicide has occurred along with crime scene analysis and evidence collection.
- Various lines of enquiry to develop and expand the police's knowledge of how the incident took place including the background of the victim and suspect and any 'history' between them.
- The selection and organisation of information and case construction, that is, translating the incident into legal discourse.

Regarding this latter stage, Innes' reference to 'case construction' (the equivalent of Stelfox's 'case management stage') reflects his more critical emphasis upon the preparation of case materials. To elaborate briefly, Innes (2002: 683) argues that the police are not engaged in simply retelling what happened, they are producing an edited and organised version of it (see also McConville et al., 1991). Moreover, the legal structure that frames the investigative process identifies that only certain elements of the story have to be provided 'for the account to be legally valid and explanatory' (Innes, 2002: 683). We will return to this, and other issues regarding the social construction of the homicide investigative process, in the second section of this chapter.

Innes suggests that *'whodunit' investigations* begin and end in the same way as self-solvers (that is, the initial response stage through to case construction). However, he also identifies a further three stages in between, namely information burst, suspect development and prime suspect targeting. Because the police do not have a suspect from the outset in whodunit killings, they have to follow many lines of enquiry in the search for the suspect, which ultimately leads to the gathering of vast amounts of information – much of which might eventually become irrelevant but, nevertheless, has to be followed up (information burst). Throughout this process certain potential suspects may be eliminated, whilst others may be further implicated. The ultimate objective is to narrow down the suspect field until the prime suspect can be identified. The main priority then becomes one of proving the involvement of the prime suspect by targeting activity toward him or her and gathering appropriate evidence. Once charged, the police go about formalising their evidence, that is, constructing a case against the prime suspect or suspects.

In summary, secondary enquiries build upon the information and evidence gathered during the initial response stage of the investigation and vary in emphasis depending upon whether a suspect has already been identified or remains 'at large'. The ultimate aim is to identify the offender (or offenders) and affect an arrest and successful prosecution. If and when a suspect is arrested, a whole new set of issues become important. For example, certain pieces of legislation, such as the Police and Criminal Evidence Act 1984 (PACE), become significant, determining the manner in which the police conduct interviews with, and searches of, the suspect. At the same time, the scientific process that began at the crime scene resumes, with samples for DNA and other testing being taken from the suspect and significant items (such as clothing or other items) being removed from the suspect and/or his or her home and place of work for forensic analysis. Throughout, the 'PACE clock' is ticking,[11] setting limits upon the police in terms of how long the suspect can be held before either being charged or released. In short, whether the police are confronted with a relatively straightforward homicide or a difficult-to-solve killing, they are often under considerable pressure to conduct their investigations speedily and within a restricted budget. Such pressures can be exacerbated when the homicide attracts intense media attention, an issue to which we now turn.

The Media and Homicide Investigations

It is well established that the media, which includes television, radio, newspapers, magazines and the Internet, have a thirst for crime stories (Williams and Dickinson,

1993; Ericson et al., 1991; Ericson, 1995; and Pearson, 2002). Much has been written about the manner in which the media report crime and the consequences of this (see Reiner, 2002 for an overview), especially violent crime, and the way in which they disproportionately focus upon violent or sexual offences (Ditton and Duffy, 1983; Soothill and Walby, 1991) as opposed to more mundane criminal offences. This is particularly so in cases where the victim is perceived as vulnerable (for example, children, elderly or disabled victims) or where the victim is well known (for example, the murder of Jill Dando).[12] Less well articulated is the manner in which the police sometimes use the media as part of their investigative strategy for serious crimes such as homicide (Innes, 1999a, 2001), and the complex issues that surround the police handling of the media. Managing the media places significant demands upon the police in the face of a serious criminal investigation such as homicide. Research conducted by Feist (1999) found that most SIOs estimate that they spend between 20 and 40 per cent of their time dealing with the media in the first two days of a serious criminal enquiry. Media interest typically declines after this time, although it may be the case that the police would welcome sustained media coverage, for example, in a difficult-to-solve case.

Preliminary Media Strategies and the Police Press Officer

The *Murder Investigation Manual* indicates the importance of the SIO contacting the force media services department at the earliest stage in a homicide enquiry in order that a preliminary media strategy can be agreed (ACPO, 1999). This will often take the form of providing a 'holding statement', which simply puts the media on alert and confirms that the police are dealing with a death that they are treating as murder or otherwise suspicious. At the same time the police may appeal for potential witnesses and provide a contact number for the incident room. Details of victims are rarely released at this stage for two key reasons: to allow immediate relatives and friends of the victim to be informed, and to await the results of formal identification. It is general practice (and clearly advocated in the *Murder Investigation Manual*) that the media are fed sufficient information to keep murder appeals 'alive'. This requires a close working relationship between the SIO the police press officer (usually civilians and ex-journalists who work for the police). Whilst the SIO is often responsible for heading up press conferences, providing interviews and making appeals, the press officer can organise each of these activities, handle all routine media enquiries and routine press briefings as well as drafting press releases for the approval of the SIO.

Objectives Within Media Strategies

Research conducted by Feist (1999) reveals various objectives within media strategies in serious crime investigations, as illustrated in Figure 10.6. Meeting these needs requires careful management of the media. To take the first point in Figure 10.6, the media represent the most effective means of alerting the public at large to crime events. Since the police are heavily reliant upon the public for information in order to solve crime, they clearly benefit from media involvement of this nature. At the same time, the police have to carefully manage the extent and

Figure 10.6   Objectives within media strategies in serious crime investigations

- To use the media in the best way possible to acquire information required by the investigation.
- To manage press interest effectively so as to minimise potential misinformation and interference with scenes, witnesses, victims' relatives and suspects.
- To provide the public with accurate information about the offence and the police response.
- To give due concern to the portrayal of victims, the feelings of victims' relatives and friends, and the response of the community.
- To minimise unnecessary community concern over the fear of crime.
- To disseminate relevant crime prevention advice.
- To demonstrate the professionalism of the police service.

Source: Feist, 1999: 3.

nature of the information they reveal to the media in case this leads, for example, to interference with witnesses, victims' relatives or suspects. Moreover, in most murder investigations some unique feature of evidence is deliberately held back from the media and the police service in general in order that the veracity of any confession evidence can be tested. Linked to this, certain pieces of legislation are appropriate in the management of information flow to and from the media. For example, after criminal proceedings commence, the press are bound by the sub-judice ruling and the provisions of the Contempt of Court Act 1981, which prevents them from publishing or broadcasting material that creates a 'substantial risk of serious prejudice' to the impending proceedings (see Feist, 1999: 28). However, the press can still have a detrimental effect on a homicide investigation and its prosecution. For example, during the investigation of the murder of Damilola Taylor, a tabloid newspaper published details of a critical piece of evidence that would otherwise only have been known by the killer(s) and investigation team. This concerned an object (possibly) lodged in Damilola's windpipe (Sentamu et al., 2002). Confessional evidence apparently existed that included mention of this particular detail. However, the fact that this evidence had been made public in the national press rendered this potentially compelling confessional evidence inadmissible. The source of the unauthorised disclosure of this piece of evidence to the press has not been determined. It is possible that the leak came from within the police service (Sentamu et al., 2002).

Innes (1999a) outlines several more 'suspect orientated' media strategies adopted by the police. These include publicising the crime in order that the offender may be overcome with guilt or recognise the futility of trying to avoid detection or that, due to psychological pressure, the offender may begin to manifest bizarre or uncharacteristic behaviours that may raise suspicions amongst close family members or friends. Alternatively, media presence can be used to exploit the conscience of anyone who might be shielding the killer. Finally, Innes cites the controversial suggestion that the police may occasionally use the media as a means of developing or enhancing suspicions they have of the involvement of an individual close to the victim, for example, a family member. In this instance, the 'grieving' relative or friend takes centre stage in a press conference, asking for public assistance in capturing the killer (see also Innes, 1999a). There have been several examples of individuals engaging in appeals of this nature who have subsequently been convicted of the murders about which they were appealing. For example, the case of Tracy Andrews in 1997, who claimed that her boyfriend had been stabbed in a road rage incident and made several emotional television pleas for her boyfriend's killer to come forward. She was ultimately convicted of his murder.

High Impact versus Low Impact Killing: Managing Information Flow

Whilst some murder enquiries, particularly those where the victim is perceived as vulnerable (for example, the murder of a child) generate intense and long-standing media and public interest, others may not. Hence, enhancing the likelihood of generating interest and information can be of paramount importance. To these ends, the *Murder Investigation Manual* emphasises that every opportunity should be taken to stress key issues surrounding the case to the public in order to 'win their hearts and minds', such as:

- The vulnerability of the victim.
- The despicable nature of the case.
- Relevant features of scenes.
- Sightings/movements of the suspect(s).
- Likelihood that the offender will re-offend.

(ACPO, 1999: 114)

On the other hand, the media can be very 'hungry' for information, and media appeals can be extremely effective and generate large amounts of information or 'leads' from the public. The difficulty is that the vast majority of this information is unlikely to be relevant to the enquiry. However, it must all be investigated in order to separate the 'wheat from the chaff'. Thus, as Innes (2001) observes, poorly managed media strategies can be detrimental to the overall effectiveness and efficiency of an investigation. Specifically, having to wade through swamps of information can lead to the delayed arrest of the suspect. The popular BBC1 crime appeal programme *Crimewatch UK* is a good example of the points made here. Often the investigating officer who makes the appeal will return in the update section of the programme and reiterate the specifics that the public should focus upon before coming forward with information and emphasise that, for example, the police do not want calls about a particular tool or item of clothing – i.e., where it can be bought from – since this is already known. So trying to manage the nature and quality of the information received into an enquiry and avoid wasting time and resources following irrelevant 'leads' is an important task.

Linked to all of this, Innes (2001) has noted that in a number of recent homicide cases, including the killing of Jill Dando, Sarah Payne and Damilola Taylor (other more recent examples include the abduction and murder of Jessica Chapman and Holly Wells[13] and the murder of Millie Dowler), the police have enlisted the media and therefore ensured that the investigation is high profile (see also Mawby, 1999). Innes (2001) observes that this creates a 'feedback loop' whereby there is an expectation from the public that the police should solve such cases, which in turn leads to large amounts of resources being directed to the investigation as the police strive to meet this demand. This raises a very important question: what happens in those investigations that are not, for whatever reasons, perceived by the media as newsworthy? For example, cases where the victim does not fulfil the media image of a 'good victim', such as drug dealers or prostitutes (see Ward Jouve, 1988). Innes asks, 'Are these cases investigated with as much care and attention as those where the victim or their relatives are particularly "media friendly"?'(2001: 43). Does the absence of a feedback loop have implications for the energy and resources fed into a murder inquiry?

Certainly some police forces, such as the Metropolitan and Greater Manchester, have encountered difficulties in securing co-operation from the public in instances where the murder victim is a drugs dealer. Yet the victims need not be involved in deviant or criminal activities to fail to sustain media interest and, by extension, high levels of information flow into the investigation. The National Missing Persons Helpline (NMPH) has noted the arbitrary manner in which vulnerable missing persons (who may have become the victim of a homicide) attract media attention. For example, Hannah Williams (aged 14) disappeared without trace from her home in Deptford in April 2001. Her body was found, wrapped in tarpaulin in a cement works, almost a year later in Kent. Hannah's disappearance never attracted the kind of headlines that followed the disappearance of Danielle Jones (a 15-year-old Essex schoolgirl who went missing two months after Hannah), nor the widespread media coverage of the disappearance of Millie Dowler (aged 13). Despite the best efforts of the NMPH to generate significant media coverage for all vulnerable missing persons, the media only tend to focus on particular cases that fit in with their publications. The vulnerable cases which generate the greatest publicity tend to be those where the missing person is white, female, from a middle-class, two-parent stable family and where there is no indication that the young person may have run away (NMPH Newsletter, Spring 2002). Hannah did not fit all of these criteria – she was not the model middle-class schoolgirl. Rather, she was from a working-class background, her parents were estranged and she wore a stud in her nose (*Guardian*, 28 March, 2002). Hannah's case has since prompted media discussions about the disparity in the amount of attention that different missing person cases receive (see, for example, *Daily Telegraph*, 6 November 2002 and *Guardian*, 28 March 2002; see also Biehal et al., 2002 for an overview of the profile of missing persons).

In summary, some homicides become high impact due to intense media interest and this can lead to difficulties in terms of managing information overflow and interrogating the quality of information received. Alternatively, other killings do not meet the media's criteria of newsworthiness and thus can necessitate (in difficult-to-solve cases) the police employing particular strategies to enhance media interest and, by extension, public interest and provision of important information. Finally, regardless of the levels of media interest, it is important that the police ensure that inappropriate details of the case are not released to the media that could hamper the development of the case, particularly at court. Hence, as Innes notes, 'a key motivation behind police co-operation with journalists is to try and control their interest and prevent them from conducting independent enquiries that may prove detrimental to the police investigation' (2003: 246).

Study Task 10.2

Conduct a review of current and archive newspaper articles of homicide investigations in the UK. You may use library archive systems or access newspapers online via the Internet. What kind of homicides are covered in these articles, that is, what are the characteristics of the victim and the circumstances of the homicide more generally? What, if anything, is known about the suspect(s) and how is he or she portrayed? How does this compare to the wider picture of homicide covered in Chapter 2 of this text in terms of the nature and extent of homicide in the UK?

A Critical Appraisal of the Homicide Investigation Process

So far we have considered the 'textbook' version of how detectives investigate a homicide, with only occasional critical reflection. In this section we cast a critical eye over this process in order to more fully appreciate the complexity of the investigation process. As Innes points out, 'detectives investigating a crime do not simply compile the facts of the case from a range of sources, rather they make interpretations and inferences which contribute to how the "facts" of the case are assembled and established' (2003: 6). It is not possible to critically review every aspect of the investigative process. Here we focus upon just some of the interesting ways in which the police and the FSS make certain decisions, interpretations and inferences throughout the investigative process, starting with a consideration of the legal context that frames the investigative process. We will end by considering how and why some homicide investigations fail to identify a suspect or 'construct' the wrong suspect.

The Legal Context of Homicide Investigations

As with all criminal investigations, detectives investigating a homicide, or potential homicide, are guided and informed by various pieces of legislation. This legislation affects all stages of the investigation process. As Innes notes, from the outset the police 'have to investigate whether "a murder" as defined in law has actually taken place and secondly, if it has, the circumstances of the killing and the identities of those involved' (2003: 81). Moreover, throughout the whole process of an investigation the police will be mindful of the rules that must guide the presentation of evidence for the CPS. Hence, examining the legal context of the homicide investigation represents one very good example of the socially constructed nature of the process in that it illustrates the way in which so-called 'facts' of the case are reconstructed in accordance with the requirements of the legal system. I do not intend to deal with the specifics of legislation that guide and inform, restrain and enable investigating officers; rather, the aim here is to provide the reader with some sense of how the police operate within and 'negotiate' the legal structure and how they work towards constructing a case that will stand up to scrutiny.[14] It is necessary to outline briefly the nature of the British Criminal Justice model.

Adversarial Justice

The Anglo-American model of criminal justice is characterised by a search for 'proof' as opposed to 'truth' (see Jackson, 1999 for an overview). The adversarial system is dominated by the prosecution and defence counsels, whose task it is to present their sides of evidence and argument and thus their version of the truth to the court. The Judge oversees proceedings, but does not directly take part in the disputes and battles between Counsel. Ultimately, the side that presents the strongest case generally wins. In short, the adversarial system 'recognises the potential for competing versions of reality between participants, and tasks defence and prosecuting counsel to construct their cases accordingly' (Innes, 2003: 57). Hence, as Jackson suggests, 'the adversarial system focuses on one event – the contested trial' (1999: 192).[15]

For the police, it is critical that their case against the defendant is 'sufficient', in terms of evidence, to meet the necessary standards of law and, ultimately, compelling enough (ideally in terms of motive and intent) first to convince the Crown Prosecution Service to take the prosecution forward to the court stage and ultimately to convince the jury of the defendant's guilt (beyond reasonable doubt). To these ends, the police are mindful, throughout the whole of the investigative process, that they gather evidence appropriately and that they ultimately compile a compelling case against the defendant. As Innes notes, the legal process is 'oriented towards the proof of guilt beyond "reasonable doubt", as opposed to the divination of "absolute proof"' (2003: 82). The important point is that the legal structure determines what is and what is not to be counted as important evidence or 'facts at issue' and, therefore, guides the police in terms of certain 'points to prove'. Two related examples will perhaps suffice: the issue of establishing intent and determining motive.

The Issue of Intent

During the custodial interview, the police aim to encourage suspects to implicate themselves in some way to the homicide. Although the sole reliance upon confession evidence as proof of guilt is no longer maintained in investigations, confession evidence remains crucial (Ainsworth, 1995). As detailed in Chapter 1 of this text, in order that a suspect be successfully convicted of murder (the most serious category of homicide), it must be proven (beyond reasonable doubt) that he or she 'intended' to kill or seriously injure the victim. It is generally the case that the police, when confronted with a homicide, proceed along the grounds of 'worst case scenario' and investigate the case as one of murder (as opposed to manslaughter) (Innes, 2003: 63). To these ends, they must set about proving intent. However, as Innes (2003: 62) notes, intent is a subjective state of mind and is more difficult to prove than that of criminal action (which itself can be difficult, of course). Shooting someone in the head at point-blank range would pose few difficulties in terms of proving intent to kill. However, as detailed in Chapter 2 of this book, very few homicides in the UK involve firearms (approximately 9 per cent). Many more are the outcome of stabbing incidents (30 per cent), or being hit/kicked to death (11 per cent). Hence, the question of intent is often not straightforward. In order to overcome the inherent difficulties involved in trying to establish intent, the police tend to take certain forms of action on the part of the killer as 'signifiers of intent' (Innes, 2003: 64). These are seen to provide an indication of the killer's internal, subjective motivations. Examples of the kinds of actions that might be considered signifiers of intent are: taking a weapon to the scene of the crime (as opposed to acquiring a 'handy' weapon at the scene); prior threats to kill or in some way harm the victim; the extent and nature of wounds and, thereby, the ferocity of the attack; and, of course, evidence of premeditation or planning. Whether each of these signifiers accurately reflects intent is open to debate. For example, a suspect may arm himself or herself with a weapon prior to seeking out the victim (who earlier that evening insulted him) with the intention of threatening the victim and exerting some control over the situation – that is, the weapon provides the offender with the 'upper-hand', or to protect their own wellbeing – not with the specific intention of using it to injure or kill.

Establishing a Motive

Establishing a clear motive for homicide can be equally difficult but is an issue that, once again, the police are keen to achieve in order to convince their audience (the CPS and ultimately a jury) of the guilt of the suspect(s). Like intent, motive is an elusive concept and represents an internal state. Unless the suspect reveals his or her motives for homicide (they may not themselves truly know why they killed), the police have to make inferences. Innes (2002: 684) notes that the police often 'fill in the missing pieces' regarding motive, by drawing upon other aspects of the case or particular bits of information about the suspect's past (such as previous convictions, evidence of prior violent relationships and so forth). For example, Innes cites the following attempt by one detective at unravelling the underlying motive for the homicide:

> We can never be absolutely certain why he did it. My guess is if you look at his relationship with his mother and the fact he beat his girlfriend up when she's pregnant and then the fact that the woman he followed and spoke to bears an uncanny physical resemblance to his mother ... it seems reasonable to think that his reasons are tied up with his feelings towards her. (Innes, 2002: 684)

The point is that whilst this account does not purport to be one of certainties, it nevertheless links and utilises factual information (that is, the beating of the girlfriend and the physical characteristics of the victim) to the hypothesised motive and is likely to be far more compelling than an account that simply conceded 'we have no idea why this individual has killed'.

Police Judgement and the 'Production' of Evidence

The police make inferences regarding issues such as motive and intent, based either upon information they can extract (via persuasion) from the suspect or from information pieced together from witnesses – whose accounts often conflict with one another and can change over time. The police are trained in various interview techniques in order to try to encourage suspects to implicate themselves to the fullest degree in relation to the crime in question. In addition, they are adept at 'helping' suspects to explain and justify their motive for the crime and will often present suspects with a 'scenario' of how and why the crime occurred. The police use very different tactics, depending upon the kind of suspect they are confronted with, enabling them to extract information, most of the time, regardless of whether they have a helpful or hostile suspect or an emotional or stable suspect (see Gudjonsson, 2002 for a comprehensive overview of police interview tactics and techniques). This might not be problematic if the police were always dealing with the killer. However, in complex investigations (that is, what Innes refers to as 'whodunits') the police may ultimately interview many 'potential' suspects before they find the killer. For some critics, the potential for 'false confessions' is an ever-real possibility under such circumstances (see Gudjonsson, 1998).

At the same time, the police are continually making judgements as to the credibility of witness statements and information. Certain witnesses are viewed as more credible and reliable than others. For example, Brookman's (1999) analysis of police covering reports[16] found many examples of judgemental language in relation to certain witnesses, the objective being to persuade the CPS that witness A was to be taken seriously (that is, was credible), whilst witnesses B and C should not be relied upon. Such statements are of course subjective, that is, they are based on the opinions of investigating officers and are not necessarily based upon any real evidence as to the reliability of particular witnesses. Moreover, such statements form part of a wider objective within these particular documents, that is, to persuade the CPS to prosecute the case. Hence, the police construct an account of events which most strongly supports their charge of murder or manslaughter (though the latter is rare), and this may involved enhancing the credibility of certain witnesses and downgrading or even denigrating information from other witnesses that does not support their version of events.

Detectives do not, then, simply discover the facts of an incident, rather they create the facts and in the process are responsible for the attribution of particular legal and social meanings to the incident concerned (see Innes, 2002; and McConville et al., 1991). For example, particular aspects of the incident are selectively emphasised whilst others are downplayed and viewed as having less influence upon how the homicide transpired. Moreover, the information that the police can glean is constructed in such a way that it can be taken as reliable and valid and thereby attributed a 'factual status' (Innes, 2002). Perhaps more so than any other form of evidence, forensic evidence is afforded primacy in the 'fact' stakes. However, as should become clear in the discussion of forensic evidence below, forensic science is not a pure fact-finding enterprise. Like most activities, it involves critical decisions and interpretations that can affect what is counted as 'evidence', how it is analysed and ultimately, how it is weighted and presented at court.

Forensic Science: The Role of Inference and Opinion in the Collection of 'Hard Facts'

Forensic evidence is often viewed and presented as 'hard fact'. Yet there are those who proceed more cautiously in their assessment of forensic evidence and recognise that laboratory science is a creative, interpretive practice (Latour, 1985; Knorr-Cetina, 1980).[17] Compared with more standard forms of laboratory science, where environmental conditions are carefully controlled and manipulated, forensic scientists work in the 'messy and chaotic' conditions of the crime scene (Innes, 2003). Arguably, this leads to a greater degree of interpretive practice as scientists are less able to rely on controlled environmental conditions in reaching their conclusions. Instead, they have to take account of the 'local conditions' in which the evidence was found. As Walker and Stockdale put it, 'the raw materials of forensic science are the stuff of everyday life, and the forensic scientist has to take them in the state that they are in and to recognise them for what they are' (1999: 121). The preservation and management of crime scenes is particularly complex where the killing has taken place in the open air and public places. Whilst there have been significant steps taken in recent years to ensure that evidence is not contaminated at crime scenes, dangers still prevail in terms of contamination and cross-contamination. Despite increased training of SOCOs, it is the case that they only attend a minority of crime scenes and arrive after other police officers have visited (Walker and Stockdale, 1999: 127).

The Relationship Between the Forensic Science Service and the Police Service

In addition to the difficulties involved in making sense of and interpreting this 'messy' form of evidence, forensic scientists working for the 'state' (that is, the police and CPS) are involved in a particular relationship. That is, a relationship whereby the police brief the forensic scientist(s) as to what they believe has occurred. For Innes, this briefing is 'significant, because it effectively provides a hypothesis to be tested and imbues the procedure of testing itself with a certain logic and purpose' (2003: 157).

Moreover, some critics have strenuously argued that the relationship between the FSS and the police can have serious implications for the quality of 'evidence' received. For example, Erzinclioglu (2002) has expressed concern about how forensic evidence is given in court, suggesting that now the FSS is an executive agency of the Home Office – paid for on an item service basis – it may be used less frequently, or inferior advice sought because it is cheaper. He argues for a system whereby a judge can commission accredited scientists drawn from a panel, bringing our justice system in line with that of France.[18]

Homicide investigations often involve the removal of hundreds of different items and exhibits from the crime scene(s) for analysis. The forensic scientist will have to make a reasoned judgement as to what items can and should be subject to analysis (that is, which would be most profitable to examine), and then has to determine what particular form of analysis to undertake and, finally, what can be inferred from the test results. Hence, forensic scientists are often confronted with difficulties in terms of identifying, extracting, processing and interpreting potential evidence.

In summary, as Walker and Stockdale recognise, 'in reality, as in every other field of professional endeavour, different forensic scientists presented with the same sets of data can and do come to different views and express different opinions based on them' (1999: 121). They also recognise that there is a 'popular misconception' that forensic science 'provides an especially pure and objective form of evidence and has the capacity to give universally accepted, clear-cut answers leaving no doubt' (1999: 126). In reality this is not the case. Hence, there has been, and continues to be, much debate and dispute regarding the evidential value of various forms of forensic evidence, not least DNA evidence (see Lander, 1989; Young, 1991; Munday, 1995; Robertson, 1995; Samuels, 1995; Chambers et al., 1997; Schklar and Diamond, 1999; Evett et al., 2000; Jowett, 2001).

In this final section of the critical overview of the investigative process we will consider those occasions where the police process 'goes very wrong' and the police fail to solve the homicide or make particular mistakes and errors that lead to the identification of the wrong suspect.

Investigative Failure: Unsolved Homicides and Constructing the Wrong Suspect

We are often informed of the very high success rate of homicide investigations in the UK – for example, a national clear-up rate of approximately 90 per cent in England and Wales. However, this success should not detract from the fact that, despite considerable resources being channelled into this particular form of police activity, some homicide cases remain unsolved.[19] In the 10-year period to 1997, over 700 offences of homicide in England and Wales had no suspect charged, or they had been acquitted (Gaylor, 2002: ii). Moreover, the detection rate for homicide varies considerably from force to force. For example, between 1989 and 1998 the Metropolitan Police Service (MPS) had an average detection rate of 84 per cent, compared to the national average of 92 per cent (HMIC, 2000: 105).[20] Unsolved homicides in the UK are never 'closed' (Innes, 2003: 251). Rather, investigative effort is ultimately withdrawn where all resources are seen to have been exhausted and the investigation is only re-opened if new information emerges which is likely to open up new lines of enquiry.[21]

At one level, it has to be acknowledged that some homicide cases are extremely difficult to solve due to the particular circumstances of the homicide. Examples might include those where the victim's identity has not been established (due to decomposition or only partial remains) or occasions where the victim is an 'unknown entity' – that is, he or she has no family or close friends and there is very little information available regarding his or her lifestyle. Innes (2003: 249) refers to these sorts of cases as posing 'extrinsic difficulties' – that is, the investigation fails due to factors beyond the actual investigation, such as the particular circumstances of the homicide. Alternatively, some homicide investigations fail due to 'intrinsic errors' and mistakes during the investigation – that is, are rooted in or inherent to the work of the detectives investigating it. So what sorts of intrinsic errors confound the investigation of certain homicides? Related to this, why do the police sometimes 'get it wrong' and identify an innocent individual as their prime suspect? On some occasions such individuals will be identified as unconnected to the homicide prior to court proceedings, in other cases they will experience a full trial and may be erroneously convicted. Even in those instances where such individuals manage to secure an appeal and are acquitted, it is extremely rare for the Court of Appeal make a declaration of a miscarriage of justice.[22] The Miscarriage of Justice Organisation (MOJO) (2002) claim that convictions for murder are the major miscarriage of justice occurrence and the least likely to be reversed. I do not intend to deal specifically with miscarriages of justice here, suffice it to say that they represent the worse case scenario of homicide investigative failure (see Walker and Starmer, 1999). We will now consider some of the factors that can contribute to investigative failure.

Factors that Can Hinder the Investigation of Homicide

Research into failed homicide investigations has been minimal, with a few exceptions (Byford Report, 1982; Macpherson Report, 1999; HMIC, 2000; Feist and Newiss (forthcoming); and Sentamu et al., 2002). In the section below we will consider some of the common themes that have emerged from these reviews and studies. It is important to recognise, however, that every murder investigation brings with it unique problems and difficulties.

Initial Response

Decisions and actions taken in the early part of an investigation can have far-reaching consequences in terms of the direction of an investigation and eventual outcome (Smith and Flanagan, 2000). In particular, the first 24 hours of a homicide investigation are critical to the eventual outcome and many homicides are solved due to activities that take place during these hours. For example, there is often only one opportunity to gather evidence that will be suitable for forensic analysis, and if this evidence is overlooked or contaminated during the initial response there is rarely an opportunity to gain lost ground. Yet the very early stages can be characterised by disorganisation and even chaos as officers try to make sense of what has occurred and as an effective command system is put into place. It is not surprising, therefore, that errors during this phase of the investigation have been identified as contributing to investigative failure. For example, the Macpherson Report (1999) criticised the lack of direction and organisation during the vital first hours after the murder of Stephen Lawrence. Specifically, the investigation team were criticised for not taking early steps to pursue the suspects, and for a general lack of imagination, co-ordination, planning and action. Along similar lines, the review of murder and race relations in the Metropolitan Police Force found that the chain of command at strategic and tactical levels was unclear to staff, and determined that the 'ownership' of murder investigation needed to be more clearly defined and understood within the MPF (HMIC, 2000: 11)

Information Overload: Interrogating the Quality of Information

Research by both Innes (2003) and Feist and Newiss (forthcoming) has identified the particular difficulties that can arise when a homicide investigation amasses large amounts of information in a short space of time (see the earlier discussion of the media and homicide investigations). Innes refers to this as 'systemic overload' (2003: 253). Much of the information coming into an enquiry may ultimately be of little value to the investigation (Feist and Newiss, forthcoming), yet it is not always a straightforward task to identify which pieces of information merit further investigation or should lead to specific lines of enquiry and in what order they should be prioritised. Distinguishing between 'good' and 'bad' information is vital to the efficient progression of a murder enquiry; establishing too many lines of inquiry or following the wrong leads can result in a low productivity spiral (Innes, 1999b).

Linked to this, if certain pieces of information are taken as particularly important and others ignored, the investigation can take a critical wrong turn and deflect attention from the real suspect. A very good example of an investigation that became seriously lengthened due to an error of judgement concerning information is the Yorkshire Ripper Investigation. Between March 1978 and June 1979, during the second half of the Yorkshire Ripper inquiry, the West Yorkshire Police received three anonymous letters and a tape recording claiming to be from the murderer, 'Jack the Ripper'. The postmarks on the letters and the voice on the tape recording indicated that the sender was from Sunderland. The tape recording became particularly significant and was played across the UK and beyond.[23] Acceptance that the author of the letters and tape was the killer led to major police resources being deployed to trace this individual (none of which were successful). More crucially, information derived from the letters and tapes was used to eliminate suspects (that is, on the basis of handwriting, accent and blood group). For example, the police and public were conditioned to believe that the killer was a native of Sunderland, with a 'Geordie' accent. This alone effectively ruled Peter Sutcliffe 'out of the frame' for some time, as he was a native of Shipley and did not speak with a Sunderland accent (see Figure 10.7).

In summary, establishing the relevance and value of information that can flow into major enquiries such as homicide is a critical skill required for the successful resolution of major investigations, particularly those that receive large quantities of information and are under pressure in terms of resources (see Smith and Flanagan, 2000; Feist and Newiss, forthcoming). Getting this wrong can lead to a very protracted investigation and/or ultimately the failure to solve the murder.

No Motive Killings and 'Competing Scenarios'

Aside from the obvious difficulties that can ensue when there is no apparent motive for a homicide, it is also the case that many hard-to-solve homicides present the

Figure 10.7   West Yorkshire Police poster appeal

SIO with competing scenarios regarding the circumstances or scenario of the killing (Feist and Newiss, forthcoming). For example, different pieces of information may suggest that the killing was linked to drug dealing or, alternatively, a gay encounter. In order to follow the most fruitful lines of enquiry, a critical task becomes making appropriate judgements regarding the relative strength of one scenario over another. However, without further probing the possibility of each scenario such a judgement may be very difficult to make.

The Major Incident Room and HOLMES

Byford (1982) found that many of the limitations of the Yorkshire Ripper investigation stemmed from the failings of the Major Incident Room (MIR). As well as being overloaded and understaffed, Byford found the MIR to be inherently rigid and incapable of being adapted to deal efficiently with the continuing murders and assaults. Hence, 'instead of being the nerve centre of the most important detective effort in history, it frustrated the work of senior officers and junior detectives alike' (1982: 144). More recently, Macpherson (1999) judged the HOLMES system to have been understaffed and inappropriately supervised during the Lawrence investigation, and various decisions by senior investigating officers were heavily criticised – such as the failure to arrest suspects named early in the enquiry. Whilst reforms that emerged as a direct result of the Byford Report, such as standardised Major Incident Room Standard Administration Procedures (MIRSAP) (see Home Office Circular 114/82) and HOLMES, have improved the co-ordination and management of major crime enquiries, it remains the case that this core element or hub of the investigative system can suffer due to information overload and understaffing. Moreover, Byford's recommendation regarding the standardisation of computer systems across MIRs has not been fully achieved in that different forces are operating different versions of HOLMES, which are not necessarily compatible.

Financial Pressures and Understaffing

Major crime investigations are extremely resource intensive and can impact upon the ability of a force to deliver other services to the public as officers are taken off other enquiries to staff the major incident (Innes, 2003). As a result, SIOs are ever aware of the need to conduct an effective and efficient investigation and to stay within the given budget. This can impact upon the investigation in a number of ways. At one level it is likely to require some officers working very long hours under considerable strain, making errors of judgement more likely. Linked to this, it may lead to understaffing, as those in command try to minimise cost to the investigation or simply are not able to secure sufficient officers due to them being engaged in other duties. The downsizing of the investigative team during the post-charge stage of the Damilola Taylor homicide investigation is a case in point. Specifically, the oversight panel that reviewed this homicide found that the investigation had 'insufficient resources to progress this aspect of the case in an effective way' (Sentamu et al., 2002: 24). At the time when the team were engaged in the intricate and time-consuming task of preparing evidence for trial, the Metropolitan Police Service (MPS) acquired a large number of new murder investigations. As a result, pressure on resources was intense and most of the inquiry team were re-deployed to meet the new demands. Sentamu et al. criticised senior managers (with resourcing responsibilities) for failing to fully understand 'the nature and scale of the preparatory work post-charge' (2002: 29). More general issues concerning a lack of resources and high caseloads being carried by SIOs in the MPS have also been raised.

The HMIC (2000) inspection team urged the MPS 'to revisit the staffing of murder investigation as there is a link between resource allocation and thorough and timely investigations' (HMIC, 2000: 11).

Linked to this, once a suspect has been identified there is often considerable pressure to discontinue costly previous lines of enquiry. This is, however, a high-risk strategy that may prevent alternative hypotheses regarding the homicide from being appropriately explored. This is particularly dangerous in those situations where the police have the wrong suspect, for whilst they focus all of their energies upon this individual, clues as to the identity of the real killer may be easily overlooked. This leads us into the final part of the chapter where we consider the sorts of factors that can lead the police to identify the wrong suspect in connection with a homicide.

Constructing the Wrong Suspect

Investigations under pressure are particularly susceptible to the mis-identification of suspects (Innes, 2003: 256). Innes notes that it is 'surprisingly easy when searching for a suspect to establish circumstantial evidence that can be interpreted so as to seemingly implicate a person in a crime' (2003: 259). Put another way, the police's suspicion of a suspect (which may involve elements of stereotyping) leads them to investigate him or her. Unless the suspect can be clearly eliminated (for example, by DNA evidence), the police's suspicion is further amplified, whereupon they 'dig deeper' in order to find more evidence to associate the suspect to the crime. At the same time, where the police become convinced they 'have their man' it is likely that they may be ignoring other pieces of information that might be pointing toward the real perpetrator. Hence, 'when an individual fits the police's "fuzzy" stereotypes about what sort of person tends to be involved in murder, and they can be connected to the crime, there is a tendency for the police to instigate a "cycle of suspicion"' (Innes, 2003: 258; see also McConville et al., 1991).

Stereotyping and suspicion are just two of a number of facets of police occupational culture (often referred to as 'cop culture') along with other traits such as cynicism, pessimism, racism, machismo, a thirst for action and a sense of mission. All these characteristics are artefacts of the pressure for results endemic to all police work but are, arguably, particularly salient where the investigation of serious crime, such as homicide, is concerned (see Reiner, 2000; and Bowling and Foster, 2002 for a comprehensive overview of the phenomenon of 'cop culture').

Departing from the 'Rules'

As argued, homicide investigations may fail due to the sheer complexity of the case, problems of information overload and the associated difficulties of determining the value and credibility of information, financial pressures and associated understaffing and certain aspects of police occupational culture. However, there is a further important issue that merits attention, namely those occasions where the police circumvent standard practice in an effort to 'get a result'. It is, once again, the intense pressures associated with the job that can lead officers to take certain 'short-cuts'.

Moreover, where these short-cuts are seen to succeed, they can become rapidly accepted and normalised as standard practice – despite the obvious dangers that such transgressions can engender.

Innes (2003: 259) uses the concept 'compliance drift' to refer to the way that deviations from standard practice can creep into the work of detectives when working under pressure on long-running cases. Specifically, compliance drift involves officers making adaptive responses in their working practices that circumvent certain forms of standard procedure and regulation. Innes identifies several causes of compliance drift, most of which revolve around the perceived need to maintain an effective and efficient investigation in the face of considerable strain. In addition, repetition and boredom during long-running investigations can lead to compliance drift. The non-standard practices that creep into detectives' work are seen by detectives to provide a quick-fix solution that can overcome factors which are hindering the progress of the investigation. In reality, such practices may only serve further to complicate and hinder the ultimate investigation – especially where these deviations come to light at court. Examples include deviating from standard operating procedures, such as failing to enter information through the HOLMES database, conducting unauthorised interviews with suspects or searching premises without the necessary search warrants, and generally bypassing any perceived unnecessarily cumbersome or onerous bureaucratic procedures. Alternatively, some of the most serious examples of compliance drift can involve deliberate and wilful actions on the part of detectives – such as the fabrication of evidence of one form or another to secure a conviction (see Ashworth, 1998). Such miscarriages of justice are well documented (see Walker and Starmer, 1999). Importantly, however, Innes' research suggests that whilst attention has tended to be focused upon these most dramatic instances of investigative failure, compliance drift explains a far greater number of 'normal errors' that can become a routine part of major crime enquiries. Hence, as Innes aptly concludes, 'the accepted presence of compliance drift in major investigations, as a normal consequence of how major investigations are resources and working practices enacted, may establish the pre-conditions for the rarer, more serious types of deviation' (2003: 262). Maguire and Norris (1992) observed the prevalence of 'rule bending', specifically in relation to the work of detectives and detective culture.[24] For example, a commonly identified feature of 'detective culture' that they encountered was detectives' willingness to regularly 'sail close to the wind' where formal rules were concerned – encapsulated in official jokes about the 'Ways and Means Act' (Maguire and Norris, 1992: 21). Moreover, Maguire and Norris observed a greater confidence amongst detectives (as compared to their uniformed colleagues) that they could safely bend (if not break) rules, which the researchers attributed to the less visible nature of their dealings with suspects, their greater legal knowledge and awareness and the overall nature of the relationship between detectives and their supervisors.

In summary, it is impossible to determine to what extent the investigation of homicide is subject to errors and malpractice. Certainly some commentators (see Innes, 2003) have argued that mistakes and errors are fairly common on murder enquiries. Moreover, the significant attention paid to high-profile cases of failure and miscarriages of justice obscure the presence of more routine and normal errors in homicide enquiries. That such a high proportion of homicides are solved is, at least in part, due to the fact that many require very little in the way of 'solving' – the perpetrators are easily and readily identified. For those that are more complex, the police often face considerable pressures to bring the investigation to a speedy conclusion. This is particularly so where the victim or victims are highly newsworthy, whereupon the pressure to produce a result becomes enormous. It is not perhaps surprising that under such circumstances, investigations can take a wrong turn.

Study Task 10.3

Secure a copy of the inquiry into the investigation of the Stephen Lawrence murder (Macpherson, 1999). The report considers a number of flaws specific to this homicide investigation, starting with one of the most basic requirements of officers attending the scene of a major crime with an injured victim – that of preserving life. The report notes that none of the officers who attended the crime scene 'did anything by way of first aid, apart from a small amount of testing to see whether Stephen Lawrence was still breathing and whether his pulse was beating' (Macpherson, 1999: 317). Overall, the report serves as a very useful example of the accumulative effect of errors and failures. Make a list of the major criticisms raised in this report. How do they compare with those considered above? To what extent do you believe that the difficulties encountered were unique to the Stephen Lawrence investigation? You may also wish to consult Innes (1999b), who argues that many of the failings of the Lawrence Investigation are characteristic of wider homicide investigations, and Brian Cathcart's (2000) *The Case of Stephen Lawrence.*

Chapter Summary and Conclusion

We began this chapter by considering the 'textbook' version of the homicide investigation process, broken down into two main phases; the initial response and secondary enquiries. We observed that a number of challenges can confront officers when they attend the scene of a potential homicide, in terms of determining whether the victim has been murdered, or met his or her death by some other means (such as suicide, accident or natural causes). At the same time, during the initial response stage, officers have to be mindful of preserving the scene and evidence within it, as well as questioning witnesses and possible suspects at the earliest opportunity. As the homicide investigation is launched, a whole host of personnel and resources are drawn upon as the investigation is formalised. Whether the investigation is comparatively simple (that is, a self-solver) or complex and protracted (that is, a whodunit), the crux of the investigation during the secondary response stage revolves around identifying the suspect and developing a case against that individual or individuals with a view to progressing the case to court. Finally, we considered the role of the media in homicide investigations, police media objectives and, in particular, the manner in which the police try to manage media interest in particular cases of homicide.

Following this, the second section took a more critical approach, focusing upon the socially constructed nature of the investigative process. Having briefly considered the legal context that frames the investigation, we considered the role of police inference in establishing intent and motive and considered the interpretive practice of forensic science, challenging the notion that forensic science necessarily produces objective evidence. Finally, we considered some of the factors that can contribute to investigative failure, noting the potential negative consequences of pressure to produce a 'result', understaffing, under-resourcing and information overload. We also considered those occasions where the police construct the 'wrong suspect', focusing upon certain facets of police occupational culture that can lead the police to instigate unfounded cycles of suspicion, as well as those occasions where detectives engage in non-standard practices during the investigation that can have potentially disastrous consequences.

Unlawful homicides are rare events in the UK, representing less than 1 per cent of all police recorded violence against the person. Yet homicide is seen as one of the most heinous crimes and hence, the police are often judged most acutely in terms of their performance and professionalism in respect of the investigation of this offence category. This is especially so for those homicides that gain significant media coverage, that is, those where the moral status of the victim and the particular circumstances of the homicide render the case to be perceived as 'especially appalling'. What this chapter has hopefully conveyed is that investigating homicide is, as Innes put it, 'primarily sense-making work' (2003: 282). Put another way, as the police are very rarely privy to a homicide event, they have to reconstruct what went on by gleaning information (termed 'evidence' to imbue it with a factual status) from the crime scene (including evidence left on the victim), witness accounts and, where possible, incriminating evidence from the suspect. Yet the evidence that they gather may not be straightforward and concrete and has to be interrogated in terms of its evidential value. Hence, the police tend to draw upon an accumulated set of knowledge in order to determine what is, and what is not, credible evidence, who is, and who is not, a credible suspect. To these ends they are naturally guided by various facets of their organisational structure and occupational culture in making sense of the killing.

It is clear that a number of important lessons have been learned from some of the high-profile homicide investigations that have failed. Most notably, the police were commended several times by the review team of the Damilola Taylor homicide investigation, particularly in terms of the primary investigation being innovative, committed and well resourced. The oversight panel suggested that the great deal of good practice that they identified demonstrated how the Metropolitan Police Service had 'moved on since its unsatisfactory investigation of the murder of Stephen Lawrence' (Sentamu et al., 2002: 5). It is an unfortunate reality that strategies and structures are often only improved in the aftermath of a negative event. In addition, the creation of the *Murder Investigation Manual* and the development of standardised investigative practices and protocols are evidence of the commitment of the police force to improve, where possible, the homicide investigative procedure. But, of course, it would not be possible to devise a handbook or manual that contained the 'perfect recipe' for the investigation of homicide, not least because every homicide is in some way unique. Moreover, no manual or set of instructions can adequately capture the 'reality' of the investigative process, the stresses and strains that it can involve or the role of inference and decision-making that determine the direction that an investigation will take – be that right or wrong. Ultimately, it would not be possible for detectives to investigate homicide (or any other crime for that matter) without some element of interpretation and inference. That said, few would argue that there is 'room for improvement' in terms of tackling some of the facets of police occupational culture and organisational structure that can lead to the mis-identification of suspects (accidentally or maliciously) or an otherwise 'failed' investigation.

Review Questions

- What difficulties confront the police during the initial response stage of a homicide (or potential homicide) investigation?
- In what ways might the media hamper the effective investigation of a homicide? Consider a recent example of a high-profile homicide investigation (such as the abductions and murders of Jessica Wells and Holly Chapman).
- What particular facets of 'cop culture' might contribute to investigative failure?
- What aspects of the organisational structure of the police force might lead to the more effective investigation of homicides in England and Wales? You may wish to consult Sentamu et al. (2002) and HMIC (2000) (both available online, see References).

Further Reading

The most central and comprehensive reference source in relation to this chapter is *Investigating Murder: Detective Work and the Police Response to Criminal Homicide* (Innes, 2003: Oxford University Press). Innes explores the practices and processes involved in the investigation of homicides and, in particular, emphasises the constructive agency of detectives in making sense of and producing accounts of homicide. For an excellent overview of crime scene investigations, refer to *Crime Scene to Court* edited by Peter White (1998: RSC). The first chapter provides an overview of the origins and development of forensic science in the UK, whilst the second provides a very accessible discussion of crime scene analysis, with specific reference to homicide. Subsequent chapters deal with specific aspects of evidence analysis. *Simpson's Forensic Medicine* (Knight, 1997: Arnold) also has two very useful opening chapters concerning the medico-legal aspects of investigating death. Regarding the use of and role of the media in the investigation of homicide, the most useful sources are *The Effective Use of the Media in Serious Crime Investigations* (Feist, 1999: Home Office) and various publications by Martin Innes, such as 'The Media as an Investigative Resource in Murder Enquiries' (*British Journal of Criminology*, 1999, Vol. 39/2, pp. 269–82).

For those interested in finding out more about the questioning of suspects by the police, a useful and up-to-date source is *The Psychology of Interrogations and Confessions* (Gudjonsson, 2002: Wiley). This text deals with the psychology of interrogation as well as the investigative and legal issues that bear upon obtaining and using evidence from interrogations of suspects in court. More general literature on the phenomenon of police occupational culture or 'cop culture' include: *The Politics of the Police* (Reiner, 2000: Oxford University Press); Bowling and Foster's chapter in the *Oxford Handbook of Criminology*, 3rd edition, 'Policing and the Police' (2002: Oxford University Press); Waddington's (1999) 'Police (Canteen) Sub-Culture: An Appreciation' (*British Journal of Criminology*, Vol. 39/2, pp. 287–309); and *Changing Police Culture: Policing in a Multicultural Society* (Chan, 1997: Cambridge University Press).

For general overviews of some of the difficulties faced by investigators involved in major crime enquiries, refer to *Major Crime Enquiries: Improving Expert Support for Detectives* (Adhami and Browne, 1996: Home Office); *The Conduct and Supervision of Criminal Investigation* (Maguire and Norris, 1992: HMSO); *Human Factors in the Quality Control of CID Investigations* (Irving and Dunninghan, 1993: HMSO); *The Police Function and the Investigation of Crime* (Brian Morgan, 1990: Avebury); and *The Effective Detective* (Smith and Flanagan, 2000: Home Office). Finally, refer to *Getting Away with Murder: The Re-investigation of Historic Undetected Homicide* (Gaylor, 2000: Crown) for an interesting study into the increasing number of undetected homicide offences and the potential for re-investigation (available from the Home Office website).

Useful Internet Sites

- The Association of Chief Police Officers of England, Wales and Northern Ireland: www.acpo.police.uk/links/index.html
- The Forensic Science Service: www.forensic.gov.uk
- The Criminal Cases Review Commission: www.ccrc.gov.uk
- Miscarriages of Justice Organisation: www.mojo.freehosting.net
- Innocent: www.innocent.org.uk
- The Police Services UK: www.police.uk
- Criminal Justice System UK: www.criminal-justice-system.gov.uk
- Review of Information on Homicide: A Discussion Document: www.homeoffice. gov.uk/rds/pdfs/provhomicideinfo.pdf
- Support after Murder and Manslaughter: www.samm.org.uk/

Notes

1 I would like to extend my gratitude to Detective Superintendent Peter Stelfox of the Greater Manchester Police for sharing with me his (as yet unpublished) PhD research into the investigation of homicide and allowing me to cite his work. In addition, many thanks to

Assistant Chief Constable Tony Rogers of South Wales Police for granting me permission (on behalf of ACPO) to use certain parts of the *Murder Investigation Manual*. Finally, my thanks to Dr Martin Innes (University of Surrey) for allowing me to use the draft of his text *Investigating Murder: Detective Work and the Police Response to Criminal Homicide* prior to publication (2003). This chapter would not have been possible without their assistance and generosity.

2 In 1999, for the first time, a *Murder Investigation Manual* was created. Prior to this time there was no single comprehensive manual or similar document upon which the police could draw to guide them in the investigation of homicide. Rather, individual Senior Investigating Officers (SIOs) drew upon their experience and passed this on to less senior investigators. The *Manual* was created by the Association of Chief Police Officers (ACPO), in conjunction with the Forensic Science Service (FSS) in order to encourage the uniform and efficient investigation of homicide. The *Murder Investigation Manual* is not in the public domain.

3 Stelfox is conducting ongoing doctoral research into homicide in the Greater Manchester Police (GMP) force. Specifically, his research aims to identify the factors that determine outcomes in homicide investigations. Every homicide recorded in the GMP force area for the financial year 1998/99 have been subject to detailed cases analysis (48 homicide investigations).

4 HOLMES (Home Office Large Major Enquiry System), which was established in 1987, is an information storage and retrieval system which allows for all information emanating from any major enquiry to be stored, indexed, cross referenced and interrogated for investigative significance (Maguire and Norris, 1992: 57). Innes (2003: 100) notes that compared to contemporary information and communication systems, HOLMES 1 is dated, overly complex and difficult to use. Many of these problems were addressed through the introduction of HOLMES 2 in 1997. However, several forces still operate the original version. HOLMES 3 was launched in September 2002 (personal communication with the Home Office).

5 See Newiss (1999) for an interesting discussion of the difficulties that the police encounter in determining whether a missing individual is likely to have come to any harm and what degree of resources should be invested in searching for a missing person.

6 The *Murder Investigation Manual* cites a number of examples of scenarios or scenes that should be treated as suspicious even though they do not obviously present as a homicide, including, reports of vulnerable missing persons, reports of abduction, cot deaths, hit-and-run accidents, suicides and fires where death occurs. The message to officers is 'THINK MURDER' – i.e. if in doubt, investigate as a murder until the evidence proves otherwise.

7 Refer to www.met.police.uk/about/organisation for further information on the structure of police ranks.

8 Like all other aspects of the investigation, this process can fall short of what is required. For example, in the Stephen Lawrence murder one of the (many) criticisms of the investigation was the failure by the FLO to keep the family of Stephen Lawrence adequately informed of the development of the investigation or to provide them with the necessary support required in the aftermath of the murder.

9 All murders that remain undetected one month after the investigation commenced are subject to what is known as a 28-Day Progress Review. These reviews are designed to ensure that adequate control measures are in place and that investigative opportunities (up to that point) have not been overlooked (Sentamu et al., 2002).

10 Despite the apparent routine nature of this phase of the investigation, it is nevertheless a vital aspect of the overall investigative strategy and one that has been subject to criticism in recent years by both HMIC (2000) and the Damilola Taylor Murder Investigation Review Team (Sentamu et al., 2002).

11 The Police and Criminal Evidence Act (PACE) 1984 stipulates clear time limits in terms of how long a suspect who has been arrested can be held at the police station before being charged. It is normally the case that the police must charge or release a suspect within 24 hours. In exceptional cases this time period can be extended to 36 hours or even 96 hours with the leave of the magistrates (Sanders and Young, 2002: 1045). A suspect who has not been arrested is free to leave the police station at any time.

12 See Soothill et al. (2002) for an interesting study of the coverage of homicide cases in *The Times* between 1977 to 1999. The study focuses upon and how and why some homicides become 'mega-cases', receiving extensive and persistent coverage.

13 This case in particular led to very intense and long-standing media coverage, which is perhaps not surprising when one considers that two vulnerable children had fallen victim to homicide.

14 For further information regarding some of the most significant pieces of legislation that frame the police investigative process, such as the Police and Criminal Evidence Act (PACE) (1984), the Criminal Justice and Public Order Act (1994), the Criminal Procedures and Investigation Act (1996), and the Crime and Disorder Act (1998), see English and Card (2001), Jason-Lloyd (2000) and Sloan (2001).

15 In contrast, the inquisitorial or inquiry system (operated in Europe, particularly France, Germany and Italy) involves the more central role of the judge and is less constrained by various formal rules of evidence (refer to Bell, 1999 and Harding et al., 1995 for overviews of the inquisitorial system).

16 Covering reports are an 'executive summary' of the circumstances of a homicide, compiled by the police and required by the CPS within 10 weeks from the time a suspect or suspects are charged with murder. They range in size from anything between 20 to 100 pages in length, depending essentially on the size and complexity of the homicide investigation.

17 Various groups criticise the objective value of scientific knowledge (such as certain feminists, environmentalists, animal rights activists and sociologists and philosophers who fall into the category of social constructivists). An example of the latter are those who write from the standpoint of the Sociology of Scientific Knowledge (SSK), who view scientific knowledge as the product of a social group (i.e., natural scientists, or of interest here, forensic scientists) influenced by social factors. As such, they recognise that the production of scientific knowledge is influenced by various factors, such as the social relations within scientific communities and between them and their social, economic and institutional contexts (for general overviews see Couvalis, 1997; Gross and Levitt, 1994; Klee, 1999; and Hacking, 1999; for discussions specifically related to forensic evidence, see Jasanoff, 1995; and Smith and Wynne, 1989).

18 See also HMIC (2000) for its criticisms of the forensic science support structure within the Metropolitan Police Service.

19 Between 1995 and 1999 there were 355 unsolved homicides in England and Wales, which translates to 8 per cent of all known homicides (4,437 cases in total) during the 5-year time period (Home Office HI). For the period 1999/00, 10 per cent of homicides in England and Wales remain unsolved (i.e., no suspect has been identified). In addition, a further 5 per cent of suspects have been acquitted at Crown Court, bringing the 'failure' figure to 15 per cent (Home Office, 2001a).

20 This could be partially attributed to the significantly higher levels of homicide experienced in this force area. Between 1988 and 1997 the homicide rate in the MPS averaged at 2.3 homicides per 100,000 population, compared to between 1.5 and 1.7 per cent for comparative forces, such as Greater Manchester, West Yorkshire, West Midlands and Merseyside (HMIC, 2000: 105). That said, the number of officers available to investigate crime in the MPS is higher than in comparison force areas. It is unlikely that homicide rates alone can explain the significant discrepancy in detection rates across metropolitan force areas. Other possible contributing variables may be the nature of particular homicides experienced (stranger homicides generally being more difficult to detect) and the size of transient populations (refer to HMIC, 2000 for further details).

21 See Gaylor (2002) for a comprehensive review of the potential to reinvestigate undetected homicides.

22 As they are a court of law, as opposed to fact, all appeals are eventually successful on some point of law and so the 'lurking finger of suspicion' always remains (personal communication, Hazel Keirle, Legal Officer, Miscarriage of Justice Organisation, MOJO).

MOJO currently have 306 applications for assistance on their files from prisoners who allege they were wrongly convicted. The major percentage of these (72 per cent) are from individuals convicted of murder (personal communication, Hazel Keirle, Legal Officer, MOJO).

23 I can vividly recall hearing the tape recording being played on the radio when I was a child living in Cyprus on an RAF base. The identity of the hoaxer has never been determined.

24 See Chan, 1997 for an overview of the distinct forms that occupational culture can take in relation to factors such as rank and policing role.

11 Preventing Homicide in the UK[1]

This chapter will consider the potential for preventing homicide. Because of the relative rarity of homicide it is a difficult crime to predict. Moreover, whilst it is possible to identify certain 'risk factors' in relation to particular forms of homicide, it is often the case that these factors are widespread, making the task of identifying with any clarity high-risk populations or locations extremely difficult. Despite such difficulties (to which we return shortly), there is much research from various regions of the world which takes as its focus the potential for preventing homicide. This chapter begins with an introduction to crime prevention approaches and a consideration of their applicability to homicide. This leads us to a brief discussion of some important distinctions between certain kinds of homicide, not least between those where the death of the victim is essentially the 'accidental' outcome of an incident of inter-personal violence and those in which the death is more deliberate or planned. This has important implications for the prevention of homicide, as different forms will undoubtedly require very different forms of intervention. In the second section of the chapter we move on to consider three distinct forms of homicide and how their incidence might be reduced. Specifically we deal with 'domestic homicide' (male-on-female), 'infanticide' (essentially focusing upon female killers) and 'alcohol-related street killings' (that is, in the context of a 'night out'). These forms of homicide are very different in terms of their underlying causes and, hence, the sorts of preventative measures that could be employed. At a conservative estimate, the three categories together account for around 50 per cent of the total number of homicides recorded in England and Wales,[2] so they clearly merit special attention. The chapter ends by drawing together a number of the lessons that can be learned about the area of crime prevention in relation to homicide.

Crime Prevention and Homicide

We begin this section of the chapter with a brief overview of crime prevention approaches.

An Introduction to Crime Prevention Approaches

There are a number of different definitions, models and typologies of crime prevention, about which there is no real consensus among criminologists (Hughes, 2001). Traditionally, a basic distinction has been made, particularly by North American writers, between 'primary', 'secondary' and 'tertiary' crime prevention strategies. Primary approaches focus upon the direct prevention of the crime event and are, therefore, *offence* rather than *offender* orientated. These often involve either target hardening or opportunity reductions. An example of the latter would be reducing the supply of lethal weapons (such as firearms) in circulation. Secondary prevention aims to combat criminal motivation before people become involved in crime (for example, through anti-poverty programmes, education or alternative activities to 'keep young people off the streets'). Tertiary prevention focuses upon halting criminal careers via the treatment or punishment of known offenders.[3] As Pease (1997) notes, in the UK the police have tended to take the lead in primary prevention, youth services in secondary prevention, and the prison and probation services in tertiary prevention. Another popular means of defining crime prevention (in the late twentieth century) has been in terms of a broad distinction between situational and social (also known as 'community') strategies (Hughes, 2001: 63).

In the UK, policy has been strongly influenced since the early 1980s by the concept of 'situational' crime prevention (an example of primary prevention), the key aim of which is to reduce the opportunities (and/or increase the likelihood of detection) for specific types of crime in specific kinds of situations or locations (see Clarke, 1995; Pease, 1997; Hughes, 1998; and Coleman and Norris, 2000). While initially based primarily upon the 'target hardening' or surveillance of geographical locations, this approach has become increasingly flexible, and has evolved to incorporate strategies which focus upon potential offenders and victims as well as locations. At the same time, there has been a revival of interest in broader 'social' crime prevention policies (including initiatives in community regeneration, literacy, parenting skills and the like) as well as in offender treatment programmes, both of which may be combined with situational approaches in the same multi-agency project. As outlined in Chapter 5, there is evidence of a strong correlation between homicide rates and levels of poverty and social inequality, and it may be that significant and lasting reductions in homicide can only be achieved by strategies which take this fully into account (an issue to which we shall return at the end of the chapter).

Finally, it is worth noting (though we will not elaborate on the issue here) that at the end of the 1990s in the UK there was a shift in emphasis in the discourse of crime control at government level from that of 'crime prevention' to 'crime reduction' (see Walklate, 2002; and Ekblom, 2000). There are clear attractions for the government in adopting this change in discourse. At one level it allows government to excuse the targeting of particular crimes on the basis of resources (that is, investing only in that which has been 'proven' by evidence to 'work') and it could also be argued that reduction is much easier to measure than prevention and, in that sense, easier to make claims of success. Linked to this, the term 'prevention' suggests somewhat grander results that may be unrealistic.

In thinking about the various ways in which homicide may be reduced, it is essential to begin by recognising its diversity. For example, domestic homicide, robbery homicide, the killing of infants, gang-related shootings and lethal fights in the context of night-time drinking are all very different in nature, and the underlying causes are different too. Hence, these distinct categories will all require very different forms of intervention. At a broader level, we could draw a distinction between those killings that are essentially accidental by-products of interpersonal violence and those that are more purposeful or planned, an issue to which we now turn.

Homicide and the Issue of Lethal Intent

There is some debate among academics regarding the extent to which homicide is a distinct phenomenon, therefore requiring very specific forms of preventative targeting or whether, on the other hand, it is essentially similar to other forms of interpersonal violence. How one conceptualises homicide in this respect has potentially important implications for prevention.

Homicides as 'Fatal Assaults'

It has been argued by a number of writers that the dynamics of homicide are basically identical to those of other forms of violence (see, for example, Fyfe et al., 1997; Harries, 1990). As Gottfredson and Hirschi point out, many violent interactions occur which, while not resulting in homicide, are very similar in aetiology and intent:

> The difference between homicide and assault may simply be the intervention of a bystander, the accuracy of a gun, the weight of a frying pan, the speed of an ambulance or the availability of a trauma centre. (1990: 34)

Harries likewise concludes that:

> The legal labels 'homicide' and 'assault' represent essentially similar behaviours differing principally in outcome rather than process ... the typical homicide is most appropriately considered a fatal assault. (1990: 48, 68)

In addition, the social correlates of homicide are not dissimilar to those of violence. As outlined in several of the preceding chapters, perpetrators (and to a lesser extent victims) belong disproportionately to particular socio-demographic groups, and homicide events display certain patterns. Perhaps more importantly, these patterns and characteristics are also, to a large extent typical of *violent crime in general*. The *British Crime Survey* (Kershaw et al., 2000) found, for example, that 80 per cent of violent incidents were perpetrated by males and in 60 per cent of cases victims were also male. In addition, in 40 per cent of incidents offenders were judged to be under the influence of alcohol, and in almost half of all violent incidents (44 per cent) offenders were aged 16–24 (for further data see Kershaw et al., 2000; Simmons, 2002; Levi and Maguire, 2002; and Stanko et al., 2002).

These similarities, then, give support to the view that, while homicide itself is relatively rare, it is not a completely separate and unique form of behaviour. Rather, it can be understood as an extreme manifestation of serious violence, with similar underlying causes and dynamics and influenced by similar situational factors. Clearly, if this is the case, strategies for preventing homicide can be developed in conjunction with those aimed at violent crime in general or, alternatively, at the most serious kinds of violent crime. Thus, for example, the 850 homicides recorded in England and Wales in 2000/01 can be considered alongside a similar number of attempted murders (708) and a much greater number of 'woundings or other acts endangering life' (15,662)[4] (Simmons, 2002).

Homicide as a Distinct Phenomenon

On the other hand, there are those who acknowledge that homicide and other forms of serious violence are not so closely linked as first appears, and that at least a proportion of homicides are of a quite different order. Some researchers have noted that homicide rates and violence rates do not always move together. For example, as discussed in Chapter 2, Soothill et al. (1999) suggest that there is an inverse relationship between violence and homicide between England and Wales and Scotland, the former having a higher rate of violence but lower rate of homicide and vice versa.[5]

It is also clear that there are some homicides in which the perpetrator fully intends to kill (as opposed to injure) the victim and ensure his or her death. These may include coldly premeditated murders, murders by people who actively 'enjoy' killing (some of whom may be serial murderers) and frenzied attacks in which the victim is stabbed or bludgeoned numerous times.[6] As Fyfe et al., point out, 'when homicides are committed by emptying high-capacity pistols and automatic weapons into victims' bodies, the offenders' intent is unmistakable' (1997: 8).

Felson and Messner (1996: 520) are among the main proponents of this alternative perspective. They claim that 'a substantial portion of homicide offenders really do intend to kill their victims and not merely injure them' and hence that we are dealing with behaviour quite different to that of assault. They cite supporting evidence for this from their regression analysis of a merged data set from the US containing information on homicides, robberies, rapes and assaults. Whilst only a minority of researchers currently adhere to this view (see, for example, Kleck, 1991; Riedel, 1993; and Block et al., 2001), it is nevertheless an important topic for further investigation. Kleck (1991), in his discussion of weapons and violent crime outcomes, notes that weapon lethality and attacker lethality are closely associated and can be easily confused. Whilst acknowledging that part of the difference in death rates of violent attacks is linked to the properties of the weapons themselves, he argues that part of the difference is also due to 'the greater "lethality" of the users of the more deadly weapons' (1991: 165). In short, he argues that individuals with more lethal intent choose more serious weaponry. Riedel (1993: 157) also notes the planned and intended nature of some killings in his discussion of robbery homicides. He cites, for example, those occasions when robbery is secondary to execution-style, gangland killings.

Ultimately, the two arguments are not incompatible. Clearly, there are homicides which are similar in dynamics to other acts of violence, and homicides which are not (Brookman and Maguire, 2003). The important point is to recognise this diversity and consider how it may impact upon a proposed crime prevention technique. Thinking back to Chapter 6 for a moment, we considered two very different forms of 'masculine homicide' which illustrate this difference well. Confrontational homicides generally arose from 'honour contests' in response to relatively trivial disagreements. The subsequent spontaneous assaults that took place were rarely intended – at least at the outset of the dispute – to result in the victim's death. In contrast, revenge killings were much more purposeful and determined in nature. Murder was often planned in advance, the offender seeking the victim out and giving him little chance to resist the lethal attack. Firearms were adopted in these revenge killings to a much greater extent than in other forms of homicide observed amongst men (see Brookman, 2003). So, whilst there are clearly some common elements between these two forms of homicide (notably in the part frequently played by 'masculine ego'), there are also fundamental differences. In short, an appreciation of the differences in nature and aetiology between homicides leads necessarily to a different focus in terms of possible intervention strategies. The broad distinction between 'accidental' and 'purposeful' killings is just one such example of this diversity.

Study Task 11.1

Make a list of at least three different techniques or tactics that could be employed to reduce homicide under the general headings of 'primary', 'secondary' and 'tertiary' prevention.

Preventing Specific Forms of Homicide

In this section of the chapter we consider the possibilities for preventing three distinct kinds of homicide, defined by a combination of the type of victim, type of offender, the motives/circumstances of the offence and the type of weapon used. The categories are:

- domestic (partner) homicide (where the victim is an adult female);
- child/infant homicide (with a focus upon parents or carers as perpetrators); and
- alcohol-related street killings (that is, in the context of a night out).

These forms of homicide are recognisable as relatively distinct and homogeneous kinds of homicide, each with its own set of 'typical' characteristics (see Chapter 2), and are also interesting because they cover both 'domestic' and 'street' offences. Finally, as indicated earlier, the three categories are significant in terms of numbers (between them covering in the region of half of all homicides in England and Wales). Each section will begin with a brief overview of the nature and extent of the particular form of homicide, followed by a consideration of the risk factors associated with it and, finally, an assessment of possible preventive strategies. We begin with a consideration of male-perpetrated domestic homicide.

Domestic (Partner) Homicide: Extent, Nature and Risk Factors

'Domestic' (or 'partner') homicide[7] makes up a significant proportion of homicides in the UK. In 2001, for example, almost one-fifth of all recorded homicides in England and Wales were of this kind. It is also clear from both national and international data and literature that killing by a partner is the form of homicide to which women are most at risk (refer to Chapter 6). According to the Homicide Index (HI), between 1997 and 2001, 42 per cent of all female homicide victims in England and Wales were killed by a current or former sexual partner. This compares to just 5 per cent of all male victims. In numerical terms, there were 533 female and 141 male victims of domestic homicide over the five years. Data from various regions of the world show similar gender differences.[8]

Researchers have consistently found that a significant proportion of female victims of domestic homicide have previously experienced domestic violence (Wallace, 1986; Campbell, 1992; Moracco et al., 1998, Smith et al., 1998). It has therefore been suggested that one important avenue for preventing domestic homicide is *to identify and intervene with female victims of domestic violence*. However, domestic violence is obviously much more widespread than domestic homicide, making it difficult to determine those women who, from the large numbers who suffer domestic violence, might be seriously 'at risk' of homicide. The 1998 British Crime Survey (Mirrlees-Black et al., 1998) found that almost one in four women aged 16–59 had fallen victim to domestic violence over their lifetime. By contrast, under 100 women aged 16–59 fell victim to domestic homicide during 1998, which translates to less than one in 100,000 across England and Wales. In short, one might have to cast the net very wide in order to prevent a small number of domestic homicides. Further evidence for this is provided by Sherman (1993), who found in his analysis of data from Minneapolis that only a tiny fraction of addresses with repeated domestic disturbance calls to the police witnessed a domestic homicide. Further, three-fifths of all domestic homicides reviewed occurred at addresses to which the police had *never* been called.[9] He concluded that 'a prediction of domestic homicide from chronic domestic disturbance calls would be wrong 997 times out of 1,000' (1993: 25).

An important research finding which may assist prediction is that a substantial proportion of domestic killings by men are in some way connected to separation or the threat of separation between the intimates (Showalter et al., 1980; Barnard et al., 1982; Campbell, 1992; Wilson and Daly, 1993). In such cases, it is often suggested that the killer was typically impassioned by sexual jealousy and/or by his concerns about losing his partner. Polk (1994a: 23) refers to such homicides as motivated by 'jealousy/control' and Wallace (1986: 96) uses similar terms when she talks of 'jealousy/sexual exclusivity'. As Polk and Ranson (1991: 18) remark, the phrase 'if I can't have you no one will' echoes through the literature on male-perpetrated spousal homicide.

The above observations fit well with other research suggesting that a particular factor which may increase the risk of serious violence from an ex-partner is evidence of *stalking*. Detailed statistical analyses of the link between femicide and stalking by ex-partners are virtually absent from the literature. A valuable exception is a study by Moracco et al. (1998) of 586 femicide victims in North Carolina. The researchers found that 36 per cent of these women had been murdered by a current or former partner who had previously committed domestic violence against them,[10] and that in 23 per cent of these latter cases – that is, about 8 per cent of the total sample of femicides – the killer had stalked the victim prior to the fatal incident. McFarlane et al. (1999) argue, on the basis of these findings, that when stalking occurs in conjunction with intimate partner violence, there is a significantly enhanced risk of severe violence and/or femicide, and they urge that both abused women and relevant agencies should be so advised (see also Sheridan et al., 2001).

Finally, some recent research from the US points to the importance of incorporating victims' perception of risk and danger into the equation. For example, the Danger Assessment Scale (DAS) (Campbell, 1986, 1995; Stuart and Campbell, 1989), which has been used for some years as a mechanism for assessing risk of escalating violence based on victims' self-reports of violence-related issues, was subjected to a careful pilot investigation by Goodman et al. (2000). Whilst the sample size adopted was small (49 women), the findings indicated that the DAS, when administered to female victims of domestic violence seeking help from the criminal justice system, can contribute significantly to the prediction of short-term abuse recurrence amongst arrested batterers (see also Campbell, 1995 for discussions of psychologically-based risk assessments for lethality within domestic violence settings). Second, Weisz et al. (2000) conducted research to assess the accuracy with which female victims of domestic violence (termed 'survivors') could predict further episodes of severe violence against themselves. Findings indicated that women who strongly predicted future violence were often likely to be correct (for the four-month follow-up period). The researchers concluded that survivors' predictions should be incorporated into existing risk assessment models and should be taken seriously even where other markers fail to identify a risk. They also stressed the importance of agencies maintaining contact with such women over the longer term. It should be noted, however, that the research examined only the risk of serious violence – no attempt was made to test women's assessment of mortal risk.

From the available evidence, much of which emanates from North America, a number of indicators can be identified as most appropriate to assessing risk of homicide within the domestic setting. From the research mentioned above, the following factors emerge:

- Recent ending of a relationship instigated by female partner.
- Evidence of stalking.
- Women's (survivors') predictions of future risk and its likely severity.

In addition, the following list, which is adapted from Campbell (1995: 111), includes a range of risk factors. Whilst some are undoubtedly more applicable to the US than the UK, such as access to guns, most are likely to be as important in the UK context as in the US, although this cannot be confirmed without further research.

- Access to/ownership of guns.
- Displaying weapons such as knives within the household.
- Threats with weapons.
- Threats to kill.
- Serious injury in prior abusive incident.
- Threats of suicide by male partner (in response to female partner's threats to leave).
- Drug and alcohol abuse by male partner.
- Forced sex of female partner.
- Obsessiveness/extensive jealousy, extensive dominance.

It is important to note, however, that the presence even of those factors that appear particularly salient as risk factors (and which may be good predictors of violence), such as threats to kill, does *not* lead to homicide in the great majority of cases. It is revealing, for example, that in their study of 15,000 domestic assault reports over a three-year period in Milwaukee, Sherman et al. (1991) found that *none* of 110 prior episodes of gun-pointing and death threats were followed by homicide. Equally, it should be remembered that a fair proportion of domestic homicides have no reported history of domestic abuse.

Possible Preventive Strategies

The research findings outlined above suggest that predictions of serious domestic violence can be refined to a sufficient extent to allow targeted interventions, but that the scope for predicting domestic homicide seems much more limited. Even so, there is evidence of some links between the two phenomena, suggesting that a significant reduction in the overall frequency of domestic violence (especially that involving serious and repeated assaults) would be accompanied by at least a small reduction in the number of homicides. For this reason, it is useful to look at possible preventive strategies which might achieve this dual purpose.

As pointed out earlier, interventions can be targeted at potential offenders, potential victims, or both. We begin with a discussion of responses within the criminal justice system (including prosecution, anti-stalking legislation and offender programmes), before moving on to look at multi-agency responses.

Criminal Justice Responses

Prosecution: One of the core weapons of the criminal justice response to domestic violence is the prosecution of offenders. However, this has always been dogged by the major problem of case attrition – most frequently through the fear or reluctance of victims to give evidence in court. Efforts to address this problem include the introduction of the Protection from Harassment Act 1997; prosecutions using section 23(3)(b) of the Criminal Justice Act 1998 (often called 'victimless prosecutions'), whereby the victim can avoid attending court and submit a written statement to take the place of an oral statement; and enhanced monitoring and evidence gathering by the police at crime scenes to support prosecutions (Edwards, 2000).

Guidelines published by the Home Office early in March 2000 included guidance to the Crown Prosecution Service (CPS) that it must consider prosecuting perpetrators of domestic violence even if their victims withdraw complaints. At the same time, the Home Office urged local authorities to evict 'wife beaters'. Such measures may prove particularly valuable in cases where there is evidence that a victim is at risk of serious assault or even that her life may be in danger. The key to effective use of these provisions, however, lies in identifying which cases pose the most significant risk and in the adoption of a co-ordinated response to women's plight, and that of their children where appropriate.

Brookman and Maguire (2003), during interviews with staff at a local Family Support Unit (FSU), found that the police encountered a number of difficulties whilst trying to assist victims of domestic violence and, in particular, ensuring their future wellbeing. Concerns revolved around the perceived inadequacy of the CPS to deal with domestic violence cases due to a lack of specialised staff, and the recurring situation of offenders receiving bail at Magistrates' court after being charged with serious assaults on their female partners. The development of specialist domestic violence courts was seen as one possible solution (a tactic which has been piloted in one court in Liverpool), as was a general 'tightening up' of the processes surrounding the handling of domestic violence cases.

Anti-stalking Legislation: The main statutory protection against stalking is provided by the Protection from Harassment Act 1997. Under the Act, victims no longer have to present evidence of physical violence in order to secure injunctions and restraining orders. Breach of a restraining order carries up to five years' imprisonment and/or a fine. The Act also recognises an offence of putting people in fear of violence (s4) and provides for a civil remedy (s3). Harris (2000) undertook an evaluation of the use and effectiveness of this Act and found that it was most often used in relation to harassment by former partners and by neighbours (as opposed to cases fitting the popular image of stalking by an obsessed stranger). Harris also reported a variety of implementation problems. For example, the police were not always clear about what constituted harassment (within the meaning of the Act), did not always take action at an appropriate time and did not always select the most appropriate charge. The publication by the Home Office of an 'Investigator's Guide' to stalking and other forms of harassment (Brown, 2000) should improve the situation in this respect. However, there is also a problem of relatively high attrition rates in harassment cases. Harris (2000: 55) found that the cases against 39 per cent of those arrested were dropped, often because of the withdrawal of complaints. Harris suggests that victims need to be better supported through the pre-trial and trial stages in order to reduce the levels of withdrawal. Finally, the research found that restraining orders were only imposed in around half of all convictions and that, even where they were imposed, there were problems with enforcement and breaches were common. The latter findings are echoed in a study by Sheridan et al. (2001), who report that, among 19 cases in which an injunction was obtained, it had been breached in 15 cases. In light of the previously-quoted findings on the risks of violence (and homicide) from *ex*-partners, this seems to be a matter for some concern.

Offender Programmes: There are around 30 perpetrator programmes currently running in the UK (Mullender and Burton, 2000). These generally incorporate a cognitive-behavioural approach and/or gender analysis. Programmes range from 20 hours over 10 weeks to 120 hours over 48 weeks. Despite some evidence of success in reducing re-offending for some specific programmes (see for example, Dobash et al., 1996; Burton et al., 1998), there remains a general lack of conclusive evidence as to their effectiveness. Howells et al. (2002) assessed the effectiveness of an anger management programme in Australia and found that the overall impact was small, and not of any real clinical significance. In addition, similar changes in a positive direction were also found for the control group (who were assessed, but did not participate in the program any further). Programmes in this field are extremely difficult to evaluate for a range of methodological reasons, including small sample sizes, lack of comparison groups, and inadequate means of measuring outcomes (Dobash et al., 1996). It may also be the case that different types of men require different types of approaches and respond very differently. Some researchers in the US suggest that specialised approaches to offender programmes are required, based on typologies of batterers (Healey and Smith, 1998). For example, offenders with mental health problems, or who regularly abuse alcohol or drugs, may require very different kind of interventions from other men without such difficulties.

Completion rates have been shown to be problematic in all countries surveyed and some thought is required as to how best to counteract this. There is some evidence to suggest that criminal justice interventions can dramatically increase compliance with perpetrator programmes – for example, prompt, rigorous and agreed action in cases of breach of conditions (Mullender and Burton, 2000). Healey and Smith (1998) suggest that probation officers are the most critical link between the criminal justice system and other interventions, and suggest that assigning them to specialised units would enhance their ability to assist both offenders and their victims effectively.

Finally, it is vital that consideration of the safety of partners and children is at the forefront of planning programmes and that perpetrator programmes do not dilute or divert attention away from services for survivors. In short, perpetrator programmes should never be set up in isolation. Rather, they need to form part of a comprehensive strategy to protect the safety of women and their children.

Multi-Agency Responses

One of the clearest messages from the literature is that criminal justice interventions alone are unlikely to produce a significant impact on the problem of domestic violence (and by inference, on domestic homicide), and hence that a well-co-ordinated multi-agency approach is vital. The agencies most likely to be involved in effective multi-agency work are the police, probation service, social services, and voluntary agencies such as those who provide domestic violence shelters. Co-ordinated programmes of intervention need to operate at various levels, starting with identifying risk of an escalation in violence, then dealing appropriately and effectively with victims and offenders, and finally continuing to monitor the effectiveness of any such interventions. There is much scope for improvement at all three levels (see Brookman and Maguire, 2003).

For example, where interventions themselves are concerned, data from the US support the notion that decreases in domestic homicide follow from increased co-operation between domestic violence service providers, police departments and professionals who work with offenders. The authors of the report *Homicide in Eight US Cities* (Lattimore et al., 1997) cite Tampa as an excellent example of such a co-ordinated approach. Tampa has a large number of services available to abuse victims and their children. The domestic violence shelter has 77 beds and 20 cribs and no-one is ever turned away – hotels and motels provide available rooms at no charge to domestic violence victims when the shelter is full to capacity. A school housed at the shelter is seen to overcome the problem of children being abducted to and from school, or whilst at school. Finally, an offender programme is also operated by the shelter and comprises an intensive 26-week course to prevent re-offending. Ninety per cent of participants have been ordered by the courts to attend. Whilst Tampa had a low number of intimate/family homicides prior to the aforementioned programmes, it is claimed that the combination of programmes has led to a significant reduction in the number of domestic-related homicides.[11]

Similar arguments regarding co-ordination and co-operation amongst relevant agencies can be made regarding the identification of risk. For example, in relation to risk assessment, an obvious starting-point is a concerted effort to make agencies such as the police, social services and voluntary agencies more fully aware of the indicators of increased risk outlined above, and to devise strategies of notification where they are present. Hospital emergency departments and general practitioners may also provide an important link in the identification of 'at risk' women. Studies have shown that victims of domestic violence consult doctors more often than they consult the police or any other groups of professionals (Dobash and Dobash, 1979; Dobash et al., 1985; Gottlieb, 1998; Stanko et al., 1998). However, the specific role that medical practitioners may adopt in relation to domestic violence is debated. For example, some researchers (Shepherd, 1998) view accident and emergency departments as an important additional route to the identification and conviction of perpetrators of domestic violence. Others, such as Morley (1995), view this as flawed, believing it may dissuade some women from seeking medical help and make others less able to disclose the cause of injury.

Study Task 11.2

In June 2003 the government released a consultation paper 'Safety and Justice' setting out their new strategy for dealing with domestic violence. Visit the Home Office website and refer to this paper. What are the key features of their proposed new strategy? You should note that the bulk of space devoted to domestic homicide relates to improving the ways in which the law on homicide in domestic violence cases operates – particularly in relation to the defences of provocation, self-defence and diminished responsibility. Assess these proposals. Do you believe that the arguments for altering the criminal law will have any impact upon the incidence of domestic homicide?

Preventing Domestic Homicide: Conclusions

Around one in five of all homicides in England and Wales are perpetrated by a co-habitant or ex-partner. Such homicides are very difficult to predict, as the vast majority of victims even of serious and repeated domestic violence are not killed, while many homicides occur without prior reports of violence. Even so, it is likely that effective measures to reduce domestic violence as a whole would have at least a small effect on the number of domestic murders.

The evidence strongly suggests that female victims of domestic violence should be treated as particularly vulnerable during and after separation from their violent partner. However, further research is required into the nature and antecedents of escalation patterns, specifically the changing frequency and severity of assaults and factors associated with this. Closer understanding is also required of the relationship between domestic violence and other forms of victimisation, such as stalking (see Walby and Myhill, 2000). Crucially, we need evaluations of risks to women before and after separation. An established body of research suggests that separation is a particularly dangerous time for battered women in terms of risks of homicide. It is important to decipher whether and how actually leaving an abusive partner merits specific forms of intervention by criminal justice agencies.

Finally, whilst we have not dealt with female perpetrators of partner homicide in this chapter, it is worth remembering (as outlined in Chapter 7) that men's violence toward their female partners is also critical when considering the problem of partner homicides committed by women. Several researchers have observed that women who kill their male partners do so in response to violence perpetrated by the male (Radford, 1993; Wilson and Daly, 1993; Jurik and Winn, 1990). Further, such violence is often linked to male sexual jealousy and propriety. Hence, regardless of the sex of the perpetrator, partner homicide often occurs as a result of a history of habitual male aggression and abuse, physical and/or sexual (see Smith et al., 1998).

The Killing of Infants: Extent, Nature and Risk Factors

This section deals with the killing of infants less than a year old. This form of homicide is commonly referred to as 'infanticide', although this is not strictly accurate. As discussed in Chapter 8, infanticide is a legal term used to describe instances where mothers kill their own babies during periods of post-natal depression. The current discussion focuses in particular upon mothers who kill their infants (though fathers are also briefly considered) and deals only with killing of infants in the context of the family unit.

Infant homicide may be regarded as a sub-group of the broader category of *child* homicide.[12] However, there are some important differences between the killing of babies and of older children, which mark the former out as worthy of special attention. First, while children as a whole have a low risk of being killed compared to adults, babies of less than 12 months old are at higher risk than any other single year age group, child or adult (see Chapters 2 and 8). Moreover, the killing of infants is the only category of homicide in which women's offending rates approximate those of males. Between 1995 and 1999 in England and Wales, 90 per cent of the known or suspected killers of children aged 10–16 were male, dropping to 62 per cent for children aged below five years, and 56 per cent for babies less than one year. Finally, the proportion of child homicides in which the perpetrator is a parent is exceptionally high among infants. Over the above-mentioned period, 80 per cent of victims under one year old were killed by a parent, compared to 49 per cent of those aged one year, and less than 5 per cent of those aged 15 or 16.[13] Research from Australia and North America has revealed similar patterns (Crittenden and Craig, 1990; Adler and Polk, 1996).

There is as yet no definitive explanation of why such young babies are at greater risk of homicide than either older children or adults. That said, most researchers suggest that their fragility and total dependence or helplessness is of key importance (Strang, 1996; NSPCC, personal communication). In addition, the very real demands and stresses placed on a family by a newborn baby are almost certainly a factor (Wallace, 1986). Some researchers have claimed that infants with feeding or sleep difficulties, firstborn children or those whose deliveries were difficult may also be associated with greater risk (Marks, 1996). Other factors identified as increasing risk include low birth weight and lack of pre-natal care (Cummings and Mueller, 1994).

In addition, there is the important sub-category of neonaticides, which refers to the killing of babies less than a day old. One of the most frequent observations made in relation to mothers who commit neonaticide (fathers rarely commit this offence) is that the pregnancy has been denied (Brozovsky and Falit, 1971; Green and Manohar, 1990). Regardless of whether the expectant mother has failed to acknowledge her pregnancy or simply ignores the reality of the situation, it is often the case that she does not seek medical help and makes no preparations for delivery (Marks, 1996). Whilst there are no available data to determine the number of 'hidden' pregnancies that result in neonaticide, the suggestion is that it may be significant.

These cases are clearly cause for concern, but their absence from public/official view makes it difficult to undertake appropriate interventions.

As with domestic violence and domestic homicide, it is widely accepted that a link exists between fatal and non-fatal child abuse (Strang, 1996).[14] Hence, literature that focuses upon the prevention of non-fatal events can provide useful insights as a starting point for consideration of policies to reduce homicide. Research in this area suggests that a number of factors are frequently present in the backgrounds of offenders. Among the most frequently cited are mental disturbance in mothers and a range of social and economic factors. These issues have been considered in some detail in Chapter 8 and will thus simply be listed below:

- *Maternal mental illness*: There is a longstanding view that mothers who kill their infants are often suffering from some sort of postpartum mental illness.
- *Male mental distress*: There is some evidence that males who kill their infants are suffering mental distress that can manifest itself in depression or rage (sometimes due to the desertion of the female partner) and the subsequent suicide or attempted suicide of the killer.
- *Socio-economic factors*: Social deprivation, single parenthood, and unstable and violent relationships are among the most frequently cited factors.
- *The combined influences of both individual and structural factors*: Many researchers argue that it is the combined effects of social-structural disadvantage and individual factors that are key to unravelling the killing of infants.

Whilst each of the above factors may help to narrow down the population at highest risk of abusive behaviour, many difficulties remain in terms of translating this knowledge into practical and effective ways of identifying particular parents who might fruitfully be made the target of prevention strategies in relation to serious abuse – let alone to homicide specifically. As Strang points out:

> It is apparent that the offenders in these incidents do not differ sufficiently from a much larger population of socially and economically disadvantaged young parents for them to be identified specifically prior to the event. (1996: 5)

Some researchers nevertheless report encouraging findings from more focused efforts to identify abusive parents. Lynch and Roberts (cited in Oates, 1982), who studied families in Australian maternity hospitals, found five factors that distinguished a control group from an abusive group. Abusive mothers were more likely to:

- be under the age of 20 when their first child was born;
- have signs of emotional disturbance recorded in their maternity notes;
- have been referred to a hospital social worker;
- have caused concern to hospital staff over their mothering capacity; and
- have had their babies admitted to the special care nursery.

Other research has suggested that health visitors who visit parents in the first year are able, with reasonable reliability, to identify families in which there is a significant risk of child abuse (Dean et al., cited in Oates, 1982).

In addition, more general studies of filicide (child-killing by parents) have identified certain risk factors that may be useful to consider in the more confined cases of the killing of infants. Wilczynski (1995, 1997a) found that filicidal parents tend to exhibit three characteristics. First, they experience multiple social stresses, such as financial and housing problems, youthful parenthood, marital conflict, lack of preparation for parenthood and children who are difficult to care for. Such factors can combine, leading to a situation of isolation, instability and misery. They are also often compounded by psychiatric problems; many offenders exhibit depressive symptoms, have received prior psychiatric treatment and have abused alcohol or drugs. The second common feature of filicidal parents is that they usually have a lack of compensatory personal and social resources with which to cope with their problems and are often extremely isolated (Goetting, 1988c; Korbin, 1986). Finally, filicidal parents tend to perceive their situation as essentially negative (Korbin, 1987).

To sum up, although it is possible to identify a number of risk factors in relation to infant homicide (drawn mainly from studies of filicide or non-fatal child abuse), there remains the perennial problem that faces anyone attempting to predict and prevent grave but low frequency offences. Even among those who exhibit the risk factors in abundance, only a tiny minority will actually kill an infant, so it is extremely difficult to target interventions at the right individuals.

Possible Preventive Strategies

Despite the difficulties of prediction, there is a fair degree of agreement within the available literature regarding the kinds of measures that need to be put into place to reduce the incidence of child and infant abuse (fatal or otherwise). Among the most often cited preventive strategies are: parental education programmes; improvements in the diagnoses and identification of infant and child abuse; more co-ordinated responses to suspected abuse cases; and improved services to parents both before and after childbirth. Each of these is discussed briefly in turn.

Parental Education Programmes

Many commentators argue that education programmes or campaigns may go some way toward reducing the incidence of infant or child maltreatment and, by extension, the number of deaths. Strang (1996) suggests that most parents, especially the very young, would benefit from education for parenting, whether at school, as part of prenatal care or through the media. The rationale being that much abuse is a consequence of ignorance of good child-rearing practices and reasonable expectations of children's behaviour. Similarly, the NSPCC, in its *5–Point Manifesto for Protecting Babies* (NSPCC, 2000) (see Table 11.1) urges improved preparation for parenthood, with better antenatal advice on how to cope with crying babies and sleep deprivation; more public education on the dangers of shaking and hitting babies; and education about family life in the national school curriculum. With this aim in mind, the NSPCC launched its 'Full Stop Campaign' in March 1999. This included a national television advertising campaign aimed at supporting parents under stress and protecting babies from harm. In addition, 600,000 parents of new millennium babies received a book entitled *Babies' First Year* and a magazine entitled *Get Ready!*, urging parents to think about the more difficult aspects of parenting before the

Table 11.1   NSPCC's 5-point manifesto for protecting babies

- Improved preparation for parenthood with better antenatal advice on how to cope with crying babies and sleep deprivation, more public education on the dangers of shaking and hitting babies and education about family life in the national school curriculum.
- Better health service support for parents, including increased resources for and expansion of midwife and health visitor support.
- Child protection awareness training for all professionals working with children and families.
- National guidelines to ensure consistent procedures in accident and emergency departments to identify and manage non-accidental injuries as soon as they occur.
- Early, thorough and consistent investigations of all child deaths.

Source: NSPCC, 2000.

baby is born and during its first year of life. *Handle with Care* and *Protecting Your Baby* are two other NSPCC publications aimed at new parents. They focus on how easily babies and toddlers can be injured if mishandled and the importance of parents getting help straight away if they think they may be driven to harm their baby. Whilst it is too early to determine whether the campaign has had any impact upon child or infant abuse or homicide, it has been found to have significantly increased public awareness of the issues surrounding child abuse. The NSPCC believe that the campaign was a great success in that research conducted after the campaign found that 8 out of 10 parents said it had made them much more aware of how easily babies can be injured if mishandled. Audience research has shown strong identification among new parents with the stressful situations portrayed in the television advertising campaign (personal communication, NSPCC).

Improvements in Diagnoses and Identification of Infant and Child Abuse

There is mounting evidence that a significant proportion (up to 20 per cent) of infant deaths may be incorrectly attributed to Sudden Infant Death Syndrome (SIDS, refer to Chapter 1). Recent research by Jayawant et al. (1998) on the incidence and clinical outcome of subdural haemorrhage in children under two years of age in South Wales and the South-West of England highlights the difficulties in attributing this condition to accident or abuse. The researchers concluded that 27 of the 33 cases of subdural haemorrhage they reviewed were highly suggestive of abuse. They also found that a significant number of these cases had not been properly investigated at the time that the child was presented at hospital. Nine of the children died and a further 15 suffered profound disability. Four of the children who died had suffered previous physical abuse. The authors argue that the high probability of child abuse in cases of subdural haemorrhage is still not being recognised and cases are not being investigated fully. They note that clinical investigations must include a full series of basic investigations and that previous child abuse in an infant is a strong risk factor for subdural haemorrhage. They urge that child protection agencies must therefore give 'high priority to the protection of all current and future children in such families' (1998: 1561). Similar conclusions were reached by Hicks and Gaughan (1995), who found that the families involved in 6 of the 14 cases of fatal child abuse they reviewed in Ohio had prior protective service involvement. The NSPCC similarly recognises the importance of identifying child abuse swiftly. Point 4 of their Manifesto requests national guidelines to ensure consistent procedures in accident and emergency departments to identify and manage non-accidental injuries without delay.

More Co-ordinated Responses to Suspected Abuse Cases

One of the principal recommendations put forward by Fleming et al. (2000) in a wide-ranging review of previous inquiries was the adoption of a partnership framework for the investigation of sudden infant deaths. For example, health care representatives, paediatric and forensic pathologists, police officers and the social services should all be involved. Similarly, point 5 of the NSPCC's manifesto stresses the need for early, thorough and consistent investigations of all child deaths. Linked to this, the above-mentioned research by Jayawant et al. indicates that a partnership approach is equally vital in identifying potentially vulnerable babies or children both at the time of injury and in the immediate aftermath (to prevent any further instances of harm). As Strang (1996) suggests, whilst it may be impractical to target families on the basis of general risk factors, it may be possible to prevent some homicides by putting in place a rapid and coherent response once cases of actual abuse and injury have been identified.

Improved Services to Parents both Before and After Childbirth

Strang (1996) suggested that home visiting services might usefully compensate for the decline of adequate family support for parents. Research into the possible preventive value of home visiting services has produced somewhat mixed findings. Roberts et al. (1996), in their review of 11 randomised controlled trials of home visiting programmes, found conflicting evidence which they attributed to differential surveillance for child abuse between intervention and control groups. However, many studies report positive findings. Olds et al. (1986) provide evidence that women at highest risk of child abuse and neglect (which they defined as teenagers, unmarried or of low socio-economic status) benefited from home visits. Amongst the high-risk women they studied, those who were visited by a nurse had fewer instances of verified child abuse and neglect during the first two years of their children's lives. MacMillan and Thomas (1993) also found that home visits can prevent physical abuse and neglect of children in high-risk families. Finally, Eckenrode et al. (2000), in a large-scale longitudinal study of socially disadvantaged pregnant women in New York, found that families receiving home visits during pregnancy and infancy (from birth to two years) had significantly fewer child maltreatment reports involving the mother as perpetrator. What these and other studies appear to indicate is the importance of sustained visiting programmes (that is, up until the child's second birthday) for effective preventive results to be fully realised.

On a somewhat broader social, cultural and policy level, it is important to highlight some promising findings from Sweden. Somander and Rammer (1991) observed a decrease in child homicide (those aged 0–14 years) in Sweden in the second half of the decade 1971–80, from 59 victims to 37. According to Belsey (1993), the Swedish rate of infant deaths from presumed abuse is now one of the lowest in the industrialised world. Whilst no specific strategies have been shown by research to be positively linked to the decrease, some important changes in laws, policies and programmes aimed at protecting children, promoting their wellbeing and recognising their rights (Durrant and Olsen, 1997) are likely to have played a part. For example, in 1979 the Parental Code was changed, forbidding all physical punishment of children. The Swedish law was the first of its kind in the world. Sweden boasts well-developed maternity and child welfare centres available to all inhabitants without exception. The killing of infants due to postnatal depression is rare, arguably due to good surveillance of mothers (Somander and Rammer, 1991). In addition, parental leave allowances (parents can share a 12 month leave from work while being compensated at 75 per cent of their salary) and extensive day care provisions for all children aged one year and older are seen to have reduced the extent of parental stress and of work–family conflicts (Durrant and Olsen, 1997). Durrant and Olsen regard it as significant that such provisions have taken place in a social and cultural climate that emphasises a collectivist approach to meeting children's needs and rights through public policy.

Finally, as far as neonaticides are concerned (where pregnancies are often denied and hidden from public view), prevention becomes extremely difficult, since no one may be aware of the woman's plight (herself included). Perhaps the most sensible approach would involve education campaigns aimed at vulnerable pregnant women and their families. Families could be alerted to the importance of recognising pregnancy and provided with relevant information, while young pregnant women could be directed towards sources of confidential assistance.[15]

Preventing Infant Homicides: Conclusions

To conclude, on the basis of research in the area of infant homicide and the associated areas of filicide and abuse of young children, the most promising preventive strategies – which may be aimed at homicide and abuse simultaneously – appear to be:

- More and better educational programmes, including advertising, aimed at improving parenting skills.
- A need to emphasise to parents the particular fragility of infants and the ease with which parents (for example, by shaking their babies) can cause their death.
- Improvements in the identification of high-risk/vulnerable families and circumstances, with an emphasis on improved co-ordinated responses across a range of professions.
- Improvements in the identification, investigation and management of cases of non-accidental injury, including more rapid and better co-ordinated multi-agency responses.
- Home visiting programmes – such as public health nurses visiting parents at home who may be at risk of abuse or neglect.
- Counselling and respite services to families suffering undue stresses/pressures.

Study Task 11.3

Visit the website of the NSPCC (www.nspcc.org.uk) and read the relevant publications, leaflets and campaigning strategies in relation to protecting babies. What
form of crime prevention strategy does the NSPCC fall into (refer back to the first
section of this chapter)? What evidence does the NSPCC put forth for the success
of its campaigns? What do you believe to be the strengths and weaknesses of the
NSPCC's strategies, and why?

Alcohol and 'Street' Homicide: Extent, Nature and Risk Factors

One of the factors strongly associated with violent behaviour is the consumption
of alcohol (see, for example, Deehan, 1999; Levi and Maguire, 2002). As we shall
see, alcohol is also an important factor in a considerable proportion of homicides.
Moreover, both alcohol-related violence and alcohol-related homicide share a number
of common features. These similarities, together with the fact that many homicides
in which the offender is intoxicated are often not pre-planned, nor involve a strong
determination to kill (as opposed to injure), make it plausible to argue that alcohol-
related homicides represent, for the most part, the 'top of the pyramid' of a common type of violent crime, rather than a distinct form of behaviour. If this is the
case it is likely that strategies which significantly reduce alcohol-related violence
will also reduce alcohol-related homicide.

It is difficult to provide accurate figures on the number of homicides occurring in
the UK that are in some way related to the use of alcohol. According to the HI database, 10 per cent of all suspects during the period 1995–2001 were under the influence of alcohol at the time of the killing (88 per cent of these being male).[16] Among
'adult male-on-adult male' homicides, the proportion was higher, at 12 per cent.
However, it would appear that the HI considerably underestimates the extent of
alcohol use in both cases, if studies using more detailed records are to be relied
upon (see Brookman and Maguire, 2003).[17] Brookman (2003) found that in over
half (52 per cent) of all adult male-on-male homicides analysed, either the victim
or the offender had consumed alcohol, often to excess. Furthermore, in 36 per cent
both the offender and victim had consumed alcohol. These findings are not dissimilar to findings from other countries (see Brookman and Maguire, 2003).

Returning to the HI (England and Wales), analysis reveals that over half (56 per
cent) of homicides involving an intoxicated suspect occurred in circumstances of
what are officially categorised as 'rage/quarrels' amongst unrelated individuals. This
rises to 64 per cent where the suspect was an intoxicated adult male. In contrast,
only 29 per cent of killings by non-intoxicated suspects were classified as such.
Whilst the category 'rage/quarrels' is clearly broad, the data are consistent with the
frequent observation that alcohol fuels quarrelsome and aggressive behaviour –
often in relation to so-called 'trivial arguments' and/or taking the form of a masculine
'honour contest' (Polk, 1994a) – amongst unrelated men. In this context, a study

by Gillies is useful in illustrating the similarity between violent incidents involving alcohol which do and do not result in homicide. Noting that nearly half of all homicide suspects had previous convictions for lesser violence, he comments:

> Most crimes were unpremeditated, unintended, impulsive and precipitated by quarrels picked over trifles when the participants were worse for drink. (1976)

The HI does not, currently, record details of the location of homicides. However, Scotland does so.[18] Fewer than 4 per cent of killings between 1979 and 1998 in Scotland occurred in pubs, clubs or restaurants. The coding scheme adopted does not allow for any measure of homicides that took place outside such buildings, so there is no indication of the extent to which 'spill out areas' from pubs and clubs were involved – although it may be relevant that about a quarter of homicides in Scotland occurred on 'streets or footpaths'.[19]

In summary, alcohol-related homicides predominantly occur amongst unrelated adult males and are the result of some kind of quarrel. Thinking back to Chapter 6 where we considered 'masculine' homicide, alcohol-related killings most closely fit the category of confrontational homicide considered, that is, they are often spontaneous and unpremeditated attacks amongst men who are, for one reason or another, protecting their masculine pride. Few of these killings appear to take place within pubs or clubs, although it is likely that larger numbers occur in 'spill out' areas or, even if committed further away, involve people still intoxicated from earlier drinking sessions. Moreover, alcohol is, of course, a transportable product, and significant numbers of killings occur where perpetrators, victims or both have been drinking in their own or other people's homes. This suggests that tackling pub/club type violence, in which considerable progress has been made recently, will only go part of the way to preventing alcohol-related homicide (and violence more generally). We will not deal here with the complex issue of the relationship between alcohol (and/or drug) consumption and violence suffice it to say, as discussed in Chapters 3 and 5, there is ample evidence of a link, albeit mediated by other factors (see, for example, Brookman, 2003; and Tomsen, 1997).

Possible Preventive Strategies

Manipulating the Physical and Social Environment in and around Licensed Premises

Significant effort has been put into finding ways of preventing violence in and around licensed premises. Moreover, many of the measures employed appear to have met with some degree of success. Most of the research in this area recognises that not all pubs and clubs are equally associated with violence (Deehan, 1999; Maguire and Nettleton, 2003). Rather, it is generally the case that towns and cities contain a number of 'hot spots' in the form of establishments with a high frequency of (and often a reputation for) violent incidents, together with a larger number of generally unproblematic venues. Research and interventions have focused mainly on the physical or social environment in and around such 'hot spots'.

One area of attention has been the physical design of pubs and clubs. For example, research conducted by Graham and Homel (1997) identified a number of factors conducive to violence in public houses and clubs, including the density of activities within such premises and indoor design (for example, the location of furniture and pool tables, pillars, walls and bars). Design features, they point out, can also affect the social environment through helping to create a particular mood or atmosphere.

Other examples of attempts to improve the social environment include training and licensing schemes for 'door staff' (who work inside clubs as well as 'on the doors'). It is claimed that properly trained staff can often spot indicators of impending trouble and take discreet action to prevent it (Deehan, 1999). Equally, there is evidence that poorly-trained and unsupervised door staff can cause violence as well as prevent it (Hobbs et al., 2002). Some areas have set up partnership arrangements to facilitate joint actions by the police, licensing magistrates and managers of licensed premises. While it may occasionally be necessary to use deterrent measures (such as threats to withdraw licenses) against 'hot spots' where managers are uncooperative, in most cases the partnership approach appears to be the best way of identifying and solving underlying problems – and hence of reducing levels of violence – in particular premises (Maguire and Nettleton, 2003).

Table 11.2 draws attention to a number of interventions concerned directly with the monitoring and control of drinkers, including controls over the numbers of people entering premises, CCTV surveillance (and, again, surveillance by well-trained security staff), refusal of drinks to intoxicated customers, and 'Pubwatch' schemes.[20] Many of these appear from early local evaluations to be promising in terms of their potential to reduce violence, although little fully reliable research evidence is available. Still less, of course, is known about their capacity for preventing homicide.

Finally – and particularly importantly – many local authorities are now beginning to recognise the emergence in the UK of the phenomenon of the 'night-time economy' (Hobbs et al., 2002) and with it their responsibility to manage this economy in a proactive fashion, rather than simply leaving it to the police. This includes preventing the late-night gathering of crowds of intoxicated individuals by staggering closing times and providing reliable transport services at times when people are leaving pubs or clubs in large numbers. Several cities have apparently reduced incidents of fighting between people under the influence of alcohol due to such measures. For example, a study by Purser (1997) in Coventry found that 70 per cent of city-centre assaults occurred in or around major entertainment centres and at licensed premises' closing times, and taxi ranks were identified as regular sites for violence. Transport facilities were subsequently organised to prevent queuing and a late-night bus service was organised. Purser reports a reduction in alcohol-related assaults as a result of these measures (see also Ramsay, 1990).

In terms of preventing *homicides* in and around licensed premises, general violence reduction measures of these kinds are clearly relevant. However, it is also important to consider measures aimed specifically at *minimising the level of harm that results from those violent incidents which are not prevented*. One obvious strategy here

Table 11.2   Summary of strategies for preventing violence in and around licensed premises

Nature of intervention	Examples
Manipulation of the physical environment of pubs/clubs	• No 'hidden' alcoves that prevent the easy monitoring of behaviour. • Attention to the spacing of furniture, including tables, chairs, stools and pool tables, to avoid customer crowding. • Raised bar-areas to permit staff monitoring of customer behaviour.
Controlling the social atmosphere	• Attractive, well-maintained premises. • Registered door staff schemes and employment of well-trained staff who discourage antisocial behaviour in a manner that does not escalate violence. • The reduction of excessively loud music.
Alcohol control	• No 'happy hours'/drinks promotions. • Serving of food and soft beverages.
Control of drinkers	• Well-ventilated premises with controls over the number of customers entering. • Well-trained and socially skilled door staff and bar staff experienced at dealing with aggressive or violent individuals (see also above). • Refusal of alcohol to already intoxicated customers. • 'Pubwatch' schemes. • Efforts to reduce 'pub hopping'. • The use of CCTV to monitor disorder and violence. • Staggered closing times to avoid large numbers of individuals gathering in the same area together. • Regular and reliable transportation away from pubs and clubs.
Injury reduction	• Use of toughened glass. • Use of plastic cups. • The banning of bottle-served alcohol. • Swift removal of any glassware used. • Weapons searches on entry to public houses and clubs.
Criminal justice policy	• Heavier penalties for breaches of licensing laws, such as serving to underage drinkers (relevant to both 'on' and 'off' licences). • Courts to divert alcohol offenders to treatment and education programmes. • Monitoring of 'problem/violent' premises. • Alcohol education schemes.

is to encourage the use of safer glassware and bottles, which has been identified by Shepherd (1994, 1997) as an important factor in reducing the seriousness of injuries from assaults in licensed premises. In this context, the wide-scale introduction of drinking glasses made either from toughened or unbreakable glass needs further consideration.[21] Some forward-looking manufacturers (for example, Bass) are starting to use specially designed plastic bottles for drinks which are often drunk from the bottle. In welcoming this, the Portman Group adds that, regardless of the policies ultimately implemented regarding glassware, 'licensees can substantially reduce the risk of "glassing attacks" on their premises by ensuring that empty bottles and glasses are regularly collected' (1998: 20). Such policies might also reduce the number of assaults that end fatally – as might other harm-minimisation strategies, including speedy intervention when violence erupts and rapid medical treatment when individuals have been injured.

Study Task 11.4

Mosher and Jerrigan (2001) developed a typology known as 'the four P's' as a way of thinking about preventing alcohol-related violence. **Price** (increased taxes), **Place** (restricting physical availability of alcohol and settings for drinking), **Promotion** (reduction of alcohol advertising) and **Product** (reduce alcoholic content, appearance and 'portions'). Consider the possible merits of each of the individual P's and their potential impact in combination.

Responses by Emergency Services

Finally, it is worth noting one final strategy that may reduce not only alcohol-related violence, but violence of any kind where the victim does not die immediately. This concerns improvements to the emergency services which may have an opportunity of saving the victim's life. As discussed at greater length by Brookman and Maguire (2003), there is a small amount of research evidence from the US to indicate that the speed and quality of post-assaultive medical care can affect the lethality of violent attacks (see Lattimore et al., 1997; and Doerner, 1988). Soothill et al. (1999), too, mention longer distances travelled to intensive care facilities as one of several possible factors accounting for the higher per capita homicide rate in Scotland than in England and Wales. In short, improvements in emergency medical services, especially in terms of the quality and quantity of vehicles and equipment, increased staff training, and more sophisticated staffing and vehicle-routing schemes could have an impact upon the number of homicides.

Preventing Alcohol-related 'Street' Homicides: Conclusions

A substantial proportion of homicides are associated with the consumption of alcohol. While around half of these occur in or around victims' or offenders' homes, many of the remainder – which are predominantly male-on-male offences – occur in licensed premises or on the streets. These are often the result of apparently trivial arguments or 'masculine honour contests', and they share many of the characteristics of the very large numbers of non-lethal assaults which occur in similar circumstances. Hence, in terms of prevention, there is a good case for arguing that a significant reduction in alcohol-related *violence* would lead also to a reduction in alcohol-related *homicide*. Summarised below are what appear to be the most promising interventions.

- More widespread manipulation of the physical and social environments of public houses and clubs to minimise the potential for violent altercations.
- The more consistent implementation of measures to reduce intoxication – such as the serving of food and promotion of lower-alcohol beers.
- More imaginative strategies to reduce alcohol consumption by under-age people.
- The establishment of co-operation and co-ordinated responses between land-lords, door staff, the police and licensing authorities, especially in responding to regular violent 'hot spots' and in ensuring speedy responses to violent disorder.
- Staggered closing times and efficient and regular transportation away from town and city centres.

A second type of strategy, aimed more directly at homicide reduction, concerns attempts to reduce the 'lethality' of those assaults which do take place. Again, although there is no clear British evidence on the effectiveness of such initiatives, some American research results give cause for cautious optimism. Suggested measures include:

- improvements in the responses of emergency services to street assaults; and
- the universal introduction of toughened (or non-glass) glassware.

However, it should be emphasised that all the above strategies can only go part of the way towards preventing alcohol-related homicide, as significant numbers of cases occur beyond the confines of public entertainment, and often in people's homes. Significant reductions may only be achieved over the long term by serious attention to ways of eroding the association between masculine bravado and the consumption of large volumes of alcohol.

Broader Strategies: Social, Cultural and Structural Factors

Through focusing on specific types of homicide, rather less attention has been paid in this chapter to the sorts of preventive strategies that tackle broader social, cultural and structural issues. This is, in part, a reflection of the lesser attention that such strategies receive, at both local, national and international levels. As Coleman and Norris note, primary prevention (which arguably has been the subject of the most attention and implementation) 'is neither concerned with the wider social structural causes of crime nor interventions aimed at fundamentally altering the individual' (2000: 147). Yet, there are many social scientists who are firmly of the belief that fundamental social and cultural change is the most promising (albeit long-term) route to preventing violence generally and homicide specifically.

For example, focusing upon violence against women, and addressing the all-important theme of masculinity addressed several times throughout this book, Snider (1998) argues that such violence can only be ameliorated by ideological and structural change which target patriarchy and capitalism (and thus dominant hegemonic masculinities and identities). She criticises what she sees as the exclusive focus upon sanctions of punishment through criminal justice interventions and argues that 'there is little evidence that increased criminalization has empowered women or made them safer in or outside the home' (1998: 10). She further argues that 'it should, it *must* be possible to find ways of being manly that are not misogynous and do not require the repression of every human emotion except anger' (1998: 24). Along similar lines, Bowker (1978) also convincingly argues that reducing domestic violence involves altering a fundamental value system that supports such violence.

Even more radically, Gil (1996) argues that we live in a structurally violent society that has developed through a long period of social evolution, from a structurally non-violent pattern of social organisation of hunter-gatherers through to hierarchical systems of domination and exploitation. Essentially, Gil argues that structurally violent societies cannot meet people's needs and fulfilments, and that blocked developmental energy is expressed destructively as counter violence – manifested in crime and violence. Gil argues that prevention requires fundamental change from a structurally violent to a non-violent society, involving changes in social attitudes and values. As such, Gil proposes extremely far-reaching transformations in preventing (and understanding) violence, including reorganisation of production and work and the distribution of provisions. Along similar lines, Buvinic and Morrison (2000) argue that globalisation has aggravated income inequalities throughout the world, spread a culture of violence through increased communications and media, and expanded trade in 'death industries' such as firearms and drugs. They argue that these developments have led to the increasing visibility of income inequality and ultimately strain, frustration and a perception of relative deprivation. In terms of prevention, they point out the tendency to resist long-term investments, focusing instead upon short-term strategies that have more political appeal.

Finally, Gilligan (2001) similarly views wide structural change as essential to reduce violence within society. He cites numerous examples of classless societies (such as the Hutteries and Kibbutzim) – which he claim are essentially free from violence due to social and economic equality – as evidence of the real possibilities of creating non-violent societies. Gilligan's proposals for preventing violence are associated with ways to reduce feelings of shame and humiliation (which he sees as the key motivations for violence; see Chapter 4). At the societal level he discusses universal access to free higher education and the elimination of poverty – both of which he sees as enhancing individuals' self-esteem. At the same time, he is an ardent advocate of substantial change to the criminal justice system, and the penal system in particular, which he views as only exacerbating the problem of violence in society. As he puts it, 'punishment increases feelings of shame and humiliation, and decreases feelings of guilt; and those are exactly the psychological conditions that give rise to violent behaviour, in which the rage that has been provoked by being humiliated is not inhibited by feelings of guilt' (2001: 16) (see also Mercy and Hammond, 1999; and Kakar, 1998 for related discussions).

Chapter Summary and Conclusions

This chapter began by outlining the different ways in which crime prevention can be defined, followed by a consideration of how the different approaches might be applied to homicide. We then moved on to consider three distinct forms of homicide and assessed the potential for their reduction or prevention. It has not been possible within one chapter to consider all different manifestations of homicide and how these might be prevented (see Brookman and Maguire, 2003 for consideration of some other categories not discussed here). Clearly though, different forms require different sorts of strategies. This is particularly important when considering the broad distinction between unintended homicides (termed 'lethal assaults' earlier) and those more purposeful killings where death is the intended outcome. However, it was also pointed out that it is important not to ignore possible preventive strategies that focus on broader social, cultural and structural conditions which also have an influence on homicide rates. As Hughes notes, 'there remains a continuing dominance of a narrow focus in administrative criminology on "what works" as crime prevention techniques (most associated with situational crime prevention "fixes")' (2001: 64). Moreover, this 'technicist focus ... runs the risk of missing the broader sociological and political context in terms of which trends in crime prevention need to be understood (2001: 64). In conclusion, what a number of criminologists are increasingly recognising is the need for more sustained cultural, structural and social changes in order to produce any significant and sustained reductions in violence. Whether crime prevention (or reduction) will move toward tackling these issues more firmly in the future remains to be seen.

Review Questions

- What are the differences between homicide prevention and homicide reduction? (You may wish to consult the Home Office web page for further information on their use of the term 'reduction').
- What are the advantages to thinking about homicide prevention in terms of specific forms of homicide?
- In what different ways might purposeful (that is, those where the offender intends the victim to die) and 'accidental' homicides (for example, assaults where death was not intended) be prevented? Think about this in relation to the three major categories of primary, secondary and tertiary prevention.
- Make a list of the arguments for and against adopting social, economic and cultural change as a means to preventing homicide.

Further Reading

For general overviews of crime prevention refer to *Understanding Crime Prevention* (Hughes, 1998: Open University Press); also Chapter 6 in *Introducing Criminology* is useful (Coleman and Norris, 2002: Willan), as is the chapter by Walklate entitled 'Community and Crime Prevention', in the edited collection *Controlling Crime* (McLaughlin and Muncie (eds), 2002: Sage). Finally, *Building a Safer Society: Strategic Approaches to Crime Prevention* (Tonry and Farrington, 1995: University of Chicago Press) is a useful resource. Regarding the prevention of violence or homicide, James Gilligan's *Preventing Violence* (2001: Thames and Hudson) is an excellent and very accessible text in relation to the social and economic changes that could facilitate the prevention of violence. Also refer to 'Preventing Violence in a Structurally Violent Society: Mission Impossible' in the *American Journal of Orthopsychiatry* (Gil, 1996: Vol. 66, pp. 77–84) and 'Living in a More Violent World' in the *Journal of Foreign Policy* (Buvinic and Morrison, 2000: Vol. 118, pp. 58–72). Further useful sources include *Reducing Homicide: A Review of the Possibilities* (Brookman and Maguire, 2003: RDS Online Report 01/03: Home Office); *Understanding and Preventing Violence* (Reiss and Roth, 1993: National Academy Press); *Homicide: Patterns, Prevention and Control* (Strang and Gerull, 1993: Australian Institute of Criminology Conference Proceedings); 'Intervention in Lethal Violence', in *Lethal Violence: A Sourcebook on Fatal Domestic, Acquaintance and Stranger Violence* (Hall, 1999: CRC Press); and 'The Police Role in Preventing Homicide: Considering the Impact of Problem-orientated Policing on the Prevalence of Murder' (White et al., 2003: *Journal of Research in Crime and Delinquency*, Vol. 40/2, pp. 194–225). Finally, *Homicidal Encounters: A Study of Homicide in Australia* (Mouzos, 2000: AIC) contains a useful section on the prevention of homicide, that deals with a number of the sub-categories considered in this chapter. In relation to the prevention of domestic homicide, it is worth consulting *Reducing Domestic Violence ... What Works? Perpetrator Programmes* (Mullender and Burton, 2000: Home Office). Also various chapters in *Assessing Dangerousness: Violence by Sexual Offenders, Batterers and Child Abusers* (Campbell, 1995: Sage) are useful to consult, as is *Research Evaluation of Programmes for Violent Men* (Dobash et al., 1996: HMSO). Regarding the killing of infants, the following texts are useful; *Child Victims of Homicide* (Adler and Polk, 2001: Cambridge University Press), which covers many of the themes also contained in Strang's *Child Abuse Homicides in Australia* (1996: Canberra: Australian Institute of Criminology). Finally, regarding alcohol and homicide, the most useful resources include: *Alcohol and Crime: Taking Stock,* Crime Reduction Research Series Paper 3 (Deehan, 1999: Home Office; *Alcohol and Homicide: A Deadly Combination of Two American Traditions* (Parker and Rebhun, 1995: State University of New York Press; and *Alcohol and Crime: From Understanding to Effective Intervention* (Giesbrecht and Nesbitt, 2001: Journal of Substance Use, Vol. 6, pp. 215–17).

Useful Internet Sites

The Home Office website www.homeoffice.gov.uk. contains sections dedicated to the prevention of domestic violence. Type 'domestic violence' in the search box on the home page to access these links. The Homicide Research Working Group contains a number of useful publications and links and can be found at www. icpsr.umich.edu/HRWG. The World Health Organisation is a very useful site to visit and includes the *Report on Violence and Health (2002)* and other related information including *Progress towards a United Nations Year for Violence Prevention in 2007* and campaigns for violence prevention, and a Guide to United Nations' resources and activities for the prevention of interpersonal violence can be found by visiting the WHO website www.who.int and conducting a search under 'violence'. The NSPCC website www.nspcc.org.uk contains a great deal of useful information in relation to measures to protect infants and children from abuse and lethal injury. The Suzy Lamplugh Trust is a useful resource regarding personal safety generally and ways of preventing violence: www.suzylamplugh.org/home. The Australian Institute of Criminology website www.aic.gov.au contains a number of useful violence and homicide reduction research papers. Also Australian-based is the New South Wales Crime Prevention Division at www.lawlink.nsw.gov.au A directory of New South Wales Government Crime Prevention Programmes can be found at www.lawlink. nsw.gov.au. Finally, typing 'preventing homicide' or 'reducing homicide' into a search engine such as Google returns a number of useful 'hits'.

Notes

1 Much of this chapter is based on previous research by Brookman and Maguire (2003) which explored the potential to reduce and/or prevent homicide in the UK and was conducted on behalf of the Home Office.

2 It has not been possible, from analysing the HI, to gain precise information regarding certain categories of homicide discussed in this chapter. The figure of around 50 per cent was arrived at by combining male-on-female domestic killings (just under 13 per cent) with the killing of babies less than one year (10 per cent); along with male-on-male 'rage-related' killings (28 per cent) – as distinct from, for example, faction fights/feuds which tend to involve male-on-male gang related killings, often in relation to 'turf' wars and drug dealing (see Chapter 2).

3 A number of other basic classifications have been developed. For example, Tonry and Farrington (1995) distinguish four strategies of crime prevention, namely law enforcement, developmental, community and situational strategies. Law enforcement is chiefly ignored by Tonry and Farrington in their discussion, despite its inclusion in their classificatory scheme.

4 The 'wounding' category refers to assaults resulting in serious injury (mainly 'GBH' cases). There were also 14,064 recorded offences of 'threat or conspiracy to murder' and 195,925 of less serious 'other wounding etc' (mainly 'ABH').

5 However, such apparent anomalies may be due mainly to differences in recording practices, particularly in the categorisation of non-lethal incidents.

6 Although as Katz (1988) points out, overkill or frenzied attacks do not necessarily mean that the sole intent was to kill; see Chapter 4.

7 Defined here, as in previous chapters, as killing by a current or former spouse, co-habitant or sexual partner.

8 There appears to be an anomaly in the US, where almost as many women kill their husbands as men kill their wives (Wilson and Daly, 1992). However, it is not clear that this holds if the data are extended to include co-habitants and other sexual partners.

9 This does not, of course, mean that incidents of domestic violence had never occurred at these addresses. It has been well established that domestic violence is often not reported to the police (Hamner and Saunders, 1984; Jones et al., 1986; Mirlees-Black, 1995; Heidensohn, 2002).

10 A further 18 per cent were killed by partners without any evidence of prior domestic violence.

11 Atlanta also experienced declines in the number of intimate/family homicides following increased co-operation between domestic violence service providers and the police since 1985. In particular, the police in Atlanta conducted more arrests than previously for domestic violence, and domestic violence services became more professional and better organised.

12 Children (that is those aged 16 years and below) comprised almost 16 per cent of the total homicide victim population in England and Wales between 1995–2000 (HI). There were 736 child victims over this period, 461 males (62 per cent) and 275 females (38 per cent).

13 Apart from parents, the other groups from which most killers of children were drawn were step-parents, 'other family' and 'friends or ex-friends'. Overall, 7 per cent were classified as 'strangers'. However, the majority of the children killed by strangers were aged 15 or 16. No infants under one year, and very few children under 10, were known to have been killed by a stranger. And even among older children, this was still a rare event. For example, over the period 1995–99, out of 117 homicides of children aged 10–16, 23 were known or suspected to have been committed by a stranger. That said, during 2001–2002, 40 per cent of babies less than a year old were killed by a stranger and 40 per cent by a parent. The reason for this change is not yet known.

14 This assumption, however, has recently been questioned by Rodriguez and Smithey (1999), who challenge the notion of a continuum of violence ranging from mild physical punishment to severe abuse and infant homicide.

15 It is also worth mentioning that claims of success have been made for the introduction of incubators in some Hungarian hospital lobbies, in response to a rise in the number of mothers abandoning their babies. Eight hospitals in five Hungarian cities offer desperate mothers an alternative to abandoning their babies in potentially dangerous locations. The Schopf-Merei Agost Hospital initiated the incubator programme in 1997 and claims to have saved the lives of nine babies. The programme also includes discreet antenatal care and counselling for mothers who do not want to keep their infants and reports that 500 mothers have participated in the programme to date (Kovac, 1999).

16 The great majority were under the influence of alcohol alone. Less than 1 per cent were recorded as under the influence of drugs and a further 2 per cent under the influence of both drink and drugs.

17 The code for alcohol consumption is only used if the suspect was said (by the police in their homicide returns to the Home Office) to have consumed large amounts of alcohol, spent a long time drinking, or shown signs of drunkenness. Of course this might be impossible to determine if a suspect is apprehended some time after the alleged homicide. In contrast, any mention of drugs is sufficient for a positive coding for drugs. Neither Scotland nor Northern Ireland routinely record information on these matters.

18 It has not been possible to determine the location of homicide in relation to alcohol consumption as none of the jurisdictions record both aspects of the homicide event.

19 The largest proportion – 53 per cent – óccurred in and around dwellings.

20 Sheffield has invested considerable effort in a city-wide Pubwatch scheme (which includes a system of communication between pubs about people likely to become violent), to which a fall in alcohol-related crime in the city has been partly attributed. Another scheme worthy of mention is a high-profile enforcement strategy in Torbay, based on frequent police visits to pubs and checks for violations of licensing laws, which has again been associated with a fall in violent crime (both schemes are described by Deehan, 1999).

21 Breweries are increasingly coming to recognise the importance of this issue (see, for example, Brewers and Licensed Retailers Association, 1997), although it is important to add that further scientific research is needed to identify the safest forms of glass. Unbreakable plastic glasses were used successfully in Cardiff City Centre during the 1999 Rugby World Cup, when considerable numbers of people drank outside pubs on the street. Instrumental in this was the Cardiff Licensees Forum, which persuaded all city centre licensed premises to use plastic glasses with a government approved design and official stamp.

12 Overview and Conclusions

In this concluding chapter, some of the most important and recurring issues and themes raised in the text as a whole will be considered with a view to identifying the key messages that should be taken away from this book. At the same time, where relevant, areas for future research will be identified. Four important issues will be addressed; the diverse nature of homicide; developing balanced explanations that take into account both macro- and micro- influences and factors; the extent to which gender is an important explanatory concept; and the socially constructed nature of homicide.

The Diversity of Homicide

One of the key messages to take away from this text is that homicide is not one kind of act or event. Far from it; homicide takes a number of very diverse forms. Ultimately, in some way or another, every single homicide event is unique; the only clear factor they have in common is the death of the victim (who may, of course, have been the initial protagonist). That said, certain categories or forms of homicide can be identified that share several characteristics in common and, more broadly, it is clear that homicide is patterned in several ways.

As noted in Chapter 2, there are numerous ways of dividing up homicide into meaningful categories. Throughout this text we have considered different categories of homicide, starting from the premise that the 'gender mix' of victims and offenders, as well as the relationships between them, are critical starting points. Within these categories we then explored the particular contexts, circumstances and dynamics of different homicides. For example, within the broad category of male-on-male homicide we identified two discrete scenarios – 'confrontational' and 'revenge' homicide. Similarly, within the categories of femicide, female-perpetrated homicide and the killing of children, a number of distinctions were noted in terms of the nature and circumstances of homicide.

The analysis undertaken throughout this book, therefore, strongly supports the statement by Wallace:

> Homicides can and should be qualitatively distinguished. Just as there is no unitary entity called 'crime', there is no unitary phenomenon of homicide. Analysis of qualitatively distinct homicides highlights the particular points of conflict between different people, in different situations at different points in time. (1986: 13)

Making Sense of Homicide: Balancing the Focus

Making sense of homicide is complex for two broad reasons. First, as already discussed, due to the diverse nature of homicide it is difficult, if not impossible, to develop one kind of theory to explain it. The factors that contribute to homicide between sexual intimates are undoubtedly different from the chain of events that culminate in homicide amongst criminal associates. Similarly, the reasons for a parent killing his or her offspring will be far removed from the circumstances surrounding a rape-murder, or a robbery-murder. Furthermore, within each of these categories there exists a mass of variation, so that the reasons why men kill their spouse will vary widely, as will the reasons why parents kills their children. As Levi and Maguire aptly note in their discussion of violence, 'what we place into the category of "violent crime" makes a big difference to the range of behaviours we have to explain' (2002: 795). Equally, what we place into the category of homicide makes a big difference to the range of behaviours we have to explain. Corporate homicide or vehicular homicide, for example, clearly require very different explanations to, for example, domestic homicide or fatal pub brawls.

Second, regardless of what particular homicide we are concerned to explain, there is no single cause. Rather, a wide variety of factors play a role, some bound up with the situational context in which lethal violence occurs (such as micro-situational dynamics) and others connected to larger structural and cultural factors that can impact upon an individuals' readiness or willingness to adopt violence as a means of dealing with interpersonal conflict.

Ultimately, different researchers adopt different emphases, depending upon their own theoretical preferences. Researchers with a particular 'bias' toward one theory or perspective could, in all probability, find a way of applying that theory to any form of homicide. However, this would not necessarily mean that they had found the most appropriate or powerful theory to explain that particular manifestation. Messerschmidt (1993, 1997), for example, has clearly demonstrated his theoretical preference in that he has attempted to explain violent acts as diverse as rape and corporate homicide within a gendered framework. Other researchers have been concerned to generate grand or general theories to explain homicide as a whole (see Gottfredson and Hirschi, 1990), whilst yet others prefer to focus upon particular manifestations of homicide. Each approach has particular strengths and weaknesses.

Regardless of what type of homicide we are interested to explain, certain structural, cultural and situational forces, when combined, seem to provide the most reasonable explanation for violence (lethal or otherwise). Human action does not take place in a vacuum. It is influenced by the structure and fabric of the society in which people live, as well as by the particular circumstances they find themselves in at a given point in time. Research has progressed substantially in terms of acknowledging the importance of the intersection between gender and other demographic factors (such as age, social class and race). However, it still remains that criminologists and social scientists tend to operate at the macro- or micro-level, when what is clearly needed is a careful consideration of the interaction between the two. Hence, as discussed in Chapter 5, relying upon explanations at the structural or cultural level (such as relative deprivation of unemployment) paints a partial picture in that many more individuals are exposed to these 'negative' social forces than commit violent crime. An appreciation of the social settings in which violence occurs and the particular kinds of social interactions and psychological processes that underpin violent interactions helps to overcome these shortcomings.

The 'Gender' Question

Gender is one of the socio-demographic variables that has received sustained attention in recent years and has been a recurring theme throughout this text. As noted in Chapter 2, of all the variables studied in relation to homicide, gender stands out as particularly important in that males (or more specifically men) are vastly over-represented as both offenders and (albeit less dramatically) victims of homicide. However, the link between homicide and gender is clearly complex. As observed in Chapter 6, feminist scholars in the 1970s posited a link between masculinity and patriarchy or male domination and were amongst the first academics to seriously analyse and theorise the 'maleness' of crime, and especially violent crime. Subsequently, researchers suggested the existence of a range of competing masculinities, some of which are subordinate to others. For example, many writers have suggested that male-perpetrated homicide can be understood as the 'situational accomplishment' of masculinity or, put another way, one mode of 'doing gender'. Moreover, many of these accounts specifically unravel violence as a way of 'doing' masculinity within particular (and distinct) social, economic and cultural contexts. What clearly separates these accounts from the earlier feminist contributions is their lesser attention to issues of power and a greater emphasis upon the differences, not only between masculinity and femininity, but also within them (see Walklate, 2001b; and Morgan, 1992). This is an important point to which we return below.

Most recently concerns have been expressed regarding the extent to which gender, and in particular masculinity (or masculinities), can adequately explain violent crime. For example, Hearn has suggested that:

> Masculinity is often a gloss on complex social processes. The concept is sometimes attributed a causal power – for example, that masculinity is said to cause a social problem, such as violence – when masculinity is rather the result of other social processes. (1998: 213)

Somewhat more radically, Wikström and Svensson (2003) challenge the extent to which gender, and in particular masculinity, should be considered a key variable in explaining violent crime. They point out that almost 90 per cent of males do not commit violent acts and that, therefore, gender is not a powerful explanatory variable in relation to predicting who will (or will not) become a violent offender. Their analysis is specifically concerned with juvenile crime, and they argue that differences in rates of juvenile offending are not due to gender differences. Instead, they seem to suggest that differences in rates of male and female offending are largely due to males being more exposed to criminogenic forces or non-restraining forces than females.

The important point, however, is that not only do males commit a much greater proportion of homicide than females, but that they also 'do it differently'. That is, males commit different kinds of homicides under different sets of circumstances than their female counterparts. Hence, even if we were to argue that males are more exposed to criminogenic (or homicidal) forces than females, this does not help to explain the distinct patterns of male and female homicide. What set of criminogenic forces could, on the one hand, lead men to be over-involved in homicide and, at the same time, engage in particular forms of homicide that women do not? If females are less exposed to criminogenic forces, why don't they just commit less of all forms of homicide, instead of being virtually absent from many kinds but approaching male rates in others (such as the killing of their own infants)?

Clearly, though, there are many unanswered questions. As discussed in Chapter 7, there remains a continued tension within the gendered approach to understanding violence and homicide when it comes to females. Theories which emphasise differences between women and men, fail to account for similarities in their experiences, and also overlook important differences *between* women, for example in terms of race, class and age. On the other hand, the gender similarities approach often results in a failure to be attentive to the importance of gender. In short, neither the 'gender difference' or 'gender similarities' approach are fully satisfactory in explaining homicide, and more research is needed clearly to unravel the extent to which female violence should be understood as distinct or similar to that of males.

Homicide: A Social Construct

Finally, as discussed in some detail in the opening chapter of this text, homicide is a socially constructed phenomenon. It is not simply the case that the taking of a life is classified as an unlawful act and universally condemned. Rather, killing is sometimes perceived as acceptable (for example, during wartime or in connection to the implementation of the death penalty), and where it is not perceived as acceptable, it is generally graded in terms of the apparent gravity of the act. Various legal categories have been created over the years that are said to comprise unlawful homicide (though these, of course, differ from one country the next). Moreover, the law attempts to distinguish different categories of homicide in terms of their seriousness, though there is some debate as to how successful the law is in achieving this aim. Issues such as the culpability of the offender and the extent to which victims are perceived as particularly vulnerable and the general context of the killing often enter into the equation. But, of course, notions of culpability and vulnerability are themselves socially constructed and change over time.

Many 'killings' occur that do not neatly fit societies' legal framework or individuals' moral framework in terms of culpability, such as deaths due to dangerous or negligent driving or those that arise through corporate negligence or neglect. One of the reasons that corporate homicide has been included for consideration in this text at several points is that it is so often ignored or downgraded in homicide texts; it is not viewed as 'real' homicide.

Linked to this, as explored in Chapter 10, the investigation of homicide is socially constructed in that the police, the CPS and the Forensic Science Service '(re)create', from a variety of sources, the homicide event and in so doing imbue a particular context and meaning to the killing that does not necessarily reflect 'reality'. The constructive nature of the homicide investigative process means that certain aspects of the cases are emphasised whilst others are downplayed and all of the time an effort is made to attribute a factual status to the evidence being presented. Hence, whether or not an individual is labelled 'a killer', and whether he or she is convicted of murder, manslaughter or some other lesser offence, involves a complex legal process.

In summary, a wide variety of individual, social and cultural influences shape our understandings and conceptions of what constitutes unlawful homicide, and it is important that future research does not take for granted the implications that this has for how we count, classify, explain and respond to homicide.

Conclusion

In conclusion, there is no simple formula, no general laws that can predict, with any degree of certainty, who will commit homicide. What is clear, however, is that homicide is patterned in several ways along such dimensions as gender, age and social class, and that certain structural factors, such as economic inequality and material deprivation, play a role in shaping the social conditions within which individuals find themselves. When confronted with particular social stresses or, as is often the case in relation to 'masculine' homicide, 'challenges to honour', these factors can create the necessary preconditions for lethal violence. That said, there are many more individuals who find themselves in any or all such circumstances who do not kill. The difficulty in making sense of homicide, then, (like any human behavior) is to strike an adequate balance between the impact of social structure and the choice of social action.

Future research needs to continue to identify meaningful categories of homicide and refine them on the basis of research. At the same time, there is clearly a need to unravel much more precisely the similarities and differences between male- and female-perpetrated homicide under a range of circumstances. Whilst gender matters, the role of gender within lethal violence is clearly complex. Some theories have been developed to account for specific manifestations of homicide – such as the 'battered women syndrome' to explain some examples of female-perpetrated partner homicide or patriarchal domination and control to explain femicide. This line of research requires further development.

Finally, one of the most practical aims of homicide research should be to move towards reducing its occurrence. As discussed in Chapter 11, reducing homicide is a complex task and those strategies that have been adopted have generally taken the form of primary prevention and ignored the more difficult and costly routes of attempting to affect cultural and structural change. There remains a great deal of work to be undertaken to determine whether and how wider societal changes could impact upon homicide rates. In addition, further consideration of how intervention strategies can be tailored to the specific nature and circumstances of different forms of homicide is required.

In conclusion, this text has undoubtedly raised many more questions than it has answered. It is hoped, however, that some progress towards unravelling the interesting but complex phenomenon of homicide has been made. The ultimate task for the future is to find ways of further illuminating the underlying causes of homicide. Clearly, though, we will have to accept that it is very unlikely that we will ever be able fully to understand every homicide or even every form of homicide. Some killings will probably always defy any logical explanation.

Appendix

Homicide in England and Wales (1997–2001): Victim/Offender Relationships, Gender Mix and Context

		Total N	Total %
DOMESTIC HOMICIDE		**1,287**	**31**
Sexual intimacy		717	17.3
Current or former spouses/lovers		*704*	*17.0*
Male offender/female victim		533	(76)

Rage/quarrel	49.2
Jealousy/revenge	7.3
Suicide pact	3.0
Reckless acts	4.2
Sexual	0.2
Financial gain	0.4
Other	9.6
Not known	26.1

Female offender/male victim		138	(19.5)

Rage/quarrel	74.6
Jealousy/revenge	2.2
Reckless acts	5.0
Other	2.3
Not known	15.9

Male offender/male victim (homosexual)	30	(4.0)
Female offender/female victim (lesbian)	3	(0.5)
Sexual rivals	*13*	*(0.3)*
Male/male	12	(93)
Male/female	1	(7)
Family intimacy	570	13.8
Parent/child	*348*	*8.4*

Male offender/male victim		131	(38)
Child abuse	51.9		
Rage	7.6		
Jealousy/revenge	4.6		
Reckless acts	3.8		
Other	10.7		
Not known	21.4		
Male offender/female victim		74	(21)
Child abuse	55.4		
Rage	5.4		
Jealousy/revenge	2.7		
Reckless acts	2.8		
Other	10.7		
Not known	23.0		
Female offender/male victim		80	(23)
Child abuse	50.0		
Suicide Pact	5		
Destruction/abortion	1.3		
Reckless act	6.3		
Other	22.4		
Not known	15.0		
Female offender/female victim		63	(18)
Child abuse	61.9		
Reckless act	4.8		
Other	20.6		
Not known	12.7		
Child/parent		**96**	**2.3**
Male offender/male victim		40	(42)
Rage	55.0		
Jealousy/revenge	2.5		
Robbery/burglary	0.5		
Suicide pact	5.0		
Other	22.0		
Not known	15.0		
Male offender/female victim		47	(49)
Rage	29.8		
Jealousy/revenge	2.1		
Suicide pact	6.4		
Other	42.6		
Not known	19.1		
Female offender/male victim		4	(4)
Female offender/female victim		5	(5)
Other (e.g. siblings/in-laws)		**126**	**3.1**
Male offender/male victim		84	(67)

{	Rage	64.3	}	
	Jealousy/revenge	3.6		
	Reckless acts	6.0		
	Other	8.2		
	Not known	17.9		
Male offender/female victim			37	(28)
{	Rage	29.7	}	
	Jealousy/revenge	5.4		
	Burglary	5.4		
	Sexual	2.7		
	Suicide pact	2.7		
	Other	29.8		
	Not known	24.3		
Female offender/male victim			1	(0.8)
Female offender/female victim			4	(3.2)

HOMICIDE IN THE COURSE OF OTHER CRIME   294   7.0

Robbery		147	(50)
Male offender/male victim	56.0		
Male offender/female victim	30.0		
Female offender/male victim	3.0		
Female offender/female victim	2.0		
Burglary		60	(20)
Male offender/male victim	63.0		
Male offender/female victim	33.0		
Female offender/male victim	4.0		
Sex Attack (unrelated individuals)		53	(18)
Male offender/male victim	14.0		
Male offender/female victim	80.0		
Female offender/male victim	4.0		
Female offender/female victim	2.0		
Other gain		28	(10)
Resisting/avoiding arrest		6	(2)

GANG HOMICIDE   43   1.0

Male offender/male victim	37	(86)
Female offender/male victim	1	(2)
Unknown offender/unsolved	5	(12)

CONFRONTATIONAL HOMICIDE (unrelated individuals)   888   22

Male offender/male victim	807	(92)
Male offender/female victim	41	(4)
Female offender/male victim	23	(2.5)
Female offender/female victim	9	(1)
Unknown offender/unsolved	8	(0.5)

JEALOUSY/REVENGE (unrelated individuals)	94	2.3
Male offender/male victim	80	(85)
Male offender/female victim	10	(11)
Female offender/male victim	2	(2)
Female offender/female victim	2	(2)
RECKLESS ACTS (unrelated individuals)	248	6
RACIAL VIOLENCE	14	<1
'OTHER' unspecified circumstances (unrelated individuals)	117	2.8
CONTEXT/MOTIVE UNKNOWN (some of which unsolved)	967	23.4
UNUSUAL CASES	171	4.1
Serial homicide	80	(47)
Mass homicide	58	(34)
Terrorism	4	(2)
Homicide amongst children (under 17) (unrelated)	29	(17)
TOTAL CASES	4,123	100

Notes:
- Percentages in brackets refer to the percentage of the subset under consideration (not the total number of homicides).
- The category 'other' includes racial violence, arson and irrational acts and, if not already stated, suicide pacts and any other category that comprised less than 1 per cent of the total circumstance category.

References

Ackers, J. (1992), 'Gendering Organizational Theory', in A. Mills and P. Tancred (eds), *Gendering Organizational Analysis*. Newbury Park, CA: Sage.

ACPO (1999), *Murder Investigation Manual*. London: ACPO. (Unpublished)

Adhami, E. and Browne, D.P. (1996), *Major Crime Enquiries: Improving Expert Support for Detectives*. Special Interest Series Paper 9. London: Home Office.

Adler, C.M. and Polk, K. (1996), 'Masculinity and Child Homicide', *British Journal of Criminology*, Vol. 36/3, pp. 396–411.

Adler, C. and Polk, K. (2001), *Child Victims of Homicide*. Cambridge: Cambridge University Press.

Adler, F. (1975), *Sisters in Crime: The Rise of the New Female Criminal*. New York: McGraw-Hill.

Agnew, R. (1992), 'Foundation for a General Strain Theory of Crime and Delinquency', *Criminology*, Vol. 30, pp. 47–87.

Agnew, R. (2001), 'Strain Theory', in E. McLaughlin and J. Muncie (eds), *The Sage Dictionary of Criminology*. London: Sage.

Aichorn, A. (1936), *Wayward Youth*. New York: Viking.

Ainsworth, P.B. (1995), *Psychology and Policing in a Changing World*. Chichester: Wiley.

Ainsworth, P.B. (2000), *Psychology and Crime: Myths and Reality*. Essex: Pearson Education.

Ainsworth, P.B. (2001), *Offender Profiling and Crime Analysis*. Devon: Willan.

Alexander, F. and Healy, W. (1935), *Roots of Crime*. New York: Knopf.

Alexander, Y. and O'Day, A. (1984), *Terrorism in Ireland*. London: Palgrave Macmillan.

Allen, N.H. (1980), *Homicide: Perspectives on Prevention*. New York: Human Sciences Press.

Alonso, R. (2001), 'The Modernization in Irish Republican Thinking Toward the Utility of Violence', *Studies in Conflict and Terrorism*, Vol. 24, pp. 131–44.

American Psychiatric Association (APA) (1994), *Diagnostic and Statistical Manual of Mental Disorders* (DSM) (4th edition, revised). Washington, DC: American Psychiatric Association.

Amir, M. (1971), *Patterns of Forcible Rape*. Chicago, IL: University of Chicago Press.

Amnesty International, (1994), *Political Killings in Northern Ireland*. London: Amnesty International.

Anderson, C.A. (1987), 'Temperature and Aggression: Effects of Quarterly, Yearly and City Rates of Violent and Non-Violent Crime', *Journal of Personality and Social Psychology*, Vol. 52, pp. 1161–73.

Anderson, K. and Umberson, D. (2001), 'Gendering Violence: Masculinity and Power in Men's Accounts of Domestic Violence', *Gender and Society*, Vol. 15/3, pp. 358–80.

Appleby, L., Shaw, J., Amos, T., McDonald, R., Harris, C., McCann, K. (1999), *Safer Services: Report of the National Confidential Inquiry into Suicide and Homicide by People with Mental Illness*. London: Stationery Office.

Archer, J. (1991), 'The Influence of Testosterone on Human Aggression', *British Journal of Psychology*, Vol. 82, pp. 1–28.

Archer, J., Jones, J., Lewis-Roylance, C. and Orr, D. (2002) 'Violence in the Northwest with Special Reference to Liverpool and Manchester 1850–1914'. *VRP Summary Findings*.

Arin, C. (2001), 'Femicide in the Name of Honour in Turkey', *Violence Against Women*, Vol. 7/7, pp. 821–5.

Artz, S. (1998), *Sex, Power and the Violent School Girl*. Toronto: Trifolium.

Ashworth, A. (1998), *The Criminal Process: An Evaluative Study*. Oxford: Oxford University Press.

Ashworth, A. (1999), *Principles of Criminal Law* (3rd edition). Oxford: Oxford University Press.

Ashworth, A. and Mitchell, B. (2000), *Rethinking English Homicide Law*. Oxford: Oxford University Press.

Athens, L.H. (1977), 'Violent Crime: A Symbolic Interactionist Study', *Symbolic Interaction*, Vol. 1, pp. 56–70.

Athens, L.H. (1980), *Violent Criminal Acts and Actors: A Symbolic Interactionist Study*. London: Routledge and Kegan Paul.

Athens, L.H. (1989), *The Creation of Dangerous Violent Criminals*. London: Routledge (reprinted in 1992, Chicago, IL: University of Illinois Press).

Athens, L.H. (1997), *Violent Criminal Acts and Actors Revisited*. Chicago, IL: University of Illinois Press.

Atkinson, M. (1979), 'Societal Reactions to Suicide: The Role of Coroners' Definitions', in S. Cohen (ed.), *Images of Deviance*. Middlesex: Penguin.

Bacon, C.J. (1997), 'Cot Death after CESDI', *Archives of Disease in Childhood*, Vol. 76, pp. 171–3.

Bain, J., Langevin, R., Dickey, R. and Ben-Aron, M. (1987), 'Sex Hormones in Murderers and Assaulters', *Behavioural Science and the Law*, Vol. 5/1, pp. 95–101.

Balkwell, J.W. (1990), 'Ethnic Inequality and the Rate of Homicide', *Social Forces*, Vol. 69, pp. 53–70.

Ball-Rokeach, S.J. (1973), 'Values and Violence: A Test of the Subculture of Violence Thesis', *American Sociological Review*, Vol. 38, pp. 736–49.

Banditt, R., Katznelson, S. and Streit, S. (1970), 'The Situational Aspects of Violence: A Research Model', *Israel Studies In Criminology*, Vol. 1, pp. 241–58. Tel-Aviv: Gomeh.

Bandura, A. (1973a), *Aggression: A Social Learning Analysis*. Englewood Cliffs, NJ: Prentice-Hall.

Bandura, A. (1973b), 'Social Learning Theory of Aggression', in J.F. Kautson (ed.), *The Control of Aggression: Implications from Basic Research*. Chicago, IL: Aldine.

Bandura, A., Ross, D. and Ross, S.A. (1963), 'Imitation of Film-Mediated Aggressive Models', *Journal of Abnormal and Social Psychology*, Vol. 66, pp. 3–11.

Barnard, G.W., Vera, H., Vera, M. and Newman, G. (1982), 'Till Death Do Us Part: A Study of Spouse Murder', *Bulletin of the American Association of Psychiatry and the Law*, Vol. 10, pp. 271–80.

Baron, L. (1993), 'Gender Inequality and Child Homicide: A State-Level Analysis', in A.V. Wilson (ed.), *Homicide: The Victim-Offender Connection*, Cincinnati, OH: Anderson.

Bartol, C.R. (1999), *Criminal Behaviour: A Psychosocial Approach* (5th edition). Englewood Cliffs, NJ: Prentice-Hall.

BBC News (2002), 'Timeline Dissident Republican Attacks', 8 February. (Accessed via http://news.bbc.co.uk/1/hi/northern_ireland/1056797.stm, 17–06–03).

Bean, C.A. (1992), *Women Murdered by the Men They Loved*. New York: Harington Park.

Beck, A.T. (1999), *Prisoners of Hate: The Cognitive Basis of Anger, Hostility, and Violence*. New York: HarperCollins.

Becker, E. (1962), 'Anthropological Notes on the Concept of Aggression', *Psychiatry*, Vol. 23, pp. 328–38.

Beckwith, J.B. (1970), 'Observations on the Pathological Anatomy of the Sudden Infant Death Syndrome', in A.B. Bergman, J.B. Beckwith and C.G. Ray (eds), *Sudden Infant Death Syndrome: Proceedings of the Second International Conference on Causes of Sudden Death in Infants*. Seattle, WA: University of Washington Press.

Bell, C. and Fox, M. (1996), 'Telling Stories of Women who Kill', *Social and Legal Studies*, Vol. 5/4, pp. 471–94.

Bell, J. (1999), 'The French Pre-Trial System', in C. Walker and K. Starmer (eds), *Miscarriages of Justice: A Review of Justice in Error*. London: Blackstone.

Belsey, M.A. (1993), 'Child Abuse: Measuring a Global Problem', *World Health Statistics Quarterly*, Vol. 46, pp. 69–77.

Benson, D. and Archer, J. (2002), 'An Ethnographic Study of Sources of Conflict Between Young Men in the Context of the Night Out', *Psychology, Evolution and Gender*, Vol. 4/1, pp. 3–30.

Bergman, D. (1994), *The Perfect Crime? How Companies Can Get Away with Manslaughter in the Workplace*. Birmingham: Health and Safety Advice Centre.

Biehal, N., Mitchell, F. and Wade, J. (2002), *Lost from View: A Study of Missing Persons in the UK*. Summary of research findings (www1.york.ac.uk/inst/swrdu/Publications/Missing Persons.pdf).

Biro, M., Vuckovic, N. and Djuric, V. (1992), 'Towards a Typology of Homicides on the Basis of Personality', *British Journal of Criminology*, Vol. 32/3, pp. 361–71.

Black, D. (1983), 'Crime as Social Control', *American Sociological Review*, Vol. 48, pp. 34–45.

Black, D. (1993), *The Social Structure of Right and Wrong*. San Diego, CA: Academic Press.

Blackburn, R. (1968), 'Personality in Relation to Extreme Aggression in Psychiatric Offenders', *British Journal of Psychiatry*, Vol. 114, pp. 821–8.

Blackburn, R. (1971), 'Personality Types among Abnormal Homicides', *British Journal of Criminology*, Vol. 11, pp. 14–31.

Blackburn, R. and Coid, J.W. (1999), 'Empirical Clusters of DSM-III Personality Disorders in Violent Offenders', *Journal of Personality Disorders*, Vol. 13/1, pp. 18–34.

Blau, J.R. and Blau, P.M. (1982), 'The Cost of Inequality: Metropolitan Structure and Criminal Violence', *American Sociological Review*, Vol. 47, pp. 114–29.

Block, C.R. (1977), *Violent Crime*. Lexington, MA: Heath.

Block, C.R. and Block, R.L. (1991), 'Beginning with Wolfgang: An Agenda for Homicide Research', *Journal of Crime and Justice*, Vol. 14, pp. 31–70.

Block, R.L. and Block, C.R. (1992), 'Homicide Syndromes and Vulnerability: Violence in Chicago's Community Areas over Twenty-Five Years', *Studies on Crime and Crime Prevention*, Vol. 1, pp. 61–87.

Block, C.R., Devitt, C.O., Donoghue, E.R., Dames, R.J. and Block, R.L. (2001), 'Are There Types of Intimate Partner Homicide?', in P.H. Blackman, V.L. Leggett and J.P. Jarvis (eds), *The Diversity of Homicide: Proceedings of the 2000 Annual Meeting of the Homicide Research Working Group*. Washington, DC: Federal Bureau of Investigation.

Blum, A. and Fisher, G. (1978), 'Women who Kill', in I. Kutash, S. Kutash and L. Schlesinge (eds), *Perspectives on Murder and Aggression*. San Francisco, CA: Jossey-Bass.

Bohman, M. (1995), 'Predispositions to Criminality: Swedish Adoption Studies in Retrospect', in *Genetics of Criminal and Antisocial Behaviour, Ciba Foundation Symposium 194*. Chichester: Wiley.

Bottoms, A. (1977) 'Reflections on the Renaissance of Dangerousness', *Howard Journal*, Vol. 16/2, pp. 70–96.

Bottoms, A. and Brownsword, R. (1982), 'The Dangerousness Debate after the Floud Report', *British Journal of Criminology*, Vol. 22/3, pp. 229–54.

Bourget, D. and Bradford, J. (1990), 'Homicidal Parents', *Canadian Journal of Psychiatry*, Vol. 35/3, pp. 233–8.

Bourgois, P. (1996), 'In Search of Masculinity: Violence, Respect and Sexuality among Puerto Rican Crack Dealers in East Harlem', *British Journal of Criminology*, Vol. 36/3, pp. 412–27.

Bowker, W.T. (1978), *Women, Crime and the Criminal Justice System*. Toronto: Lexington.

Bowling, B. (1999) 'The Rise and fall of New York Murder', *British Journal of Criminology*, Vol. 39/4, pp. 531–54.

Bowling, B. and Foster, J. (2002), 'Policing and the Police', in M. Maguire, R. Morgan and R. Reiner (eds), *The Oxford Handbook of Criminology* (3rd edition). Oxford: Oxford University Press.

Box, S. (1983), *Power, Crime and Mystification*. London: Tavistock.

Box, S. (1996), 'Crime, Power and Ideological Mystification', in J. Muncie, E. McLaughlin and M. Langan (eds), *Criminological Perspectives: A Reader*. London: Sage.

Brain, P. (1990), *Hormonal Aspects of Aggression and Violence*. Symposium on the Understanding and Control of Violent Behaviour. Destin, Florida. 1–4 April.

Braithwaite, J. (1984), *Corporate Crime in the Pharmaceutical Industry*. London: Routledge and Kegan Paul.

Brennan, P.A., Mednick, S.A. and Volavka, J. (1995), 'Biomedical Factors in Crime', in J.Q. Wilson and J. Petersilia (eds), *Crime*. Oakland, CA: ICS.

Brewers and Licensed Retailers Association (1997), *Statement on Toughened Glass*. London: BLRA.

Brewster, A.L., Nelson, J.P. and Hymel, K.P. (1998), 'Victim, Perpetrator, Family and Incident Characteristics of 32 Infant Maltreatment Deaths in the US Airforce', *Child Abuse and Neglect*, Vol. 22, pp. 91–101.

Brian Morgan, J. (1990), *The Police Function and the Investigation of Crime*. Aldershot: Avebury.

Brittain, R.P. (1970), 'The Sadistic Murderer', *Medicine, Science and the Law*, Vol. 10, pp. 198–207.

Brod, H. (1987), *The Making of Masculinities*. Boston, MA: Allen and Unwin.

Brody, S. and Tarling, R. (1980), *Taking Offenders out of Circulation*. Home Office Research Study No. 64. London: HMSO.

Brookman, F. (1999), 'Accessing and Analysing Police Murder Files', in F. Brookman, L. Noaks and E. Wincup (eds), *Qualitative Research in Criminology*. Aldershot: Ashgate.

Brookman, F. (2000a) 'Dying for Control: Men, Murder and Sub-Lethal Violence', *British Criminology Conference: Selected Proceedings, Volume 3*. (http://www.lboro.ac.uk/departments/ss/bsc/bccsp/vol03/brookman.html)

Brookman, F. (2000b), *Dying for Control: Men, Murder and Sub-Lethal Violence in England and Wales*. Unpublished PhD Thesis. Cardiff University.

Brookman, F. (2003), 'Confrontational and Revenge Homicides in England and Wales', *The Australian and New Zealand Journal of Criminology*, Vol. 36/1, pp. 34–59.

Brookman, F. and Maguire, M. (2003), *Reducing Homicide: A Review of the Possibilities*. RDS Online Report 01/03. London: Home Office.

Brown, H. (2000), *Stalking and other Forms of Harassment: An Investigator's Guide*. Metropolitan Police. London: Home Office.

Browne, K.D. and Lynch M.A. (1995), 'The Nature and Extent of Child Homicide and Fatal Abuse', *Child Abuse Review*, Special Issue, December, Vol. 4, pp. 309–316.

Browne, A. and Williams, K.R. (1989), 'Exploring the Effect of Resource Availability and the Likelihood of Female-Perpetrated Homicides', *Law and Society Review*, Vol. 23/1, pp. 75–94.

Browne, A. and Williams, K.R. (1993), 'Gender, Intimacy, and Lethal Violence: Trends from 1976 through 1987', *Gender and Society*, Vol. 7, pp. 78–98.

Browne, A., Williams, K.R. and Dutton, D.G. (1999), 'Homicide Between Intimate Partners: A 20-Year Review', in M.D. Smith and M.A. Zahn (eds), *Homicide: A Sourcebook of Social Research*. London: Sage.

Brownfield, D. (1986), 'Social Class and Violent Behaviour', *Criminology*, Vol. 24/3, pp. 421–38.

Brownstein, H.H., Spunt, B.J., Crimmins, S., Goldstein, P.J. and Langley, S. (1994), 'Changing Patterns of Lethal Violence by Women', *Women and Criminal Justice*, Vol. 5, pp. 99–118.

Brozovsky, M. and Falit, H. (1971), 'Neonaticide: Clinical and Psychodynamic Considerations', *Journal of American Academy of Child Psychiatry*, Vol. 10, pp. 673–83.

Bruce, D.D. (1979), *Violence and Culture of the Antebellum South*. Austin, TX: University of Texas Press.

Brumm, H.J. and Cloninger, D.O. (1995), 'The Drug War and the Homicide Rate: A Direct Correlation?' *Cato Journal*, Vol. 14/3, pp. 509–517.

Bukowski, N.T. and Gehrke, R. (1979), 'The Rorschach in Homicides', *Psicologia*, Vol. 16, pp. 5–27.

Bull, R. and McAlpine, S. (1998), 'Facial Appearance and Criminality', in A. Vrij and R. Bull, *Psychology and Law: Truthfulness, Accuracy and Credibility*. Maidenhead: McGraw-Hill.

Bunch, B.J., Foley, L.A. and Urbina, S.P. (1983), 'The Psychology of Violent Female Offenders: A Sex-Role Perspective', *The Prison Journal*, Vol. 63, pp. 66–79.

Burgess, E.W. (1928), 'The Growth of the City', in R.E. Park, E.W. Burgess and McKenzie, R.D. (eds), *The City*. Chicago, IL: University of Chicago Press.

Burgess, R. and Draper, P. (1989), 'The Explanation of Family Violence: The Role of Biological, Behavioural and Cultural Selection', in L. Ohlin and M. Tonry (eds), *Family Violence*. Chicago, IL: University of Chicago Press.

Burman, M., Brown, J., Tisdall, K. and Batchelor, S. (2000), *A View from the Girls: Exploring Violence and Violent Behaviour*. Swindon: Economic and Social Research Council.

Burton, S., Regan, L. and Kelly, L. (1998), *Supporting Women and Challenging Men: Lessons from the Domestic Violence Intervention Project*. Bristol: Policy.

Busch, A.L. (1999), *Finding Their Voices: Listening to Battered Women Who've Killed*. New York: Kroshka.

Buss, D. (1999), *Evolutionary Psychology*. Boston, MA: Allyn and Bacon.

Butler, Lord (1975), *Report of the Committee on Mentally Abnormal Offenders* (Butler Report). Cmnd. 6244. London: HMSO.

Buvinic, M. and Morrison, A.R. (2000), 'Living in a More Violent World', *Foreign Policy*, Vol. 118, Spring, pp. 58–72.

Byford, L. (1982), *The Yorkshire Ripper Enquiry*. (unpublished).

Cameron, D. and Frazer, E. (1987), *The Lust to Kill*. Cambridge: Polity.

Campbell, A. (1991), *The Girls in the Gang* (2nd edition). Oxford: Basil Blackwell.

Campbell, A. (1993), *Out of Control: Men, Women and Aggression*. London: Harper Collins.

Campbell, J. (1981), 'Misogyny and Homicide of Women', *Advances in Nursing Science*, Vol. 3/2, pp. 67–85.

Campbell, J. (1986), 'Assessing the Risk of Homicide for Battered Women', *Advances in Nursing Science*, Vol. 8/4, pp. 36–51.

Campbell, J. (1992), 'If I Can't Have You, No One Can: Power and Control in Homicide of Female Partners', in J. Radford and D.E.H. Russell (eds), *Femicide: The Politics of Woman Killing*. Buckingham: Open University Press.

Campbell, J. (1995), 'Prediction of Homicide of and by Battered Women', in J.C. Campbell (ed.), *Assessing Dangerousness: Violence by Sexual Offenders, Batterers and Child Abusers*. London: Sage.

Campbell, J. and Runyan, C.W. (1998), 'Femicide: Guest Editors' Introduction', *Homicide Studies*, Vol. 2/4, pp. 347–52.

Canaan, J.E. (1996), '"One Thing Least to Another": Drinking, Fighting and Working-Class Masculinities', in M. Mac An Ghaill (ed.), *Understanding Masculinities*. Buckingham: Open University Press.

Canter, D. and Alison, L. (1999), *Profiling in Policy and Practice: Offender Profiling Series*. Dartmouth: Ashgate.

Capsi, A., McClay, J., Moffitt, T., Mill, J., Martin, J., Craig, I., Taylor, A. and Pulton, R. (2002), 'Role of Genotype in the Cycle of Violence in Maltreated Children', *Science*, Vol. 297, pp. 851–4.

Caputi, J. (1987), *The Age of Sex Crime*. London: Harper Collins.

Caputi, J. and Russell, D.E.H. (1992), 'Femicide: Sexist Terrorism Against Women', in J. Radford and D.E.H. Russell (eds), *Femicide: The Politics of Woman Killing*. Buckingham: Open University Press.

Card, R. (1998), *Criminal Law* (14th edition). London: Butterworth.

Cathcart, B. (2000), *The Case of Stephen Lawrence*. London: Viking (Penguin).

Cavadino, P. (1996), *Children Who Kill*. Winchester: Waterside.

CESDI (1998), *Confidential Inquiry into Still Births and Deaths in Infancy*. Fifth Annual Report. London: Maternal and Child Health Research Consortium.

Chadwick, K. and Scraton, P. (2001), 'Critical Criminology', in E. McLaughlin and J. Muncie (eds), *The Sage Dictionary of Criminology*. London: Sage.

Chambers, G.K., Cordiner, S.J., Buckleton, J.S., Robertson, B. and Vignaux, G.A. (1997), 'Forensic DNA Profiling: The Importance of Giving Accurate Answers to the Right Questions', *Criminal Law Forum*, Vol. 8/3, pp. 445–59.

Chan, J. (1997), *Changing Police Culture: Policing in a Multicultural Society*. Cambridge: Cambridge University Press.

Chan, W. (2001), *Women, Murder and Justice*. Basingstoke: Palgrave.

Chapple, C. (1998), 'Dow Corning and the Silicone Breast Implant Debacle: A Case of Corporate Crime Against Women', in L.H. Bowker (ed.), *Masculinities and Violence*. London: Sage.

Charlton, P. and Bolger, M. (1999), *Irish Criminal Law*. Dublin: Butterworths.

Chesney-Lind, M. (1997), *The Female Offender: Girls, Women, and Crime*. London: Sage.

Childs, P. (1996), *Nutcases Criminal Law* (1st edition). London: Sweet and Maxwell.

Christiansen, K. and Winkler, E.M. (1992), 'Hormonal, Anthropometrical, and Behavioural Correlates of Physical Aggression in Kuang San Men of Namibia', *Aggressive Behaviour*, Vol. 18, pp. 271–80.

Christie, S. (2002), *Introduction to Scots Criminal Law*. Essex: Pearson.

Clarke, C. (2001), 'Social Constructionism', in E. McLaughlin and J. Muncie (eds), *The Sage Dictionary of Criminology*. London: Sage.

Clarke, R. (1995) 'Situational Crime Prevention', in M. Tonry and D. Farrington (eds), *Building a Safer Society: Strategic Approaches to Crime*. Chicago, IL: University of Chicago Press.

Clarkson, C.M.V. (2000), 'Context and Culpability in Involuntary Manslaughter: Principle or Instinct?', in A. Ashworth and B. Mitchell (eds), *Rethinking English Homicide Law*. Oxford: Oxford University Press.

Clinard, M.B. and Meier, R.F. (1979), *The Sociology of Deviant Behaviour*. New York: Holt, Rinehart and Winston.

Cloward, R. and Ohlin, L. (1960), *Delinquency and Opportunity: A Theory of Delinquent Gangs*. New York: Free Press.

Clutterbuck, R. (1986), *The Future of Political Violence: Destabilization, Disorder and Terrorism*. London: Macmillan.

Clutterbuck, R. (1990), *Terrorism, Drugs and Crime in Europe after 1992*. London: Routledge.

Cohen, A.K. (1966), *Deviance and Control*. Englewood Cliffs, NJ: Prentice-Hall.

Cole, T.B. (1999), 'Ebbing Epidemic: Youth Homicide Rate at a 14-Year Low', *The Journal of the American Medical Association*, Vol. 281/1, pp. 25–6.

Coleman, C. and Moynihan, J. (1996), *Understanding Crime Data: Haunted by the Dark Figure*. Philadelphia, PA: Open University Press.

Coleman, C. and Norris, C. (2000), *Introducing Criminology*. Cullompton: Willan.

Coleman, J. (1987), 'Towards an Integrated Theory of White Collar Crime', *American Journal of Sociology*, Vol. 93, pp. 406–439.

Collier, R. (1998), *Masculinities, Crime and Criminology*. London: Sage.

Collier, R. (2000), 'Masculinities and Violence', *Criminal Justice Matters*, Vol. 42, Winter, pp. 8–10.

Collins, J.J. (1989), 'Alcohol and Interpersonal Violence: Less Than Meets the Eye', in N.A. Weiner and M.E. Wolfgang (eds), *Pathways to Criminal Violence*. London: Sage.

Committee on the Penalty for Homicide (1993), *The Report of an Independent Inquiry into the Mandatory Life Sentence for Murder*. London: Prison Reform Trust.

Conklin, J.E. (1998), *Criminology* (6th edition). London: Allyn and Bacon.

Connell, R.W. (1987), *Gender and Power*. Cambridge: Polity.

Connell, R.W. (2002), 'On Hegemonic Masculinity and Violence: Response to Jefferson and Hall', *Theoretical Criminology*, Vol. 6/1, pp. 89–99.

Cooney, M. (1997), 'The Decline of Elite Homicide', *Criminology*, Vol. 35/3, pp. 381–407.

Copp, P. (1998), 'Forensic Science', in P. White (ed.), *Crime Scene to Court: The Essentials of Forensic Science*. Cambridge: Royal Society of Chemistry.

Cordelia, A. (1985), 'Alcohol and Property Crime: Explaining the Causal Nexus', *Journal of Studies on Alcohol*, Vol. 46, pp. 161–71.

Cortes, J.B. and Gatti, F.M. (1972), *Delinquency and Crime: A Biopsychosocial Approach*. New York: Seminar Press.

Corzine, J., Huff-Corzine, L. and Whitt, H.P. (1999), 'Cultural and Subcultural Theories of Homicide', in M.D. Smith and M.A. Zahn (eds), *Homicide: A Sourcebook of Social Research*. London: Sage.

Cotton, J. (2003), 'Homicide', in C. Flood-Page and J. Taylor (eds), *Crime in England and Wales: Supplementary Volume 01/03*. London: Home Office.

Couvalis, G. (1997), *The Philosophy of Science: Science and Objectivity*. London: Sage.

Crawford, D.A. (1977), 'The HDHQ Results of Long Term Prisoners: Relationships with Criminal and Institutional Behaviour', *British Journal of Social and Clinical Psychology*, Vol. 16, pp. 391–4.

Crenshaw, M. (1984), 'The Persistence of IRA Terrorism', in Y. Alexander and A.O'Day (eds), *Terrorism in Ireland*. London: Croom Helm.

Crimmins, S., Langley, S., Brownstein, H.H. and Spunt, B.J. (1997), 'Convicted Women Who Have Killed Children: A Self-Psychology Perspective', *Journal of Interpersonal Violence*, Vol. 12/1: 49–69.

Crittenden, P. and Craig, S. (1990), 'Development Trends in the Nature of Child Homicide', *Journal of Interpersonal Violence*, Vol. 5/2, pp. 202–16.

Croall, H. (1992), *White Collar Crime*. Buckingham: Open University Press.

Croall, H. (1998), *Crime and Society in Britain*. London: Longman.

Cummings, P. and Mueller, B.A. (1994), 'Infant Injury Death in Washington State, 1981 through 1990', *Archives of Pediatric and Adolescent Medicine*, Vol. 148, pp. 1021–6.

Curtis, G.C. (1963), 'Violence Breeds Violence – Perhaps?', *American Journal of Psychiatry*, Vol. 120, pp. 386–7.

Curtis, L.A. (1975), *Violence, Race and Culture*. Lexington, MA: Heath.

Daily Telegraph (2002), 'Why Police have Poured all their Resources into the Hunt', 6 November. Reporter: Nicole Martin. (www.telegraph.co.uk)

Dalgaard, S.O. and Kringlen, E. (1976), 'A Norwegian Twin Study of Criminality', *British Journal of Criminology*, Vol. 16, pp. 213–33.

Dalton, K. (1961), 'Menstruation and Crime', *British Medical Journal*, Vol. 2, pp. 1752–3.

Dalton, K. (1990), *Pre-menstrual Syndrome goes to Court*. Worcestershire: Peter Andrew.

Daly, K. and Chesney-Lind, M. (1988), 'Feminism and Criminology', *Justice Quarterly*, Vol. 5/4, pp. 497–538.

Daly, M. and Wilson, M. (1988), *Homicide*. New York: De Gruyter.

Daly, M. and Wilson, M. (1996), 'The Evolutionary Psychology of Homicide', *Demos*, December 8, pp. 39–45.

Daly, M. and Wilson, M. (1990), 'Killing the Competition: Female/Female and Male/Male Homicide', *Human Nature*, Vol. 1/1, pp. 81–107.

Daly, M., Wilson, M. and Weghorst, S.J. (1982), 'Male Sexual Jealousy', *Ethology and Sociobiology*, Vol. 3, pp. 11–27.

Danson, L. and Soothill, K. (1996), 'Multiple Murder and the Media: A Study of the Reporting of Multiple Murders in *The Times* (1887–1990)', *Journal of Forensic Psychiatry*, Vol. 7/1, pp. 114–29.

Darwin, C. (1859), *The Origin of the Species*. Danbury, CT: Grolier.

Darwin, C. (1872), *Expressions of Emotion in Man and Animals*. London: John Murray.

Davidson, G.C. and Neale, J.M. (2001), *Abnormal Psychology*. Chichester: Wiley.

Dawson, M. (2001), '*Examination of Declining Intimate Parner Homicide Rates: A Literature Review*'. Research and Statistics Division, Canada: Department of Justice.

Decker, S. (1995), 'Reconstructing Homicide Events: The Role of Witnesses in Fatal Encounters', *Journal of Criminal Justice*, Vol. 23/5, pp. 439–50.

Deehan, A. (1999), *Alcohol and Crime: Taking Stock*. Crime Reduction Research Series Paper 3. London: Home Office.

Dengerink, H.A., Schnedler, R.W. and Covey, M.V. (1978), 'The Role of Avoidance in Aggressive Responses to Attack and No Attack', *Journal of Personality and Social Psychology*. Vol. 36, pp. 1044–53.

Denno, D. (1990), *Biology and Violence: From Birth to Adulthood*. Cambridge: Cambridge University Press.

DETR (2000), *Road Traffic Penalties: A Consultation Paper*. London: Department of the Environment, Transport and the Regions.

Dewar, M. (1996), *The British Army in Northern Ireland*. London: Arms and Armour.

Dine, J. and Gobert, J. (1998), *Cases and Materials on Criminal Law* (2nd edition). London: Butterworth.

Dingley, J. (2001), 'The Bombing of Omagh, 15 August 1998: The Bombers, Their Tactics, Strategy, and Purpose Behind the Incident', *Studies in Conflict and Terrorism*, Vol. 24, pp. 451–65.

Ditton, J. and Duffy, J. (1983), 'Bias in the Newspaper Reporting of Crime News', *British Journal of Criminology*, Vol. 23/2, pp. 159–65.

d'Orban, P.T. (1979), 'Women Who Kill Their Children', *British Journal of Psychiatry*, Vol. 134, pp. 560–71.

d'Orban, P.T. (1990), 'Female Homicide', *Irish Journal of Psychological Medicine*, Vol. 7, pp. 64–70.

d'Orban, P.T. and Dalton, J. (1980), 'Violent Crime and the Menstrual Cycle', *Psychological Medicine*, Vol. 10, pp. 353–9.

Dobash, R.E. (1990), Shaping Gender Through Violence. International Symposium: the Construction of Sex/Gender: What is a Feminist Perspective? Stockholm, 4–6 October.

Dobash, R.P. and Dobash, R.E. (1979), *Violence Against Wives*. New York: Free Press.

Dobash, R.E. and Dobash, R.P. (1992), *Women, Violence and Social Change*. London: Routledge.

Dobash, R.E., Dobash, R.P. and Cavanagh, K. (1985), 'The Contact Between Battered Women and Social and Medical Agencies', in J. Pahl (ed.), *Private Violence and Public Policy*. London: Routledge and Kegan Paul.

Dobash, R.P, Dobash, R.E., Cavanagh, K. and Lewis, R. (1996), *Research Evaluation of Programmes for Violent Men*. Edinburgh: HMSO.

Dobash, R.P., Dobash, R.E., Cavanagh, K. and Lewis, R. (1998), 'Separate and Intersecting Realities: A Comparison of Men's and Women's Accounts of Violence against Women', *Violence Against Women*, Vol. 4, pp. 382–414.

Dobash, R.E., Dobash, R.D., Cavanagh, K. and Lewis, R. (2001), *Homicide in Britain*. Research Bulletin No. 1, University of Manchester.

Dobash, R.E., Dobash, R.P., Cavanagh, K. and Lewis, R. forthcoming, 'Not an Ordinary Killer – Just an Ordinary Guy: When Men Murder an Intimate Woman Partner', *Violence Against Women* (Special Issue).

Doerner, W.G. (1983), 'Why Does Johnny Reb Die When Shot? The Impact of Medical Resources Upon Lethality', *Sociological Inquiry*, Vol. 53, pp. 1–15.

Doerner, W.G. (1988), 'The Impact of Medical Resources on Criminally Induced Lethality: A Further Examination', *Criminology*, Vol. 26, pp. 171–80.

Dooley, E. (1995), *Homicide in Ireland, 1972–1991*. Dublin: Stationery Office.

Dooley, E. (2001), *Homicide in Ireland, 1992–1996*. Dublin: Stationery Office.

Drapkin, I. and Viano, E. (eds) (1974), *Victimology*. Lexington, MA: Heath.

Dugan, L., Nagin, D.S. and Rosenfeld, R. (1999), 'Explaining the Decline in Intimate Partner Homicides: The Effects of Changing Domesticity, Women's Status and Domestic Violence Resources', *Homicide Studies*, Vol. 3/3, pp. 187–214.

Durkheim, E. (1951), *Suicide*. Trans. J.A. Spaulding and G. Simpson. New York: Free Press (first published 1897).

Durrant, J.E. and Olsen, G.M. (1997), 'Parenting and Public Policy: Contextualizing the Swedish Corporal Punishment Ban', *Journal of Social Welfare and Family Law*, Vol. 19/4, pp. 443–61.

Easteal, P.W. (1993), *Killing the Beloved: Homicide Between Adult Sexual Intimates*. Canberra: Australian Institute of Criminology.

Eaton, M. (1986), *Justice for Women? Family; Court and Social Control*. Milton Keynes: Open University Press.

Eckenrode, J., Ganzel, R., Henderson, C.R., Smith, E., Olds, D.L., Powers, J., Cole, R., Kitzman, H. and Sidora, K. (2000), 'Preventing Child Abuse and Neglect with a Program of Nurse Home Visitation: The Limiting Effects of Domestic Violence', *JAMA*, Vol. 284/11, pp. 1385–91.

Edgell, S. (1980), *Middle Class Couples*. London: George Allen and Unwin.

Edwards, S. (1996), *Sex and Gender in the Legal Process*. London: Blackstone.

Edwards, S. (2000), 'Reducing Domestic Violence ... What Works? Use of the Criminal Law'. *Policing and Reducing Crime Unit Briefing Notes*. London: Home Office.

Egger, S.A. (1990), 'Serial Murder: A Synthesis of Literature and Research', in S.A. Egger (ed.), *Serial Murder: An Elusive Phenomenon*. London: Praeger.

Ekblom, P. (2000), 'The Conjunction of Criminal Opportunity' in S. Ballintyre, K. Pease and V. Mclaren (eds), *Secure Foundations: Key Issues in Crime Prevention, Crime Reduction and Community Safety*. London: IPPR.

Elias, N. (1982), *State Formation and Civilization*. Oxford: Blackwell.

Elliott, D.S., Ageton, S.S. and Canter, R. (1979), 'An Integrated Theoretical Perspective on Delinquent Behaviour', *Journal of Research in Crime and Delinquency*, Vol. 16, pp. 3–27.

Emmerichs, E. (1999), 'Getting Away with Murder?: Homicide and the Coroners in Nineteenth-Century London', in P. Blackman, V. Leggett, B. Olson and J. Jarvis (eds), *The Varieties of Homicide and Its Research*. Proceedings of the 1999 Meeting of the Homicide Research Working Group. Washington, DC: FBI.

English, J. and Card, R. (2001), *Butterworths Police Law* (7th edition). London: Butterworth.

Ericson, R. (1995), *Crime and the Media*. Aldershot: Dartmouth.

Ericson, R., Baranek, P. and Chan, J. (1991), *Representing Crime: Crime, Law and Justice in the News Media*. Toronto: Toronto University Press.

Eronen, M. (1995), 'Mental Disorders and Homicidal Behavior in Female Subjects', *American Journal of Psychiatry*, Vol. 152, pp. 1216–18.

Erzinclioglu, Z. (2002), *Maggots, Murder and Men: Memories and Reflections of a Forensic Entomologist*. New York: St Martin's.

Evans, C.M. (1980), 'Alcohol, Violence and Aggression', *Journal of Alcohol and Alcoholism*, Vol. 15/3, pp. 104–117.

Evett, I.W., Foreman, L.A., Jackson, G. and Lambert, J.A. (2000), 'DNA Profiling: A Discussion of Issues Relating to the Reporting of Very Small Match Probabilities', *Criminal Law Review*, May, pp. 341–55.

Ewing, P. (1990), *When Children Kill*. Toronto: Lexington.

Ewing, P. (1997), *Fatal Families: The Dynamics of Intra-Familial Homicide*. Thousand Oaks, CA: Sage.

Eysenck, H.J. (1959), *Manual of the Maudsley Personality Inventory*. London: University of London Press.

Eysenck, H.J. (1964), *Crime and Personality*. London: Routledge and Kegan Paul.

Eysenck, H.J. and Eysenck, S.B.G. (1968), 'A Factorial Study of Psychoticism as a Dimension of Personality', *Multivariate Behavioural Research*, (Special Issue), pp. 15–31.

Eysenck, H.J. and Eysenck, S.B.G. (1976), *Psychoticism as a Dimension of Personalty*. London: Hodder and Stoughton.

Eysenck, H.J. and Gudjonsson, G.H. (1989), *The Causes and Cures of Criminality*. New York: Plenum.

Fagan, J. (1990), 'Intoxificication and Aggression', in M. Tonry and J. Wilson (eds), *Drugs and Crime*. Chicago, IL: University of Chicago Press.

Falk, G. (1990), *Murder: An Analysis of its Forms, Conditions and Causes*. London: McFarland and Company.

Falkov, A. (1996), *A Study of Working Together Part 8 Reports: Fatal Child Abuse and Parental Psychiatric Disorder*. London: Department of Health.

Farrington, D.P. (1997), 'The Relationship Between Low Resting Heart Rate and Violence', in A. Raine, P.A. Brennan, D.P. Farrington and S.A. Mednick (eds), *Biosocial Basis of Violence*. New York: Plenum.

Farrington, D.P. (1998), 'Individual Differences in Offending', in M. Tonry (ed.), *The Handbook of Crime and Punishment*. Oxford: Oxford University Press.

Farrington, D.P. (2002), 'Developmental Criminology and Risk-Focussed Prevention', in M. Maguire, R. Morgan and R. Reiner (eds), *The Oxford Handbook of Criminology* (3rd edition). Oxford: Clarendon.

Fattah, E.A. (1991), *Understanding Criminal Victimization*. Scarborough, Ontario: Prentice-Hall.

Fava, M. (1998), 'Depression with Anger Attacks', *Journal of Clinical Psychiatry*, Vol. 59, pp. 18–22.

Fay, M.T., Morrissey, M. and Smyth, M. (1997), *Mapping Troubles-Related Deaths in Northern Ireland, 1969–1994*. Derry, Londonderry: INCORE (Initiative on Conflict Resolution and Ethnicity).

Feist, A. (1999), *The Effective Use of the Media in Serious Crime Investigations*. Policing and Reducing Crime Unit Paper 120. London: Home Office.

Feist, A. and Newiss, G. (forthcoming), *Watching the Detectives: Analysing Hard to Solve Homicide Investigations*. Police Research Series. Home Office Research, Development and Statistics and Directorate. London: HMSO.

Felson, M. (1998), *Crime and Everyday Life* (2nd edition). Thousand Oaks, CA: Pine Forge.

Felson, R.B. (1978), 'Aggression as Impression Management', *Social Psychology*, Vol. 41, pp. 205–213.

Felson, R.B. (1984), 'Patterns of Aggressive Social Interactions', in A. Mummendey (ed.), *Social Psychology and Aggression: From Individual Behaviour to Social Interaction*. Berlin: Springer-Verlag.

Felson, R.B. and Messner, S.F. (1996) 'To Kill or Not to Kill? Lethal Outcomes in Injurious Attacks', *Criminology*, Vol. 34/4, pp. 519–45.

Felson, R.B. and Steadman, H.J. (1983), 'Situational Factors in Disputes Leading to Criminal Violence', *Criminology*, Vol. 21/1, pp. 59–74.

Ferri, E. (1902), *Les Criminels dans l'Art et la Litterature*. Trans. Laurent. Paris: Alcan.

Field, S. (1990), *Trends in Crime and Their Interpretation*. London: HMSO.

Filley, C., Price, B., Nell, V., Antoinette, T., Morgan, A., Bresnahan, J., Pincus, J., Gelbort, M., Weissberg, M. and Kelly, J. (2001), 'Toward an Understanding of Violence: Neurobehavioural Aspects of Unwarranted Physical Aggression: Aspen Neurobehavioural Conference Consensus Statement'. *Neuropsychiatry, Neuropsychology and Behavioural Neurology*, Vol. 14/1, pp. 1–14.

Fishbein, D.H. (1992), 'The Psychobiology of Female Aggression', *Criminal Justice and Behaviour*, Vol. 19, pp. 99–126.

Fishbein, D.H. (1996), 'The Biology of Antisocial Behaviour', in J.E. Conklin (ed.), *New Perspectives in Criminology*. Boston, MA: Allyn and Bacon.

Fleming, P., Blair, P., Bacon, C. and Berry, J. (eds) (2000), *Sudden Unexplained Deaths in Infancy: The CESDI SUDI Stories*. London: Stationery Office.

Flood-Page, C. and Taylor, J. (2003), *Crime in England and Wales 2001/2002: Supplementary Volume*. London: National Statistics.

Floud, J. (1982), 'Dangerousness and Criminal Justice', *British Journal of Criminology*, Vol. 22/3, pp. 213–28.

Floud, J. and Young, W. (1981), *Dangerousness and Criminal Justice*. London: Heinemann.

Follingstad, D.R., Brondino, M.J. and Kleinfelter, K.J. (1996), 'Reputation and Behavior of Battered Women who Kill their Partners: Do These Variables Negate Self-Defense?', *Journal of Family Violence*, Vol. 11/3, pp. 251–67.

Foote, W. (1999), 'Victim-Precipitated Homicide', in H.V. Hall (ed.), *Lethal Violence: A Sourcebook on Fatal Domestic, Acquaintance and Stranger Violence*. London: CRC.

Forde, R.A. (1978), 'Twin Studies, Inheritance and Criminality', *British Journal of Criminology*, Vol. 18/1, pp. 71–4.

Fox, J.A. and Levin, J. (1998), 'Multiple Homicide: Patterns of Serial and Mass Murder', *Crime and Justice – A Review of Research*, Vol. 23, pp. 407–455.

Freedman, D. and Hemenway, D. (2000), 'Precursors of Lethal Violence: A Death Row Sample', *Social Science and Medicine*, Vol. 50, pp. 1757–70.

Freud, S. (1920), *A General Introduction to Psychoanalsys*. New York: Boni and Liveright.

Freud, S. (1927), *The Ego and the Id*. London: Hogarth.

Freud, S. (1930), *Civilization and its Discontents*. New York: Cape and Smith.

Friedlander, K. (1947), *The Psycho-Analytical Approach to Juvenile Delinquency*. London: Routledge and Kegan Paul.

Friere, P. (1971), *Pedagogy of the Oppressed*. New York: Continuum.

Frieze, I. and Brown, A. (1989), 'Violence in Marriage', in L. Ohlin and M. Tonry (eds), *Family Violence*. Chicago, IL: University of Chicago Press.

Fuller, N. (2001), 'She Made Me Go Out of My Mind: Marital Violence From the Male Point of View', *Development*, Vol. 44/3, pp. 25–9.

Fyfe, J., Goldkamp, J. and White, M. (1997), *Strategies for Reducing Homicide: The Comprehensive Homicide Initiative in Richmond, California*. Washington, DC: US Department of Justice.

Gallagher, B.J. (1987), *The Sociology of Mental Illness*. Englewood Cliffs, NJ: Prentice-Hall.

Gallop, A. and Stockdale, R. (1998), 'Trace and Contact Evidence', in P. White (ed.), *Crime Scene to Court: The Essentials of Forensic Science*. Cambridge: Royal Society of Chemistry.

Gane, C. and Stoddart, C. (1988), *A Casebook on Scottish Criminal Law* (2nd edition). Edinburgh: Green.

Garofalo, R. (1914), *Criminology*. Boston, MA: Little, Brown.

Garriott, J.C., DeMaio, V. and Rodriguez, R.G. (1986), 'Detection of Cannabinoids in Homicide Victims and Motor Vehicle Fatalities', *Journal of Forensic Sciences*, Vol. 31, pp. 1274–82.

Gaylor, D. (2002), *Getting Away with Murder: The Re-investigation of Historic Undetected Homicide*. London: Crown.

Geberth, V.J. (1996), *Practical Homicide Investigation: Tactics, Procedures and Forensic Techniques* (3rd edition). New York: CRC.

Gee, D.J. (1988), 'A Pathologist's View of Multiple Murder', *Forensic Science International*, Vol. 38/1–2, pp. 53–65.

Gelles, R.J. (1991), 'Physical Violence, Child Abuse and Child Homicide: A Continuum of Violence or Distinct Behaviours?', *Human Nature*, Vol. 2/1, pp. 59–72.

Gerson, L.W. (1978), 'Alcohol-Related Acts Of Violence: Who Was Drinking and Where the Acts Occurred', *Journal of Studies on Alcohol*, Vol. 39/7, pp. 1294–6.

Gibbons, D.C. (1992), *Society, Crime and Criminal Behaviour*. Englewood Cliffs, NJ: Prentice-Hall.

Gibson, E. (1975), *Homicide in England and Wales 1967–1971*. Home Office Research Study No. 31. London: HMSO.

Giesbrecht, N. and Nesbitt, S. (2001), 'Alcohol and Crime: From Understanding to Effective Intervention', *Journal of Substance Use*, Vol. 6, pp. 215–17.

Gil, D.G. (1970), *Violence Against Children: Physical Child Abuse in the United States*. Cambridge, MA: Harvard University Press.

Gil, D.G. (1996), 'Preventing Violence in a Structurally Violent Society: Mission Impossible', *American Journal of Orthopsychiatry*, Vol. 66/Jan., pp. 77–84.

Gillies, H. (1976), 'Homicide in the West of Scotland', *British Journal of Psychiatry*, Vol. 128, pp. 105–127.

Gilligan, J. (2000), *Violence: Reflections on Our Deadliest Epidemic*. London: Jessica Kingsley.

Gilligan, J. (2001), *Preventing Violence*. London: Thames and Hudson.

Gilmore, D.D. (1990), *Manhood in the Making: Cultural Concepts of Masculinity*. New Haven, CT: Yale University Press.

Glueck, S. and Glueck, E.T. (1956), *Physique and Delinquency*. New York: Harper and Row.

Goetting, A. (1987), 'Homicidal Wives', *Journal of Family Issues*, Vol. 8, pp. 332–41.

Goetting, A. (1988a), 'Patterns of Homicide Among Women', *Journal of Interpersonal Violence*, Vol. 3, pp. 3–20.

Goetting, A. (1988b), 'When Females Kill One Another', *Criminal Justice and Behavior*, Vol. 15, pp. 179–89.

Goetting, A. (1988c), 'When Parents Kill their Young Children: Detroit 1982–1986'. *Journal of Family Violence*, Vol. 3/4, pp. 339–46.

Goetting, A. (1989), 'Patterns of Marital Homicide: A Comparison of Husbands and Wives', *Journal of Comparative Family Studies*, Vol. 20, pp. 341–54.

Goffman, E. (1967), *Interaction Ritual: Essays on Face-to-Face Behaviour*. New York: Doubleday.

Golden, R.M. and Messner, S.F. (1987), 'Dimensions of Racial Inequality and Rates of Violent Crime', *Criminology*, Vol. 25, pp. 525–54.

Goldstein, P.J. (1985), 'The Drugs/Violence Nexus: A Tripartite Conceptual Framework', *Journal of Drug Issues*, Vol. 15, pp. 493–506.

Gondolf, E.W. (2002), *Batterer Intervention Systems: Issues, Outcomes and Recommendations*. Thousand Oaks, CA: Sage.

Goodman, L.A., Dutton, M.A. and Bennett, L. (2000), 'Predicting Repeat Abuse Among Arrested Batterers: Use of the Danger Assessment Scale in the Criminal Justice System', *Journal of Interpersonal Violence*, Vol. 15/1, pp. 63–73.

Goodman, R.A., Mercy, J.A., Loya, F., Rosenberg, M.L., Smith, J.C., Allen, M.H., Vargas, L. and Kotts, R. (1986), 'Alcohol Use and Interpersonal Violence – Alcohol Detected in Homicide Victims', *American Journal of Public Health*, Vol. 762, pp. 144–9.

Gottfredson, M.R. and Hirschi, T. (1990), *A General Theory of Crime*. Stanford, CA: Stanford University Press.

Gottlieb, S. (1998), 'Doctors Could Have Greater Role in Spotting Domestic Violence', *British Medical Journal*, Vol. 317, pp. 99.

Gove, W.R. (1972), 'The Relationship between Sex Roles, Marital Status and Marital Illness', *Social Forces*, Vol. 51, pp. 34–44.

Graham, K. and Homel, R. (1997), 'Creating Safer Bars', in M. Plant, E. Single and T. Stockwell (eds), *Alcohol: Minimising the Harm – What Works?*. London: Free Association.

Gramsci, A. (1971), *Selection from the Prison Notebooks*. London: Lawrence and Wishart.

Grann, M., Langstrom, N.J., Tengstrom, A. and Kullgren, G. (1999), 'Psychopathy (PCL-R) Predicts Violent Recidivism among Criminal Offenders with Personality Disorders in Sweden', *Law and Human Behaviour*, Vol. 23/2, pp. 205–217.

Grant, B. and Curry, G.D. (1993), 'Women Murderers and Victims of Abuse in a Southern State', *American Journal of Criminal Justice*, Vol. 17, pp. 73–83.

Green, C.M. and Manohar, S.V. (1990), 'Neonaticide and Hysterical Denial of Pregnancy', *British Journal of Psychiatry*, Vol. 156, pp. 121–3.

Green, M.A. and Limerick, S. (1999), 'Debate: Time to Put Cot Death to Bed?/Not Time to put Cot Death to Bed', *British Medical Journal*, Vol. 319, pp. 697–700.

Greenberg, D. (1977), 'Delinquency and the Age Structure of Society', *Contemporary Crises*, Vol. 1, pp. 189–224.

Greenberg, D. (1981), *Crime and Capitalism*. Palo Alto, CA: Mayfield.

Greenwood, P., Chaiken, J. and Petersilia, J. (1977), *The Criminal Investigation Process*. Lexington, MA: Heath.

Gresswell, D.M. (1991), 'Psychological Models of Addiction and the Origins and Maintenance of Multiple Murder', in M. McMurran and C. McDougall (eds), *Proceedings of the First DCLP Annual Conference* (Volume 2) pp. 86–91. Leicester: British Psychological Association.

Gresswell, D.M. (1994), *Multiple Murder in England and Wales, 1982–1991: An Analysis*. PhD Thesis, University of Birmingham.

Gresswell, D.M. and Hollin, C.R. (1994), 'Multiple Murder: A Review', *British Journal of Criminology*, Vol. 34/1, pp. 1–14.

Gross, P. and Levitt, M. (1994), *Higher Superstition: The Academic Left and its Quarrels with Science*. Baltimore, MD: Johns Hopkins.

Grover, C. and Soothill, K. (1997), 'British Serial Killing: Towards a Structural Explanation', *The British Criminology Conferences: Selected Proceedings, Volume 2*. Papers from the British Criminology Conference, Queens University, Belfast, 15–19 July.

Grubin, D. (1994), 'Sexual Murder', *British Journal of Psychiatry*, Vol. 165, pp. 624–9.

Guardian (2002), 'The Girl who Vanished', 28 March. Reporter: Raekha Prasad. (www.guardian. co.uk)

Gudjonsson, G. (1998), 'Retracted Confessions', *Medicine, Science and the Law*, Vol. 28/3, pp. 187–94.

Gudjonsson, G. (2002), *The Psychology of Interrogations and Confessions*. London: Wiley.

Gunn, T. and Taylor, D. (1995), 'Clinical, Legal and Ethical Issues', *Forensic Psychiatry*, Vol. 8, pp. 49–53.

Guttmacher, M. (1973), *The Mind of the Murderer*. New York: Arno.

Guze, S.B. (1976), *Criminality and Psychiatric Disorders*. New York: Oxford University Press.

Hacking, I. (1999), *The Social Construction of What?* Cambridge, MA: Harvard University, Press.

Hackney, S. (1969), 'Southern Violence', *American Historical Review*, Vol. 39, pp. 906–925.

Hall, H.V. (1999), *Lethal Violence: A Sourcebook on Fatal Domestic, Acquaintance and Stranger Violence*. London: CRC.

Hall Williams, J.E. (1982), *Criminology and Criminal Justice*. London: Butterworth.

Hammersley, M. and Atkinson, P. (1995), *Ethnography: Principles in Practice* (2nd edition). London: Routledge.

Hamner, J. and Saunder, S. (1984), *Well Founded Fear: A Community Study of Violence to Women*. London: Hutchison.

Hanly, C. (1999), *An Introduction to Irish Criminal Law*. Dublin: Gill and Macmillan.

Harding, C., Fennell, P., Jorg, N. and Swart, B. (eds) (1995), *Criminal Justice in Europe*. Oxford: Oxford University Press.

Harlan, H. (1950), 'Five Hundred Homicides', *Journal of Criminal Law and Criminology*, Vol. 40, pp. 736–52.

Harries, K.D. (1990), *Serious Violence: Patterns of Homicide and Assault in America*. Springfield, IL: Thomas.

Harris, J. (2000), *An Evaluation of the Use and Effectiveness of the Protection from Harassment Act 1997*. Home Office Research Study 203. London: Home Office.

Hathaway, S.R. and McKinley, J.C. (1967), *Manual for the Minnesota Multiphasic Personality Inventory* (Revised edition). New York: Psychological Corporation.

Hayes, S.C., Rincover, A. and Volosin, D. (1980), 'Variables Influencing the Acquisition and Maintenance of Aggressive Behaviour: Modelling Versus Sensory Reinforcement', *Journal of Abnormal Psychology*, Vol. 89, pp. 254–62.

Healey, K.M. and Smith, C. (1998), 'Batterer Programs: What Criminal Justice Agencies Need to Know', Research in Action. *National Institute of Justice*. Washington, DC: US Department of Justice, Office of Justice Programs.

Hearn, J. (1998), *The Violences of Men*. London: Sage.

Heide, K. (1999), *Young Killers*. London: Sage.

Heidensohn, F. (1996), *Women and Crime* (2nd edition). London: Macmillan.

Heidensohn, F. (2000), 'Women and Violence: Myths and Reality in the 21st Century', *Criminal Justice Matters*, Vol. 42, Winter 2000/2001, pp. 20.

Heidensohn, F. (2002), 'Gender and Crime', in M. Maguire, R. Morgan and R. Reiner (eds), *The Oxford Handbook of Criminology* (3rd edition). Oxford: Oxford University Press.

Henderson, M. (1983), 'An Empirical Classification of Non-Violent Offenders using the MMPI', *Personality and Individual Differences*, Vol. 4, pp. 671–7.

Henn, F.A., Herjanic, M. and Vanderpearl, R.H. (1976), 'Forensic Psychiatry: Profiles of Two Types of Sex Offenders', *American Journal of Psychiatry*, Vol. 133, pp. 694–6.

Hepburn, J.R. (1973), 'Violent Behaviour in Interpersonal Relationships', *Sociological Quarterly*, Vol. 14, pp. 419–29.

Hernstein, R.J. (1995), 'Criminogenic Traits', in J. Wilson and J. Petersilia (eds), *Crime*. San Francisco, CA: ICS.

Hernstein, R.J. and Murray, C. (1994), *The Bell Curve*. New York: Basic Books.

Heskin, K. (1984), 'The Psychology of Terrorism in Northern Ireland', in Y. Alexander and A. O'Day (eds), *Terrorism in Ireland*. London: Croom Helm.

Hickey, E.W. (1991), *Serial Murderers and Their Victims*. Belmont, CA: Wadsworth.

Hicks, R.A. and Gaughan, D.C. (1995), 'Understanding Fatal Child Abuse', *Child Abuse and Neglect*, Vol. 19/7, pp. 855–63.

Hindelang, M., Gottfredson, M. and Garofalo, J. (1978), *Victims of Personal Victimization: An Empirical Foundation for a Theory of Personal Victimization*. Cambridge, MA: Ballinger.

HMIC (Her Majesty's Inspectorate of Constabulary) (2000), *Policing London: 'Winning Consent'. A Review of Murder Investigation and Community and Race Relations Issues in the Metropolitan Police Service*. London: HMIC. (www.homeoffice.gov.uk/hmic/pollondn.pdf)

Hobbs, D. (1988), *Doing the Business*. Oxford: Oxford University Press.

Hobbs, D., Hadfield, P., Lister, S. and Winlow, S. (2002) '"Door Lore": The Art and Economics of Intimidation', *British Journal of Criminology*, Vol. 42/ 2, pp. 352–70.

Hollin, C.R. (1989), *Psychology and Crime: An Introduction to Criminological Psychology*. London: Routledge.

Holmes, R.M. and De Burger, J. (1988), *Serial Murder*. Newbury Park, CA: Sage.

Holmes, R.M. and Holmes, S.T. (1996), *Profiling Violent Crimes: An Investigative Tool*. London: Sage.

Holmes, R.M. and Holmes, S.T. (1998), *Serial Murder* (2nd edition). London: Sage.

Holmes, R.M. and Holmes, S.T. (2001a), *Murder in America* (2nd edition). London: Sage.

Holmes, R.M. and Holmes, S.T. (2001b), *Mass Murder in the United States*. London: Prentice-Hall.

Homel, R. and Tomsen, S. (1993), 'Hot Spots for Violence: The Environment of Pubs and Clubs', in H. Strang and S.A. Gerull (eds), *Homicide : Patterns, Prevention and Control*. AIC Conference Proceedings, No. 17. Canberra: Australian Institute of Criminology.

Home Office (1981), *The Yorkshire Ripper Case: Review of the Police Investigation of the Case* by Lawrence Byford, Esq., Her Majesty's Inspector of Constabulary. London: Home Office.

Home Office (1982), Circular 114/82. The *Investigation of Series of Major Crimes*. London: Home Office.

Home Office (1998a), *Criminal Statistics, England and Wales 1997*. London: HMSO.

Home Office (1998b), *Statistics on the Operation of Prevention of Terrorism Legislation*. Home Office Statistical Bulletin No. 04/98. London: Home Office.

Home Office (2000), *Reforming the Law on Involuntary Manslaughter*. Consultation Paper. London: Home Office.

Home Office (2001a), *Criminal Statistics England and Wales 2000*. London: HMSO.

Home Office (2001b), *Statistics on the Operation of Prevention of Terrorism Legislation*. Home Office Statistical Bulletin No. 16/01. London: Home Office.

Home Office Department for Transport (2002), *Report on the Review of Road Traffic Penalties*. Home Office Communication Directorate. London: Home Office.

Home Office (2003), *Safety and Justice: The Government's Proposals on Domestic Violence*. London: Home Office.

Hood, R. (1996), *The Death Penalty: A World-Wide Perspective*. Oxford: Clarendon.

Hooton, E.A. (1939), *Crime and the Man*. Cambridge, MA: Harvard University Press.

Hopkins Burke, R. (2001), *An Introduction to Criminological Theory*. Devon: Willan.

Horder, J. (1991), *Provocation and Responsibility*. Oxford: Clarendon.

Horney, J. (1978), 'Menstrual Cycles and Criminal Responsibility', *Law and Human Behaviour*, Vol. 2, pp. 139–50.

House of Commons (2000), *Select Committee on Health: Fourth Report*. London: HMSO. (www.parliament.the-stationery-office.co.uk)

Howells, K., Day, A., Bubner, S., Jauncey, S., Williamson, P., Parker, A. and Heseltine, K. (2002), *Anger Management and Violence Prevention: Improving Effectiveness*. Trends and Issues in Crime and Criminal Justice, No. 227. Canberra: Australian Institute of Criminology.

Howells, K. and Hollin, C.R. (eds) (1989), *Clinical Approaches to Violence*. Chichester: Wiley.

Howitt, D. (1998), *Crime, the Media and the Law*. Chichester: Wiley.

HSE (2000), *Health and Safety Statistics 1999/2000*. London: HMSO.

HSE (2001), *Health and Safety Statistics 2000/2001*. London: HMSO.

HSE (2003), *Statistics of Fatal Injuries to Workers 2001/02*. London: Health and Safety Executive. (www.hse.gov.uk/statistics)

Huesmann, L.R. (1997), 'Observational Learning of Violent Behaviour', in A. Raine, P.A. Brennan, D. Farrington and S.A. Mednick (eds), *Biosocial Bases of Violence*. London: Plenum.

Huesmann, L.R. and Eron, L. (1989), 'Individual Differences and the Trait of Aggression', *European Journal of Personality*, Vol. 3, pp. 95–106.

Huff-Corzine, L., Corzine, J. and Moore, D.C. (1991), 'Deadly Connections: Culture, Poverty and the Direction of Lethal Violence', *Social Forces*, Vol. 69, pp. 715–32.

Hughes, G. (1998), *Understanding Crime Prevention: Social Control, Risk and Late Modernity*. Buckingham: Open University Press.

Hughes, G. (2001), 'Crime Prevention', in E. McLaughlin and J. Muncie (eds), *The Sage Dictionary of Criminology*. London: Sage.

Hughes, G. and Langan, M. (2001), 'Good or Bad Business?: Explaining Corporate and Organized Crime', in J. Muncie and E. McLaughlin (eds), *The Problem of Crime* (2nd edition). London: Sage in association with The Open University. (pp. 239–82).

Hutchings, B. and Mednick, S.A. (1977), 'Criminality in Adoptees and their Adoptive and Biological Parents: A Pilot Study', in S.A. Mednick and K.O. Christensen (eds), *Biosocial Bases of Criminal Behaviour*. New York: Gardner.

Hyams, E. (1975), *Terrorists and Terrorism*. London: Aldine.

Innes, M. (1999a), 'The Media as an Investigative Resource in Murder Enquiries'. *British Journal of Criminology*, Vol. 39/2, pp. 269–82.

Innes, M. (1999b), 'Beyond the Macpherson Report: Managing Murder Inquiries in Context', *Sociological Research Online*, 4/1. (http://www.socresonline.org.uk/socresonline/4/lawrence/innes.html)

Innes, M. (2001), '"Crimewatching": Homicide Investigations in the Age of Information', *Criminal Justice Matters*, Vol. 43, pp. 42–3.

Innes, M. (2002), 'The "Process Structures" of Police Homicide Investigations', *British Journal of Criminology*, Vol. 42/4, pp. 669–88.

Innes, M. (2003), *Investigating Murder: Detective Work and the Police Response to Criminal Homicide*. Oxford: Oxford University Press.

International Commission of Jurists (1996), *Administration of the Death Penalty in the USA: Report of a Mission*. Geneva: United Nations.

Irving, B. and Dunninghan, C. (1993), *Human Factors in the Quality Control of CID Investigations*. Commission on Criminal Justice Research Study No. 21. London: HMSO.

Jackson, D. (1995), *Destroying the Baby in Themselves: Why Did The Two Boys Kill James Bulger?* Nottingham: Mushroom.

Jackson, J. (1999), 'Trial Procedures', in C. Walker and L. Starmer (eds), *Miscarriages of Justice: A Review of Justice in Error*. London: Blackstone.

Jackson, M. (2002), *Infanticide: Historical Perspectives on Child Murder and Concealment, 1550–2000*. Aldershot: Ashgate.

Jacobs, P.A., Brunton, M. and Melville, M.M. (1965), 'Aggressive Behaviour, Mental Subnormality and the XYY Male', *Nature*, Vol. 208, pp. 1351–64.

James, A. and Jenks, C. (1996), 'Public Perceptions of Childhood Criminality', *The British Journal of Sociology*, Vol. 47, pp. 315–31.

Jarvik, L.F., Klodin, V. and Matsyama, S.S. (1973), 'Human Aggression and the Extra Y Chromosome', *American Psychologist*, Vol. 28, pp. 674–82.

Jasanoff, S. (1995), *Science at the Bar*. Cambridge, MA: Harvard University Press.

Jason-Lloyd, L. (2000), *An Introduction to Policing and Police Powers*. London: Cavendish.

Jayawant, S., Rawlinson, A., Gibbon, F., Price, J., Schulte, J., Sharples, P., Sibert, J.R. and Kemp, A.M. (1998), 'Subdural Haemorrhages in Infants: Population Based Study', *British Medical Journal*, Vol. 317, pp. 1558–61.

Jefferson, M. (1999), *Criminal Law* (4th edition). London: Pearson Education.

Jefferson, T. (1989), 'On Men and Masculinity', *Changes*, Vol. 7, pp. 124–8.

Jefferson, T. (1994), 'Theorising Masculine Subjectivity', in T. Newburn and E.A. Stanko (eds), *Just Boys Doing Business? Men, Masculinities and Crime*. London: Routledge.

Jefferson, T. (1996), 'Introduction', in *British Journal of Criminology*, Special Issue, Vol. 36/3, pp. 337–47.

Jefferson, T. (1997), 'Masculinities and Crime', in M. Maguire, R. Morgan and R. Reiner (eds), *The Oxford Handbook of Criminology* (2nd edition). Oxford: Clarendon.

Jenkins, P. (1988), 'Serial Murder in England 1940–1985', *Journal of Criminal Justice*, Vol. 16, pp. 1–15.

Jenkins, P. (1991), 'Changing Perceptions of Serial Murder in Contemporary England', *Journal of Contemporary Criminal Justice*, Vol. 7/4, pp. 210–231.

Jenkins, P. (1994), *Using Murder: The Social Construction of Serial Homicide*. New York: Aldine de Gruyter.

Jensen, V. (2001), *Why Women Kill: Homicide and Gender Equality*. London: Lynne Reiner.

Jesse, F.T. (1952), *Murder and its Motives*. London: Harrap.

Jones, S. (2000), *Understanding Violent Crime*. Buckingham: Open University Press.

Jones, T., Maclean, B. and Young, T. (1986), *The Islington Crime Survey*. Aldershot: Gower.

Jowett, C. (2001), 'Lies, Damned Lies and DNA Statistics: DNA Match Testing, Bayes' Theorem and the Criminal Courts', *Medicine Science and the Law*, Vol. 41/3, pp. 194–205.

Jurik, N.C. and Gregware, P. (1992), 'A Method for Murder: The Study of Homicides by Women', *Perspectives on Social Problems*, Vol. 4, pp. 179–201.

Jurik, N.C. and Winn, R. (1990), 'Gender and Homicide: A Comparison of Men and Women who Kill', *Violence and Victims*, Vol. 5, pp. 227–42.

Kakar, S. (1998), 'Delinquency Prevention through Family and Neighborhood Empowerment', *Studies on Crime and Crime Prevention*, Vol. 7/1, pp. 107–125.

Kanarek, R.B. (1994), 'Nutrition and Violent Behaviour', in A.J. Reiss (ed.), *Understanding and Preventing Violence: Volume 2 Biobehavioural Influences*. Washington, DC: National Academy Press.

Karmen, A. (1984), *Crime Victims: An Introduction to Victimology*. Pacific Grove, CA: Brooks/Cole.

Katz, J. (1988), *The Seductions of Crime: the Moral and Sensual Attractions of Doing Evil*. New York: Basic Books.

Keeney, B.T. (1995), 'Serial Murder: A More Accurate and Inclusive Definition', *International Journal of Offender Therapy and Comparative Criminology*, Vol. 39 (Winter), pp. 298–306.

Kemshall, H. (2001), *Risk Assessment and Management of Known Sexual and Violent Offenders: A Review of Current Issues*. Police Research Series Paper 140. London: Home Office.

Kershaw, C., Budd, T., Kinshott, G., Mattinson, J., Mayhew, P. and Myhill, A. (2000), *The 2000 British Crime Survey*. Home Office Statistical Bulletin 18/00. London: Home Office.

Kiger, K. (1990), 'The Darker Figure of Crime: The Serial Murder Enigma', in S.A. Egger (ed.), *Serial Murder: An Elusive Phenomenon*. London: Praeger.

Kleck, G. (1991), *Point Blank: Guns and Violence in America*. New York: Aldine de Gruyter.

Klee, R. (1999), *Scientific Enquiry: Readings in the Philosophy of Science*. Oxford: Oxford University Press.

Knight, B. (1997), *Simpson's Forensic Medicine* (11th edition). London: Arnold.

Knorr-Cetina, K. (1980), *The Manufacture of Knowledge*. Oxford: Pergamon.

Korbin, J.E. (1986), 'Childhood Histories of Women Imprisoned for Fatal Child Maltreatment', *Child Abuse and Neglect*, Vol. 10, pp. 331–8.

Korbin, J.E. (1987), 'Incarcerated Mothers Perceptions and Interpretations of their Fatally Maltreated Children', *Child Abuse and Neglect*, Vol. 11, pp. 397–407.

Kordvani, A.H. (2002), 'Hegemonic Masculinity, Domination and Violence Against Women'. Paper Presented to the *Expanding our Horizons Conference: Understanding the Complexities of Violence Against Women*. University of Sydney, Australia, 18–22 February.

Kovac, C. (1999), 'Incubators in Hungarian Hospital Lobbies Allow Babies to be Abandoned More Safely', *British Medical Journal*, Vol. 319, p. 214.

Kowalski, G.S. and Petee, T.A. (1991), 'Sunbelt Effects on Homicide Rates', *Sociology and Social Research*, Vol. 75, pp. 73–9.

Kposowa, A.J., Harrison, B.M. and Breault, K.D. (1995), 'Reassessing the Structural Covariates of Violent and Property Crimes in the USA: A County Level Analysis', *British Journal of Sociology*, Vol. 46/1, pp. 79–105.

Kretschmer, E. (1925), *Physique and Character* (trans. W.J.H. Sprott). New York: Harcourt, Brace.

Kunz, J. and Bahr, S.J. (1996), 'A Profile of Parental Homicide against Children', *Journal of Family Violence*, Vol. 11/4, pp. 347–62.

Lacey, N. (2002), 'Legal Constructions of Crime', in M. Maguire, R. Moran and R. Reiner (eds), *The Oxford Handbook of Criminology* (3rd edition). Oxford: Oxford University Press.

Lacey, N. and Wells, C. (1998), *Reconstructing Criminal Law: Texts and Materials* (2nd edition). London: Butterworth.

Lambie, I. (2001), 'Mothers who Kill: The Crime of Infanticide', *International Journal of Law and Psychiatry*, Vol. 24, pp. 71–80.

Land, K.C., McCall, P.L. and Cohen, L.E. (1990), 'Structural Covariates of Homicide Rates: Are There Any Invariances Across Time and Space?', *American Journal of Sociology*, Vol. 95, pp. 922–63.

Lander, E. (1989), 'DNA Fingerprinting on Trial', *Nature*, Vol. 339, pp. 501–505.

Lange, J. (1929), *Verbrechen als Shicksal: Studien an Kriminellen Zwillingen*, (trans. Charlotte Haldane, 1930), *Crime as Destiny: A Study of Criminal Twins*. New York: Boni.

Latour, B. (1985), *Science in Action*. Milton Keynes: Open University Press.

Lattimore, P.K., Trudeau, J., Riley, K.J., Leiter, J. and Edwards, S. (1997), *Homicide in Eight US Cities: Trends, Context and Policy Implications*. An Intramural Research Project. Washington, DC: United States Department of Justice.

Law Commission (1995), *Legislating the Criminal Code: The Year and a Day Rule in Homicide*. Report No. 230, London: HMSO.

Law Commission (1996), *Legislating the Criminal Code: Involuntary Manslaughter*. Report No. 237. London: HMSO.

Lea, S. and Auburn, T. (2001), 'The Social Construction of Rape in the Talk of a Convicted Rapist', *Feminism and Psychology*, Vol. 11/1, pp. 11–33.

Leary, J. (1976), 'Fists and Foul Mouths – Fights and Fight Stories in Contemporary Rural American Bars', *Journal of American Folklore*, Vol. 89, pp. 27–39.

Leather, P. and Lawrence, C. (1995), 'Perceiving Pub Violence: The Symbolic Influence of Social and Environmental Factors', *British Journal of Social Psychology*, Vol. 34, pp. 395–407.

Lester, D. (1995), *Serial Killers: The Insatiable Passion*. Philapdelphia, PA: Charles Press.

Levi, K. (1980), 'Homicide as Conflict Resolution', *Deviant Behaviour*, Vol 1/3–4, pp. 281–307.

Levi, M. (1997), 'Violent Crime', in M. Maguire., R. Morgan. and R. Reiner (eds), *The Oxford Handbook of Criminology* (2nd edition). Oxford: Clarendon.

Levi, M. and Maguire, M. (2002), 'Violent Crime', in M. Maguire, R. Morgan and R. Reiner (eds), *The Oxford Handbook of Criminology* (3rd edition). Oxford: Oxford University Press.

Levinson, D. (1989), *Family Violence in Cross-Cultural Perspective*. Beverley Hills: CA: Sage.

Lewis, C. (1992), 'Crime Statistics: Their Use and Misuse', *Social Trends*, Vol. 22, pp. 13–23.

Lewis, R., Dobash, R.E., Dobash, R.P. and Cavanagh, K. (2003), 'Researching Homicide', in R.M. Lee and E.A. Stanko (eds), *Researching Violence: Essays in Methodology and Measurement*. London: Routledge.

Leyton, E. (1986), *Compulsive Killers: The Story of Modern Multiple Murder*. New York: New York University Press.

Leyton, E. (1995) *Men of Blood: Murder in Modern England*. London: Constable.

Lilly, J.R., Cullen, F.T. and Ball, R.A. (1995), *Criminological Theory: Context and Consequences*. London: Sage.

Lindquist, P. (1986), 'Criminal Homicide in Northern Sweden, 1970–1981 – Alcohol Intoxification, Alcohol Abuse and Mental Disease', *International Journal of Law and Psychiatry*, Vol. 8, pp 19–37.

Linnoila, M. and Virkunnen, M. (1992), 'Aggression, Suicidality and Serotonin', *Journal of Clinical Psychiatry*, Vol. 53, pp. 46–51.

Linnoila, M., Virkkunen, M., Roy, A. and Potter, W.Z. (1990), 'Monoamines, Glucose Metabolism and Impulse Control', in H.M. Van Praag, R. Plitchik and A. Apter (eds), *Violence and Suicidality: Perspectives in Clinical and Psychobiological Research*. New York: Brunner/Mazel.

Locard, E. (1920), *L' enquete Criminelle et les Methodes Scientifique*. Paris: Ernest Flammarion.

Loftin, C. and Hill, R.H. (1974), 'Regional Subculture and Homicide: An Examination of the Gastil-Hackney Thesis', *American Sociological Review*, Vol. 39, pp. 714–24.

Logan, J.R. and Messner, S.F. (1987), 'Racial Residential Segregation and Suburban Violent Crime', *Social Science Quarterly*, Vol. 68, pp. 510–527.

Lombroso, C. (1911), *Crime: Its Causes and Remedies*. Boston, MA: Little Brown.

Lucas, B. (1988), *Project Brahms: A Qualitative Study of Drink Related Violence*. Unpublished paper prepared for the Home Office by Questel Ltd.

Luckenbill, D.F. (1977), 'Criminal Homicide as a Situated Transaction', *Social Forces*, Vol. 25, pp..176–86.

Luckenbill, D.F. and Doyle, D.P. (1989), 'Structural Position and Violence: Developing a Cultural Explanation', *Criminology*, Vol. 27/3, pp. 419–35.

Lyons, H.A. and Harbinson, H.J. (1986), 'A Comparison of Political and Non-Political Murderers in Northern Ireland, 1974–1984', *Medicine, Science and the Law*, Vol. 6/3, pp. 193–8.

McCaghy, C.H. and Chernkovich, S.A. (1987), *Crime in American Society*. New York: Macmillan.

McConville, M., Sanders, A. and Leng, R. (1991), *The Case for the Prosecution*. London: Routledge.

McFarlane, J.M., Campbell, J.C., Wiot, S., Sachs, C., Ulrich, Y. and Xu, X. (1999), 'Stalking and Intimate Partner Femicide', *Homicide Studies*, Vol. 3/4, pp. 300–317.

McGurk, B.J. and McGurk, R.E. (1979), 'Personality Types among Prisoners and Prison Officers: An Investigation of Megargee's Theory of Control', *British Journal of Criminology*, Vol. 19/1, pp. 31–49.

McHugh, M. and Thompson, C. (1991), *The Role of Alcohol in the Commission of Crimes of Violence*. Unpublished paper presented to the British Criminology Conference, University of York, July.

McLaughlin, E. and Muncie, J. (2001), *The Sage Dictionary of Criminology*. London: Sage.

MacCulloch, M.J., Snowden, P.R., Wood, P.J.W. and Mills, H.E. (1983), 'Sadistic Fantasy, Sadistic Behaviour and Offending', *British Journal of Psychiatry*, Vol. 143, pp. 20–29.

Mackay, R.D. (1993), 'The Consequences of Killing Very Young Children', *Criminal Law Review*, January, pp. 21–30.

Mackay, R.D. (2000), 'Diminished Responsibility and Mentally Disordered Killers', in A. Ashworth and B. Mitchell (eds), *Rethinking English Homicide Law*. Oxford: Oxford University Press.

MacMillan, H.L. and Thomas, B.H. (1993), 'Public Health Nurse Home Visitation for the Tertiary Prevention of Child Maltreatment: Results of a Pilot Study', *Canadian Journal of Psychiatry*, Vol. 38/6, pp. 436–42.

Macpherson, W. (1999), *The Stephen Lawrence Inquiry*. Report of an Inquiry by Sir William Macpherson of Cluny. London: Home Office. (www.official-documents.co.uk/document/cm42/4262/4262.htm)

Maguire, M. and Nettleton, H. (2003), *Reducing Alcohol-Related Violence and Disorder: An Evaluation of the 'TASC' Project*. Home Office Research Study 265. London: Home Office.

Maguire, M. and Norris, C. (1992) *The Conduct and Supervision of Criminal Investigation*. Royal Commission on Criminal Justice Research Study No. 5. London: HMSO.

Maier-Katkin, D. and Ogle, R.S. (1993), 'A Rational for Infanticide Laws', *The Criminal Law Review*, December, pp. 903–914.

Mann, C.R. (1996), *When Women Kill*. New York: State University of New York Press.

Marongui, P. and Newman, G. (1987), *Vengeance*. Totowa, NJ: Rowman and Littlefield.

Marks, M.N. (1996), 'Characteristics and Causes of Infanticide in Britain', *International Review of Psychiatry*, Vol. 8, pp. 99–106.

Marks, M.N. and Kumar, R. (1993), 'Infanticide in England and Wales', *Medicine, Science and the Law*, Vol. 33/4, pp. 329–39.

Martin, D. (1983), *Battered Wives*. New York: Pocket Books.

Matthews, R. and Young, J. (1986), 'Editor's Introduction', in R. Matthews and J. Young (eds), *Confronting Crime*. London: Sage.

Mattinson, J. (2001), *Stranger and Acquaintance Violence: Practice Messages from the British Crime Survey*. Briefing Note 7/01. London: Home Office.

Matza, D. (1964), *Delinquency and Drift*. London: Wiley.

Mawby, R. (1999), 'Visibility, Transparency and Police Media Relationships', *Policing and Society*, Vol. 9, pp. 263–86.

Mawby, R. and Walklate, S. (1994), *Critical Victimology*. London: Sage.

Mawson, A.R. and Jacobs, K.W. (1978), 'Corn Consumption, Tryptophan and Cross-National Homicide Rates', *Journal of Orthomolecular Psychiatry*, Vol. 7/4, pp. 227–30.

Maxfield, M.G. (1989), 'Circumstances in Supplementary Homicide Reports: Variety and Validity', *Criminology*, Vol. 27/4, pp. 671–95.

May, H. (1999), 'Who Killed Whom?: Victimization and Culpability in the Social Construction of Murder', *British Journal of Sociology*, Vol. 50/3, pp. 489–506.

Meadow, R. (1999), 'Unnatural Sudden Infant Death', *Archives of Disease in Childhood*, Vol. 80, pp. 7–14.

Mednick, S.A., Gabrielli, T.W.F. and Hutchings, B. (1984), 'Genetic Influences on Criminal Convictions: Evidence from an Adoption Cohort', *Science*, Vol. 224, pp. 891–4.

Mednick, S.A., Moffitt, T.E. and Stack, S. (eds) (1987), *The Causes of Crime: New Biological Approaches*. Cambridge: Cambridge University Press.

Megargee, E.I. (1966), 'Undercontrolled and Overcontrolled Personality Types in Extreme Antisocial Aggression', *Psychological Monographs*, Vol. 80/3, pp. 1–29.

Megargee, E.I. (1972), *The Psychology of Violence and Aggression*. Morristown, NJ: General Learning.

Megargee, E.I. (1982), 'Psychological Determinants and Correlates of Criminal Violence', in M. Wolfgang and N. Weiner (eds), *Criminal Violence*. London: Sage.

Mendelsohn, B. (1956), 'Une nouvelle branche de la science bio-psycho-sociale: Victimologie', *Revue Internationale de Criminology et de Police Technique*, Vol. 10, pp. 31.

Menzies, R.J. and Webster, C.D. (1989), 'Mental Disorder and Violent Crime', in N.A. Weiner and M.E. Wolfgang (eds), *Pathways to Criminal Violence*. London: Sage.

Mercy, J.A. and Hammond, W.R. (1999), 'Combining Action and Analysis to Prevent Homicide: A Public Health Perspective', in M.D. Smith and M.A. Zahn (eds), *Homicide: A Sourcebook of Social Research*. London: Sage.

Merton, R.K. (1938), 'Social Structure and Anomie', *American Sociological Review*, Vol. 3, pp. 672–82.

Messerschmidt, J. (1986), *Capitalism, Patriarchy and Crime: Towards a Socialist Feminist Criminology*. Totowa, NJ: Rowan and Littlefield.

Messerschmidt, J. (1993), *Masculinities and Crime*. Lanham, MD: Rowman and Littlefield.

Messerschmidt, J. (1995), 'From Patriarchy to Gender: Feminist Theory, Criminology and the Challenge of Diversity', in N. Rafter and F. Heidensohn (eds), *International Feminist Perspectives in Criminology*. Buckingham: Open University Press.

Messerschmidt, J. (1997), *Crime as Structured Action: Gender, Race, Class and Crime in the Making*. London: Sage.

Messner, S.F., Raffalovich, L.E. and McMillan, R. (2001), 'Economic Deprivation and Changes in Homicide Arrest Rates for White and Black Youths, 1967–1998: A National Time Series Analysis', *Criminology*, Vol. 39/3, pp. 591–614.

Messner, S.F. and Rosenfeld, R. (1999), 'Social Structure and Homicide', in M.D. Smith and M.A. Zahn (eds), *Homicide: A Sourcebook of Social Research*. London: Sage.

Messner, S.F. and Tardiff, K. (1985), 'The Social Ecology of Urban Homicide: An Application of the "Routine Activities" Approach', *Criminology*, Vol. 23/2, pp. 241–67.

Michalowski, R.J. (1975), 'Violence in the Road: The Crime of Vehicular Homicide', *Journal of Research in Crime and Delinquency*, Vol. 12/1, pp. 30–43.

Miethe, T.D. and Meier, R.F. (1994), *Crime and its Social Context: Towards an Integrated Theory of Offenders, Victims and Situations*. Albany, NY: State University of New York Press.

Milgram, S. (1974), *Obedience to Authority: An Experimental View*. New York: Harper Row.

Miller, J. (2001), *One of the Guys: Girls, Gangs and Gender*. Oxford: Oxford University Press.

Miller, W.B. (1958), 'Lower Class Culture as a Generating Milieu of Gang Delinquency', *Journal of Social Issues*, Vol. 14/3, pp. 5–19.

Millington, N. and Smith, N. (1999), *Investigating Suspicious Infant Deaths: A Literature Review*. Unpublished Briefing Note.

Milne, R. and Bull, R. (1999), *Investigative Interviewing: Psychology and Practice*. Chichester: Wiley.

Milovanovic, D. (1996), 'Postmodern Criminology', *Justice Quarterly*, Vol. 13/4, pp. 567–609.

Milovanovic, D. (ed.) (1997), *Chaos, Criminology and Social Justice: The New Orderly (Dis)Order*. Westport, CT: Prager.

Milovanovic, D. (2001a), 'Chaos Theory', in E. McLaughlin and J. Muncie (eds), *The Sage Dictionary of Criminology*. London: Sage.

Milovanovic, D. (2001b), 'Postmodernism', in E. McLaughlin and J. Muncie (eds), *The Sage Dictionary of Criminology*. London: Sage.

Mirrlees-Black, C. (1995), *Estimating the Extent of Domestic Violence: Findings from the 1992 BCS*. Home Office Research Bulletin, 37, pp. 1–10. London: Home Office Research and Statistics Directorate.

Mirrlees-Black, C., Budd, T., Partridge, S. and Mayhew, P. (1998), *The 1998 British Crime Survey England and Wales*. Issue 21/98. London: Home Office.

Miscarriage of Justice Organisation (MOJO) (2002), *Are Miscarriages of Justice being Remedied? Is the Court of Appeal Dispensing Fair Justice? Can Miscarriages of Justice be*

Prevented? A MOJO Critical Analysis and Review of the Efficiency of the Criminal Cases Review Commission and the Criminal Court of Appeal. Birmingham: MOJO.

Mitchell, B. (1990), *Murder and Penal Policy*. London: Macmillan.

Mitchell, B. (1991), 'Distinguishing Between Murder and Manslaughter', *New Law Journal*, Vol.141, pp. 935–7.

Mitchell, E.W. (1997), *The Aetiology of Serial Murder: Towards an Integrated Model*. Unpublished MPhil thesis, University of Cambridge.

Moir, A. and Jessel, D. (1995), *A Mind to Crime: The Controversial Link between the Mind and Criminal Behaviour*. London: Michael Joseph.

Molof, M.J. (1967), *Differences Between Assaultive and Non-Assaultive Juvenile Offenders in the California Youth Authority*. Research Report Number 51, Division of Research, State of California, Department of Youth Authority.

Monahan, J. (1981) *Predicting Violent Behaviour*. Beverly Hills, CA: Sage.

Monahan, J. (1997) 'Clinical and Actuarial Predictions of Violence', in D. Faigman, D. Kaye, M. Saks and J. Sanders (eds), *West's Companion to Scientific Evidence*. St Pauls, MN: West.

Monahan, J. and Steadman, H. (eds) (1994), *Violence and Mental Disorder: Developments in Risk Assessment*. Chicago, IL: University of Chicago Press.

Monahan, J., Steadman, H., Silver, E., Appelbaum, P., Robbins, P., Mulvey, E., Roth, L., Grisso, T. and Banks, S. (2001), *Rethinking Risk Assessment: The Macarthur Study of Mental Disorder and Violence*. Oxford: Oxford University Press.

Mones, P. (1991), *When a Child Kills*. London: Pocket Books.

Moracco, K., Runyan, C.W. and Butts, J.D. (1998), 'Femicide in North Carolina, 1991–1993: A Statewide Study of Patterns and Precursors', *Homicide Studies*, Vol. 2/4: 422–46.

Morgan, D. (1992), *Discovering Men*. London: Routledge.

Morley, R. (1995), 'The Sociologist's View: More Convictions Won't Help Victims of Domestic Violence', *British Medical Journal*, Vol. 311, pp. 1618–19.

Morris, A. (1987), *Women, Crime and Criminal Justice*. Oxford: Basil Blackwell.

Morris, T. (1966), *The Criminal Area*. New York: Humanities Press.

Morris, T. and Blom-Cooper, L. (1964), *A Calendar of Murder: Criminal Homicide in England Since 1957*. London: Michael Joseph.

Morrisey, B. (2003), *When Women Kill: Questions of Agency and Subjectivity*. London: Routledge.

Morrison, W. (1995), *Theoretical Criminology*. London: Cavendish.

Moseley, K.L. (1986), 'The History of Infanticide in Western Society', *Issues in Law and Medicine*, Vol. 1, pp. 345–61.

Mosher, J. and Jerrigan, D. (2001), 'Making the Link: A Public Health Approach to Preventing Alcohol-related Violence and Crime', *Journal of Substance Use*, Vol. 6/4, pp. 273–92.

Motz, A. (2001), *The Psychology of Female Violence: Crimes Against the Body*. Hove: Brunner-Routledge.

Mouzos, J. (1999a), *Mental Disorder and Homicide in Australia*, Trends and Issues in Crime and Criminal Justice, Vol. 133. Canberra: Australian Institute of Criminology.

Mouzos, J. (1999b), *Femicide: The Killing of Women in Australia 1989–1998*. Research and Public Policy Series No. 18. Canberra: Australian Institute of Criminology. (www.aic.gov.au/publications/rpp/18/full_report.pdf)

Mouzos, J. (1999c), *Femicide: An Overview of Major Findings*. Report No. 124: Trends and Issues in Crime and Criminal Justice. Canberra: Australian Institute of Criminology. (www.aic.gov.au/publications/tandi/ti124.pdf)

Mouzos, J. (2000), *Homicidal Encounters: A Study of Homicide in Australia, 1989–1999*, Australian Institute of Criminology Research and Public Policy Series No. 28. Canberra: Australian Institute of Criminology.

Mouzos, J. (2001), *Homicide in Australia: 1999–2000*. Report No. 187: Trends and Issues in Crime and Criminal Justice. Canberra: Australian Institute of Criminology. (www.aic.gov.au/publications/tandi/ti187.pdf)

Mouzos, J. (2003), *Homicide in Australia: 2001–2002*. Report No. 46: National Homicide Monitoring Program (NHMP) annual report. Canberra: Australian Institute of Criminology.

Mowat, F. (1951), *The People of the Deer*. New York: Pyramid.

Moxon, D. (2001), *A Review of Information on Homicide: A Discussion Document.* London: Home Office.

Muncer, S., Campbell, A., Jervis, V. and Lewis, R. (2001), 'Ladettes', Social Representations and Aggression, *Sex Roles,* Vol. 44, pp. 33–44.

Muncie, J. (1996), *Reader Guide 1: The Search for the Causes of Crime.* Milton Keynes: The Open University.

Mullender, A. and Burton, S. (2000), 'Reducing Domestic Violence ... What Works? Perpetrator Programmes'. *Policing and Reducing Crime Unit Briefing Notes.* London: Home Office.

Munday, R. (1995), 'Section 78 of PACE and Improperly Obtained DNA Evidence', *Justice of the Peace and Local Government Law,* Vol. 159/40, pp. 663–8.

Murray, D.J. (1989), *Review of Research on Re-Offending of Mentally Disordered Offenders,* Research and Planning Unit Paper 55. London: Home Office.

National Missing Persons Helpline Newsletter (2002), *Missing* (Spring). London: NMPH.

NCIS (2002), *UK Threat Assessment 2002: The Threat from Serious and Organised Crime.* London: National Criminal Intelligence Service.

Needleman, H.L., Riess, J.A., Tobin, M.J., Biesecker, G.E. and Greenhouse, J.B. (1996), 'Bone Lead Levels and Delinquent Behaviour', *JAMA,* Vol. 275, pp. 363–9.

Nelken, D. (1997), 'White-Collar Crime', in M. Maguire, R. Morgan and R. Reiner (eds), *The Oxford Handbook of Criminology* (2nd edition). Oxford: Oxford University Press.

Nelken, D. (2002), 'White-Collar Crime', in M. Maguire, R. Morgan and R. Reiner (eds), *The Oxford Handbook of Criminology* (3rd edition). Oxford: Oxford University Press.

Newburn, T. and Stanko, B. (1994), *Just Boys Doing Business.* London: Routledge.

Newiss, G. (1999), *Missing Presumed ... ? The Police Response to Missing Persons.* Police Research Series Paper 114. London: Home Office.

Nicolson, D. and Sanghvi, R. (1993), 'Battered Women and Provocation: the Implications of R. V. Ahluwalia', *Criminal Law Review,* October, pp. 728–38.

Niehoff, D. (1999), *The Biology of Violence.* New York: Free Press.

Norris, J. (1988), *Serial Killers: The Growing Menace.* New York: Doubleday.

Northern Ireland Office (2002), *Criminal Statistics Northern Ireland, 2001/02.* Statistics and Research Branch. Belfast: Northern Ireland Office.

NSPCC (2000), 'Powerful TV Ads Launch Campaign to Protect Babies', NSPCC website www.nspcc.org.uk/html/home/informationresources/powerfultvadslaunchcampaigntoprotectbabies.htm, 03/05/00.

NSPCC (2001), *Out of Sight: NSPCC Report on Child Deaths from Abuse 1973 to 2000* (2nd edition). London: NSPCC.

O'Boyle, G. (2002), 'Theories of Justification and Political Violence: Examples from Four Groups', *Terrorism and Political Violence,* Vol. 14/2, pp. 23–46.

O'Carroll, P.W. and Mercy, J.A. (1989), 'Regional Variation in Homicide Rates: Why is the West so Violent?', *Violence and Victims,* Vol. 4/1, pp. 17–25.

O'Keefe, M. (1997), 'Incarcerated Battered Women: A Comparison of Battered Women who Killed their Abusers and those Incarcerated for other Offences', *Journal of Family Violence,* Vol. 12, pp. 1–19.

O'Leary, B. and McGarry, J. (1996), *The Politics of Antagonism: Understanding Northern Ireland* (2nd edition). London: Athlone.

Oates, K. (1982), *Child Abuse: A Community Concern.* Sydney: Butterworth.

Oberman, M. (1996), 'Mothers who Kill: Coming to Terms with Modern American Infanticide', *American Criminal Law Review,* Vol. 34, pp. 1–110.

Ogle, R.S. and Jacobs, S. (2002), *Self-Defense and Battered Women Who Kill.* London: Praeger.

Olds, D.L., Henderson, C.R., Chamberlin, R. and Tatelbaum, R. (1986), 'Preventing Child Abuse and Neglect: A Randomized Trial of Nurse Home Visitation', *Pediatrics,* Vol. 78/1, pp. 65–78.

Olweus, D., Matterson, A., Shalling, D. and Low, H. (1988), 'Circulating Testosterone Levels and Aggression in Adolescent Males: A Causal Analysis', *Psychosomatic Medicine,* Vol. 50, pp. 261–72.

OPCS (2001) *Mortality Statistics: Injury and Poisoning.* Series DH4, No. 24. London: HMSO.

Padfield, N. (1998), *Criminal Law*. London: Butterworth.

Parker, K.E. and Pruitt, M.V. (2000), 'How the West Was One: Explaining the Similarities in Race-Specific Homicide Rates in the West and South', *Social Forces*, Vol. 78/4, pp. 1483–1508.

Parker, K.F. and McCall, P.L. (1997), 'Adding Another Piece to the Inequality-Homicide Puzzle: The Impact of Structural Inequality on Racially Disaggregated Homicide Rates', *Homicide Studies*, Vol. 1/1, pp. 35–60.

Parker, K.F. McCall, P.K. and Land, K.C. (1999), 'Determining Social-Structural Predictors of Homicide: Units of Analysis and Related Methodological Concerns', in M.D. Smith and M.A. Zahn (eds), *Homicide: A Sourcebook of Social Research*. London: Sage.

Parker, R.N. and Rebhun, L.A. (1995), *Alcohol and Homicide: A Deadly Combination of Two American Traditions*. Albany, NY: State University of New York Press.

Parker, R.N. and Smith, M.D. (1979), 'Deterrence, Poverty and Type of Homicide', *American Journal of Sociology*, Vol. 85, pp. 614–24.

Passas, N. (1990), 'Anomie and Corporate Deviance', *Contemporary Crises*, Vol. 14, pp. 157–78.

Patterson, E.B. (1991), 'Poverty, Income Inequality and Community Crime Rates', *Criminology*, Vol. 29, pp. 755–76.

Pearson, J. (2002), *The Cult of Violence*. London: Orion.

Pease, K. (1997), 'Crime Prevention', in M. Maguire, R. Morgan and R. Reiner (eds), *The Oxford Handbook of Criminology* (2nd edition). Oxford: Oxford University Press.

Peay, J. (1997), 'Mentally Disordered Offenders', in M. Maguire, R. Morgan and R. Reiner (eds), *The Oxford Handbook of Criminology* (2nd edition). Oxford: Oxford University Press.

Peterson, E.S.L. (1999), 'Murder as Self-Help: Women and Intimate Partner Homicide', *Homicide Studies*, Vol. 3/1, pp. 30–46.

Peterson, R.D. and Krivo, L.J. (1993), 'Racial Segregation and Black Urban Homicide', *Social Forces*, Vol. 71, pp. 1001–1026.

Police Service Northern Ireland (PSNI) (2002), *Recorded Crime in Northern Ireland, 2001/2002*. Central Statistics Unit. Northern Ireland: PSNI.

Police Service Northern Ireland (PSNI) (2003a), *Recorded Crime in Northern Ireland, 2002/2003*. Central Statistics Unit. Northern Ireland: PSNI.

Police Service Northern Ireland (PSNI), (2003b), *Deaths Due to the Security Situation in Northern Ireland, 1969–2003*. Central Statistics Unit. Northern Ireland: PSNI.

Police Service Northern Ireland (PSNI), (2003c), *Casualties as a Result of Paramilitary-Style Attacks, 1973–2003*. Central Statistics Unit. Northern Ireland: PSNI.

Police Service Northern Ireland (PSNI), (2003d), *Number of Persons Charged with Terrorist and Serious Public Order Offences, 1972–2003*. Central Statistics Unit. Northern Ireland: PSNI.

Police Service Northern Ireland (PSNI), (2003e), *Security-Related Incidents, 1969-2003*. Central Statistics Unit. Northern Ireland: PSNI.

Polk, K. (1991), 'Homicide: Women as Offenders', in P.W. Easteal. and S. McKillop (eds), *Women and the Law*, Proceedings of the Women and the Law Conference, Sydney, 24–26 September.

Polk, K. (1994a), *When Men Kill: Scenarios of Masculine Violence*. Cambridge: Cambridge University Press.

Polk, K. (1994b), 'Masculinity, Honour and Confrontational Homicide', in T. Newburn and E.A. Stanko (eds), *Just Boys doing the Business?* London: Routledge.

Polk, K. (1995), 'Lethal Violence as a Form of Masculine Conflict Resolution'. *The Australian and New Zealand Journal of Criminology*, Vol. 28/1, pp. 93–115.

Polk, K. (1997a), 'A Reexamination of the Concept of Victim-Precipitated Homicide', *Homicide Studies: An Interdisciplinary and International Journal*, Vol.1/2, pp. 141–68.

Polk, K. (1997b), When Men Kill: A Comparison of Everyday Homicide with Images of Media Violence'. Paper Presented at the Violence, Crime and the Entertainment Media Conference, Sydney, December.

Polk, K. (1998), 'Violence, Masculinity and Evolution: A Comment on Wilson and Daly', *Theoretical Criminology*, Vol. 2/4, pp. 461–9.

Polk, K. (1999), 'Males and Honour Contest Violence'. *Homicide Studies*, Vol. 3/1, pp. 6–29.

Polk, K. and Ranson, D. (1991), 'The Role of Gender in Intimate Homicide', *Australian and New Zealand Journal of Criminology*, Vol. 24, pp. 15–24.

Pollock, V., Mednick, S.A. and Gabrielli, W.E. (1983), 'Crime Causation: Biological Theories', in S.H. Kadish (ed.), *Encyclopedia of Crime and Justice*, Vol. 1. New York: Free Press.

Poole, M. (1993), 'The Spatial Distribution of Political Violence in Northern Ireland: An update to 1993', in A. O'Day (ed.), *Terrorism's Laboratory: The Case of Northern Ireland*, Aldershot: Dartmouth.

Portman Group (1998), *Keeping the Peace*. London: Working Solutions.

Prentky, R.A., Burgess, A.W., Rokous, F., Lee, A., Hartman, C., Ressler, R. and Douglas, J. (1989), 'The Presumptive Role of Fantasy in Serial Sexual Homicide', *American Journal of Psychiatry*, Vol. 146/7, pp. 887–91.

President's Commission (1986), *Report of the Presidential Commission on the Space Shuttle Challenger Accident*. Washington, DC: Government Printing Office.

Prins, H. (1986), *Dangerous Behaviour, the Law and Mental Disorder*. London: Tavistock.

Ptacek, J. (1988), 'Why do Men Batter their Wives?', in K. Yllö and M. Bograd (eds), *Feminist Perspectives on Wife Abuse*. Newbury Park, CA: Sage.

Punch, M. (1996), *Dirty Business: Exploring Corporate Misconduct*. London: Sage.

Purser, R.M. (1997) *Prevention Approaches to Alcohol-Related Crime: a Review of a Community-Based Initiative from a UK Midlands City*. Birmingham: Aquarius.

Putkonen, H., Collaner, J., Honkasalo, M.L. and Lonnqvist, J. (1998), 'Finnish Female Homicide Offenders 1982–1992', *Journal of Forensic Psychiatry*, Vol. 9/3, pp. 672–84.

Putkonen, H., Collander, J., Honkasalo, M.L. and Lonnqvist, J. (2001), 'Personality Disorders and Psychoses Form Two Distinct Subgroups of Homicide Among Female Offenders', *Journal of Forensic Psychiatry*, Vol. 12/2, pp. 300–312.

Quinn, S.E. (1998), *Criminal Law in Ireland*. Ireland: Irish Genealogy Press.

Radelet, M. and Pierce, G. (1985), 'Race and Prosecutorial Discretion in Homicide Cases', *Law and Society Review*, Vol. 19/4, pp. 918–27.

Radford, J. (1992), 'Introduction', in J. Radford and D.E.H. Russell (eds), *Femicide: The Politics of Woman Killing*. Buckingham: Open University Press.

Radford, L. (1993), 'Pleading for Time: Justice for Battered Women Who Kill', in H. Birch (ed.), *Moving Targets: Women, Murder and Representation*. London: Virago.

Radford, J. and Russell, D.E.H. (1992), *Femicide: The Politics of Woman Killing*. New York: Twayne.

Rafter, N.H. (1992), *Criminal Anthropology* (2nd edition). New York: Holt, Rinehart and Winston.

Raine, A. (1993), *The Psychopathology of Crime: Criminal Behaviour as a Clinical Disorder*. London: Academic Press.

Raine, A., Brennan, P.A., Farrington, D. and Mednick, S.A. (1997a), *Biosocial Bases of Violence*. London: Plenum.

Raine, A., Buchsbaum, M., LaCasse, L. (1997b), 'Brain Abnormalities in Murderers Indicated by Positron Emission Tomography', *Biological Psychiatry*, Vol. 42, pp. 495–508.

Raine, A., Buchsbaum, M., Stanely, J., Lottenberg, S., Abel, L. and Stoddard, J. (1994), 'Selective Reductions in Prefrontal Glucose Metabolism in Murderers Assessed with Positron Emission Tomography', *Biological Psychiatry*, Vol. 36/1, pp. 365–73.

Ramsay, M. (1990), *Lagerland Lost? An Experiment in Keeping Drinkers off the Streets in Central Coventry and Elsewhere*. Crime Prevention Unit Paper 22. London: Home Office.

Rappaport, R.G. (1988), 'The Serial and Mass Murderer: Patterns, Differentiation, Pathology', *American Journal of Forensic Psychiatry*, Vol. 9, pp. 38–48.

Redl, F. and Wineman, D. (1951), *Children Who Hate*. New York: Free Press.

Reed, J.S. (1982), *One South: An Ethnic Approach to Regional Culture*. Baton Rouge, LA: Louisiana State University Press.

Reid, S.T. (1979), *Crime and Criminology* (2nd edition). New York: Holt, Rinehart and Winston.

Reiner, R. (2000), *The Politics of the Police* (3rd edition). Oxford: Oxford University Press.

Reiner, R. (2002), 'Media Made Criminality: The Representation of Crime in the Mass Media', in M. Maguire, R. Morgan and R. Reiner (eds), *The Oxford Handbook of Criminology* (3rd edition). Oxford: Oxford University Press.

Reiss, A.J. (1994) (ed.), *Understanding and Preventing Violence: Volume 2 Biobehavioural Influences*. Washington, DC: National Academy Press.

Reiss, A.J. and Roth, J.A. (1993), *Understanding and Preventing Violence*. Washington, DC: National Academy Press.

Remy, J. (1990), 'Patriarchy and Fratriarchy as Forms of Androcracy', in J. Hearn and D. Morgan (eds), *Men, Masculinities and Social Theory*. London: Unwin and Hyman.

Resnick, P.J. (1972), 'Infanticide', in J.G. Howells (ed.), *Modern Perspectives in Psycho-Obstetrics*. Edinburgh: Oliver and Boyd.

Ressler, R., Burgess, A. and Douglas, J. (1988), *Sexual Homicide: Patterns and Motives*. New York: Lexington.

Richards, P. (1999), *Homicide Statistics*. Research Paper 99/56, London: House of Commons Library.

RIDDOR (1995), *The Reporting of Injuries, Diseases and Dangerous Occurrences Regulations*. London: HMSO.

Riedel, M. (1993), *Stranger Violence: A Theoretical Inquiry*. New York: Garland.

Ritsher, J. and Luckstead, A. (2000), 'What Do You Call Your Problem', *Psychiatric Rehabilitation Journal*, Vol. 23/4, pp 393–5.

RoadPeace (2001), *Towards Justice: RoadPeace's Response to the Government's Consultation Paper on Road Traffic Penalties*. London: RoadPeace.

Roberts, A.R. (1996), 'Battered Women who Kill: A Comparison Study of Incarcerated Participants with a Community Sample of Battered Women', *Journal of Family Violence*, Vol.11/3, pp. 291–304.

Roberts, I., Kramer, M. and Suissa, S. (1996), 'Does Home Visiting Prevent Childhood Injury? A Systematic Review of Randomised Controlled Trials', *British Medical Journal*, Vol. 312, pp. 29–33.

Roberts, S. (1983), 'Oppressed Group Behaviour: Implications for Nursing', *Advances in Nursing Science*, July, pp. 22–30.

Robertson, B. (1995), *Interpreting Evidence: Evaluating Forensic Science in the Courtroom*. Chichester: Wiley.

Rock, P. (1998), *After Homicide*. Oxford: Clarendon.

Rock, P. (2002), 'Sociological Theories of Crime', in M. Maguire, R. Morgan and R. Reiner (eds), *The Oxford Handbook of Criminology* (3rd edition). Oxford: Oxford University Press.

Rodriguez, S.F. and Smithey, M. (1999), Infant and Adult Homicide. Incompatibility of Predictive Models', *Homicide Studies*, Vol. 3/2, pp. 170–84.

Rosenfeld, R. (1997), 'Changing Relationships Between Men and Women: A Note on the Decline in Intimate Partner Homicide', *Homicide Studies*, Vol. 1/1, pp. 72–83.

Rosenfeld, R., Jacobs, B. and Wright, R. (2003), 'Snitching and the Code of the Streets', *British Journal of Criminology*, Vol. 43/2, pp. 291–309.

Rosenhahn, D. (1973), 'On Being Sane in Insane Places', *Science*, Vol. 179, pp 250–58.

Roshier, B. (1989), *Controlling Crime: The Classical Perspective in Criminology*. Milton Keynes: Open University Press.

ROSPA (2001), *Response to the Home Office and Department of Environment Transport and the Regions (DETR) Consultation Paper 'Road Traffic Penalties – A Consultation Paper'*. (www.rospa.co.uk/pdfs/road/consultation/sentencing.pdf)

Rossmo, D.K. (1999), 'Geographic Profiling', in J.L. Jackson and D.A. Bekerian (eds), *Offender Profiling: Theory, Research and Practice*. London: Wiley.

Rotter, J.B. (1954), *Social Learning and Clinical Psychology*. Englewood Cliffs, NJ: Prentice-Hall.

Rotton, J. and Frey, J. (1985), 'Air Pollution, Weather and Violent Crimes: Concomitant Time-Series Analysis of Archival Data', *Journal of Personality and Social Psychology*, Vol. 49, pp. 1207–1220.

Rowbotham, J., Stevenson, K. and Pegg, S. (2003), 'Children of Misfortune: Parallels in the Cases of Child Murderers Thompson and Venables, Barratt and Bradley', *The Howard Journal*, Vol. 42/2, pp. 107–122.

Rowe, D.C. (1990), 'Inherited Dispositions Towards Learning Delinquency and Criminal Behaviour: New Evidence', in L. Ellis and H. Hoffman (eds), *Crime in Biological, Social and Moral Context*. New York: Praeger.

Rowe, D.C. and Rogers, J.L. (1989), 'Behaviour Genetics, Adolescent Development and "d": Contributions and Issues', in G.R. Adams, R. Montemayor and T.P. Gullotta (eds), *Advances in Adolescent Development*. Beverley Hills, CA: Sage.

Royal Ulster Constabulary (RUC) (2000), *Homicide in Northern Ireland, 1987–1999*, Personal Communication, Central Statistics Unit.

Russell, D. and Harmes, R. (2001) (eds), *Femicide in Global Perspective*. London: Teachers College Press.

Sampson, R. (1992), 'Family Management and Child Development: Insights from Social DisorganisationTheory', in J. McCord (ed.), *Facts, Frameworks and Forecasts*. New Brunswick, NJ: Transaction.

Sampson, R. and Lauristen, J. (1990), 'Deviant Lifestyles, Proximity to Crime and the Offender-Victim Link in PersonalViolence', *Journal of Research in Crime and Delinquency*, Vol. 27, pp. 7–40.

Sampson, R. and Lauristen, J. (1994), 'ViolentVictimization and Offending: Individual-, Situational- and Community-Level Risk Factors', in A.J. Reiss and J.A. Roth (eds), *Understanding and Preventing Violence: Vol. 3, Social Influences*. Washington, DC: National Academy Press.

Samuels, A. (1995), 'Challenging DNA Evidence', *Justice of the Peace and Local Government Law*, Vol. 159/10, pp. 156.

Sanders, A. and Young, R. (2002), 'From Suspect to Trial', in M. Maguire, R. Morgan and R. Reiner (eds), *The Oxford Handbook of Criminology* (3rd edition). Oxford: Oxford University Press.

Sarbin, T.R. and Miller, J.E. (1970), 'Demonism Revisited: The XYY Chromosome Anomaly', *Issues in Criminology*, Vol. 5, pp. 199–218.

Schklar, J. and Diamond, S.S. (1999), 'Jurors Reactions to DNA Evidence: Errors and Expectancies', *Law and Human Behaviour*, Vol. 23/2, pp. 159–84.

Schneider, E.M. (2000), *Battered Women and Feminist Lawmaking*. New Haven, CT: Yale University Press.

Scott, P.D. (1973), 'Parents Who Kill Their Children', *Medicine, Science and Law*, Vol. 13, pp. 120–26.

Scottish Council on Crime (1975), *Crime and the Prevention of Crime*. London: HMSO.

Scottish Executive (1999), *Homicide in Scotland 1998*. Edinburgh: Scottish Executive.

Scottish Executive (2001), *Homicide in Scotland 2000*. Edinburgh: Scottish Executive.

Scottish Executive (2002), *Homicides in Scotland in 2001*. Edinburgh: Scottish Executive.

Segal, L. (1990), *Slow Motion: Changing Masculinities, Changing Men*. London: Virago.

Seidler, V.J. (1989), *Rediscovering Masculinity: Reason, Language and Sexuality*. New York: Routledge.

Sentamu, Rt Revd J., Blakey, D. and Nove, P. (2002), *The Damilola Taylor Murder Investigation Review: The Report of the Oversight Panel*. (www.met.police.uk/damilola/damilola.pdf)

Shah, S.A. and Roth, L.H. (1974), 'Biological and Psychological Factors in Criminality', in, D. Glaser (ed.), *Handbook of Criminology*. Chicago, IL: Rand McNally.

Shaw, C.R. and McKay, H.D. (1969), *Juvenile Delinquency and Urban Areas*. Chicago, IL: University of Chicago Press.

Sheldon, W.H. (1940), *The Varieties of Human Physique*. New York: Harper.

Shepherd, J.P. (1994), 'Prevention of Bar Glass Injuries', *British Medical Journal*, Vol. 308, pp. 932–3.

Shepherd, J.P. (1997), 'Injury Research Leads to a National Glass Replacement Initiative', *British Journal of Oral and Maxillofacial Surgery*, Vol. 35/6, pp. 454.

Shepherd, J.P. (1998), 'Tackling Violence: Interagency Procedures and Injury Surveillance are Urgently Needed', *British Medical Journal*, Vol. 316, pp. 879–80.

Sheridan, L., Davies, G.M. and Boon, J.C.W. (2001), 'The Course and Nature of Stalking: A Victim Perspective', *The Howard Journal of Criminal Justice*, Vol. 40, pp. 215–34.

Sherman, L.W. (1993), 'Preventing Homicide Through Trial and Error', in H. Strang and S.A. Gerull (eds), *Homicide: Patterns, Prevention and Control*. Australian Institute of Criminology Conference Proceedings. Canberra: AIC.

Sherman, L.W., Gartin, P.R. and Buerger, M.E. (1989), 'Hot Spots of Predatory Crime: Routine Activities and the Criminology of Place', *Criminology*, Vol. 27/1, pp. 27–55.

Sherman, L.W., Schmidt, J.D., Rogarn, D.P. and DeRiso, C. (1991), 'Predicting Domestic Homicide', in M. Steinman (ed.), *Woman Battering: Policy Responses*. Cincinnati, OH: Anderson.

Shihadeh, E.S. and Maume, M.O. (1997), 'Segregation and Crime: The Relationship Between Black Centralization and Urban Black Homicide', *Homicide Studies*, Vol. 1/3, pp. 254–80.

Shoemaker, D.J. (1996), *Theories of Delinquency: An Examination of Explanations of Delinquent Behaviour*. Oxford: Oxford University Press.

Shoham, S., Ben-David, S., Vadmani, R., Atar, J. and Fleming, S. (1973), 'The Cycles of Interaction in Violence', in S. Shoham (ed.), *Israel Studies in Criminology*, Vol. II, pp. 69–87. Jerusalem: Jerusalem Academic Press.

Showalter, C.R., Bonnie, R.J. and Roddy, V. (1980), 'The Spousal Homicide Syndrome', *International Journal of Law and Psychiatry*, Vol. 3, pp. 117–41.

Shumaker, D.M. and Prinz, R.J. (2000), 'Children who Murder: A Review', *Clinical Child and Family Psychology Review*, Vol. 3/2, pp. 97–115.

Siann, G. (1985), *Accounting for Aggression: Perspectives on Aggression and Violence*. London: Allen and Unwin.

Siddiqui, H. (2001), 'Domestic Violence and Black/Minority Women: Enough is Enough!', *Criminal Justice Matters*, Vol. 42, Winter 2000/2001, pp. 14–15.

Silke, A. (2002), 'Understanding Terrorism', *Psychology Review*, Vol. 9/1, pp. 17–19.

Silke, A. and Taylor, M. (2000), 'War Without End: Comparing IRA and Loyalist Vigilantism in Northern Ireland', *The Howard Journal*, Vol. 39/3, pp. 249–66.

Silverman, R.A. (1974), 'Victim Typologies: Overview, Critique and Reformulation', in I. Drapkin and E. Viano (eds), *Victimology*. Lexington, MA: Heath.

Silverman, R. and Kennedy, L. (1988), 'Women who Kill their Children', *Violence and Victims*, Vol. 3, pp. 113–27.

Silverman, R. and Kennedy, L. (1993), *Deadly Deeds: Murder in Canada*. Ontario: Nelson Canada.

Simmons, J. (ed.) (2002), *Crime in England and Wales 2001/2002*. Home Office Statistical Bulletin 07/02. London: Home Office.

Simon, R.J. (1975), *Women and Crime*. Toronto: Lexington.

Simpson, M.E. (1985), 'Violent Crime, Income Inequality and Regional Culture: Another Look', *Sociological Focus*, Vol. 18, pp. 199–208.

Sinclair, R. and Bullock, R. (2002), *Learning from Past Experience – A Review of Serious Case Reviews*. London: Department of Health.

Skrapec, C. (2001), 'Phenomenology and Serial Murder', *Homicide Studies*, Vol. 5/4, pp. 46–63.

Slapper, G. (1993), 'Corporate Manslaughter: An Examination of the Determinants of Prosecutorial Policy', *Social and Legal Studies*, Vol. 2, pp. 423–43.

Slapper, G. and Tombs, S. (1999), *Corporate Crime*. London: Longman.

Sloan, K. (2001), *Police Law Primer*. London: Butterworth.

Smith, D., Ray, L. and Wastell, L. (2002), 'Racial Violence in Manchester', *VRP Summary Findings*. Egham: Royal Holloway.

Smith, J. (1989), 'There's Only One Yorkshire Ripper', in J. Smith (ed.), *Misogynies*. London: Faber.

Smith, J. (1999), *Homicide in England and Wales*. Unpublished PhD thesis. Brunel University: Uxbridge.

Smith, J. (unpublished), *What's the Honour Among Men? Exploring Male on Male Confrontational Homicides in England and Wales*.

Smith, N. and Flanagan, C. (2000), *The Effective Detective: Identifying the Skills of an Effective SIO*. Police Research Series No. 122. London: Home Office.

Smith, P.H., Moracco, K. and Butts, J. (1998), 'Partner Homicide in Context: A Population-Based Perspective', *Homicide Studies*, Vol. 2/4, pp. 400–421.

Smith, R. and Wynne, B. (1989), *Expert Evidence*. London: Routledge.

Smithey, M. (1998), 'Infant Homicide: Victim/Offender Relationship and Causes of Death', *Journal of Family Violence*, Vol. 13/3, pp. 285–97.

Snider, L. (1998), 'Towards Safer Societies: Punishment, Masculinities and Violence Against Women', *British Journal of Criminology*, Vol. 38/1, pp. 1–39.

Somander, L.K. and Rammer, L. (1991), 'Intra- and Extrafamilial Child Homicide in Sweden 1971–1980', *Child Abuse and Neglect*, Vol. 15, pp. 45–55.

Sommier, I. (2002), 'Terrorism as Total Violence', *International Social Science Journal*, Vol. 54/174, pp. 473–81.

Soothill, K. (1993), 'The Serial Killer Industry', *Journal of Forensic Psychiatry*, Vol. 4, pp. 341–54.

Soothill, K., Francis, B., Ackerley, E. and Collett, S. (1999), *Homicide in Britain: A Comparative Study of Rates in Scotland and England and Wales*. Edinburgh: Scottish Executive Central Research Unit.

Soothill, K., Peelo, M., Francis, B., Pearson, J. and Ackerley, E. (2002), 'Homicide and the Media: Identifying the Top Cases in The Times', *Howard Journal*, Vol. 41/5, pp. 401–421.

Soothill, K. and Walby, S. (1991), *Sex Crime in the News*. London: Routledge.

Sorenson, S.B., Shen, H.K. and Kraus, J.F. (1997), 'Undetermined Manner of Death – A Comparison with Unintentional Injury, Suicide and Homicide Death', *Evaluation Review*, Vol. 211, pp. 43–57.

South Wales Echo (2001), 'Attack on Pill Pilot', 11 August.

Spatz Widom, C. (1989), 'The Intergenerational Transmission of Violence', in N.A. Weiner and M.E. Wolfgang (eds), *Pathways to Criminal Violence*. London: Sage.

Spierenberg, P. (1998), *Men and Violence: Gender, Honour and Rituals in Modern Europe and America*. Columbas, OH: Ohio State University.

Spunt, B., Brownstein, H., Crimmins, S. and Langley, S. (1996), 'Drugs and Homicide by Women', *Substance Use and Misuse*, Vol. 31/7, pp. 825–45.

Spunt, B., Brownstein, H., Goldstein, P., Fendrich, M. and Liberty, H.J. (1995), 'Drug Use by Homicide Offenders', *Journal of Psychoactive Drugs*, Vol. 27/2, pp. 125–34.

Stanko, B., O'Beirne, M. and Zaffuto, G. (2002), *Taking Stock: What Do We Know About Interpersonal Violence*. The ESRC Violence Research Programme. Egham: ESRC.

Stanko, E.A., Marian, L., Crisp, D., Manning, R., Smith, J. and Cowan, S. (1998), *Taking Stock: What Do We Know About Violence?* Egham: ESRC Violence Research Programme.

Stark, M.J.A., Raine, W.J., Burbeck, S.L. and Davis, K.K. (1974), 'Some Empirical Patterns in a Riot Process', *American Sociological Review*, Vol. 39, pp. 865–6.

Steffensmeier, D. and Allen, E. (1996), 'Gender and Crime: Toward a Gendered Theory of Offending', *Annual Review of Sociology*, Vol. 2, pp. 459–87.

Steffensmeier, D. and Haynie, D.L. (2000), 'The Structural Sources of Urban Female Violence in the United States: A Macrosocial Gender-Disaggregated Analysis of Adult and Juvenile Homicide Offending Rates', *Homicide Studies*, Vol. 4/2, pp. 107–134.

Stelfox, P. (unpublished) *Homicide Investigation*. PhD thesis.

Stone, M.H. (2001), 'Serial Sexual Homicide: Biological, Psychological and Sociological Aspects', *Journal of Personality Disorders*, Vol. 15/1, pp. 1–18.

Stout, K.D. (1993), 'Intimate Femicide: A Study of Men Who Have Killed Their Mates', *Journal of Offender Rehabilitation*, Vol. 19/3–4, pp. 81–94.

Strang, H. (1996), *Child Abuse Homicides in Australia: Incidence, Circumstances, Prevention and Control*. Australian Institute of Criminology, Trends and Issues No.53. Canberra: Australian Institute of Criminology.

Strang, H. and Gerull, S.A. (eds) (1993), *Homicide: Patterns, Prevention and Control*. Australian Institute of Criminology Conference Proceedings. Canberra: AIC.

Stretesky, P.B. (2001), 'The Relationship Between Lead Exposure and Homicide', *Archives of Pediatric Adolescent Medicine*, Vol. 155, pp. 579–82.

Stroud, J. (1997), 'Mental Disorder and the Homicide of Children: A Review', *Social Work and Social Sciences Review*, Vol. 6/3, pp. 149–62.

Stroud, J. and Pritchard, C. (2001), 'Child Homicide, Psychiatric Disorder and Dangerousness: A Review and an Empirical Approach', *British Journal of Social Work*, Vol. 31/2, pp. 249–69.

Stuart, E. and Campbell, J. (1989), 'Assessment of Patterns of Dangerousness with Battered Women', *Issues in Mental Health Nursing*, Vol. 10, pp. 245–60.

Sutherland, E.H. (1939), *Criminology* (2nd edition). Philadelphia, PA: Lippincott.

Swanson, C.R., Chamelin, N.C. and Territo, L. (1999), *Criminal Investigation* (7th edition). New York: McGraw-Hill.

Tanay, E. (1976), 'Reactive Patricide', *Journal of Forensic Sciences*, Vol. 21, pp. 76–82.

Tarde, G. (1912), *Penal Philosophy*. Boston, MA: Little, Brown.

Tardiff, K., Marzu, P., Leon, A. Hirsch, C., Stajic, M., Portera, L. and Hartell, N. (1995) 'A Profile of Homicides on the Streets and Homes of New York City', *Public Health Reports*, Jan-Feb, Vol. 10/1, p. 13.

Taylor, I., Walton, P. and Young, J. (1973), *The New Criminology: For a Social Theory of Deviance*. London: Routledge and Kegan Paul.

Taylor, P.J. and Gunn, J. (1999), 'Homicides by People with Mental Illness: Myth and Reality', *British Journal of Psychiatry*, Vol. 174, pp. 9–14.

Taylor, S.P. and Hulsizer, M.R. (1998), 'Psychoactive Drugs and Human Aggression', in R.G. Green and E. Donnerstein (eds), *Human Aggression: Theories, Research and Implications for Social Policy*. San Diego, CA: Academic Press.

Tedeschi, J.T. and Felson, R.B. (1994), *Violence, Aggression and Coercive Actions*. Washington: American Psychological Association.

Tierney, J. (1996), *Criminology: Theory and Context*. London: Prentice-Hall.

Toch, H. (1969), *Violent Men: An Inquiry into the Psychology of Violence*. Chicago, IL: Aldine.

Toch, H. and Adams, K. (1994), *The Disturbed Violent Offender*. Washington, DC: American Psychological Association.

Tolson, A. (1977), *The Limits of Masculinity*. New York: Harper and Row.

Tomsen, S. (1997), 'A Top Night. Social Protest, Masculinity and the Culture of Drinking Violence', *The British Journal of Criminology*, Vol. 37/1, pp. 90–102.

Tonry, M. and Farrington, D. (1995), *Building a Safer Society: Strategic Approaches to Crime Prevention*. Chicago, IL: University of Chicago Press.

Topalli, V., Wright, R. and Fornango, R. (2002), 'Drug Dealers, Robbery and Retaliation', *British Journal of Criminology*, Vol. 42, pp. 337–51.

Totman, J. (1978), *The Murderess: A Psychosocial Study of Criminal Homicide*. San Francisco, CA: R and E Research Associates.

Trasler, G. (1987), 'Some Cautions for the Biological Approach to Crime Causation', in S.A. Mednick, T.A. Moffitt and S.A. Stack (eds), *The Causes of Crime: New Biological Approaches*. Cambridge: Cambridge University Press.

Travis, A. (2003), 'Life Means Life for Child Killers, Says Blunkett', *Guardian Online* www.guardian.co.uk, 7/05/03.

Turvey, B. (1999), *Criminal Profiling: An Introduction to Behavioural Evidence Analysis*. London: Academic Press.

Unnithan, N.P. (1997), 'Child Homicide in Developed Countries', *International Review of Victimology*, Vol. 4/4, pp. 313–26.

Venables, P.H. (1987), 'Autonomic and Central Nervous System Factors in Criminal Behaviour', in S.A. Mednick, T.E. Moffitt and S. Stack (eds), *The Causes of Crime: New Biological Approaches*. Cambridge: Cambridge University Press.

Vetter, H. (1990), 'Dissociation, Psychopathy and the Serial Murderer', in S.A. Egger (ed.), *Serial Murder: An Elusive Phenomenon*. London: Praeger.

Virkkunen, M. (1986), 'Reactive Hypoglycaemic Tendency Among Habitually Violent Offenders', *Nutrition Reviews*, Vol. 44. (Suppl.), pp. 94–103.

Virkkunen, M. and Huttunen, M.O. (1982), 'Evidence for Abnormal Glucose Tolerance Test Among Violent Offenders', *Neuropsychoiology*, Vol. 8, pp. 30–34.

Volavka, J. (1987), 'Electroencephalogram among Criminals', in S.A. Mednick, T.E. Moffitt and S. Stack (eds), *The Causes of Crime: New Biological Approaches*. Cambridge: Cambridge University Press.

Volavka, J. (1999), 'The Neurobiology of Violence: An Update', *Journal of Neuropsychiatry and Clinical Neuroscience*, Vol. 11, pp. 307–314.

Vold, B., Bernard, T. and Snipes, J. (1998), *Theoretical Criminology* (4th edition). Oxford: Oxford University Press.

Von Hentig, H. (1938), 'Some Problems Regarding Murder Detection', *Journal of Criminal Law and Criminology*, Vol. 29, pp. 108–118.

Von Hentig, H. (1948), *The Criminal and His Victim: Studies in the Sociobiology of Crime*. New Haven, CT: Yale University Press.

Waddington, P.A.J. (1999), 'Police (Canteen) Sub-Culture: An Appreciation', *British Journal of Criminology*, Vol. 39/2, pp. 287–309.

Walby, S. and Myhill, A. (2000), 'Reducing Domestic Violence ... What Works? Assessing and Managing the Risk of Domestic Violence'. *Policing and Reducing Crime Unit Briefing Notes*. London: Home Office.

Walker, C. and Stockdale, R. (1999), 'Forensic Evidence', in C. Walker and K. Starmer (eds), *Miscarriages of Justice: A Review of Justice in Error*. London: Blackstone.

Walker, C. and Starmer, K. (1999), *Miscarriages of Justice: A Review of Justice in Error*. London: Blackstone.

Walker, L.E. (1979), *The Battered Woman*. London: Harper and Row.

Walker, L.E. (1984), *The Battered Woman Syndrome*. New York: Springer.

Walker, L.E. (1989), *Terrifying Love: Why Battered Women Kill and How Society Responds*. New York: Harper and Row.

Walker, L.E. and Browne, A. (1985), 'Gender and Victimization by Intimates', *Journal of Personality*, Vol. 53/2, pp. 179–95.

Walker, N. (1978), 'Dangerous People', *International Journal of Law and Psychiatry*, Vol. 11, pp. 37–50.

Walklate, S. (1989), *Victimology*. London: Unwin Hyman.

Walklate, S. (1995), *Gender and Crime: An Introduction*. London: Prentice-Hall/Harvester Wheatsheaf.

Walklate, S. (2001a), 'Victimology', in E. McLaughlin and J. Muncie (eds), *The Sage Dictionary of Criminology*. London: Sage.

Walklate, S. (2001b), *Gender, Crime and Criminal Justice*. Cullompton: Willan.

Walklate, S. (2002), 'Community and Crime Prevention', in E. McLaughlin and J. Muncie (eds), *Controlling Crime*. London: Sage.

Wallace, A. (1986), *Homicide: The Social Reality*. Bureau of Crime Statistics and Research. Research Study No. 5. Sydney: BCSR.

Wallace, S.E. (1964), 'Patterns of Violence in San Juan', in W.C. Reckless and C.L. Newman (eds), *Interdisciplinary Problems in Criminology: Papers of the American Society of Criminology*. Columbus, OH: Ohio State University Press.

Ward, T. (1999), 'The Sad Subject of Infanticide: Law, Medicine and Child Murder, 1860–1938', *Social and Legal Studies*, Vol. 8/2, pp. 163–80.

Ward Jouve, N. (1988), *'The Street-Cleaner': The Yorkshire Ripper Case on Trial*. London: Boyars.

Waring, E., Weisburd, D. and Chayet, E. (1995), 'White-Collar Crime and Anomie', in F. Adler and W.S. Laufer (eds), *The Legacy of Anomie Theory: Advances in Criminological Theory*, (Volume 6). New Brunswick, NJ: Transaction.

Watkin, H.A. (1977), 'XYY and XXY Men: Criminality and Aggression', in S.A. Mednick and K.O. Christiansen (eds), *Biosocial Bases of Criminal Behaviour*. New York: Gardner.

Weatherson, D. and Moran, J. (2003), 'Terrorism and Mental Illness: Is there a Relationship?', *International Journal of Offender Therapy and Comparative Criminology*, Vol. 47/6, pp. 698–714.

Websdale, N. (1999), *Understanding Domestic Violence*. Boston, MA: Northeastern University Press.

Websdale, N. and Chesney-Lind, M. (1998), 'Dong Violence to Women', in L.H. Bowker (ed.), *Masculinities and Violence*. London: Sage.

Weisz, A.N., Tolman, R.M. and Saunders, D. (2000), 'Assessing the Risk of Severe Domestic Violence: The Importance of Survivors' Predictions', *Journal of Interpersonal Violence*, Vol. 15/1, pp. 75–90.

Welham, M.G. (2002), *Corporate Killing: A Managers' Guide to Legal Compliance*. London: Tolley.

Wells, C. (1995), 'Cry in the Dark: Corporate Manslaughter and Cultural Meaning', in L. Loveland (ed.), *Criminality*. London: Sweet and Maxwell.

Wells, C. (2000), 'Provocation: the Case for Abolition', in A. Ashworth and B. Mitchell (eds), *Rethinking English Homicide Law*. Oxford: Oxford University Press.

Wells, C. (2001), *Corporations and Criminal Responsibility* (2nd edition). Oxford: Oxford University Press.

West, C. and Fenstermaker, S. (1995), 'Doing Difference', *Gender and Society*, Vol. 9, pp. 8–37.

Weston, N. (1998), 'The Crime Scene', in P. White (ed.), *Crime Scene to Court: The Essentials of Forensic Science*. Cambridge: Royal Society of Chemistry.

White, C. (1999), 'Some "Cot Deaths" are Child Abuse', *British Medical Journal*, Vol. 318, pp. 147.

White, P. (1995), 'Homicide', in M. Walker (ed.), *Interpreting Crime Statistics*. Oxford: Clarendon.

White, P. (1998), *Crime Scene to Court: The Essentials of Forensic Science*. Cambridge: Royal Society of Chemistry.

White, M.D., Fyfe, J.J., Campbell, S.P. and Goldkamp, J.S. (2003), 'The Police Role in Preventing Homicide: Considering the Impact of Problem-orientated Policing on the Prevalence of Murder', *Journal of Research in Crime and Delinquency*, Vol. 40/2, pp. 194–225.

Wikström, P. and Svensson, R. (2003), Does Gender Matter? A Study of Adolescent Criminality and Substance Use. Paper presented at the Annual Lecture of the Centre for Criminology, University of Glamorgan, 21 May 2003 and the American Society of Criminology Conference in Chicago, 2002.

Wilczynski, A. (1995), 'Child Killing by Parents: Social, Legal and Gender Issues', in R.E. Dobash, R.P. Dobash and L. Noaks (eds), *Gender and Crime*. Cardiff: Open University Press.

Wilczynski, A. (1997a), *Child Homicide*. London: Greenwich Medical.

Wilczynski, A. (1997b), 'Prior Agency Contact and Physical Abuse in Cases of Child Homicide', *British Journal of Social Work*, Vol. 27/2, pp. 241–53.

Wilczynski, A. and Morris, A. (1993), 'Parents who Kill their Children', *Criminal Law Review*, Vol. 793 (January), pp. 31–6.

Wilkey, I., Pearn, J., Petrie, G. and Nixon, J. (1982), 'Neonaticide, Infanticide and Child Homicide', *Medicine Science and the Law*, Vol. 22/1, p. 31–4.

Wilkinson, P. (1974), *Political Terrorism*. London: Macmillan.

Wilkinson, P. (1986), *Terrorism and the Liberal State* (2nd edition). London: Macmillan.

Wilkinson, P. (2001), *Terrorism versus Democracy*. London: Frank Cass.

Wille, W. (1974), *Citizens Who Commit Murder*. St Louis, MO: Warren Green.

Williams, G. (1983), *Textbook of Criminal Law*. London: Stevens.

Williams, K. (1991), *Textbook on Criminology*. London: Blackstone.

Williams, K. (1996), *Textbook on Criminology*. London: Blackstone.

Williams, K. (2001), *Textbook on Criminology*. London: Blackstone.

Williams, K.R. and Flewelling, R.L. (1988), 'The Social Production of Homicide: A Comparative Study of Disaggregated Rates in American Cities', *American Sociological Review*, Vol. 53, pp. 421–31.

Williams, P. and Dickinson, J. (1993), 'Fear of Crime: Read All About It', *British Journal of Criminology*, Vol. 33/1, pp. 33–56.

Willis, P.E. (1977), *Learning to Labour*. Farnborough: Saxon House.

Wilson, J.Q. and Hernstein, R.J. (1985), *Crime and Human Nature*. New York: Simon and Schuster.

Wilson, J.Q. and Petersilia, J. (1995), *Crime*. Oakland, CA: ICS.

Wilson, M. and Daly, M. (1985), 'Competitiveness, Risk Taking and Violence: The Young Male Syndrome', *Ethology and Sociology*, Vol. 6/1, pp. 59–73.

Wilson, M.I. (1989) 'Marital Conflict and Homicide in Evolutionary Perspective', in R.W. Bell and N.J. Bell (eds), *Sociobiology and the Social Sciences*. Lubbock, TX: Texas Tech University Press.

Wilson, M.I. and Daly, M. (1992), 'Till Death us Do Part', in J. Radford and D.E.H. Russell (eds), *Femicide: The Politics of Woman Killing*. Buckingham: Open University Press.

Wilson, M. and Daly, M. (1993), 'Spousal Homicide Risk and Estrangement', *Violence and Victims*, Vol. 8/1, pp. 3–16.

Wilson, M. and Daly, M. (1998), 'Sexual Rivalry and Sexual Conflict: Recurring Themes in Fatal Conflicts', *Theoretical Criminology*, Vol. 2/3, pp. 291–310.

Wilson, M.I, Daly, M. and Daniele, A. (1995), 'Familicide: The Killing of Spouse and Children', *Aggressive Behaviour*, Vol. 21/4, pp. 275–91.

Wilson, N.K. (1993), 'Gendered Interaction in Criminal Homicide', in A.V. Wilson (ed.), *Homicide: The Victim/Offender Connection*. Cincinnati, OH: Anderson.

Wolfgang, M. (1958), *Patterns in Criminal Homicide*. Montclair, NJ: Patterson Smith.

Wolfgang, M.E. and Ferracuti, F. (1967), *The Subculture of Violence: Towards an Integrated Theory in Criminology*. London: Tavistock.

Workman, L. and Reader, W. (2003), *Evolutionary Psychology*. Cambridge: Cambridge University Press.

World Health Organisation (WHO) (1992), *ICD-10: The ICD-10 Classification of Mental and Behavioural Disorders: Clinical Descriptions and Diagnostic Guidelines*. Geneva: World Health Organisation.

World Health Organisation (WHO) (2001), *Mental Health: New Understanding, New Hope*. World Health Organisation. (www.who.int)

Yarvis, R.M. (1994), 'Patterns of Substance Abuse and Intoxication Among Murderers', *Bulletin of the American Academy of Psychiatry and the Law*, Vol. 22/1, pp. 133–44.

Young, S.J. (1991), 'DNA Evidence – Beyond Reasonable Doubt?' *Criminal Law Review*, (April) pp. 264–7.

Young, J. and Matthews, R. (1992), *Rethinking Criminology: The Realist Debate*. London: Sage.

Zahn, M.A. (1990), 'Intervention Strategies to Reduce Homicide', in M. Weiner, R. Zahn and R. Sagi (eds), *Violence*. San Diego, CA: Harcourt, Brace, Jovanovich.

Zimbardo, P.G., Banks, W.C., Craig, H. and Jaffe, D. (1973), 'A Pirandellian Prison: The Mind is a Formidable Jailor', *New York Times Magazine*, (April 8), pp. 38–60.

Index